Digital Technologies for Entrepreneurship in Industry 4.0

Elena G. Popkova
MGIMO University, Russia

A volume in the Advances in E-Business Research (AEBR) Book Series

IGI Global
PUBLISHER of TIMELY KNOWLEDGE

Published in the United States of America by
IGI Global
Business Science Reference (an imprint of IGI Global)
701 E. Chocolate Avenue
Hershey PA, USA 17033
Tel: 717-533-8845
Fax: 717-533-8661
E-mail: cust@igi-global.com
Web site: http://www.igi-global.com

Library of Congress Cataloging-in-Publication Data

Names: Popkova, Elena G., editor.
Title: Digital technologies for entrepreneurship in industry 4.0 / Elena G. Popkova, editor.
Description: Hershey, PA : Business Science Reference, [2023] | Includes bibliographical references and index. | Summary: "This book substantiates digital entrepreneurship, discussing the practical experience of its implementation, and developing the scientific and methodological recommendations for development of its infrastructural provision and ways to control its regulation and provision of its competitiveness"-- Provided by publisher.
Identifiers: LCCN 2022021796 (print) | LCCN 2022021797 (ebook) | ISBN 9781668442654 (hardcover) | ISBN 9781668442852 (paperback) | ISBN 9781668442661 (ebook)
Subjects: LCSH: Information technology--Economic aspects. | Technological innovations--Economic aspects. | Entrepreneurship. | Industry 4.0.
Classification: LCC HC79.I55 D574 2023 (print) | LCC HC79.I55 (ebook) | DDC 303.48/33--dc23/eng/20220519
LC record available at https://lccn.loc.gov/2022021796
LC ebook record available at https://lccn.loc.gov/2022021797

This book is published in the IGI Global book series Advances in E-Business Research (AEBR) (ISSN: 1935-2700; eISSN: 1935-2719)

British Cataloguing in Publication Data
A Cataloguing in Publication record for this book is available from the British Library.

Advances in E-Business Research (AEBR) Book Series

ISSN:1935-2700
EISSN:1935-2719

Editor-in-Chief: In Lee Western Illinois University, USA

MISSION

Technology has played a vital role in the emergence of e-business and its applications incorporate strategies. These processes have aided in the use of electronic transactions via telecommunications networks for collaborating with business partners, buying and selling of goods and services, and customer service. Research in this field continues to develop into a wide range of topics, including marketing, psychology, information systems, accounting, economics, and computer science.

The **Advances in E-Business Research (AEBR) Book Series** provides multidisciplinary references for researchers and practitioners in this area. Instructors, researchers, and professionals interested in the most up-to-date research on the concepts, issues, applications, and trends in the e-business field will find this collection, or individual books, extremely useful. This collection contains the highest quality academic books that advance understanding of e-business and addresses the challenges faced by researchers and practitioners.

COVERAGE

- Semantic Web
- Economics of e-business
- Trust, Security, and Privacy
- Sustainable E-business
- Virtual organization
- Outsourcing and e-business technologies
- E-business models and architectures
- Evaluation methodologies for e-business systems
- Valuing e-business assets
- Web Service-Based Business Systems

IGI Global is currently accepting manuscripts for publication within this series. To submit a proposal for a volume in this series, please contact our Acquisition Editors at Acquisitions@igi-global.com or visit: http://www.igi-global.com/publish/.

The Advances in E-Business Research (AEBR) Book Series (ISSN 1935-2700) is published by IGI Global, 701 E. Chocolate Avenue, Hershey, PA 17033-1240, USA, www.igi-global.com. This series is composed of titles available for purchase individually; each title is edited to be contextually exclusive from any other title within the series. For pricing and ordering information please visit http://www.igi-global.com/book-series/advances-business-research/37144. Postmaster: Send all address changes to above address.

Titles in this Series

For a list of additional titles in this series, please visit:
http://www.igi-global.com/book-series/advances-business-research/37144

Virtual Technologies and E-Collaboration for the Future of Global Business
Jingyuan Zhao (University of Toronto, Canada) and Joseph Richards (California State University, Sacramento, USA)
Business Science Reference • © 2022 • 273pp • H/C (ISBN: 9781668450277) • US $250.00

Navigating Digital Communication and Challenges for Organizations
José Gabriel Andrade (University of Minho, Portugal) and Teresa Ruão (University of Minho, Portugal)
Business Science Reference • © 2022 • 325pp • H/C (ISBN: 9781799897903) • US $230.00

Handbook of Research on Smart Management for Digital Transformation
Belem Barbosa (University of Porto, Portugal) Sandra Filipe (University of Aveiro, Portugal) and Claudia Amaral Santos (University of Aveiro, Portugal)
Business Science Reference • © 2022 • 614pp • H/C (ISBN: 9781799890089) • US $325.00

Handbook of Research on Digital Transformation, Industry Use Cases, and the Impact of Disruptive Technologies
Martin George Wynn (University of Gloucestershire, UK)
Business Science Reference • © 2022 • 487pp • H/C (ISBN: 9781799877127) • US $360.00

Handbook of Research on Pathways and Opportunities Into the Business of Esports
Sharon Andrews (University of Houston-Clear Lake, USA) and Caroline M. Crawford (University of Houston-Clear Lake, USA)
Business Science Reference • © 2021 • 473pp • H/C (ISBN: 9781799873006) • US $380.00

Complex Systems and Sustainability in the Global Auditing, Consulting, and Credit Rating Agency Industries
Michael I. C. Nwogugu (Independent Researcher, Nigeria)
Business Science Reference • © 2021 • 320pp • H/C (ISBN: 9781799874188) • US $215.00

For an entire list of titles in this series, please visit:
http://www.igi-global.com/book-series/advances-business-research/37144

IGI Global
PUBLISHER of TIMELY KNOWLEDGE

701 East Chocolate Avenue, Hershey, PA 17033, USA
Tel: 717-533-8845 x100 • Fax: 717-533-8661
E-Mail: cust@igi-global.com • www.igi-global.com

Table of Contents

Detailed Table of Contents

digital technologies, and the related development of Industry 4.0, acknowledging the need to embrace ideas and concepts from multiple fields and integrate different research areas. The other related theme is digital transformation, which implies a structural change of the economies and organizations requiring a technological and cultural shift. In addition, the chapter's analysis highlights that digital transformation and its profound changes can generate imbalances if not addressed with awareness and the right mastery of digital skills. Reaping the digital revolution's benefits, and avoiding its pitfalls, will require organizations and economies to manage an unprecedented structural transformation for which the world seems still unprepared.

Digital technologies offer a great opportunity to small and medium-sized enterprises (SMEs) as they can adopt digital transformation more rapidly than large enterprises due to their greater flexibility and lean decision-making processes. So far there is no universal vision for a potential organizational model or design for Industry 4.0 SMEs. The research aimed to address this important gap by exploring the impact of digital technologies on organizational design in Industry 4.0 SMEs. The research builds on culture, staff, processes, and governance framework and follows a qualitative embedded case study design drawing on both employees' interviews and company documentation. The study provides insights about the main features, opportunities, and risks that are characterizing the current digital revolution in Industry 4.0 SMEs. Furthermore, the analysis of a notable Italian entrepreneurial reality revealed a set of practical suggestions and guidelines for other international SMEs that need to face the Industry 4.0 revolution with confidence and a proactive approach.

New digital technology has revolutionized the uncertainty inherent in entrepreneurial processes, results, and the methods for coping with such delay. This has sparked discussion on digital entrepreneurship and the relationship between digital technology and entrepreneurship. The survey was distributed online using Google Forms between January 2022 and February 2022. The target population for the study included entrepreneurs and young graduates in Lebanon. The survey was administered in English, considered the second language used in Lebanon. Additionally, the

Preface

The research object in this book is digital technologies for entrepreneurship in Industry 4.0. The very notion of "Industry 4.0" is rather actively used in the existing scientific literature – but in different treatments. The universal notion of "Industry 4.0" in theory defines it as the creation, functioning, and development of cyber-physical systems – hybrid economic systems, in which a flexible and highly effective symbiosis of physical objects and smart technologies, unified into a common intellectual network through the Internet of Things (IoT) and under the control of artificial intelligence (AI) is achieved.

The most popular criteria for determining the boundaries of Industry 4.0 are as follows. 1st criterion – from the position of markets – implies assigning to Industry the sectoral markets in which automatization covers not only production but also distribution and managerial economic processes. A drawback of this criterion is the fact that in practice, total automatization is achieved at the scale of an entire market rather rarely. As a rule, this happens only in separate market segments. At that, segments in the market are strongly differentiated by the level of automatization. In some segments, the companies' activities are almost entirely automatized, in other segments automatization is partial, and in other segments, automatization is not profitable and not available, so it is not implemented. That is why, the use of this criterion leads to the situation when, even in the case of achievement of total automatization in certain segments only, the whole market is assigned to Industry 4.0, though, in fact, Industry 4.0 is presented in this market in a limited way.

2nd criterion – from the position of the industry – is based on the initial focus of the economy's neo-industrialization on the industry. Thus, according to this criterion, Industry 4.0 includes hi-tech spheres of industry, e.g., the pharmaceutical industry, IT, and other sectors of industry with a high share of expenditures for R&D and a high share of personnel who are directly involved in R&D and implementation of technological innovations into production. A drawback of this criterion is that total automatization and technological innovations are actively implemented in all spheres of the modern economy. So limiting the coverage of Industry 4.0 by the sectors of industry is not correct, for Industry 4.0 is presented in most spheres of the economy – hi-tech segments of various markets, including smart agriculture, online commerce, hi-tech finance, digital (e.g., robotized) education, etc.

3rd criterion – from the position of the Fourth Industrial Revolution – implies assigning to Industry 4.0 the entire economic systems, which joined the Fourth Industrial Revolution. According to this criterion, Industry 4.0 includes smart cities/regions (at the scale of territories: meso-level economic systems) and digital economies (at the level of countries: macro-level economic systems). A drawback of this criterion is the insufficient precision due to the focus on the process with insufficient attention to results. The start of the neo-industrialization processes in an economic system does not mean and does not guarantee its factual transition to total automatization, which might be not achieved at all or achieved only by certain economic subjects.

This book deals with the drawbacks of the mentioned criteria and proposes a new criterion for identifying the boundaries of Industry 4.0 – from the position of using digital technologies in entrepreneurship. Digital technologies are treated as "11 frontier technologies" (so-called "digital frontiers"), distinguished in "Technology and Innovation Report 2021: Catching Technological Waves" United Nations Conference on Trade and Development (UNCTAD): artificial intelligence (AI), the Internet of Things (IoT), big data, blockchain, 3D print, robots, drones, gene editing, 5G, nanotechnologies, and solar PV. The use of digital technologies in entrepreneurship is aimed at raising its effectiveness, competitiveness, and sustainability.

According to this, Industry 4.0 is treated as a cyber-physical system of any (micro, meso, or macro) level in any sphere (not limited by industry) and in any market (including separate market segments), which are characterized by hi-technology, active implementation of technological innovations, and total automatization, achieved in the process of the Fourth Industrial Revolution. The main subject of the economy in this system is entrepreneurship. Entrepreneurship of Industry 4.0 is treated as a subject of business activity that conducts economic activities in Industry 4.0 that relate to the use of digital technologies.

The topic of implementing and using digital technologies in entrepreneurship of Industry 4.0 is very important in the modern world. First, in the course of the Fourth Industrial Revolution, economic systems (countries and territories) and economic subjects (companies) cannot stay aside under the pressure of technological competition; to stand it and overcome the growing technological barriers of many sectoral markets, they move to Industry 4.0. An open economy and free trade around the world in the modern conditions of globalization facilitate the appearance of Industry 4.0 in almost all economic systems. According to the forecast by UNCTAD, by 2025, the world volume of Industry 4.0 will be assessed at $3.2 trillion, i.e., it will grow by more than 9 times over 7 years, compared to 2018, when it was assessed at $350 billion. This is a sign of the growing popularity of digital technologies in entrepreneurship of Industry 4.0.

Second, the development of Industry 4.0 will stimulate future technological progress and global competitiveness of economic systems and economic subjects. IMD has been assessing global digital competitiveness since 2013, and since 2019 it ousted the practice of calculation of general competitiveness that was performed by the World Economic Forum; in 2019, it was changed to "Competitiveness 4.0". This means that management of competitiveness in the modern world is based on the dissemination and use of digital technologies in entrepreneurship of Industry 4.0. The quality of life and implementation of the Sustainable Development Goals more and more depend on the use of digital technologies in entrepreneurship, which ensures responsible (social and environmental) innovations.

Third, digital technologies in entrepreneurship are often disruptive innovations (according to C. Christensen). In the changing world, companies have to manage the changes. The very formulation of the Fourth Industrial Revolution says that it does not supplement but replaces the previous technological mode. Therefore, implementation and use of digital technologies in entrepreneurship of Industry 4.0 becomes an objective necessity, without which companies risk bearing losses or being ousted from the market. Against the background of the Fourth Industrial Revolution, intense social progress also takes place – the information society becomes more selective, demanding, and responsible as to suppliers of goods and services. A new market situation supports, even more, the companies' transition to Industry 4.0 through the implementation of digital technologies.

This book is devoted to the systematic research and comprehensive discussion of all aspects connected with the dissemination and use of digital technologies in entrepreneurship of Industry 4.0: organizational & economic and managerial, social and technological, and the aspects of state regulation and economic security (including cyber security). The main (primary) audience of this book is scholars who study entrepreneurship and Industry 4.0. In this book, they will find the fundamental basis of entrepreneurship in Industry 4.0 and methodological recommendations on identifying the boundaries of Industry 4.0 by the criterion of using digital technologies in entrepreneurship. The book is multidisciplinary and thus poses interest to the representatives of various spheres of scientific knowledge, including entrepreneurial economics, management, microeconomics, innovation economics, state regulation of the economy, and the use of information and communication technologies in economy and entrepreneurship.

The additional (secondary) target audience of this book is practicing experts who are interested in the issues of dissemination and use of digital technologies in entrepreneurship of Industry 4.0. State regulators of entrepreneurship (representatives of public authorities of countries and their regions) will find in this book a systematic view of the current needs of entrepreneurship of Industry 4.0 for digital technologies, as well as conditions at which dissemination and more active use of these technologies is achieved. These conditions are legal regulation of entrepreneurship in Industry 4.0, its infrastructural provision, and provision of state services, and in some cases – the use of the public-private partnership mechanisms.

Representatives (entrepreneurs, shareholders, investors, and managers) of entrepreneurship in Industry 4.0 will find in the book useful examples from international practice, as well as the authors' applied recommendations on improving the corporate management of the processes of implementing and using digital technologies in entrepreneurship of Industry 4.0. For them, the book also forms a comprehensive and clear view of the essence, regularities, and causal connections of companies' transition to Industry 4.0, as well as the role of digital technologies in this process. This will allow interested companies to perform an accelerated, more predictable, less risky, and safer transition to Industry 4.0 through the implementation and use of digital technologies.

Each chapter presented in this book makes an important contribution to the discussion of the book's topic and increase in scientific knowledge. One of the chapters studies the impact of the COVID-19 pandemic and crisis on e-business in Industry 4.0. This chapter elaborates on the specifics of the pandemic and crisis context for the dissemination of the use of digital technologies in the practice of entrepreneurship of Industry 4.0. This chapter also contains an empirical study, which sheds light on the lead practice of e-business in Industry 4.0.

Another chapter considers digital technologies for institutional investors in the environment of Industry 4.0. Institutional investors play an important role in Industry 4.0, for they provide financial support to the implementation and use of digital technologies in entrepreneurship. Institutional investors also stimulate the movement of investments to the most perspective (attractive for investments) innovative projects, which are connected to the use of digital technologies in entrepreneurship of Industry 4.0. As is shown in the chapter, to perform these important functions, institutional investors of Industry 4.0 require digital technologies. This chapter also proposes recommendations for the increase in accessibility and effectiveness of the use of digital technologies by institutional investors in the environment of Industry 4.0.

Another chapter is devoted to the modernization of corporate reporting under the conditions of the digital economy. The authors demonstrate that for the most precise determination of the limits of Industry 4.0 it is expedient to use corporate reporting, which should contain information on the use of digital technologies in entrepreneurship. This chapter also offers authors' recommendations on improving the modern practice of filing and publication in open access of corporate reporting by companies of Industry 4.0 based on digital technologies.

The book also contains a chapter devoted to the trends of digitalization of corporate governance. This chapter is important for the book's contribution to the selected topic since it vividly shows that the boundaries of Industry 4.0 go beyond industrial production and cover the governance of entrepreneurship. This chapter substantiates that the use of digital technologies in the process of corporate governance allows assigning a company to Industry 4.0. Recommendations on the increase in activity and effectiveness of using digital technologies in the practice of corporate governance of entrepreneurship in Industry 4.0 are offered.

Another chapter dwells on the investment attractiveness of "young" companies in the context of global changes associated with the new industrial revolution. The considered experience of "young" companies is very important, for it shows the cause-and-effect links of the companies' transition to Industry 4.0 and the contribution of digital technologies to this. The chapter also describes the life cycle of companies of Industry 4.0 and the transition from "young" to "mature" companies of Industry 4.0 and so on – at each stage, the specific features of using digital technologies in entrepreneurship are described.

The book also has a chapter on the digitalization of infrastructure development based on the use of public-private partnership mechanisms. The chapter sets a research question "Is Russia in trend"? Russia's experience, described in this chapter, is important for the book's contribution to the literature since it specifies the features of the transition of dynamically developing countries (considering Russia as a member of BRICS) to Industry 4.0. The chapter shows that public-private partnership has a significant role in the digital modernization of the infrastructural provision of entrepreneurship and facilitates Russia's transition to Industry 4.0.

There is also a chapter on the role of management of innovations in the digital transformation age. The chapter's significance for the book is due to its demonstrating a critically important role of management of innovations for the companies' transition to Industry 4.0. This chapter proves that the dissemination and use of digital technologies in entrepreneurship of Industry 4.0 envisages the management of innovations. The authors also offer a set of recommendations to improve the modern practice of managing innovations in the age of digital transformation for the successful transition of companies to Industry 4.0.

Another chapter is devoted to digitalization as a factor in improving the competitiveness of the national economy, which describes the opportunities and prospects of the agro-industrial complex of the Russian Federation. This chapter is important for the book for it describes the sectoral features of companies' transition to Industry 4.0. The chapter focuses on the agro-industrial complex as a strategically important sphere of the modern economy and substantiates that the dissemination and use of digital technologies in entrepreneurship facilitates the transition of the agro-industrial complex to Industry 4.0 and supports food security.

There is also a chapter that elaborates on the digital economy and digital transformation. The correlation between these notions is critically important for the given book and its subject sphere on the whole since it specifies their categorical apparatus. As is substantiated in the chapter, digital transformation is a process, and the digital economy is a result of the transition to Industry 4.0. The chapter contains an important theoretical study, which contributes to the development of the fundamental basis of using digital technologies in entrepreneurship of Industry 4.0.

Another chapter discusses organizational design for digital technologies in Industry 4.0 and dwells on the "best practice" from Italy. The significance of this chapter for the book is due to the analysis of the organizational and managerial aspects of entrepreneurship in Industry 4.0. The lead experience of entrepreneurial structures of Italy is useful for companies from other developed countries, for it reflects the specifics and prospects for improving the use of digital technologies in entrepreneurship of Industry 4.0 in these countries.

The last, but not the least, chapter of this book is devoted to the digital technology perspective of entrepreneurship, with the case of small and medium enterprises in Lebanon. This chapter describes the specific features of the subjects of small and medium entrepreneurship and forms the scientific and methodological framework, proposing applied recommendations for improving the use of digital technologies to support these companies' transition to Industry 4.0. The experience of small and medium enterprises in Lebanon would be useful for such types of companies in other developing countries.

The book contributes to the subject matter by specifying the boundaries of Industry 4.0, which are vague in the existing literature. The book offers a technological criterion to identify the boundaries of Industry 4.0. The advantage of the authors' criterion is that it allows, for the first time, for a clear and objective designation of Industry 4.0 as an economic sphere in which digital technologies в entrepreneurship are widely used. The technological criterion allows dealing with the drawback of other existing criteria that is connected with the errors of the first (excessive generalization, unjustified expansion of borders of Industry 4.0 – as in the criteria from the position of markets and the position of the Fourth Industrial Revolution) and second (excessive narrowing of the borders of Industry 4.0 – as in the criterion from the position of industry) ones.

The book reinvents the essence of the Fourth Industrial Revolution and the logic of the change of technological modes. Instead of the previous basis of technological shifts, connected with spontaneous technological progress, the book proposes a new basis, which consists in the dissemination and use of the lead (revolutionary) technologies in entrepreneurship. Due to this, the book forms a novel view of the Fourth Industrial Revolution as a manageable process, the key to which management lies in the sphere of entrepreneurship: it is connected with state and corporate governance of entrepreneurship. The proposed basis allows raising the precision of forecasting future industrial revolutions (the next one relates to the transition to Industry 5.0: the Fifth Industrial Revolution) and provides opportunities for managing them.

The book impacts the field through the identification and substantiation of the specifics of disseminating and using digital technologies in the activities of various entrepreneurial structures of Industry 4.0: subjects of e-business, “young” companies, companies that participate in public-private partnership, and small and medium enterprises. The book’s originality and its contribution to the literature consist in the deep research of isolated measures and the formation of a systematic view of the complex use of the measures of state and corporate management of entrepreneurship for further development of Industry 4.0. The book also has a high practical significance since it describes, compares, and analyses in detail the international experience of using digital technologies in entrepreneurship of Industry 4.0. The book considers the specifics of developed (e.g., Italy) and developing (e.g., Russia and Lebanon) countries.

The book’s contribution to the increase in scientific knowledge is also ensured due to the consideration of a special context in which entrepreneurship of Industry 4.0 functions and develops. This modern context is connected with the COVID-19 pandemic and crisis, the next waves of which are still ongoing around the world. The book considers, systemically, the impact of the pandemic context on entrepreneurship in Industry 4.0. It is demonstrated that, on the one hand, the COVID-19 pandemic and crisis complicated entrepreneurial activities in Industry 4.0, reducing the resource potential of companies and limiting their capabilities for R&D, implementation of innovations, and further automatization. On the other hand, it is substantiated that, under the conditions of the COVID-19 pandemic and crisis, there were created powerful stimuli for technological modernization of entrepreneurship, and the requirements from state and society to it grew. Companies of Industry 4.0 did not stand by idly – they used their lead capabilities for a hi-technology response to the viral threat, which allows achieving serious success in the slowdown of the rate of its dissemination and the breakdown in the fight against COVID-19 with the help of vaccination.

All described aspects of using digital technologies in entrepreneurship of Industry 4.0 are consistently analyzed in this book by the lead scholars from different countries, experts in the sphere of digital technologies and entrepreneurship of Industry 4.0.

Elena G. Popkova
MGIMO University, Russia

Introduction

The Current Problems of Using Digital Technologies in Entrepreneurship in Industry 4.0 and Their Solutions

The Fourth Industrial Revolution made possible the transition to Industry 4.0 and started it. However, lie all technological shifts, this transition is uneven. At the beginning of the Fourth Industrial Revolution, it was expected that the created new "rules of the game" in the emerging world hi-tech markets would ensure equal opportunities for the development for all participants (countries and companies) and allow achieving the well-balanced development of the world economic system.

However, in the course of the Fourth Industrial Revolution, the differences between countries do not reduce but even grow. By now, there emerged a new form of global inequality – technological gap – which is treated as differences in the access of economic subjects and economic systems to technologies, as well as in the opportunities and results of their use. This is manifested at all levels of economic activities.

At the level of countries, the technological gap relates to the underrun of some countries from other countries by the level of digital competitiveness. Though the Fourth Industrial Revolution was an additional impulse for the development of the quickly growing economics of BRICS, in particular China's economy which has become of the world's leading hi-tech economies, other developing countries demonstrated less vivid progress. Developed countries (Global North) preserved, overall, their key positions in the global arena, acquiring leadership in the formed world markets of high technologies and hi-tech products. Underdeveloped countries (Global South), despite their success in neo-industrialization (transition to Industry 4.0), are the periphery of the considered hi-tech markets.

At the level of households, the technological gap is manifested in the reduced and limited accessibility of digital technologies of Industry 4.0 to rural and remote areas. The technological gap adds to other forms of inequality (e.g., income inequality and ageism) and aggravates the general social tension. At the level of companies, the technological gap is manifested in different levels of automatization of economic processes among companies and different levels of technology – a large difference between companies is often retained in modern markets, from low-tech to mid-tech and hi-tech.

Entrepreneurship is a link between the state and society in Industry 4.0. It is the most flexible subject and thus plays the main role in overcoming the technological gap. Still, the problem is that entrepreneurship cannot overcome the technological gap all by itself, it needs support. This requires well-coordinated actions of all participants of the Industry 4.0 markets.

This book is to demonstrate that Industry 4.0 can still justify the expectations associated with it regarding the overcoming of inequality and provision of a balance of economic systems at all levels. This requires a new approach, which implies more active and well-coordinated state and corporate management. The novelty of this book consists in its offering a transition from the spontaneous to controlled Fourth Industrial Revolution and forms the necessary scientific and methodological framework for this.

Enterprises should receive direct access to digital technologies, a powerful market stimulus for their implementation, and capabilities (resources, regulatory environment, and scientific and methodological recommendations) for their effective practical use. Marketing conditions have a decisive role here since as long as consumers prefer products with the lowest price, being unable to pay for and assess the advantages of hi-tech products, companies will minimize the use of digital technologies. Accordingly, in a progressive information society with high incomes, companies will strive toward high technologies.

Institutional investors should take into account the level of high technologies of companies and investment projects when making decisions on the provision of financing. Here it is important to stimulate the development of venture investments in breakthrough digital innovations, since, from the positions of profitability and risk, regular investors with a low-risk appetite and striving toward the quick return of investments, may prefer less technological projects.

State regulators of entrepreneurship must ensure the wide accessibility of the telecommunication infrastructure. To stimulate responsible and socially oriented digital innovations, it is expedient to develop public-private partnership in Industry 4.0. This partnership will be also useful for attracting private investments in breakthrough innovative projects in Industry 4.0 due to the expanded government guarantees of investment return and the distribution of risks and financial burden between public and private partners.

Finally, all mentioned economic subjects – hi-tech entrepreneurship, information society, venture investors, and state regulators of Industry 4.0 – should act in a coordinated manner and common interest. This will allow turning Industry 4.0 into a macro-economic cyber-physical system, which acts as a mechanism for increasing the global competitiveness of this system overall and its individual participants. Here an important role belongs to the "healthy" international competition and free trade.

All mentioned components of the success of Industry 4.0 are described and studied in detail in this book. The book is aimed at researching the international experience, developing the theory of entrepreneurship in Industry 4.0, identifying the perspectives, and developing the scientific & methodological and applied recommendations to raise accessibility, activity, and effectiveness of using digital technologies in entrepreneurship in Industry 4.0.

The book's originality consists in the reinterpretation of the concept of entrepreneurship's development in Industry 4.0: substantiation of the expedience of the approach from spontaneous to controlled, predictable and targeted development and formation of a scientific view of the controlled Fourth Industrial Revolution. The book's uniqueness lies in consideration of the specifics of different subjects of entrepreneurship in Industry 4.0, in particular online business, "young" companies, companies participating in public-private partnership, and small and medium companies.

The novelty of the book is due to the comprehensive study, complex consideration, and formation of a systemic view of the state and corporate management of entrepreneurship's development in Industry 4.0. The book's practical significance consists in the wide research and discussion of the international experience of using digital technologies in entrepreneurship in Industry 4.0 given the specifics of developed (e.g., Italy) and developing (e.g., Russia and Lebanon) countries. A special chapter is devoted to the study of the use of digital technologies in entrepreneurship in Industry 4.0 in the special context of the COVID-19 pandemic and crisis.

Elena G. Popkova
MGIMO University, Russia

Chapter 1
The Impact of the COVID-19 Pandemic and Crisis on Doing E-Business in Industry 4.0

Elena G. Popkova
https://orcid.org/0000-0003-2136-2767
MGIMO University, Russia

Elvira A. Khalikova
Ufa State Petroleum Technological University, Russia

Inna V. Andronova
Peoples' Friendship University of Russia, Russia

Yan Y. Grigoriev
Komsomolsk-on-Amur State University, Russia

ABSTRACT

The chapter aims to determine the impact of the COVID-19 pandemic and crisis on e-business in Industry 4.0. Dynamic modeling by regression and trend analysis methods found that e-business in Industry 4.0 showed a decline in the COVID-19 pandemic and crisis. The regression analysis method reveals that doing e-business in Industry 4.0 in the COVID-19 pandemic and crisis environment is determined by the demand of information society and the factors of telecommunication infrastructure, the management of which allows supporting e-business in Industry 4.0 in these conditions. The contribution of this research to the literature lies in the development of scientific positions of e-business theory by clarifying the effects of the COVID-19 pandemic and crisis on doing e-business in Industry 4.0, as well as identifying the managerial apparatus for mitigating these effects.

DOI: 10.4018/978-1-6684-4265-4.ch001

INTRODUCTION

In an Industry 4.0 environment, today's markets are dominated by e-business, the features and benefits of which include continuous and flexible digital transformation (Astafeva et al., 2020), application of advanced technology (Digilina et al., 2022), and improved cross-sectoral interaction s and optimized value chains (Zharikova et al., 2021). The COVID-19 pandemic and crisis have changed the business environment, which is covered by many contemporary authors (Nguyen & Hoang Dinh, 2021; Wang et al., 2021). The specifics of doing e-business in Industry 4.0 in the COVID-19 pandemic and crisis are poorly understood and are still ambiguous.

Some scholars draw attention to the overall economic downturn in 2020, the total restrictions caused by the COVID-19 pandemic that hold back entrepreneurial development, and the reduced availability of innovation for business. Thus, Engidaw (2022) noted that small businesses in developing countries faced particularly great problems during the COVID-19 pandemic (shown by the example of Ethiopia). Gao (2022) also noted that COVID-19 has made the activity of small businesses more difficult. Fairlie and Fossen (2022) indicated a marked decline in business sales under the impact of the COVID-19 pandemic.

Zhou et al. (2022) pointed to a direct link between the potential risk of COVID-19 incidence and urban density with doing business in a pandemic setting, highlighting serious spatial differences. Vazirani and Bhattacharjee (2022) proved the necessity, possibility, and high complexity of launching new businesses (start-ups) during the COVID-19 pandemic. B. H. Meyer et al. (2022) also substantiated the significant impact of the COVID-19 pandemic on business expectations, leading to a revision of business strategies toward less ambitious goals.

Other researchers point out that e-commerce has received a new impetus for development in the context of social distance. In their study, Giantari et al. (2022) pointed out the important role of digital marketing in mediating the impact of the COVID-19 pandemic and the intensity of competition on business performance. Vardari et al. (2022) pointed to the positive impact of information technology on business during the COVID-19 pandemic outbreak, associated with increased business resilience.

Xie et al. (2022) proved the relationship between business networks and the potential for organizational resilience in the digital age during COVID-19, outlining a perspective using organizational information processing theory. Popkova et al. (2021b) substantiated that corporate social responsibility can support business sustainability in conditions of social distancing during the COVID-19 crisis using the experience of BRICS and OECD countries as an example, considering their specifics.

Nevertheless, the impact of the COVID-19 pandemic and crisis on e-business in Industry 4.0 is only indirectly and fragmentedly addressed in the existing literature, which constitutes a considerable gap. Using a systemic analysis of cause-and-effect relationships, this paper aims to fill an identified gap and form a holistic view of how the practice of doing e-business in Industry 4.0 has changed under the influence of the COVID-19 pandemic and crisis. The paper aims to determine the impact of the COVID-19 pandemic and crisis on doing e-business in Industry 4.0.

BACKGROUND

This research is based on the provisions of the theory of e-business and uses the following categorical apparatus:

- Industry 4.0 – an advanced technological way of life associated with a high degree of automation of economic processes, the high level and rapid pace of development of high technology and its mass distribution, and the organization of economic activity in the form of cyber-physical systems (Faheem & Butt, 2022; Kunkel et al., 2022; Liu et al., 2022; Mei et al., 2022; Osipov et al., 2021; Yankovskaya et al., 2021);
- E-business is a cyber-physical system in which information technology is integrated into the practice of socio-economic relations, and interactions of economic actors (employees, sellers, and buyers in the market) and a high degree of automation of business processes based on advanced digital technologies are achieved, the main ones being robots, big data, and Artificial Intelligence (AI) (Alsheyadi, 2022; Gómez et al., 2022; Korolev et al., 2022; Krishnakumar et al., 2022; Kumaran & Jeyachandran, 2022; Pashentsev & Antonova, 2022; Patel et al., 2018);
- Doing e-business in Industry 4.0 is the process of doing business as a Business 4.0 in Industry 4.0 markets (Al-Khateeb, 2019; Gorelikov et al., 2021; Margherita & Braccini, 2021; Niemczyk et al., 2021; Popkova et al., 2021a; Popkova et al., 2021c; Sergi & Popkova, 2022; Silva et al., 2021; Tavera Romero et al., 2021; Verdoliva & Schiavone, 2021).

The existing literature details the benefits of using Industry 4.0 to fight the COVID-19 pandemic and conduct crisis management in these conditions. Valdez-Juárez et al. (2022) demonstrated the benefits of innovative business strategies in the face of COVID-19 (using the Sonora region of Mexico as an example) and proposed a promising approach to open innovation for SMEs. Peñarroya-Farell and Miralles (2022) justified the need to adapt the business model to the COVID-19 crisis as a strategic response to an unfavorable business environment) using Spanish cultural and creative firms as an example.

Clauss et al. (2022) proposed a temporary innovative business model as an innovative response of SMEs to the COVID-19 crisis. Cugno et al. (2022) linked the prospects for manufacturing recovery in the era of COVID-19 to unlocking the potential of Industry 4.0. Gadekar et al. (2022) also substantiated the relationship between Industry 4.0 drivers, risk reduction, and sustainable organizational performance in manufacturing industries. Hussain et al. (2021) have proven that Industry 4.0 technologies can help ensure business continuity in response to the challenges of COVID-19.

Mutingi (2018) substantiated the feasibility of a pathway to a customer-centered e-health quality evaluation to increase its resilience to the COVID-19 pandemic and crisis. However, the reverse impact of the COVID-19 pandemic and crisis on doing e-business in Industry 4.0 is underdeveloped and not clearly defined. This is a research gap that raises two research questions (RQ).

RQ_1: What impact has the COVID-19 pandemic and crisis had on doing e-business in Industry 4.0? The economic point of this question is to identify the strength of this influence and its nature. The answer to this question is important to provide a highly accurate prediction of further changes in e-business in Industry 4.0 in the context of the ongoing COVID-19 pandemic and post-crisis recovery of the world's economic systems, as well as to clarify the cyclical development of e-business in Industry 4.0. Based on Childs et al. (2022) and Hansson et al. (2022), who note the overall negative impact of the COVID-19 pandemic and crisis on entrepreneurship, we set hypothesis H_1, which is that e-business in Industry 4.0 has shown a decline in the COVID-19 pandemic and crisis.

RQ_2: How to manage (support) doing e-business in Industry 4.0 in the COVID-19 pandemic and crisis? The economic point of this question is to determine how to mitigate the negative impact of the adverse context of the COVID-19 pandemic and crisis on doing e-business in Industry 4.0, which is critical to the digital competitiveness of the economy. The answer to the posed question is important to identify perspectives and applied solutions (management mechanisms) to the current problems of doing e-business in Industry 4.0 in the context of the COVID-19 pandemic and crisis.

Based on Beninger and Francis (2022), Chhatwani et al. (2022), Guckenbiehl and Corral de Zubielqui (2022), Siby and George (2022), Tao et al. (2022), and Zhai and Yue (2022), who point to the key role of demand and infrastructure factors in the development of entrepreneurship in a market economy, we put forward hypothesis H_2, which is that doing e-business in Industry 4.0 in the COVID-19 pandemic and crisis environment is determined by demand factors of the information society and factors of telecommunications infrastructure, the management of which allows supporting (stimulating development) e-business in Industry 4.0 in this environment.

MAIN FOCUS OF THE CHAPTER

Research Strategy and Sampling

For the research, we formed a sample of the top five developed countries (OECD) leading in the international ranking of digital competitiveness in 2021 and developing countries (BRICS). The advantages of the sample obtained for this research are as follows. The first advantage is the representativeness of the research sample due to its coverage of developed and developing countries. Second, the sample includes countries that are global leaders in doing e-business in Industry 4.0. The IMD rating (2022) for 2021 places the USA in 1st place, Switzerland in 6th place, the Netherlands in 7th place, Brazil in 51st place, China in 15th place, India in 46th place, Russia in 42nd place, and South Africa in 60th place. Third, the sample is well suited to study the impact of the COVID-19 pandemic and crisis because it includes countries with some of the most tangible effects of that impact. Thus, according to World Health Organization (2022) Coronavirus (COVID-19) Dashboard, globally, as of 8:36 pm CEST, April 14, 2022, the USA has the highest incidence of COVID-19 in the world (79716960 cases). India has the second-highest incidence (43039023 cases). Brazil is in third place (30183929 cases). Russia is in seventh place (18041927 cases). The Netherlands detected 8006753 cases of COVID-19, South Africa – 3735578 cases, Switzerland – 3551798 cases, Denmark – 3091899 cases, Sweden – 2491980 cases, and China – 954346 cases.

According to the International Monetary Fund (2022) estimates, in 2020, a decline in economic growth was observed in all countries of the research sample; the COVID-19 crisis clearly manifested in these countries. The deepest recession was observed in India, where the gross domestic product, constant prices percent change was -7.252%. In South Africa, the figure was -6.432%, in Brazil -4.059%, in the Netherlands -3.825%, in the USA -3.405%, in Russia -2.951%, in Sweden -2.795%, in Switzerland -2.506%, and in Denmark -2.061%. In 2020, the rate of economic growth in China was positive (2.342%); however, it was down markedly from 2019, when it was 5.951%.

The strategy (order and methodology) of the research is as follows. To find the answer to RQ_1 and determine the impact of the COVID-19 pandemic and crisis on e-business in Industry 4.0, we conducted a dynamic analysis of changes in e-commerce indicators (e-participation and Internet retailing), general indicators of business innovation activity (agility of companies and entrepreneurial fear of failure), and high-tech business indicators. The research is conducted using horizontal (estimating growth in 2020 compared to 2019, and 2021 compared to 2020) and trend analysis (estimating growth in 2021 compared to 2019). Hypothesis H_1 is considered proven if the increase is negative in most cases (i.e., there is a decrease in the values of these indicators).

To find the answer to RQ_2 and determine the prospects of managing (supporting) e-business in Industry 4.0 in the COVID-19 pandemic and crisis, we conducted a factor analysis. Regression analysis is used to determine the impact of demand factors (tablet possession, smartphone possession, and attitudes toward globalization) and development factors of telecommunications infrastructure on the indicators mentioned above (technological framework). Hypothesis H_2 is considered proven if a positive correlation of indicators is found and the regression models are reliable. Based on economic-mathematical modeling, we applied the least-squares method to determine the prospects for crisis management of e-business in Industry 4.0 for mitigating the negative impact of the COVID-19 pandemic on it.

Dynamic Change Analysis of Doing E-Business in Industry 4.0 in the COVID-19 Pandemic and Crisis Conditions

To determine the impact of the COVID-19 pandemic and crisis on doing e-business in Industry 4.0, we conducted a dynamic analysis of changes in e-business development indicators: e-commerce in Table 1 and Table 2, business innovation activity in Table 3 and Table 4, and high-tech business in Table 5 and Table 6 in 2019–2020. Given that the indicators in Tables 1–6 are measured in places, and, therefore, the smaller their values, the better, an improvement of indicators is indicated by their negative growth, and deterioration of indicators, respectively, by their positive growth.

The results from Table 1 show that e-participation in developed countries will decline by an average of 175.57% in the COVID-19 pandemic and crisis (in 2020–2021 compared to 2019). In developing countries, this indicator also worsened but less markedly, with a decline of 21.37%. The largest declines were observed in Denmark (800%) and the Netherlands (125%). There was an increase in the considered indicator in some individual countries, for example, in the USA by 80%, in Switzerland by 51.35%, and in China by 67.86%. In 2020–2021, the values of this indicator remained unchanged in all countries of the sample.

The results from Table 2 show that Internet retailing activity in developed countries increased throughout the entire period under consideration. It averaged a 6.67% increase in 2020 over 2019, a 3.22% increase in 2021 over 2020, and a 10.33% increase over 2019. In developing countries, this figure worsened under the impact of the COVID-19 pandemic and crisis. Despite an initial modest increase of 1.94% in 2020 compared to 2019, after that, there was a decline: in 2021, the value of this indicator decreased by 4.45% compared to 2020 and by 2.23% compared to 2019. The largest decline in 2021 compared to 2019 was in Denmark (25%); the largest increases were in the USA (50%) and Switzerland (20%).

Table 1. E-participation statistics for 2019–2021 (place 1–64) and analysis of its dynamics

Category of countries	Country	Before the pandemic (2019)	During the COVID-19 pandemic and crisis		Horizontal analysis		Trend analysis
			2020	2021	Increase in 2020 compared to 2019, %	Increase in 2021 compared to 2020, %	Increase in 2021 compared to 2019, %
Top 5 developed countries (OECD)	USA	5	1	1	-80.00	0.00	-80.00
	Sweden	19	35	35	84.21	0.00	84.21
	Denmark	1	9	9	800.00	0.00	800.00
	Switzerland	37	18	18	-51.35	0.00	-51.35
	Netherlands	4	9	9	125.00	0.00	125.00
Developing countries (BRICS)	Brazil	12	18	18	50.00	0.00	50.00
	China	28	9	9	-67.86	0.00	-67.86
	India	15	28	28	86.67	0.00	86.67
	Russia	23	26	26	13.04	0.00	13.04
	South Africa	36	45	45	25.00	0.00	25.00

Source: Calculated and compiled by the authors based on IMD (2022)

According to Table 3, initially (in 2020 compared to 2019), the agility of companies decreased by 4.78% in developed countries and by 10.44% in developing countries. Subsequently, it improved. In developed countries, the increase in this indicator was 16.29% in 2021 compared to 2020 and 25.56% compared to 2019. In developing countries, the increase in this indicator was 12.96% in 2021 compared to 2020 and 5.63% compared to 2019. Denmark (66.67%) and the USA (61.11%) saw the largest increases in 2021 compared to 2019.

The statistical accounting of entrepreneurial fear of failure was launched in 2020 due to the increasing importance of this indicator in the COVID-19 pandemic and crisis; it continued in 2021. According to Table 4, in 2021, there was an 18.51% decline in entrepreneurial fear of failure compared to 2020 in developed countries and a 3.02% decline in developing countries. The greatest decline in this indicator was observed in Switzerland (50%) and the Netherlands (33.33%).

According to Table 5, in developed countries, world robots distribution decreased by 3.77% in 2020 compared to 2019 and by 0.95% in 2021 compared to 2020 and 4.78% compared to 2019. In the developing countries, the rate increased by 3.57% in 2020 compared to 2019 and by 0.04% in 2021 compared to 2020 and by 3.73% compared to 2019. Sweden (23.53%) and the Netherlands (11.11%) saw the largest

Table 2. Statistics of Internet retailing in 2019–2021 (place 1–64) and analysis of its dynamics

Category of countries	Country	Before the pandemic (2019)	In the conditions of the COVID-19 pandemic and crisis		Horizontal analysis		Trend analysis
			2020	2021	Increase in 2020 compared to 2019, %	Increase in 2021 compared to 2020, %	Increase in 2021 compared to 2019, %
Top 5 developed countries (OECD)	USA	2	2	1	0.00	-50.00	-50.00
	Sweden	15	14	14	-6.67	0.00	-6.67
	Denmark	4	4	5	0.00	25.00	25.00
	Switzerland	10	9	8	-10.00	-11.11	-20.00
	Netherlands	6	5	6	-16.67	20.00	0.00
Developing countries (BRICS)	Brazil	42	43	45	2.38	4.65	7.14
	China	21	19	22	-9.52	15.79	4.76
	India	55	56	57	1.82	1.79	3.64
	Russia	41	37	37	-9.76	0.00	-9.76
	South Africa	56	59	59	5.36	0.00	5.36

Source: Calculated and compiled by the authors based on IMD (2022)

declines in 2021 compared to 2019, while Russia (8.82%) and India (7.69%) saw the largest increases.

The results from Table 6 show that the dynamics of the use of big data and analytics were inconsistent over the reviewed period. First, there was a 21.36% decline in developed countries and a 19.29% decline in developing countries in 2020 compared to 2019. Then, there was an increase of 3.25% in developed countries and 6.84% in developing countries in 2021 compared to 2020. The trend was negative in both categories of countries, with a decline of 10.39% in developed countries and 7% in developing countries in 2021 compared to 2019. South Africa (100%), the Netherlands (70%), and Sweden (42.86%) had the largest decline in 2021 compared to 2019, while India had the largest increase (50%).

Thus, the peculiarities of the selected categories of countries are considered. The global economy (for the entire sample) saw mainly a negative change (decline) in doing e-business in Industry 4.0 in the COVID-19 pandemic and crisis (in 2021 compared to 2019):

- E-commerce indicators deteriorated by 47.21% on average (e-participation decreased by 98.47%, although Internet retailing increased by 4.05%);

Table 3. Statistics on the agility of companies in 2019–2021 (place 1–64) and analysis of its dynamics

Category of countries	Country	Before the pandemic (2019)	In the conditions of the COVID-19 pandemic and crisis		Horizontal analysis		Trend analysis
			2020	2021	Increase in 2020 compared to 2019, %	Increase in 2021 compared to 2020, %	Increase in 2021 compared to 2019, %
Top 5 developed countries (OECD)	USA	18	15	7	-16.67	-53.33	-61.11
	Sweden	12	7	10	-41.67	42.86	-16.67
	Denmark	6	2	2	-66.67	0.00	-66.67
	Switzerland	9	17	6	88.89	-64.71	-33.33
	Netherlands	10	16	15	60.00	-6.25	50.00
Developing countries (BRICS)	Brazil	57	39	44	-31.58	12.82	-22.81
	China	25	29	19	16.00	-34.48	-24.00
	India	32	35	24	9.38	-31.43	-25.00
	Russia	60	61	57	1.67	-6.56	-5.00
	South Africa	37	58	55	56.76	-5.17	48.65

Source: Calculated and compiled by the authors based on IMD (2022)

- Overall business innovation performance improved by an average of 2.41% (agility of companies increased by 15.59%, but entrepreneurial fear of failure decreased by 10.76%);
- High-tech business indicators deteriorated by an average of 4.61% (world robots distribution by 0.52% and use of big data and analytics by 8.70%).

Consequently, the increase turned out to be negative in most cases (a decrease in the values of almost all indicators was revealed), proving hypothesis H_1.

Factor Analysis of Doing E-Business in Industry 4.0 in the COVID-19 Pandemic and Crisis

We conduct a factor analysis to determine the prospects of managing (supporting) e-business in Industry 4.0 in the COVID-19 pandemic and crisis. The demand factors (tablet possession, smartphone possession, and attitudes toward globalization) shown in Table 7 and the telecommunications infrastructure development factors (technological framework) shown in Table 8 were selected as potential factors.

*Table 4. Entrepreneurial fear of failure statistics for 2019–2021 (place 1–64) and analysis of its dynamics**

Category of countries	Country	In the conditions of the COVID-19 pandemic and crisis		Trend analysis
		2020	2021	Increase in 2021 compared to 2020, %
Top 5 developed countries (OECD)	USA	17	18	5.88
	Sweden	30	31	3.33
	Denmark	n/d**	n/d**	n/d**
	Switzerland	2	3	50.00
	Netherlands	3	4	33.33
Developing countries (BRICS)	Brazil	18	19	5.56
	China	35	36	2.86
	India	54	55	1.85
	Russia	37	38	2.70
	South Africa	47	48	2.13

Note: * There was no statistical record of this indicator before the COVID-19 pandemic (2019).

** n/d – *the data is not available in the source; so it is replaced by the worst possible values to fill the gaps in the array of information (64 place).*

Source: Calculated and compiled by the authors based on IMD (2022)

According to Table 7, the level of tablet possession in 2021 was high in developed countries (9.20 place on average). It ranked 47.80 in developed countries and 28.50 in the overall sample. However, during the COVID-19 pandemic, it declined (2021 compared to 2019) by 21.05% in developed countries, 1.27% in developing countries, and 4.01% for the overall sample. The smartphone possession rate was also high in developed countries (11.80 on average). It ranked 34.80 in developed countries and 23.30 in the overall sample. During the COVID-19 pandemic (2021 compared to 2019), it decreased by 6.43% in developed countries and 6.43% in the overall sample. However, in developing countries, this indicator saw an increase of 12.56%.

According to Table 8, in 2021, attitudes toward globalization were high in developed countries (13.80 place on average). It ranked 38.40 in developed countries and 26.10 in the overall sample. This indicator increased in the COVID-19 pandemic (in 2021 compared to 2019) by 25% in developed countries, 4.74% in the overall sample, but decreased by 5.49% in developing countries. The level of the technological framework was also high in developed countries (an average of 9.80 place). It ranked 49.40 in developed countries and 29.60 in the overall sample. It increased in the COVID-19

Table 5. World robots' distribution statistics for 2019–2021 (place 1–64) and analysis of its dynamics

Category of countries	Country	Before the pandemic (2019)	In the conditions of the COVID-19 pandemic and crisis		Horizontal analysis		Trend analysis
			2020	2021	Increase in 2020 compared to 2019, %	Increase in 2021 compared to 2020, %	Increase in 2021 compared to 2019, %
Top 5 developed countries (OECD)	USA	4	4	4	0.00	0.00	0.00
	Sweden	17	18	21	5.88	16.67	23.53
	Denmark	30	30	29	0.00	-3.33	-3.33
	Switzerland	27	26	25	-3.70	-3.85	-7.41
	Netherlands	18	21	20	16.67	-4.76	11.11
Developing countries (BRICS)	Brazil	19	17	18	-10.53	5.88	-5.26
	China	1	1	1	0.00	0.00	0.00
	India	13	12	12	-7.69	0.00	-7.69
	Russia	34	32	31	-5.88	-3.13	-8.82
	South Africa	32	34	33	6.25	-2.94	3.13

Source: Calculated and compiled by the authors based on IMD (2022)

pandemic (in 2021 compared to 2019) in developed countries by 2% and decreased in developing countries by 3.35% and in the overall sample by 2.42%.

We applied regression analysis to determine the impact of the factors in Tables 7–8 on e-business in Industry 4.0 in Tables 1–6. The results are shown in Table 9. The dashes ("-") on Table 9 mean that there is no close connection between the indicators.

The results of regression analysis from Table 9 revealed the following relationships:

- E-participation increases by 0.32 places with an increase in the technological framework by one place. The change in this factor explains the change in e-participation by 52.40%. The model successfully passed the F-test and is therefore reliable at the 0.01 significance level.
- Internet retailing increases by 0.06 places with smartphone possession and by 0.93 places with a one-place increase in the technological framework. The change of 98.25% is due to a change in selected factors. The model successfully passed the F-test and is therefore reliable at the 0.01 significance level.
- The agility of companies increases by 0.30 places with a one-place increase in tablet possession, by 0.0006 places with a one-place increase in smartphone possession, by 0.50 places with a one-place increase in attitudes

Table 6. Statistics on the use of big data and analytics in 2019–2021 (place 1–64) and analysis of its dynamics

Category of countries	Country	Before the pandemic (2019)	In the conditions of the COVID-19 pandemic and crisis		Horizontal analysis		Trend analysis
			2020	2021	Increase in 2020 compared to 2019, %	Increase in 2021 compared to 2020, %	Increase in 2021 compared to 2019, %
Top 5 developed countries (OECD)	USA	6	9	5	50.00	-44.44	-16.67
	Sweden	7	7	10	0.00	42.86	42.86
	Denmark	17	12	13	-29.41	8.33	-23.53
	Switzerland	29	25	23	-13.79	-8.00	-20.69
	Netherlands	10	20	17	100.00	-15.00	70.00
Developing countries (BRICS)	Brazil	60	58	56	-3.33	-3.45	-6.67
	China	12	8	11	-33.33	37.50	-8.33
	India	30	32	15	6.67	-53.13	-50.00
	Russia	31	33	31	6.45	-6.06	0.00
	South Africa	20	44	40	120.00	-9.09	100.00

Source: Calculated and compiled by the authors based on IMD (2022)

toward globalization, and by 0.18 places with a one-pace increase in the technological framework. The 90.99% change in the agility of companies is due to a change in the selected factors. The model successfully passed the F-test and is therefore reliable at the 0.01 significance level.

- Entrepreneurial fear of failure increases by 0.48 places with a one-place increase in tablet possession. The 51.28% change in the entrepreneurial fear of failure is due to a change in the selected factors. The model successfully passed the F-test and is therefore reliable at the 0.05 significance level.
- World robots' distribution increases by 0.13 places with a one-place increase in attitudes toward globalization. The change in world robots' distribution by 25.38% is due to a change in selected factors. The model did not pass the F-test and therefore is insufficiently reliable.
- The use of big data and analytics increases by 0.35 places with a one-place increase in tablet possession and by 0.29 places with a one-place increase in attitudes toward globalization. The 72.01% change in the use of big data and analytics is due to a change in selected factors. The model successfully passed the F-test and is therefore reliable at the 0.01 significance level.

Table 7. Statistics on tablet possession and smartphone possession in 2019–2021 (place 1–64) and analysis of its dynamics

Category of countries	Country	Tablet possession			Smartphone possession		
		Before the pandemic (2019)	In the conditions of the COVID-19 pandemic and crisis		Before the pandemic (2019)	In the conditions of the COVID-19 pandemic and crisis	
			2020	2021		2020	2021
Top 5 developed countries (OECD)	USA	2	1	1	12	13	14
	Sweden	6	2	2	5	4	6
	Denmark	9	19	20	7	10	11
	Switzerland	8	9	9	2	3	4
	Netherlands	13	13	14	24	24	24
Developing countries (BRICS)	Brazil	48	47	47	28	34	35
	China	31	31	36	16	17	14
	India	61	60	60	55	53	52
	Russia	39	40	39	60	29	29
	South Africa	57	57	57	40	45	44

Source: IMD (2022)

Table 8. Statistics about globalization and technological framework in 2019–2021 (place 1–64) and analysis of its dynamics

Category of countries	Country	Attitudes toward globalization			Technological framework		
		Before the pandemic (2019)	In the conditions of the COVID-19 pandemic and crisis		Before the pandemic (2019)	In the conditions of the COVID-19 pandemic and crisis	
			2020	2021		2020	2021
Top 5 developed countries (OECD)	USA	46	53	38	11	7	9
	Sweden	4	2	1	12	11	13
	Denmark	9	1	3	8	6	6
	Switzerland	27	26	21	9	14	11
	Netherlands	6	9	6	10	12	10
Developing countries (BRICS)	Brazil	47	44	42	47	50	51
	China	10	8	11	32	32	28
	India	22	22	22	62	62	62
	Russia	60	59	61	39	41	45
	South Africa	43	52	56	59	57	61

Source: IMD (2022)

Table 9. Results of regression analysis of the impact of selected factors on doing e-business in Industry 4.0 in 2019–2021

Regression statistics	Parameters of the linear regression model					
	E-participation	**Internet retailing**	**Agility of companies**	**Entrepreneurial fear of failure**	**World robots distribution**	**Use of big data and analytics**
Multiple R	0.5240	0.9825	0.9099	0.5128	0.2538	0.7201
Constant	9.90 (3.52)	-3.39 (1.30)	-1.21 (2.99)	17.63 (6.66)	15.91 (3.22)	5.52 (3.87)
Tablet possession	-	-	0.30 (0.31)	0.48 (1.19)	-	0.35 (0.11)
Smartphone possession	-	0.06 (0.08)	0.0006 (0.19)	-	-	-
Attitudes toward globalization	-	-	0.50 (0.10)	-	0.13 (0.09)	0.29 (0.11)
Technological framework	0.32 (0.10)	0.93 (0.07)	0.18 (0.32)	-	-	-
Observations	30	30	30	20	30	30
Significance of F	0.003*	$1.9\text{-}10^{-20}$*	$3.2\text{-}10^{-0.9}$*	0.021**	0.176***	$5.2*10^{-0.5}$*
F-table	7.636 (at k_1=30-1-1=28; k_2=1)	5.488 (at k_1=30-2-1=27; k_2=2)	4.140 (at k_1=30-4-1=26; k_2=4)	8.285 (at k_1=20-1-1=18; k_2=1)	The model is not reliable enough	5.488 (at k_1=30-2-1=27; k_2=2)
F-observed	10.60	376.41	30.06	6.42	1.93	14.54

Note: Robust standard errors are given in parentheses.
*p < 0.01, **p < 0.05, ***p < 0.2.
Source: Calculated and compiled by the authors

Thus, a positive relationship between all indicators was revealed; almost all regression models were reliable, which proved hypothesis H_2. This allows us to rely on the obtained regression models further in this research. The greatest contribution to doing e-business in Industry 4.0 in the COVID-19 pandemic and crisis was demonstrated by the technological framework. The second most important factor was tablet possession, and the third most important was attitudes toward globalization; smartphone possession was not a significant factor.

SOLUTIONS AND RECOMMENDATIONS

Using economic-mathematical modeling and the method of least squares, we determine the prospects of e-business in Industry 4.0 crisis management to mitigate the negative impact of the COVID-19 pandemic on it. To assess the management potential of the identified factors in support of doing e-business in Industry 4.0, let us consider the maximum possible improvement of all factor variables (bringing them to the first place): tablet possession by 96.42% compared to the current value in 2021, smartphone possession by 95.80%, attitudes toward globalization by 96.30%, and technological framework by 96.58%. The benefits of optimizing the impact of factors by stimulating demand from the information society and developing a telecommunications infrastructure for doing e-business in Industry 4.0 are demonstrated in Figure 1.

According to Figure 1, by managing demand factors from the information society and telecommunications infrastructure, instead of a decline, an increase in all e-business in Industry 4.0 could be achieved, in particular (an increase compared to 2021 is shown):

- E-participation by 48.38%;
- Internet retailing by 109.45%;
- Agility of companies by 100.96%;
- Entrepreneurial fear of failure by 42.69%;
- World robots distribution by 17.32%;
- Use of big data and analytics by 72.13%.

Therefore, the stimulation of demand from the information society and the development of telecommunication infrastructure is recommended to solve the problem of doing e-business in Industry 4.0 during the COVID-19 pandemic and crisis and in future pandemics and economic crises.

FUTURE RESEARCH DIRECTIONS

The limitation of the obtained results is the desire of this research to cover the world economy as fully as possible, identify general patterns and perspectives, and develop universal recommendations. In this regard, the characteristics of developed and developing countries are considered only partially – from the point of view of dynamics. In further research, it is advisable to conduct an in-depth study of the experience and characteristics of developed and developing countries in their expanded samples, as well as to develop special recommendations for them, considering their specifics. Further research can be based on the differences in the dynamics of e-business in Industry 4.0 during the COVID-19 pandemic and crisis identified in this paper.

It is also necessary to continue the study begun in 2022 and possibly beyond throughout the COVID-19 pandemic. It is necessary to comprehensively consider

Figure 1. The benefits of optimizing the impact of demand factors and infrastructure on doing e-business in Industry 4.0
Source: Calculated and constructed by the authors

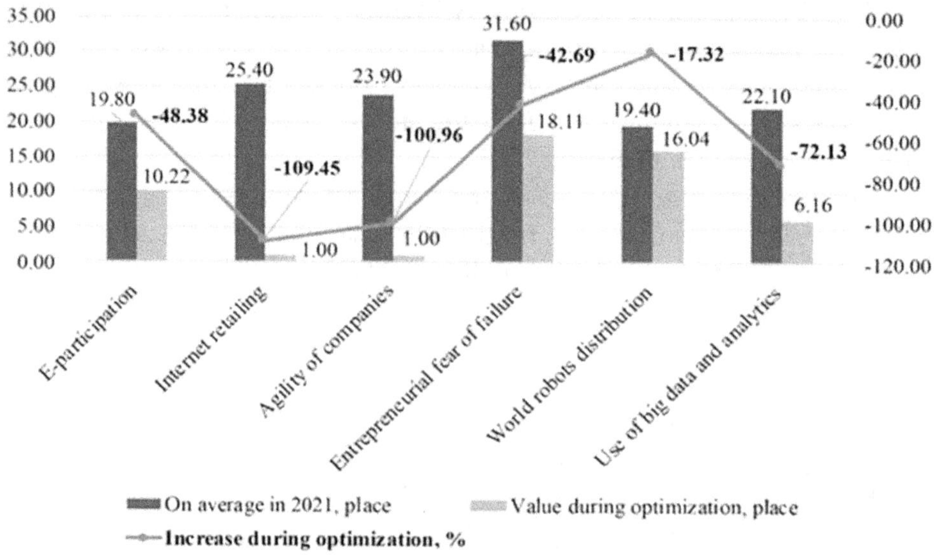

the experiences and characteristics of the world economic system affected by the COVID-19 pandemic. A starting point for this could be the results of regression and trend analyses of the 2019–2021 data, which should be supplemented in future studies with dynamic analyses of later data (for 2022 and beyond).

CONCLUSION

Thus, the answers to both research questions (RQ) are obtained, and the hypotheses put forward are confirmed. As part of RQ_1, we found that e-business in Industry 4.0 showed a decline in the COVID-19 pandemic and crisis (hypothesis H_1 is proved). Thus, in the COVID-19 pandemic and crisis (in 2021 compared to 2019), e-commerce indicators deteriorated by an average of 47.21% (e-participation decreased by 98.47%). The overall index of business innovation – entrepreneurial fear of failure decreased by 10.76%. The indicators of high-tech business deteriorated by an average of 4.61% (world robots distribution by 0.52% and the use of big data and analytics by 8.70%).

As part of RQ_2, we revealed that doing e-business in Industry 4.0 in the COVID-19 pandemic and crisis environment is determined by demand factors from the information society and telecommunication infrastructure factors, the management of which can support (stimulate the development of) e-business in Industry 4.0 in these conditions (hypothesis H_2 is proved). The greatest contribution to doing e-business in Industry 4.0 in the COVID-19 pandemic and crisis was demonstrated by the technological framework. The second most important factor was tablet possession, and the third most important was attitudes toward globalization; smartphone possession was not a significant factor.

The contribution of the study to the literature lies in the development of the scientific positions of e-business theory through clarification of the consequences of the COVID-19 pandemic and the crisis it caused for e-business in Industry 4.0, as well as identifying the managerial apparatus to mitigate them. The practical significance of the author's findings is that the proposed recommendations for managing the demand factors of information society and factors of telecommunications infrastructure are useful for stimulating the development of e-business in Industry 4.0 in the ongoing COVID-19 pandemic.

Policy implications are related to the fact that the author's recommendations are also useful to support doing e-business in Industry 4.0 in case of future pandemics and economic crises. The findings opened up the prospect of flexible and highly efficient management of demand and infrastructure factors to drive the development of e-business in Industry 4.0. Since this research is based on a representative sample, the proposed recommendations are universal – they are useful and can be applied in practice in developed and developing countries.

ACKNOWLEDGMENT

The study was conducted as part of the Consortium for Sustainable Development and Technological Leadership.

REFERENCES

Al-Khateeb, B. A. A. (2019). The conceptual framework for the examination of a successful digital entrepreneurship in 21st century. In K. Mezghani & W. Aloulou (Eds.), *Business transformations in the era of digitalization* (pp. 126–141). IGI Global. doi:10.4018/978-1-5225-7262-6.ch008

Alsheyadi, A. (2022). Collaborative e-business efforts and firm performance. *International Journal of Productivity and Performance Management, 71*(1), 100–124. doi:10.1108/IJPPM-11-2019-0516

Astafeva, O. V., Astafyev, E. V., Khalikova, E. A., Leybert, T. B., & Osipova, I. A. (2020). XBRL reporting in the conditions of digital business transformation. In S. Ashmarina, M. Vochozka, & V. Mantulenko (Eds.), *Digital age: Chances, challenges and future* (pp. 373–381). Springer. doi:10.1007/978-3-030-27015-5_45

Beninger, S., & Francis, J. N. P. (2022). Resources for business resilience in a COVID-19 world: A community-centric approach. *Business Horizons, 65*(2), 227–238. doi:10.1016/j.bushor.2021.02.048

Chhatwani, M., Mishra, S. K., Varma, A., & Rai, H. (2022). Psychological resilience and business survival chances: A study of small firms in the USA during COVID-19. *Journal of Business Research, 142*, 277–286. doi:10.1016/j.jbusres.2021.12.048

Childs, M., Turner, T., Sneed, C., & Berry, A. (2022). A contingency theory approach to understanding small retail business continuity during COVID-19. *Family and Consumer Sciences Research Journal, 50*(3), 216–230. doi:10.1111/fcsr.12434 PMID:35600319

Clauss, T., Breier, M., Kraus, S., Durst, S., & Mahto, R. V. (2022). Temporary business model innovation – SMEs' innovation response to the COVID-19 crisis. *R & D Management, 52*(2), 294–312. doi:10.1111/radm.12498

Cugno, M., Castagnoli, R., Büchi, G., & Pini, M. (2022). Industry 4.0 and production recovery in the covid era. *Technovation, 114*, 102443. doi:10.1016/j.technovation.2021.102443

Digilina, O. B., Teslenko, I. B., & Andronova, I. V. (2022). New management technologies in the context of digitalization. In E. G. Popkova (Ed.), *Imitation market modeling in digital economy: Game theoretic approaches* (pp. 333–339). Springer. doi:10.1007/978-3-030-93244-2_37

Engidaw, A. E. (2022). Small businesses and their challenges during COVID-19 pandemic in developing countries: In the case of Ethiopia. *Journal of Innovation and Entrepreneurship, 11*(1), 1. doi:10.118613731-021-00191-3 PMID:35036286

Faheem, M., & Butt, R. A. (2022). Big datasets of optical-wireless cyber-physical systems for optimizing manufacturing services in the Internet of things-enabled Industry 4.0. *Data in Brief, 42*, 108026. doi:10.1016/j.dib.2022.108026 PMID:35330737

Fairlie, R., & Fossen, F. M. (2022). The early impacts of the COVID-19 pandemic on business sales. *Small Business Economics, 58*(4), 1853–1864. doi:10.100711187-021-00479-4

Gadekar, R., Sarkar, B., & Gadekar, A. (2022). Investigating the relationship among Industry 4.0 drivers, adoption, risks reduction, and sustainable organizational performance in manufacturing industries: An empirical study. *Sustainable Production and Consumption*, *31*, 670–692. doi:10.1016/j.spc.2022.03.010

Gao, J. (2022). Has COVID-19 hindered small business activities? The role of Fintech. *Economic Analysis and Policy*, *74*, 297–308. doi:10.1016/j.eap.2022.02.008

Giantari, I. G. A. K., Yasa, N. N. K., Suprasto, H. B., & Rahmayanti, P. L. D. (2022). The role of digital marketing in mediating the effect of the COVID-19 pandemic and the intensity of competition on business performance. *International Journal of Data and Network Science*, *6*(1), 217–232. doi:10.5267/j.ijdns.2021.9.006

Gómez, J., Salazar, I., & Vargas, P. (2022). Production outsourcing, technological cooperation and E-business adoption by Spanish manufacturing firms. *Journal of Engineering and Technology Management*, *63*, 101677. doi:10.1016/j.jengtecman.2022.101677

Gorelikov, K. A., Komarov, A. V., & Bezsmertnaya, E. R. (2021). A paradigm shift in business management in the context of Industry 4.0. In E. G. Popkova & V. N. Ostrovskaya (Eds.), *Meta-scientific study of artificial intelligence* (pp. 469–476). Information Age Publishing.

Guckenbiehl, P., & Corral de Zubielqui, G. (2022). Start-ups' business model changes during the COVID-19 pandemic: Counteracting adversities and pursuing opportunities. *International Small Business Journal: Researching Entrepreneurship*, *40*(2), 150–177. doi:10.1177/02662426211055447 PMID:35250144

Hansson, J., Landstad, B. J., Vinberg, S., Hedlund, M., & Tjulin, Å. (2022). Small business managers and COVID-19 – The role of a sense of coherence and general resistance resources in coping with stressors. *PLoS One*, *17*(3), e0265029. doi:10.1371/journal.pone.0265029 PMID:35302995

Hussain, A., Farooq, M. U., Habib, M. S., Masood, T., & Pruncu, C. I. (2021). COVID-19 challenges: Can industry 4.0 technologies help with business continuity? *Sustainability*, *13*(21), 11971. doi:10.3390u132111971

IMD. (2022). *World digital competitiveness rankings 2019–2021*. Retrieved April 17, 2022, from https://www.imd.org/centers/world-competitiveness-center/rankings/world-digital-competitiveness/

International Monetary Fund. (2022). *World Economic Outlook Database: October 2021*. Retrieved April 18, 2022, from https://www.imf.org/en/Publications/WEO/weo-database/2021/October

Korolev, O. G., Yankovskaya, V. V., Grazhdankina, O. A., Tkachenko, V. V., & Kuchko, S. A. (2022). Financial model of digital cooperation in business. In A. V. Bogoviz, A. E. Suglobov, A. N. Maloletko, & O. V. Kaurova (Eds.), *Cooperation and sustainable development* (pp. 175–182). Springer. doi:10.1007/978-3-030-77000-6_21

Krishnakumar, S. K., Kishore, R., & Suresh, N. C. (2022). Expansive or focused attention? An exploration–exploitation perspective on e-Business systems and firm performance. *Production and Operations Management, 31*(5), 2038–2066. Advance online publication. doi:10.1111/poms.13664

Kumaran, L. A., & Jeyachandran, H. (2022). Modelling e-business influencing factors for supply chain performance of Indian MSMEs: An ISM approach. *International Journal of Process Management and Benchmarking, 12*(1), 28–45. doi:10.1504/IJPMB.2022.120444

Kunkel, S., Matthess, M., Xue, B., & Beier, G. (2022). Industry 4.0 in sustainable supply chain collaboration: Insights from an interview study with international buying firms and Chinese suppliers in the electronics industry. *Resources, Conservation and Recycling, 182*, 106274. doi:10.1016/j.resconrec.2022.106274

Liu, Z., Sampaio, P., Pishchulov, G., Mehandjiev, N., Cisneros-Cabrera, S., Schirrmann, A., Jiru, F., & Bnouhanna, N. (2022). The architectural design and implementation of a digital platform for Industry 4.0 SME collaboration. *Computers in Industry, 138*, 103623. doi:10.1016/j.compind.2022.103623

Margherita, E. G., & Braccini, A. M. (2021). Managing industry 4.0 automation for fair ethical business development: A single case study. *Technological Forecasting and Social Change, 172*, 121048. doi:10.1016/j.techfore.2021.121048

Mei, S., Yuan, M., Cui, J., Dong, S., & Zhao, J. (2022). Machinery condition monitoring in the era of industry 4.0: A relative degree of contribution feature selection and deep residual network combined approach. *Computers & Industrial Engineering, 168*, 108129. doi:10.1016/j.cie.2022.108129

Meyer, B. H., Prescott, B., & Sheng, X. S. (2022). The impact of the COVID-19 pandemic on business expectations. *International Journal of Forecasting, 38*(2), 529–544. doi:10.1016/j.ijforecast.2021.02.009 PMID:35185229

Mutingi, M. (2018). Towards a customer-centric framework for evaluation of E-health service quality. In N. Gwangwava & M. Mutingi (Eds.), *E-manufacturing and e-service strategies in contemporary organizations* (pp. 199–218). IGI Global. doi:10.4018/978-1-5225-3628-4.ch008

Nguyen, L. T. M., & Hoang Dinh, P. (2021). Ex-ante risk management and financial stability during the COVID-19 pandemic: A study of Vietnamese firms. *China Finance Review International*, *11*(3), 349–371. doi:10.1108/CFRI-12-2020-0177

Niemczyk, J., Trzaska, R., Wilczyński, M., & Borowski, K. (2021). Business models 4.0 using network effects: Case study of the cyfrowy polsat group. *Sustainability*, *13*(21), 11570. doi:10.3390u132111570

Osipov, V. S., Larionova, E. I., Sigarev, A. V., & Mishchenko, V. V. (2021). The key types of economic activities in the pleasure economy in the context of developing countries' transition to Industry 4.0. *International Journal of Trade and Global Markets*, *14*(4-5), 413–422. doi:10.1504/IJTGM.2021.116739

Pashentsev, D. A., & Antonova, N. V. (2022). Ensuring economical resilience in the conditions of developing penetrative (digital) technologies: Mechanisms for Protecting Rights and Legitimate Interests of Economic Subjects. In A. O. Inshakova & E. E. Frolova (Eds.), *The transformation of social relationships in Industry 4.0: Economic security and legal prevention* (pp. 75–84). Information Age Publishing.

Patel, D., Goyal, S., & Agarwal, R. (2018). E-commerce business model. In G. Sreedhar (Ed.), *Improving E-commerce web applications through business intelligence techniques* (pp. 110–129). IGI Global. doi:10.4018/978-1-5225-3646-8.ch005

Peñarroya-Farell, M., & Miralles, F. (2022). Business model adaptation to the COVID-19 crisis: Strategic response of the Spanish cultural and creative firms. *Journal of Open Innovation*, *8*(1), 39. doi:10.3390/joitmc8010039

Popkova, E., Bogoviz, A. V., & Sergi, B. S. (2021a). Towards digital society management and 'capitalism 4.0' in contemporary Russia. *Humanities and Social Sciences Communications*, *8*(1), 77. doi:10.105741599-021-00743-8

Popkova, E., DeLo, P., & Sergi, B. S. (2021b). Corporate Social Responsibility Amid Social Distancing During the COVID-19 Crisis: BRICS vs. OECD Countries. *Research in International Business and Finance*, *55*, 101315. doi:10.1016/j.ribaf.2020.101315 PMID:34173410

Popkova, E. G., Inshakova, A. O., & Sergi, B. S. (2021c). Venture capital and Industry 4.0: The G7's versus BRICS' experience. *Thunderbird International Business Review*, *63*(6), 765–777. doi:10.1002/tie.22235

Sergi, B. S., & Popkova, E. G. (2022). Towards a 'wide' role for venture capital in OECD countries' industry 4.0. *Heliyon*, *8*(1), e08700. doi:10.1016/j.heliyon.2021.e08700 PMID:35028473

Siby, A., & George, J. P. (2022). Influence of customer relationship management for the success of E-business. In A. Joshi, M. Mahmud, R. G. Ragel, & N. V. Thakur (Eds.), *Information and communication technology for competitive strategies* (pp. 473–481). Springer., doi:10.1007/978-981-16-0739-4_45

Silva, A. J., Cortez, P., Pereira, C., & Pilastri, A. (2021). Business analytics in Industry 4.0: A systematic review. *Expert Systems: International Journal of Knowledge Engineering and Neural Networks*, *38*(7), e12741. doi:10.1111/exsy.12741

Tao, H., Sun, X., Liu, X., Tian, J., & Zhang, D. (2022). The impact of consumer purchase behavior changes on the business model design of consumer services companies over the course of COVID-19. *Frontiers in Psychology*, *13*, 818845. doi:10.3389/fpsyg.2022.818845 PMID:35310236

Tavera Romero, C. A., Ortiz, J. H., Khalaf, O. I., & Prado, A. R. (2021). Business intelligence: Business evolution after Industry 4.0. *Sustainability*, *13*(18), 10026. doi:10.3390u131810026

Valdez-Juárez, L. E., Castillo-Vergara, M., & Ramos-Escobar, E. A. (2022). Innovative business strategies in the face of COVID-19: An approach to open innovation of SMEs in the Sonora Region of Mexico. *Journal of Open Innovation*, *8*(1), 47. doi:10.3390/joitmc8010047

Vardari, L., Bytyqi, Q., & Lumi, A. (2022). The impact of information technologies on business during the COVID-19 pandemic outbreak. *Contemporary Studies in Economic and Financial Analysis*, *108B*, 143–158. doi:10.1108/S1569-37592022000108B038

Vazirani, A., & Bhattacharjee, T. (2022). Necessity or opportunity: A case of business venturing decision during COVID-19 pandemic. *Managerial and Decision Economics*, *43*(3), 768–778. doi:10.1002/mde.3417

Verdoliva, V., & Schiavone, F. (2021). Technologies 4.0 and business development. *European Management Journal*, *39*(3), 315–316. doi:10.1016/j.emj.2021.05.001

Wang, S. S., Goh, J. R., Sornette, D., Wang, H., & Yang, E. Y. (2021). Government support for SMEs in response to COVID-19: Theoretical model using Wang transform. *China Finance Review International*, *11*(3), 406–433. doi:10.1108/CFRI-05-2021-0088

World Health Organization (WHO). (2022). *WHO Coronavirus (COVID-19) dashboard: Globally, as of 8:36 pm CEST, 14 April 2022*. Retrieved April 18, 2022, from https://covid19.who.int/?gclid=Cj0KCQjwrIf3BRD1ARIsAMuugNsIqvkZsmIoto8RJ964Wv1YdYlla CbKloYu2Z9HLeUkZuatNROZyzgaAvEiEALw_wcB

Xie, X., Wu, Y., Palacios-Marqués, D., & Ribeiro-Navarrete, S. (2022). Business networks and organizational resilience capacity in the digital age during COVID-19: A perspective utilizing organizational information processing theory. *Technological Forecasting and Social Change*, *177*, 121548. doi:10.1016/j.techfore.2022.121548

Yankovskaya, V. V., Kelina, K. G., Chutcheva, Y. V., & Alekseev, A. N. (2021). The consumer economy and the pleasure economy: Similarities and differences in developing countries in industry 4.0. *International Journal of Trade and Global Markets*, *14*(4-5), 507–515. doi:10.1504/IJTGM.2021.116737

Zhai, W., & Yue, H. (2022). Economic resilience during COVID-19: An insight from permanent business closures. *Environment and Planning A. Economy and Space*, *54*(2), 219–221. doi:10.1177/0308518X211055181

Zharikova, E. P., Grigoriev, Y. Y., & Grigorieva, A. L. (2021). Applications of computer vision in cross-sectoral tasks. In O. G. Shakirova, O. V. Bashkov, & A. A. Khusainov (Eds.), *Current problems and ways of industry development: Equipment and technologies* (pp. 415–426). Springer., doi:10.1007/978-3-030-69421-0_45

Zhou, L., Li, S., Li, C., Shen, G., Yang, H., Zhu, P., Han, H., & Li, B. (2022). Spatial congruency or mismatch? Analyzing the COVID-19 potential infection risk and urban density as businesses reopen. *Cities (London, England)*, *123*, 103615. doi:10.1016/j.cities.2022.103615 PMID:35095162

ADDITIONAL READING

Al-Omoush, K. S., Simón-Moya, V., & Sendra-García, J. (2020). The impact of social capital and collaborative knowledge creation on e-business proactiveness and organizational agility in responding to the COVID-19 crisis. *Journal of Innovation and Knowledge*, *5*(4), 279–288. doi:10.1016/j.jik.2020.10.002

Chandak, S., & Kumar, N. (2020). Development of a framework to improve supply chain performance through e-business and sustainability enablers: An emerging economy perspective. *Management of Environmental Quality*, *31*(5), 1045–1070. doi:10.1108/MEQ-07-2019-0150

Cristofaro, M. (2020). E-business evolution: An analysis of mobile applications' business models. *Technology Analysis and Strategic Management*, *32*(1), 88–103. doi:10.1080/09537325.2019.1634804

Häckel, B., Übelhör, J., & Voit, C. (2020). Creating competitive advantage in E-business value chains by using excess capacity via IT-enabled marketplaces. *The Data Base for Advances in Information Systems, 51*(3), 97–118. doi:10.1145/3410977.3410983

Ismailova, B., Kurmanova, A., Alimpiyeva, T., Balabiyev, K., Altynbekkyzy, A., & Altynbekuly, A. (2020). The viewpoint on legislation and guidelines on E-business and E-commerce: Kazakhstan's approach. *Journal of Advanced Research in Law and Economics, 11*(3), 856–862. doi:10.14505/jarle.v11.3(49).19

Sufian, A., Sedek, M., Qi, T. J., & Mohamed, M. A. (2020). The influence of e-business adoption on business performance of micro-entrepreneurs. *International Journal of Advanced Science and Technology, 29*(8s), 2026-2037. Retrieved April 18, 2022, from http://sersc.org/journals/index.php/IJAST/article/view/12800

Valinurova, L. S., Leibert, T. B., & Khalikova, E. A. (2020). Innovative approaches to corporate financial management in business systems. In E. Popkova & B. Sergi (Eds.), *The 21st century from the positions of modern science: Intellectual, digital and innovative aspects* (pp. 83–95). Springer. doi:10.1007/978-3-030-32015-7_11

Yelikbayev, K., & Andronova, I. (2022). The interaction of the EEU member states and risks of their mutual trade during the COVID-19 Pandemic: Implications for the management of corporate social responsibility. *Risks, 10*(2), 27. doi:10.3390/risks10020027

KEY TERMS AND DEFINITIONS

BRICS: A group of five fast-growing economies that determine the current and future growth of the world economy. The organization includes Brazil, Russia, India, China, and South Africa.

COVID-19 Crisis: The global economic recession that erupted in 2020 against the backdrop of the COVID-19 pandemic.

Cyber-Physical System: Economic system of any level (from nano- and micro- to meso-, macro-, and global levels), in which information technology is integrated into socio-economic interactions.

Doing E-Business in Industry 4.0: The process of doing business as a Business 4.0 in Industry 4.0 markets.

E-Business: A cyber-physical system in which information technology is integrated into the practice of socio-economic relations and interactions of economic actors (employees, sellers, and buyers in the market) and a high degree of automation of business processes based on advanced digital technologies is achieved, the main ones being robots, big data, and Artificial Intelligence (AI).

Industry 4.0: An advanced technological way of life associated with a high degree of automation of economic processes, the high level and rapid pace of development of high technology and its mass distribution, and the organization of economic activity in the form of cyber-physical systems.

OECD: Organization for Economic Cooperation and Development – an international intergovernmental economic organization with open borders, bringing together developed countries that recognize the principles of representative democracy and free market economy.

Pandemic: The highest degree of viral threat in which disease has spread throughout the world. For example, the COVID-19 pandemic, in which hundreds and thousands of people in all countries fall ill and die from a new coronavirus infection.

Chapter 2
Digital Economy and Digital Transformation

Daniele Schiliro
University of Messina, Italy

ABSTRACT

The chapter's main objective is to analyze the digital economy and its characteristics. In a time of overlapping disruptions, the chapter describes the fast growth of the digital environment, the emergence of digital platforms, the diffusion of innovative digital technologies, and the related development of Industry 4.0, acknowledging the need to embrace ideas and concepts from multiple fields and integrate different research areas. The other related theme is digital transformation, which implies a structural change of the economies and organizations requiring a technological and cultural shift. In addition, the chapter's analysis highlights that digital transformation and its profound changes can generate imbalances if not addressed with awareness and the right mastery of digital skills. Reaping the digital revolution's benefits, and avoiding its pitfalls, will require organizations and economies to manage an unprecedented structural transformation for which the world seems still unprepared.

INTRODUCTION

The digital economy and the related digital transformation process transform everything: the nature of markets and products, how to produce, how to deliver goods and services and pay for them, the human capital requirement, and the scale of capital to operate globally. The digital economy is also adopting new technologies and boosting productivity, creating new business models, and new market access channels influencing consumer behavior.

DOI: 10.4018/978-1-6684-4265-4.ch002

The process of digitalization is developing rapidly, also influencing the way to create and exchange value. Companies investing in digital technologies and digital solutions aim to boost productivity and competitiveness. In turn, digital technologies are redefining the competition in every industry and developing Industry 4.0. In addition, coupled with macroeconomic uncertainties, they are causing significant changes in the structure of industries, markets, and the future of work. In addition, the COVID-19 pandemic contributed to fuel digitalization efforts, the realignment of supply chains, and rethinking of how connectivity and other disruptive technologies can benefit organizations and the entire economy. In this time of overlapping disruptions, analyzing the digital economy and the related digital transformation becomes very important and can enrich the literature on this topic. In addition, the theme of digital transformation, accelerated by the evolution of digital technologies and the blooming of startups, is becoming transversal to different business disciplines. Understanding digital transformation needs to acknowledge the role of digital technologies in transforming organizations, consumer behaviors, and social relationships. It also needs to embrace ideas and concepts from multiple fields and integrate different research areas. All this will be useful to reap the benefits of the digital revolution and avoid its pitfalls. The contribution aims to analyze the digital economy and its characteristics, including the emergence of digital platforms, and examine the digital transformation process as a structural change that affects organizations, economies, and societies.

THE DIGITAL ECONOMY

The digital economy includes all those economic processes, transactions, interactions, and activities based on digital technologies (Schilirò, 2021). A digital economy is where consumers, companies, and governments live in a digital society that interacts and creates value benefitting all stakeholders. The digital economy has firmly established itself since 2010 with the growth and massive progress in the sophistication of semiconductors, the internet, and its service providers.

As UNCTAD (2021, p. 25) highlights in its report, the digital economy is data driven and is rapidly evolving amid huge divides in terms of digital readiness. As a result, data play an increasingly important role as an economic and strategic resource, a trend reinforced by the COVID-19 pandemic as many activities moved online. Two countries stand out as the frontrunners in harnessing the value of data: the United States and China. Together these two countries cover 90% of the market capitalization of the world's largest digital platforms and 94% of all funding of artificial intelligence (AI) start-ups. Moreover, the largest digital platforms increasingly control all stages of the global data value chain: collection, transmission, storage, processing, and use of data.

According to Acs et al. (2021), software programs often make economic decisions instead of managers in the digital economy. In addition to cost reductions, sophisticated algorithms, big data, and enormous computing power allow market transactions, mediated through multi-sided platforms, to reduce the need for hierarchy and hierarchical power and exploit the positive effects of the networks. Thus, coordination in the twenty-first-century economy shifts from the visible hand of management to the digital hand of platforms. Furthermore, the onset of the COVID-19 pandemic in 2020 gave rise to the global acceleration of digital platforms so that digital is now the new normal. The role of the platform business is to provide a governance structure and a set of standards and protocols that facilitate interactions at scale so that we can unleash network effects.

Digital platforms change the economics of doing business across borders, decreasing the cost of international interactions and transactions. They create increasingly efficient, transparent markets and user communities on a global scale (Schilirò, 2020). Thus, the main institutional difference of the platform economy is the role of the platform-based ecosystem that is immediately global.

Platform organizations develop the digital platform, while the entrepreneurs-owners of the platform firms determine its governance and the rules. Thus, the platform organization replaces the vertically integrated firm via network effects[1] (Acs et al., 2021, p. 1622).

Microprocessors have become the primary tool to enjoy several cost reductions in the digital economy.[2] According to Goldfarb and Tucker (2019), the key driver of the digital economy is the representation of information in bits. Information in bits reduces the cost of storage, computation, and data transmission. Thus, an important characteristic of the digital economy is that digitization reduces specific economic costs. Goldfarb and Tucker (2019) point out that digital technology featuring the digital economy reduce search, replication, transportation, tracking, and verification costs that affect economic activities. Search costs, defined as the costs of looking for information, are lower in digital environments, allowing expanding the potential scope of the search and the quality of the search itself. Furthermore, digital goods can be replicated at zero costs because they are often non-rival. As a result, we can provide these goods free, determining an increase in the supply of public goods (e.g., Wikipedia). In addition, the cost of transportation of information in bits is near zero. The other two cost changes that become lower are tracking and verification costs. "Tracking costs are the costs associated with connecting a person or firm with information about them. Low tracking costs enable novel forms of price discrimination as well as new ways to targeting advertising and other information" (Goldfarb and Tucker, 2019, p.4).[3] Digital technologies, by making it easier to verify identity and create a digital reputation, also reduce the verification costs, i.e., costs associated with the verification of identity and reputation. However, in their literature review of the digital economy, Goldfarb and Tucker (2019) criticize traditional economic models. They argue that changes in economic behavior resulting from a shift in costs are not as apparent as those models might imply.

Moreover, there is a need for a digital infrastructure anchored in digital technologies to capture the effects of digitization. As a building block of the digital platform economy, the digital infrastructure must be open, global, inclusive, and flexible. The digital infrastructure links systems and networks distributed across multiple actors, such as designers, developers, and users. Moreover, because the digital infrastructure is an open system, it can become an enabler for individual innovators.

Thus, openness is one central theme related to digitization and digital technologies and, simultaneously, is important for the innovation and entrepreneurship literature. For example, Nambisan, Wright, and Feldman (2019) observe that digitization has transformed the nature and degree of openness in innovation and entrepreneurship. For instance, the openness of the ecosystem implies that individuals and organizations can pursue innovation or entrepreneurship collaboratively and participate in joint decision-making.

NEW DIGITAL TECHNOLOGIES AND INDUSTRY 4.0

Several digital technologies characterized the new digital environment, especially the second decade (2010-2020) of the 21st century (Popkova et al., 2021), such as smartphones, mobile apps, artificial intelligence (AI), machine learning, cloud computing, big data, digital platforms, Internet of Things, robotics, blockchain, advanced realities, and digital twin, among others. These have already led to transformative advances in many domains, notably transforming services and manufacturing businesses. In addition, technologies such as broadband, internet, smartphones, cloud computing, online payment system, Web 2.0 have contributed to the development of e-commerce. They all have implications for value creation and value capture, while operational efficiency and information gathering are improved.

The novel digital technologies also change how the public sector provides services and communicates. Among these digital technologies revolutionizing contemporary business is cloud-computing services, where users access remote servers over a network (Acs et al., 2021). Smart technologies like AI and machine learning allow analyzing and storing vast quantities of data, converting them into valuable business. In the past decades, AI and deep learning, in particular, have experienced a wide range of applications spanning from manufacturing to self-driving cars, healthcare, business, education, government, gaming, and finance. But, of course, there are downsides to AI. Every day, people create data extracted from algorithms and create profiles to predict behaviors and trackers. Moreover, they often sell the data to third parties. As AI applications grow exponentially, the negative effects of bias will be more far-reaching.

Yet, AI represents a fundamental digital technology for Industry 4.0. It enhances productivity through process automation, transforms the supply of products and services, adds higher quality, and meets demand with personalized offerings tailored to individual consumers. However, AI alters the employment landscape, changing the labor force structure (Acemoglu and Restrepo, 2019). In addition, the 3D printing is one of the leading emerging technologies of Industry 4.0. In combination with other technologies, the use and implementation of additive manufacturing determine the industry evolution towards an intelligent production system where machines, systems, and networks can exchange information and respond to production management systems. 3D printing has a fundamental role in turning a 3D design into a product without intervention. Internet of Things (IoT) is another key technology for developing the digital economy and Industry 4.0 in particular. IoT refers to any technology connected to a network, such as the internet. IoT is based on the idea of 'intelligent' objects interconnected with each other to exchange information owned, collected, and processed. IoT uses cloud services and makes increasing use of AI. Popkova and Sergi (2021) highlighted that IoT, and AI could be applied successfully in managing big data implementing solutions for 'smart' digital public health, as with the COVID-19 pandemic.

The marriage between IoT and Industry 4.0 allows the industrial sector to leap forward in efficiency, safety, and environmental impact. Industry 4.0 represents a technological and cultural paradigm change that involves the manufacturing system in all its forms, merging automation technologies (e.g., AI, IoT, robots, cobots, and digital twins) and the internet with the conventional industry. Industry 4.0 introduces new development concepts for digital transformation, which is usually synonymous with disruption. Industry 4.0 involves a paradigm shift from a centralized production model to a decentralized, intelligent, flexible, and connected production model. It changes the way firms operate and the relationship between suppliers, customers, and third parties (Schilirò, 2021).

Industry 4.0 has four core principles paving the way: i) *Interconnection*, machines, sensors, devices, and people in the manufacturing process, all connecting and communicating; ii) *Decentralized decisions*, cyber-physical systems can decide independently and perform tasks autonomously; iii) *Information transparency*, the manufacturing process permits a comprehensive collection of data and information, allowing for more informed decisions; and, iv) *Technical assistance*, improved technological facility of systems assisting humans in decision-making, problem-solving, and difficult or unsafe tasks.

Much of the underlying technology of Industry 4.0 has been available for decades, including robotics and networks, but adequately using them together unlocks a massive stride in manufacturing capabilities. The digital economy and related digital technologies entail a real revolution in the industrial system and interpersonal relationships. Organizations, in particular, are under increasing pressure to apply digital technologies to transform their business models (Kohli and Melville, 2019). In such an economy, digitized data allows automating processes and enables better accessibility, leading to efficiency benefits.

As highlighted in Acs et al. (2021), the digital economy is subjected to profound changes. Radical innovations and highly innovative start-ups characterize these transformations. For instance, the birth and massive growth of multi-sided digital platform firms, especially in the U.S. and China, such as Apple, Microsoft, Alphabet, Amazon, Facebook, Alibaba, Tencent, and PayPal (i.e., the most relevant and essential in terms of market capitalization), are the evidence of the dynamism and radical transformation created in the digital economy.

Although the emergence of the digital economy has implications concerning critical issues such as data privacy and security across different levels of analysis (e.g., individual or organization ecosystem), studies focused primarily on one aspect. For instance, Goldfarb and Tucker (2012) argue that digital activity has made privacy policy a part of innovation policy. Likewise, Martin (2018) highlights the risks of information misuse and how privacy violations may place firms in a downward trust spiral.

Cybersecurity is, however, a matter of concern for the top management in companies across the world. As the report on Global cybersecurity (World Economic Forum, 2022) suggests, top managers should prioritize cyber in business decisions and aim for the support of the cybersecurity leadership since they do not want to leave companies vulnerable to cyberattacks because of inconsistent security choices and policies. Moreover, they should recruit and retain cybersecurity talent. Still, business executives seem to be unaware of the gaps, while unfortunately, the threat of ransomware continues to develop as a threat to public safety. There is a consensus that we need clear and productive regulations that enable information sharing and collaboration.

At the same time, public institutions and government authorities are trying to manage several issues concerning the digital economy and the organizations involved, such as intellectual property rights, data privacy and security, consumer rights, but also worker skills and training, incubator and accelerator programs through laws, regulations, and policies. Therefore, we should conduct further research on policies and rules focusing on these issues and examining the different levels of analysis.

DIGITAL TRANSFORMATION

Digital transformation is related to expanding the digital economy and digital technology and has become increasingly important for businesses and as a research topic in academia. Digital transformation is a different phase regarding digitization and digitalization. The latter describes how information technology (IT) or digital technologies can alter the existing business processes. Digital transformation, instead, marks a rethinking of how an organization uses technology, people, and techniques in pursuit of new business models and additional revenue streams, driven by changes in customer expectations around products and services (Boulton, 2021). According to Verhoef et al. (2021, p. 889), digital transformation comprises a change in how a firm employs digital technologies to develop a new digital business model that helps to create and appropriate more value for the firm. Digital transformation signifies disruptive implications of digital technologies for businesses: new business models, new types of products and services, new types of customer experiences. (Nambisan et al., 2019; Li, 2020). As a result, digital technologies can serve as an active ingredient in fueling innovative activities (Lusch and Nambisan, 2015; Nambisan et al., 2019). Furthermore, Kraus et al. (2022, p. 2) argue that digital transformation can be defined as integrating digital technology into all aspects and operations of an organization, which leads to infrastructural changes in how the organization is operated and delivers value to its customers.

Digital transformation implies a profound change, particularly a structural change, i.e., changes in organizations, processes, and business models in the firms, and changes in consumer behavior, not just a digitalization of business processes. Thus, the key elements of digital transformations are changing the business model, transforming operational procedures, and improving customer experience. Other scholars focused instead on the importance of business strategy. Kane et al. (2015) think that strategy, not technology, drives digital transformation. They argue that the ability to reimagine the business digitally is determined by a clear digital strategy supported by leaders who foster a culture able to change and invent the new. Warner and Wäger (2019, p. 344) maintain that digital transformation is an ongoing process of strategic renewal that uses advances in digital technologies to build capabilities that refresh or replace an organizational business model, collaborative approach, and culture. Rêgo et al. (2021), who investigate how business strategy influences digital transformation, underline that it is very important to understand the relation between digital transformation and business strategy.

While we can find many definitions of digital transformation in the scholarly literature, digital transformation is multidisciplinary by nature; it involves changes in strategy, organization, capabilities, information technology, the adoption of innovative digital technologies, big changes in the supply chain, and marketing, but also a different culture and mindset. In addition, new digital technologies blur market boundaries and change agent roles (customers become co-producers, competitors become collaborators, and firms that vertically integrate).

Digital transformation seems inevitable in many sectors, however necessary, but it is not an end, as it involves significant changes and high associated risks. Moreover, there are risks not only for the economies but also for organizations. Therefore, the latter must carefully evaluate the decision to undertake a digital transformation, considering their available talents and capabilities. Above all, they must clearly define the strategy to follow and redesign their business model.

However, digital transformation has received the most attention within specific business disciplines, with little multidisciplinary discussion in the literature. The increasing interest in digital transformation in business and management, in particular, gained considerable momentum since 2019 and accelerating during the COVID-19 pandemic. In the early years, the study of digital transformation had a primary focus on B2C, while more recently, the focus has shifted to studying the impact of digital transformation on B2B (Vial, 2019; Kraus et al., 2022).

The external factors driving digital transformation are digital technology, digital competition, and digital consumer behavior. The new digital technologies also affect firms' cost structures by replacing costlier humans during service delivery with robots, virtual agents, optimizing logistic streams, and reducing supply chain costs using AI and blockchain.

Competition is changing dramatically because of these new digital technologies. Not only has the competition become more global, but the intensity has also increased as big, information-rich firms from U.S. and China dominate many industries. At the same time, consumer behavior is changing as a response to the digital revolution. Consumers have become more connected, informed, empowered, and active. Consumers also strongly rely on apps and AI-based technologies (e.g., Amazon's Echo and Google home) entering consumers' lives. As a result, those new digital technologies will likely structurally change consumer behavior.

Because of digital transformation, firms compete and try to attain a competitive advantage through new business models, which have changed dramatically with the growth of the internet, e-commerce, and the restructuring of the financial services industry worldwide.

Teece (2010) maintains that a business model embodies nothing less than the organizational and financial 'architecture' of a business. "The notion refers in the first instance to a conceptual, rather than a financial, model of a business. It makes implicit assumptions about customers, the behavior of revenues and costs, the changing nature of user needs, and likely competitor responses. It outlines the business logic required to earn a profit (if one is available to be earned) and, once adopted, defines the way the enterprise 'goes to market' " (Teece, 2010, p. 173). No matter the sector, a good business model yields value propositions compelling to customers, achieves advantageous cost and risk structures, and enables significant value capture by the business that generates and delivers products and services.

Verhoef et al. (2021, p. 891) suggest that digital transformation introduces a new business model by implementing new business logic to create and capture value. They inherently linked digital transformation to strategic changes in the business models because of implementing digital technologies.

However, digital transformation is itself a process in continuous evolution also because new frontiers in digital technology are emerging, which are announced to be even more disruptive. Think of quantum computing or the adoption of quantum logic to allow the simultaneous management of multiple algorithms. Think also of the advancement of the 'metaverse.' The metaverse is a collective virtual open space created by the convergence of virtually enhanced physical and digital reality. Activities in isolated environments (such as buying digital land and participating in a virtual social experience) will eventually occur in the metaverse. Of course, the adoption of metaverse technologies is still at an early stage. However, the metaverse is one such technology that affects strategic business innovations.

In sum, digital transformation is a company-wide phenomenon with broad organizational implications. In pursuit of digital transformation, firms search for and implement business model innovation. Therefore, digital transformation needs both technological and cultural shifts. Digital transformation is not a short-term-tactic but a long-term process requiring a well-planned strategy. Moreover, digital transformation is relevant for incumbent firms. Given their legacy, incumbents will face challenges or barriers when searching and implementing business model innovation for digital transformation. They are often forced to deal with conflicts and trade-offs between existing and new business practices. The move to digital may usually require a marked departure from the status quo and may lead to the obsolescence of existing business models.

We relate some strategic imperatives to digital transformations. Particularly, in pursuit of digital transformation, the firm's redefinition of how it creates and delivers value to customers often requires accessing, acquiring, or developing new digital assets and capabilities. Among the essential digital assets and capabilities needed for digital change are digital assets. Firms require digital assets, like data storage, information and communication infrastructure, and accompanying technologies to compete effectively in the digital era. For instance, a firm can leverage big data as a digital asset by using its data capabilities to personalize services and offers. In addition, firms need digital agility to seize market opportunities provided by digital technologies. Digital agility is required to recombine digital assets with other organizational resources to change business practices. Digital agility is also vital for incumbent survival. Another digital asset is the digital networking capability, which refers to the firm's ability to bring together and match distinct users to address their mutual needs via digital means. Most executives indicated that their competitive advantage is not determined internally but by the strength of partners and ecosystems with which they choose to work. Furthermore, for digital transformation, extensive data analytics capability for decision-making is crucial since strategies rely on data; thus, the reliability of these data becomes crucial. Firms should have big data teams with analytical, data management, data visualization, and business skills. Pure digital firms like Amazon and Bookings.com constantly use analytics to tailor new customer offerings and optimize revenues with dynamic pricing and revenue management.

Finally, digital transformation has implications for the organizational structure favoring a flexible system composed of separate business units, forms of agile organizations, and digital functional areas. An essential feature of digital transformation is the increased reliance on IT and analytical functions.

Among the digital growth strategies for digital firms, the most prominent one involves using digital platforms. Platform strategies are common for digital transformation. Two are the key drivers behind the growth of digital platforms: platforms' high scalability and the reinforcing network effects (Verhoef et al., 2021, p. 894).

Platforms can leverage their digital and disruptive technologies to achieve significant growth by attracting non-users. Sometimes, this may create entirely new markets. Large, successful platforms often deploy this growth strategy to develop new markets with new products. This approach expands the platform to serve unique needs, update the product and service assortment, and open the firm to co-create value by partnering with sponsors (Google and Android) or other interoperable platforms, suppliers, consumers, and complimentary services providers.

In summary, digital transformation occurs in response to changes in digital technologies, increasing digital competition and resulting in digital customer behavior. Therefore, firms aiming to digitally transform must acquire digital assets, digital agility, and networking, build agile structures with low hierarchy levels, and acquire or develop big data analytics capabilities.

A GLANCE TO DIGITAL TRANSFORMATION OF THE ECONOMIES

Companies and governments worldwide adopted national programs and strategies for the digital transformation of the economies, under the pressure of competition because of the initiative of market players (Popkova et al., 2021). As argued in the previous section 2, new digital technologies have changed how the public sector provides services and communicates. To better grasp the capabilities and readiness of economies to undertake the digital transformation process, it is possible to look at the IMD World Digital Competitiveness Ranking (2021). The IMD ranking captures the digital transformation process of 64 economies through three factors: knowledge, technology, and future-readiness. Knowledge refers to know-how necessary to discover, understand and build new technologies: talent, training and education, and scientific concentration. Technology refers to the overall context that enables the development of digital technologies, including three subsectors such as regulatory framework, capital, and technological framework. Finally, future-readiness interprets the level of country preparedness to exploit digital transformation, including adaptive attitudes, business agility, and IT integration.

The IMD ranking encompasses organizational, institutional, and structural elements (technological innovation and sector changes). Based on a mixture of hard data and survey replies from business and government executives,[4] the digital rankings help organizations and governments understand best practices when embarking on digital transformation. The report by IMD (2021) highlights that technology proved to be the saving force in transforming government and business practices and social interconnection, providing a way to quantify the capacity of an economy to adapt and explore new digital technologies. Table 1 shows the digital competitiveness ranking 2021 of the top 20 countries.

The IMD World Competitiveness Center (2021, p. 23) suggests that countries with a strong presence in future-readiness, with individuals and firms that are flexible and agile, and who have integrated IT technologies in their daily practices, seem to have performed better. In addition, strong performances in training and education characterize leading economies. Those leading economies can allocate capital towards learning and developing new technologies. Finally, there have been increasing concerns regarding the ownership of private versus public data and the transparency of how data are used.

The U.S. remains at the top of the 2021 IMD World Digital Competitiveness Ranking. It performs strongly in the knowledge (3rd place) and future readiness (1st) factors. Regarding knowledge, the U.S. excels in the scientific concentration sub-factor and the future readiness performance is boosted by the leading ranking in both the adaptive attitudes and business agility subfactors.

However, to assess a country's digital transformation progress, human capital, connectivity, and the integration of digital technologies and public services must be considered. In many countries, the most critical factor is still linked to the overall backwardness of digital skills, the characteristics of human capital.

Popkova et al. (2022) point out the challenges of the diffusion of digital technology advancement in terms of sustainable development. These challenges and risks concern the ecological costs of increased energy consumption since automation often raises production and consumption energy intensity. However, these authors support the

Table 1. Digital competitiveness ranking 2021 Top 20 showing overall and factors ranking

Overall Rank	*Country*	*Knowledge Ranking*	*Technology Ranking*	*Future Readiness Ranking*
1	U.S.A.	3	4	1
2	Hong Kong SAR	5	1	10
3	Sweden	2	8	6
4	Denmark	8	9	2
5	Singapore	4	3	11
6	Switzerland	1	11	3
7	Netherlands	11	7	4
8	Taiwan, China	16	2	7
9	Norway	17	6	8
10	UAE	18	5	12
11	Finland	9	12	9
12	Korea Rep.	15	13	5
13	Canada	7	15	15
14	United Kingdom	13	17	13
15	China	6	20	17
16	Austria	10	32	16
17	Israel	12	27	21
18	Germany	14	31	18
19	Ireland	23	28	14
20	Australia	19	18	22

Source: (IMD World Competitiveness Center, 2021)

hypothesis that digital technologies improve the achievement of specific SDGs, and institutions play an important role. Furthermore, digital technologies have a mediating influence by increasing the effectiveness of social institutions. The novelty of the contribution from Popkova et al. is that it performs an indirect study of the influence of digital technology development on sustainable development through technological support. This contribution allows the correct and more complete characterization of the impact of digital technologies on implementing the SDGs, acknowledging that it is possible to improve only a minor part of them via simple digital technology development.

To conclude on digital transformation, a critical area of future research is investigating how digital resources facilitate digital transformation, for instance, in which assets and capabilities organizations must invest. Another one is to organize the resources to avoid the pitfalls of digital transformation, both regarding the goals related to sustainable development and cybersecurity. Again, the role of institutions seems fundamental. Thus, it is necessary to implement rules and an institutional framework under the government authorities appropriate for multilateral, multi-stakeholder, and multidisciplinary engagement (UNCTAD, 2021; Popkova et al., 2022).

CONCLUSION

This chapter has focused on the digital economy, its characteristics, and the digital transformation process. The role of emerging innovative digital technologies has proved fundamental in digital transformation, which manifests itself as a structural change for companies, economies, and societies, also boosting the development of Industry 4.0. In addition, the COVID-19 pandemic has greatly contributed to driving digital transformation in recent years.

Digital technologies such as AI, cloud systems, big data, predictive analysis, interactive platforms, and blockchain can dramatically improve the economy. However, they pose severe risks to companies and individuals in their roles as consumers, workers, and citizens. Reaping the digital revolution's benefits, and avoiding its pitfalls, will require managing a structural transformation for which all the stakeholders should be prepared. This chapter's analysis highlights that digital transformation, and its profound changes can generate imbalances if not addressed with awareness and the right mastery of digital skills.

These smart tools should help augment intelligence and skills by supporting rather than replacing the workforce skills. Zysman and Kenney (2018) underline that, as a community, it is possible to choose the type of society that will result from the digital economy, where digital platforms are the main protagonists. In their view, digital technology does not impose, in and of itself, a single answer. From the perspective of advancing research, it would be convenient to embrace ideas and concepts from multiple fields and integrate different areas.

Another important proviso emerging from the analysis is that, given the effects of digital transformation, it may seem prudent to think through the risks before allowing new technologies to take hold. However, this is not a simple task since digital technologies are increasing at an unprecedented rate, forcing businesses and consumers at the global level to accept them uncritically. The adoption is because, unlike industrialization, digitization is sweeping across the planet practically simultaneously; over 60% of people in low-income countries already own a mobile phone. Moreover, unlike in the advanced economies, developing countries adopt mobile internet simultaneously as they acquire smartphones, computers, and electricity.

However, a critical area of future research regarding the digital transformation of the economies must focus more on the digital divide, policy for digital education, digital infrastructures, and legislation on data protection.

REFERENCES

Acemoglu, D., & Restrepo, P. (2019). Artificial intelligence, automation, and work. In A. Agrawal, J. Gans, & A. Goldfarb (Eds.), *The economics of artificial intelligence: An agenda* (pp. 197–236). The University of Chicago Press.

Acs, Z. J., Song, A. K., Szerb, L., Audretsch, D. B., & Komlósi, E. (2021). The evolution of the global digital platform economy: 1971-2021. *Small Business Economics, 57*(4), 1629–1659. doi:10.100711187-021-00561-x

Boulton, C. (2021, June 24). *What is digital transformation? A necessary disruption.* CIO. https://www.cio.com/article/230425/what-is-digital-transformation-a-necessary-disruption.html

Goldfarb, A., & Tucker, C. (2011). Online display advertising: Targeting and obtrusiveness. *Marketing Science, 30*(3), 389–404. doi:10.1287/mksc.1100.0583

Goldfarb, A., & Tucker, C. (2012). Privacy and Innovation. *Innovation Policy and the Economy, 12*, 65–89. doi:10.1086/663156

Goldfarb, A., & Tucker, C. (2019). Digital Economics. *Journal of Economic Literature, 57*(1), 3–43. doi:10.1257/jel.20171452

IMD World Competitiveness Center. (2021). *IMD World Digital competitiveness ranking 2021.* https://www.imd.org/centers/world-competitiveness-center/rankings/world-digital-competitiveness/

Kane, G. C., Palmer, D., Phillips, A. N., Kiron, D., & Buckley, N. (2015). Strategy, not technology, drives digital transformation. *MIT Sloan Management Review and Deloitte University Press, 14*, 1–25.

Kohli, R., & Melville, N. P. (2019). Digital innovation: A review and synthesis. *Information Systems Journal, 29*(1), 200–223. doi:10.1111/isj.12193

Kraus, A., Durst, S., Ferreira, J. J., Veiga, P., Kailer, N., & Weinmann, A. (2022). Digital transformation in business and management research: An overview of the current status quo. *International Journal of Information Management, 63*, 102466. doi:10.1016/j.ijinfomgt.2021.102466

Li, F. (2020). Leading digital transformation: Three emerging approaches for managing the transition. *International Journal of Operations & Production Management, 40*(6), 809–817. doi:10.1108/IJOPM-04-2020-0202

Lusch, R. F., & Nambisan, S. (2015). Service innovation: A service-dominant logic perspective. *Management Information Systems Quarterly, 39*(1), 155–175. doi:10.25300/MISQ/2015/39.1.07

Martin, K. (2018). The penalty for privacy violations: How privacy violations impact trust online. *Journal of Business Research, 82*, 103–116. doi:10.1016/j.jbusres.2017.08.034

Nambisan, S., Wright, M., & Feldman, M. (2019). The digital transformation of innovation and entrepreneurship: Progress, challenges and key themes. *Research Policy, 48*(8), 103773. doi:10.1016/j.respol.2019.03.018

Popkova, E. G., De Bernardi, P., Tyurina, Y. G., & Sergi, B. S. (2022). A theory of digital technology advancement to address the grand challenges of sustainable development. *Technology in Society, 68*, 101831. doi:10.1016/j.techsoc.2021.101831

Popkova, E. G., Krivtsov, A. I., & Bogoviz, A. V. (2021). Digital economy in the 21st century: An introduction to the institutional approach. In E. G. Popkova, A. I. Krivtsov, & A. V. Bogoviz (Eds.), *The institutional foundations of the digital economy in the 21st century* (pp. ix–xi). De Gruyter. doi:10.1515/9783110651768-203

Popkova, E. G., & Sergi, B. S. (2021). Digital public health: Automation based on new datasets and the Internet of Things. *Socio-Economic Planning Sciences.* Advance online publication. doi:10.1016/j.seps.2021.101039

Rêgo, B. S., Jayantila, S., Ferreira, J. J., & Carayannis, E. G. (2021). Digital transformation and strategic management: A systematic review of the literature. *Journal of the Knowledge Economy*. Advance online publication. doi:10.100713132-021-00853-3

Schilirò, D. (2020). Towards digital globalization and the COVID-19 challenge. *International Journal of Business Management and Economic Research, 11*(2), 1710–1716.

Schilirò, D. (2021). Digital transformation, COVID-19, and the future of work. *International Journal of Business Management and Economic Research, 12*(3), 1945–1952.

Teece, D. (2010). Business models, business strategy and innovation. *Long Range Planning, 43*(2-3), 172–194. doi:10.1016/j.lrp.2009.07.003

UNCTAD. (2021). *Digital Economy Report 2021. Cross-border data flows and development: For whom the data flow*. United Nations.

Verhoef, P. C., Broekhuizen, T., Bart, Y., Bhattacharya, A., Qi Dong, J., Fabian, N., & Haenlein, M. (2019). Digital transformation: A multidisciplinary reflection and research agenda. *Journal of Business Research, 122*, 889–901. doi:10.1016/j.jbusres.2019.09.022

Vial, G. (2019). Understanding digital transformation: A review and a research agenda. *The Journal of Strategic Information Systems, 28*(2), 118–144. doi:10.1016/j.jsis.2019.01.003

Warner, K. S., & Wäger, M. (2019). Building dynamic capabilities for digital transformation: An ongoing process of strategic renewal. *Long Range Planning, 52*(3), 326–349. doi:10.1016/j.lrp.2018.12.001

World Economic Forum. (2022). *Global Cybersecurity Outlook 2022*. World Economic Forum. https://www3.weforum.org/docs/WEF_Global_Cybersecurity_Outlook_2022.pdf

Zysman, J., & Kenney, M. (2018). The next phase in the digital revolution: Intelligent tools, platforms, growth, employment. *Communications of the ACM, 61*(2), 54–63. doi:10.1145/3173550

ENDNOTES

1 Network effects refer to the fact that the value of a product or service increases with the number of other users. The term 'network effect' applies to positive network externalities as the utility for the individual is greater.

2 A microprocessor is a computer processor where the data processing logic and control are included on a single integrated circuit or a small number of integrated circuits.

3 For insight into targeting in online advertising and related issues, readers should see Goldfarb and Tucker (2011).

4 The rankings are calculated based on the 52 ranked criteria: 32 hard and 20 survey data.

Chapter 3
Organizational Design for Digital Technologies in Industry 4.0:
"Best Practice" From Italy

Irene Borreca
University of Sannio, Italy

Stefano Di Lauro
University of Sannio, Italy

ABSTRACT

Digital technologies offer a great opportunity to small and medium-sized enterprises (SMEs) as they can adopt digital transformation more rapidly than large enterprises due to their greater flexibility and lean decision-making processes. So far there is no universal vision for a potential organizational model or design for Industry 4.0 SMEs. The research aimed to address this important gap by exploring the impact of digital technologies on organizational design in Industry 4.0 SMEs. The research builds on culture, staff, processes, and governance framework and follows a qualitative embedded case study design drawing on both employees' interviews and company documentation. The study provides insights about the main features, opportunities, and risks that are characterizing the current digital revolution in Industry 4.0 SMEs. Furthermore, the analysis of a notable Italian entrepreneurial reality revealed a set of practical suggestions and guidelines for other international SMEs that need to face the Industry 4.0 revolution with confidence and a proactive approach.

DOI: 10.4018/978-1-6684-4265-4.ch003

INTRODUCTION

Digital technologies are causing a transformation in the way the business operates and is carried out (Llopis-Albert et al., 2021) and companies that are aware of the potential of these technologies are promised to grow faster and have a competitive advantage over those who do not use them (Bean, 2021).

Also, the industrial environment has radically changed in recent years thanks to the introduction of the "*Fourth Industrial Revolution*" related concepts and technologies. Since the term "Industry 4.0" refers to a technological mixture of robotics, sensor technology, high levels of connection, and programming tools (Javaid et al., 2021), there seems to be a further revolution in manufacturing products and organizing work. Indeed, the suffix "4.0" corresponds to the steps of a specific evolution: from the introduction of the steam engine to the increasing use of automation, interconnection, computerization, and digitalization (Liu et al., 2020). Thus, companies are moving towards a new dimension called "*bimodal*", which is characterized by both physical and virtual resources (Parmentola et al., 2021). Furthermore, *environment 4.0* is characterized by two key factors: 1) Integration and 2) Interoperability (Bousdekis & Mentzas, 2021). The former allows to enrich innovative functionalities through the network among various stakeholders within the organizational structure and along the production chain. It enables a tighter connection of physical reality operations with virtual reality. Interoperability, instead, allows new productions, even without any kind of interruption, within and beyond the boundaries of the company thanks to the interconnection among production systems and the exchange of knowledge and skills among production structures and different companies. Integration and interoperability, thus, enable some phenomena such as mass production, mass customization, and mass personalization.

Industry 4.0 is at the heart of digital transformation (Butt, 2020).

Digital technologies, often defined as a collection of various intelligent and innovative technologies in the era of Industry 4.0 (Li, Dai, & Cui, 2020), offer a great opportunity to both large and small and medium-sized enterprises (SMEs). The latter, in particular, adopt digital transformation more rapidly than large enterprises as they can easily develop and implement new information technology structures (Deloitte, 2015) and are characterized by greater flexibility and by lean decision-making processes (Garzoni et al., 2020). Though, previous literature has also underlined the complexity of the Industry 4.0 perspective for SMEs as digital technologies have implications for their organizational design (Garzoni et al., 2020). Nevertheless, there is a limited understanding of how or what organizations (including SMEs) need to change to embrace digital technologies and how these technologies can bring a business value (Mikalef et al., 2017), while there is a recognized urgency for supporting new technologies with appropriate organizational design and models.

Thus, today there is no universal vision for a potential organizational model or design for Industry 4.0 (Maimone, 2022).

The Boston Consulting Group (2015) classifies technologies of Industry 4.0, or so-called nine pillars of Industry 4.0, in Additive Manufacturing, Augmented Reality, Autonomous Robots, Big Data and Analytics, The Cloud, Cybersecurity, Horizontal and vertical system integration, The Industrial Internet of Things, and Simulation, which can transform the factory in a fully integrated, automated and "smart" factory, with an optimized production process (Silvestri et al., 2020; Zolotová et al., 2020).

Indeed, all the Industry 4.0 elements are based on a large container of data and information collected at any time and of any kind. Obtaining and using data is one of the main challenges for analysts and managers; in fact, they can support business decisions in the long term, but, above all, in the short term thanks to data and information available in real-time. However, to get a proper strategic value from a huge amount of data, any kind of organization requires the ability to extract useful information for managing businesses and processes. The overused term "Big Data", which appeared with the advent of web 2.0 and the development of mobile tools, tablets, and smartphones, summarizes the key points about the new value of data and information. Historically, three dimensions mainly characterized the Big Data phenomenon, but current experts are still introducing numerous features. Today, some of the most relevant dimensions are:

- Volume: nowadays the amounts of data that are produced, collected, and analyzed are particularly remarkable as well as their different sources. For instance, everyone produces and share data through their smartphones on a daily basis;
- Velocity: it is a typical feature of all the modern technological changes that characterize the society. At the same time, that speed also refers to the timing linked to the availability and processing of data; in particular, information needs to be met in real-time more and more;
- Variety: sources, formats, and types of the data are multiple and characterized by great confusion and disaggregation, which require revisions and interpretations to transform what is only a potential value into actual and profitable value;
- Veracity: it concerns the quality and security of data;
- Value: knowing how to exploit Big Data means being able to increase the productivity and competitiveness of companies and, at the same time, create value for consumers (Daft, 2021).

Companies and other kinds of organizations have already used large databases and analytics in recent decades, but the news in this regard is relevant. For instance, there are *greater quantities and types* of data since in the past were processed mainly structured data: such data came largely from transactions and were stored in rows and columns. Today, instead, *unstructured data* are mainly stored from a variety of sources: photos from a mobile phone, maps from a GPS, video from a surveillance camera, audio from a call center, emails, tweets, messages, and so on. Firstly, big data can be digitized, analyzed, stored and, secondly, can be accessed in real-time. Real-time data allows the staff to influence results and prevent negative results before they happen again. This is a new feature, but it's only possible with an organization designed to work in real-time. The ideal process is 1) *using* the real-time data, 2) *analyzing* it to produce instant information, 3) *processing* that information to achieve real-time decisions.

As a result, new analytics have evolved from the current new degrees of information visibility (Burton et al., 2014). These analytics are based on new parallel technologies that process large amounts of data at a low cost. In addition, big data analytics leverage new technologies, such as in-memory databases, that analyze massive data sets in real-time. These developments mark the beginning of the use of big data in everyday operations. In the past, access to systems such as data warehouses was reserved for strategic decision support, while process-centric systems, such as Enterprise Resource Planning (ERP), supported day-to-day operations. Recently, however, big data technologies, such as in-memory databases, make such separation obsolete because transactional and decision-making data are managed in an integrative way. To summarize, by increasing the visibility of information with data-driven decision-making at both strategic and operational levels, big data will trigger numerous changes in decision-making and organizational design. Big data analytics includes Descriptive Analytics (tools for representing and describing situations or processes are used to lead descriptive analysis as it happens with graphical tools for business processes); Predictive Analytics (using mathematical models and techniques such as forecasting to anticipate or at least imagine future scenarios); Prescriptive Analytics (tools for the management of decision-making processes by providing strategic guidelines or operational solutions based on the analyzes described above); and Automated Analytics (compared to what is obtained from descriptive and predictive analyzes, Automated Analytics generate predefined actions. The same rules to be respected could derive from an analysis process such as, for example, the study of the operation of machinery placed in predefined situations) (Sheng et al., 2020).

The literature on the Information Systems has long discussed how IT technologies are still reshaping work and organizational structures with new forms of work-sharing and cooperation in enterprises. It often focuses on a growing disconnection of work processes from specific places (factories/offices) or fixed schedules since technology enables flexible spatial and temporal organizations. Through digitalization and big data analytics, cross-location teams are emerging while traditional hierarchical work structures dissolve and are turned into more flexible, in-house, and networked forms. In addition, the emerging design of new forms of work offers new opportunities for flexible integration of external freelancers or labor, on the one hand, and for the organization and development of cooperation between enterprises, on the other. An example of such IT-driven developments is the crowdsourcing of financial ideas, processes, or funds. The new crowdsourcing activities allow bigger incorporation of outside resources far beyond traditional outsourcing, but, probably, with fewer businesses or even social commitments. Incremental improvements to established business models based on digitization and big data analytics aim to optimize existing processes to increase the overall efficiency and quality of products and services. The significant increase of digitalization reduces transaction costs for information gathering, communication, and control activities. Through easy access to an almost infinite complexity of information and sophisticated big data analytics, companies can, for example, analyze the interdependence of users' online and purchasing behavior to personalize advertisements and, thus, increase overall demand. However, with an increasing level of standardization and widespread adoption across the economy, "commodified" big data solutions may not be sufficient for lasting competitive advantage. Indeed, innovative startups take advantage of low barriers to entry that allow them to revolutionize the business models of incumbents. They overcome existing markets by either exploiting digital distribution channels, creating, and serving the demand of new customers, establishing new forms of engagement and relationships with customers, or through any combination of all of them (Loebbecke & Picot, 2015).

All in all, each company coordinates and controls its activities, but above all faces uncertainty, thanks to the information it has. A fundamental problem of organizational design is precisely to provide the company with an adequate organizational structure to face uncertainty. Indeed, uncertainty means a situation in which the company has only partial knowledge of the environment in which it fits and operates. According to the theory of the Information Processing View, a higher degree of uncertainty corresponds to a greater need for the acquisition, processing, and transmission of information (Burton et al., 2020). Since nowadays fast social and technological changes are increasing uncertainty, each organizational structure might need a new design to become more and more adequate. Therefore, companies are often called upon to adopt a compromise between reducing the *need* for information to be processed and increasing the *ability* to process it.

Talking about cutting down the amount of data to be processed, the so-called "slack resources" could be the solution, i.e., excess or reserve resources. For instance, in a Just in time company with zero stocks, there is a huge amount of data about production processes, clients, and supplies to process in real-time. In that case, the company could introduce some warehouses for goods and semi-finished products "in excess" to replace the need to process all the additional information required by the Just in time approach. However, this option could have a downside such as an increase in costs. For example, a company could create autonomous organizational units to reduce the information to be processed, transferred, and coordinated, but a considerable difficulty could arise in exploiting economies of scale.

Some businesses, thus, are more oriented towards the second option so that they try to improve their ability to process information. General best practices are:

1. The update of staff skills
2. The recruitment of new skilled human resources
3. Engagement of consultants or other external partners
4. Face-to-face meetings
5. Significant use of *digital devices*

As a result of the analysis of these two alternatives emerged that while the costs of digital technologies tend to decrease, the costs of slack resources are increasing. In this way it is possible to understand and affirm that digitalization proposes to adopt lean organizational structures (fewer warehouses, less staff, less middle managers). However, the discussion does not end by identifying in the second option exposed the best and simplest solution: digital information systems, as well as the other elements of the organizational structure, have to align with the same other elements. The main challenges deal with avoiding misfits and at the same time avoiding resisting change unhappily (Burton et al.,2020).

Nevertheless, there is not one best way that can be shared by any digital organization. A standard digital model would not be very effective and could threaten the business's success. Rather, it would seem that organizations need to be able to self-organize, recruit talent, leverage information and transparency from technology, forge partnerships, and so much more to quickly and effectively jump at opportunities (Kotter, 2014). Experts talk about a withdrawal from the more *rational-centralized approach*, based on the power of a few people (the so-called top management) as it tends to restrain organizations, compared, instead, to an organizational *agility* approach. According to Venier's definition, organizational agility is the "*ability of a company to change rapidly and adapt to dynamic changes in markets*" (Venier, 2017). By the way, organizational agility is not only a productive approach, but also an organizational-managerial approach, and technology is the tool that helps to seize various digital opportunities. In this context, one of the fundamental factors is *the organizational ambidexterity* and within it the *IT ambidexterity* since ambidexterity is a phenomenon for which a company or other organization manages to simultaneously exploit (*exploitation*) the assets already present and to search for opportunities and innovations to respond to change (*exploration*).

AIMS AND OBJECTIVES

The need of supporting new technologies with an appropriate organizational design and the lack of a universal vision for potential organizational models for Industry 4.0 create a relevant literature gap.

Thus, the main objective of this research was set to explore the impact of digital technologies on organizational design in Industry 4.0 SMEs. Specifically, through a case study of a "best practice" Italian manufacturing SME, a leader in the production of innovative components for household appliances, the aim is to explore types of organizational changes that were necessary to: 1) design a proper "Big Data & Analytics business function"; 2) identify and involve skilled data scientists for this function; 3) improve data analytics processes by Industry 4.0 platforms; and 4) lead and support analytics governance.

These questions have been used in this research as a sort of guidelines to analyse how the main organisational elements are influenced by digital technologies. The dominant literature about culture and human resources, governance and structure, information, and coordination systems, working environment and leadership has been enriched by the study of the digital technologies pointed out by the Boston Consulting Group (2020), on one hand, and has been translated into practice through a case study of a "best practice" Italian manufacturing SME, on the other hand.

The main organizational design challenges in reshaping the business to respond strategically to the Industry 4.0 innovations, as well as suggestions on how to avoid potential misfit among organizational elements and digital technologies will be presented.

THEORETICAL FRAMEWORK

All the mentioned organizational elements have been discussed in the Culture, Staff, Processes, and Governance (CSPG) framework proposed by Grossman and Siegel (2014). Especially, the CSPG framework focuses on the adoption of enabling technologies and in particular Big Data Analytics within an organization.

How to Spread a Culture for Big Data and Analytics

Firstly, the CSPG framework guides managers and organizational designers to establish a culture for big data and analytics.

Bean's study (2021) based on a survey of 85 Fortune 1000 and industry-leading firms reports how most of these companies (over 90%) are straggling with issues mostly related to culture, which is considered their biggest barrier, more than technological challenges. Indeed, these organizations reported to make limited efforts or underestimate the time required by these types of business transformations. A list of recommendations was therefore proposed, including the way companies need to re-examine their way of thinking about data (Bean, 2021). Indeed, business leaders must recognize the need to organize big data and analytics as an organizational function with responsibility and authority, similarly to other major functions in the organization (Burton et al., 2014). Burton and colleagues (2014) described three basic models, that involve compromises between centralization and decentralization, to identify the Big Data and Analytics function within the organization.

The first model centralizes analytics by placing data scientists in a single unit (see Figure 1). (Daft, 2021). This model is the easiest way to reach a critical mass of scientists, get the needed data, drive an integrated infrastructure, and gain the skills you need to efficiently test and spread various statistical, predictive, and mining models. When analytics is centralized, however, data scientists can be far from the business units they are supposed to support. In addition, another issue is related to the report department within the organization. The question is whether to submit each report to a functional area such as finance, research and development, marketing and so on or whether to contact the top management of the organization. The problem of the first solution, however, is the risk that specific reports about data and analytics go unnoticed or are not completely solved by a different business function (Daft, 2021).

A second organizational approach is to decentralize analytics and place a group of data scientists in each business unit (Figure 2) (Daft, R. (2021). This approach makes it easier for data scientists to collaborate with their business units and adapt their models to the needs of each unit. However, there is a certain difficulty in reaching a critical mass of experts and skills necessary to create enough datasets and deploy enough analytical models (Daft, 2021).

The third model is a hybrid approach in which a critical mass of data scientists is hosted in a central unit and the remaining data scientists are distributed throughout the organization (Figure 3). The central unit, led by a Chief Data Officer, deals with coordination, needs assessment, projects and so on. Graphically, it can be described as a "*radial structure*" where each unit is concerned with specific analytical priorities while the center constitutes an expertise with transversal applicability (Daft, 2021).

Finally, the outsourcing business solution is a very common scenario for those companies that do not possess neither the essential experience and knowledge to build a critical mass of data scientists, nor the financial resources necessary to set up dedicated units. In general, in case of tough recruiting activities, some companies prefer to rely on other organizations which, in addition, often offer training programs to the staff of the contracting company. Speaking of outsourcing, another option is the so-called "*data intermediaries*". They are companies that deal, specifically or in

Figure 1. First model for identifying the Big Data and analytics function within the organization
Source: Authors' own elaboration

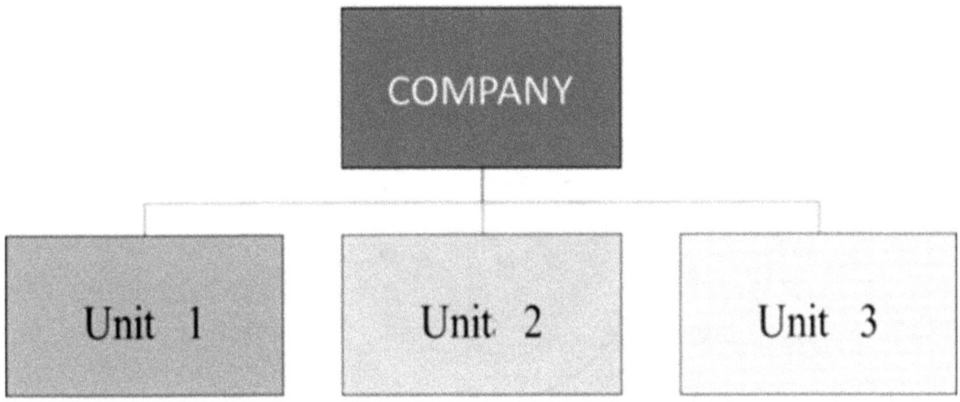

addition to their core business, with collecting data from different organizations and analyzing them as a whole. Besides the numerous existing "*data centers*", another example is given by Visa and MasterCard. They have the possibility to collect and

Figure 2. Second model for identifying the Big Data and analytics function within the organization
Source: Authors' own elaboration

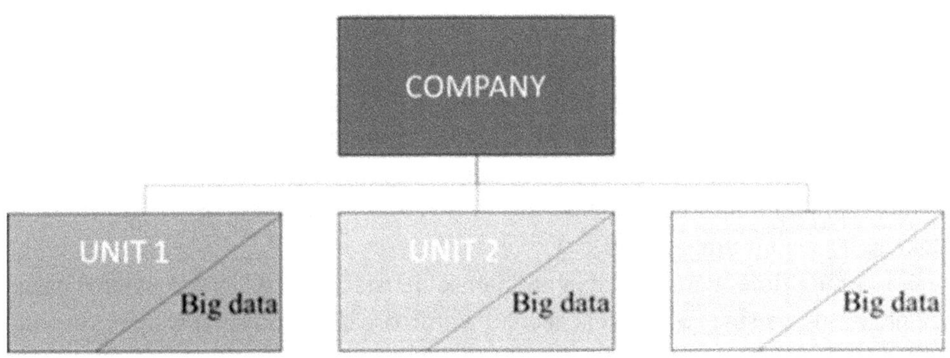

Figure 3. Third model for identifying the Big Data and analytics function within the organization
Source: Authors' own elaboration

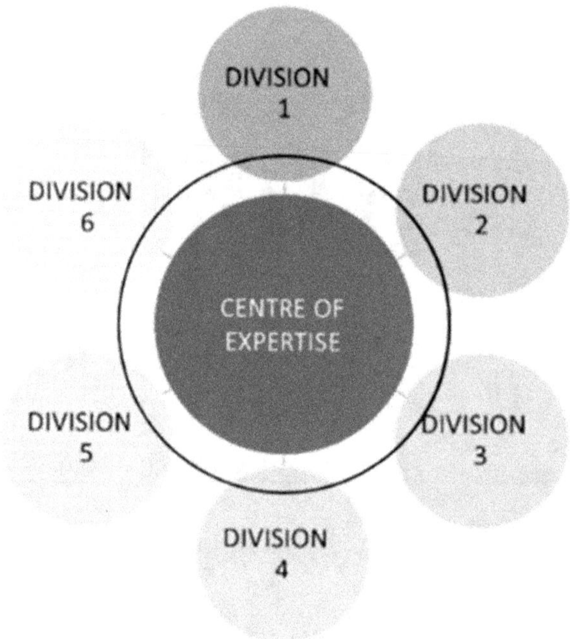

sell different data on consumer trends by analyzing the transactions made by users (Daft, 2021). All in all, today there is no universal vision for a potential organizational model or design for Industry 4.0 (Maimone, 2022).

Emerging Professionals, Debates, Roles, and Skills

The "S" of the CSPG framework refers to the fundamental presence of staff even in an organization that is increasingly pushing towards digitization. However, the blurry conception around the terms of *data science* and *data scientist* is having two negative consequences: 1) the data scientist is seen as the most important player in the process of creating economic value through the use of data, while 2) there is a sort of contempt for the other fundamental actors that actually contribute to a mature exploitation of data (De Mauro et al.,2018). Thus, it is necessary to try to make at least a minimum of clarity.

For a long time there has been an intense debate about what is meant by "data scientist" and what set of skills is needed within organizations that want to respond strategically to change. Among the most debated questions, Burton and colleagues

(2014) discussed the data science qualification, individual or group skills, and basic skills.

Currently, both data scientists' recruitment and training are expected to be more and more challenging for both the industrial and academic worlds. Businesses need data professionals with in-depth analytical skills that enable them to address the current full range of data management technologies and challenges, including security, privacy, master data, real-time streaming data, real-time predictive analytics, cloud, and mobile devices. For instance, the *Data Engineer* is a remarkable emerging job position related to big data (Miller, 2014). The data engineer has a deep understanding of relational databases, can integrate data from different data sources, and can design data-driven services. Data engineers work in collaboration with other data scientists. In general, all big data and analytics professionals will be required to have skills to work in an organization including the ability to influence co-workers, collaborate and develop creative solutions to complex business problems. Finally, the challenge is not simply about IT and technology since the different business functions, including legal, sales, marketing, finance, product development, production, and operations, are affected by the phenomenon of big data and digital technologies in general.

Academia, industry, and government should collaborate to address the challenge of big data and analytical skills (Burton et al.,2014), creating formal definitions of professional figures such as data scientist, information strategist, big data architect, and data governance professional; Establish curriculum requirements and minimum standards for data and analytics literacy of all students; Partner with industry organizations such as IT and the National Consortium for Data Science to establish strong internship programs and increase collaboration between business and academia;_Establish online communities and working groups to address key issues such as information security, individual privacy, and the ethical use of big data (Burton et al., 2014).

The literature provides multiple and partially concordant descriptions of Data Scientists' features. A macro-classification of the main figures necessary for an organization for the exploitation of big data could be the following (De Mauro et al.,2018):

1. The first group includes the skills of transforming raw data into insights, with a focus on technology and methods. Accordingly, this group includes more technical skills, such as the ability to use Big Data tools, statistical skills, and machine learning methods. The focus is on more complex skills and specific knowledge of data and analysis;
2. The second group consists of the ability to transform insights into organizational value, involving the right people and core business processes in the organization. As mentioned above, when a company transforms into a digital organization,

employees who do not have great digital skills mostly prefer to train within the same organization rather than looking for a new job elsewhere. A study by the MIT Sloan School of Management (2014) showed that more than half of employees and senior management reflected on their resignation in the following three years in case of a lack of opportunities for digital development at the early stages of transformation. However, not all companies have the same resources and opportunities to train staff while the most successful companies are those that manage talent by going beyond training. They create a perfect set of cultural rules that stimulates ambition so has to be able to retain employees in the company. Since technological transformation is moving at a remarkable speed, companies prefer to focus on the development of employees' soft skills rather than exclusively on properly technical skills. This includes famous soft skills such as communication and the ability to develop and maintain a network, flexibility, and curiosity. The tendency to prefer structures that favor inter functionality certainly explains the importance of soft skills: participating in a cross-functional group means getting out of one's cultural baggage and having a broader look; it is no coincidence that even in the interview phase interview schemes are adopted such as to verify the success in team building. More concretely, a possibility that companies have to motivate their employees lies in encouraging their participation in digital platforms and communities even outside the work context: it is one of the techniques of further training of employees by different and new external experts (Daft, 2021).

De Mauro and colleagues (2018), after retrieving the full list of jobs offered, applied basic text mining techniques, accompanied by expert judgment, to identify four essential groups of job roles: 1) ***Business Analysts*** (project/program manager, Business Consultants), whose primary skills are in the domain of project management and business impact (*effective communication, business process transformation, financial acumen, capacity for technical understanding* of analytical methods and related technologies); 2) ***Data Scientist*** (quantitative analysts, statisticians), whose primary skills are analysis and classification techniques, collaborative filtering, association rules, heuristic approaches, scripting or programming languages and statistical platforms; 3) ***Developers*** (programmers, machine learning implementers), whose primary expertise is undoubtedly the *coding*, but they also need solid experience in systems management, cloud computing, and distributed technologies; and 4) ***Big Data Engineers*** (System managers, architects/engineers) whose their primary skill refers to data architecture and includes the *skills needed to build and manage the enterprise big data ecosystem* in a sustainable way.

Essential Features of Analytics Processes

In general, the Analytics function consists of analysis, infrastructure, and operations models. Analytics operations refer to the various processes that result in output, i.e., models used to make decisions and take actions that bring business value. Analytics operations ensure that model results are integrated into an organization's products, services, and operations. In an analytics department, data scientists identify the data they need, capture the data, work collaboratively with business units to create models, and then collaborate with the IT group to deploy the models in the organization's operations. The IT department is normally involved if data is generated by the organization or collected by the organization and requires a critical mass of data scientists so that their experience extends to all analysis processes. Therefore, more parts of an organization can be involved in analytics processes. Typically, a business unit sponsors the model, an analytics department creates the model, an IT unit provides and manages the data, and an operating unit deploys the model. Since many different components are involved, an analytics governance structure is essential.

A Governance Structure for Analytics

In addition to the aforementioned "analytics function", Galbraith (2014) postulates that big data and analytics can provide a basis for a *new structural dimension* that will be "*concatenated*" to the organizational structures of the future.

The concept of "*concatenation*" had already been theorized by Chandler (1962), defining structural evolution as the cumulative result of several basic strategies: Each new dimension of the organizational structure concerns a new strategy linked to the previous ones (Chandler, 1962). Finally, it is useful to point out that Chandler spoke of four strategic dimensions: volume expansion, geographical dispersion, vertical integration, and diversification.

Regarding the organizational complexity, due to both strategy and structure, in his rigorous research, Jaques (1998) recognized that organizations show a hierarchical order of work complexity, mirroring differences in human capabilities. According to Korhonen (2014), any concatenation of a new strategy, that is, any structural evolution, requires precisely an additional organizational "layer". Incorporating a big data and analytics strategy into the organizational structure would be a sort of test to understand whether big data represents a basis for a new strategic dimension, the fifth. However, Galbraith wonders if new strategic dimensions can be added and incorporated into already complex global enterprises. The enterprise would be therefore divided into "business organization" and "analytics organization", where the second informs the first.

Beyond the discussed structural dimension, the role of an analytics governance lays on choosing a leader with sufficient authority to face the main challenges in this field. Analytics governance structure has also to includes tools and skills to be able to game sufficient resources for analytics projects, to balance done with older business projects, to catch, refer and solve any problem that stuck these projects. In this phase of evolution, it is not possible to talk about a real complete set of parameters for the design of an analytics governance structure. However, at least some preliminary parameters have been identified by Grossman and colleagues (2014):

1. Ensure the achievement of valid long-term decisions;
2. Ensure that investments in analytics generate value;
3. Ensure protection and security of data and products;
4. Ensure that criteria of accountability, transparency, and traceability are respected by funders and users of resources;

An idea of articulation (Grossman & Siegel, 2014) of the governance structure can be the establishment of multiple governance committees:

- A governance committee that includes senior managers, representatives of the IT organization and various business stakeholders. This committee helps prioritize emerging opportunities, therefore, to obtain resources for analytics projects and data required for analytics models;
- A technical committee that determines which data, applications, processes, best practices, and standards to use;
- A committee for analytical data management and data quality;
- A Compliance and Security Committee;

METHOD

This research follows a qualitative embedded case study design using both employees' interviews and internal and external company documentation. This case study approach was used as it allows access to rich and detailed contextualized data (Cuccinello et al., 2015).

Case Selection and Description

An Italian family-business SME has been selected for this case study as it is a rising leader in the field of Industry 4.0 technologies. Indeed, it has been identified as one of the 16 "lighthouse businesses" of the future by the World Economic Forum

(2019) (among more than 1000 leading manufacturers from different industries and geographical areas). Its remarkable position makes this company a clear example of a digital evolution path based on technologies with significant operational, human, and economic results.

The company was founded in 1963 as a producer of components for household appliances, but, going through a path of digitization, in 2019 it came up with a new business division/department, which is now the second most important line of business. More precisely, the company has a total of three plants and an innovation laboratory involving more than 240 full-time employees for the management of two business lines:

1. Innovative components for household appliances: components for household appliances (door lock, rotator, and other security systems hence the need for stringent quality parameters) for big brands.
2. Digital solutions for manufacturing companies: the company has an original internal software house and offers the same digital solutions to those firms that share the same issues: a significant number considering the Italian industrial environment.

Data Collection

To put the CSPG framework into practice, a semi-structured interview was conducted with two current Case Company employees with different job positions. In addition, thanks to the participation of the Head of Customer Care & Communication, it was possible to access company documentation about companies' story, digital technologies it uses, and its digital evolution path.

Considering that sometimes complex questions cannot be addressed effectively without more open-ended questions than a standardized survey (Adams, 2015), a semi-structured type of interview was chosen to exploit its main advantage, i.e., to conduct a dialogue regarding both foreseen and unforeseen issues. In respect of the order and meaning given to the elements of the CSPG framework, guiding questions have been built for each element (culture, staff, processes, governance) to have: 1) on the one hand, the freedom to expand the dialogue spontaneously (Ritchie et al., 2003); 2) on the other hand, to collect the data strictly necessary for the application of the CSPG framework to the case study. The interview lasted about forty-five minutes and was conducted both with the head of Customer care and Communication and a Project Engineer (graduated in statistics). The former gave an all-embracing vision of the company, starting from the business story to the future prospects, while the latter has made it possible to accurately collect more technical elements related to the company and its digital evolution path.

Data Analysis

First, having obtained consent to records interviews and to process the data, it was possible at a later time to transcribe verbatim the responses, translate them to English and then to conduct the analysis. All the collected data were triangulated with the company's internal (e.g., organization chart, reports, policy documentation) and external (company website, public interviews available on the Internet, news articles, etc.) documentation. Having an overall view of the case study, a proper analysis was conducted in compliance with the Boston Consulting Group classification of enabling technologies and based on the CSPG framework. Talking of enabling technologies, this case study provides some insights and information about the practical implementation of four of the nine pillars of Industry 4.0 (big data and analytics, cloud computing, Internet of Things, and augmented reality). Finally, all collected data and information were organized to fit perfectly in the four elements of the adopted theoretical framework.

RESULTS

The analysis revealed the CSPG framework (Grossman and Siegel, 2014) as an effective tool for locating, classifying, and sorting data collected, and for revealing main organizational elements affected due to the introduction of digital technologies. Indeed, the analysis revealed that all four elements of the framework were affected in this case study.

Digitalization as a Path and Cultural Approach

The analysis reveals that *cultural challenges* often represent an obstacle for organizations that underestimate the efforts and time required, while, faced with commitment and patience as in the following case study, they can lead to success.

Since 2009, thanks to the external presence of the Chief Sales & Innovation Officer, which is a new and particular figure for a family business, the Case Company has started a path of digital evolution based on customers' needs and requests and the solicitation of a big partner. The company was, thus, oriented to Lean Management and in general to the Industry 4.0 approach. As the project engineer tells during the interview,

Digitization is a journey, not an event. We started with a "pilot project" in one of our plants, in the most automated, newest and most technological plant of the

company - so that in essence it was simpler - on one machine, then on others, then on the whole department to get to the whole company.

This approach has been extended to the oldest areas so that today there are about fifteen industrial protocols for the management, programming, and control of instruments, applied to old machines (such as control over the shot counters of blanking machines) up to the most advanced assembly machines that start from the semi-finished product and give a finished product. Below are reported the salient moments of the "*path*" of digitization to have a more complete schematized vision:

- **2012 Adoption of the Lean methodology:** thanks to the Lean Manufacturing methodology, the company has developed consistent skills to increase its productivity; the Kaizen meetings, periodically dedicated to evaluating and concretely implementing the ideas collected, have increased productivity by 14%.
- **2013 Development of the digital team**
- **2015/2016 Conception and adoption of an internal software house**: qualified between a MOM (Manufacturing Operations Management) and a MES (Manufacturing Execution Systems), the digital solution created by the analyzed company is an Industry 4.0 platform that, in essence, monitors in real time the performance of the machines (almost 100). These machines perform different operations, but, regardless of the type of production and age, they are all interfaced. In collaboration with one of the world's largest producers of electronic devices, the internal software house was developed as an internal project, but it is also a technological solution perfectly suited to the whole industrial context.
- **2017 The digital solution was placed on the market**: the response of the first customers, including long-standing customers, was positive. The Case Company begins to position itself on the market not only as a manufacture, but also as a supplier of industrial software.
- **2019 Birth of a new Industrial division**: this is one of the key steps that have transformed the firm from a manufacturing company to a real Tech Company. From this moment on, the company can be qualified as a technological player that accompanies each of its customers on a digital transformation journey.
- **2020 On Azure cloud**: to date, the original digital solution is available both on-premises (continues to be adopted locally by the Case Company itself) and on cloud, thanks to Microsoft technology.
- **2021 Post Covid-19 recovery actions and strategic developments**: To recover after the slowdown caused by the Covid-19 pandemic, which also affected the household appliance production sector, the Case Company signed

a strategic partnership agreement with a global consulting company and joined the General Confederation of Italian Industry in Poland. The aim was to expand into a dynamic and thriving market, which is experiencing a phase of great development. In particular, Poland represents great development opportunities for the Digital business area of the Case Company, which has developed an innovative platform that allows monitoring production from an industrial IoT perspective, making production plants more intelligent.

In addition, in this case study a consolidated *cultural approach oriented to digitization* emerged, also because the Case Company recognizes to the digital area great autonomy and responsibility. As mentioned, this is a hub of innovation with no production, where digital technologies are concentrated. Accordingly, it refers to a centralized organizational model.

People: The Leading Element of Digitalization

The current president of the Case Company firmly states that *people* are the fundamental starting point for every evolutionary path, thus transmitting the importance of employee training. Indeed, it is often used the expression *"empowerment of employees"*. Employees know how to read indexes, use platforms, as well as, more trivially, exploit technologies to reduce the use of paper. It is often thought that technology steals work, instead, in this case, the operators have been trained on Lean Management by the same software engineers who produced the tools used today. The head of customer care and communication said:

The goal was to improve everyday reality. A sort of healthy competition was triggered between the plants and within the plants between the operators of the various shifts. I remember an episode: when the production manager was in Germany to visit a fair and on his mobile phone he received a message with the efficiency data of the machine, an exaggerated number the concept of the value of technology was transferred, which was not seen as an enemy a waste of time; it is a bit our added value to have made sure that everyone has accepted these technologies in the company.

The internal software-house based on *simplicity* has allowed it to be used easily, also because it was born from the same computer and communication engineers operating within the Case Company. Regarding the characteristics of the Digital Team, there is no distinct group in front-end and back-end, but they often refer to "full stack" (i.e., experts who know how to move easily between back-end languages and different aspects and technologies of front-end programming). Moreover, there are Sales Business employees, softwarists, an engineering manager of digital IT solutions, and a graduate in statistics with a master's degree in Industry 4.0.

Regarding the selection and recruiting process, there are strong relations with universities and higher technical institutes. Technologies (e.g., Bot systems) are not used, preferring to traditionally evaluate aspects such as flexibility and adaptation. Always looking to the future, the Case Company has created collaborations with universities and professional training institutes to grow new talents, with specific and advanced skills, to effectively introduce them into the world of work.

We go to find them (Talents) while they are doing training, and we "cuddle" them from there. [Name of an employee] is an example, as many others who entered the marketing office, of an internship path during university studies: it is from there that the leap was made, and we kept them with us. (Interviewee 1)

This is how an original Case Company Academy was born: it is a physical and virtual place where knowledge is produced and the encounter between people, the contamination of ideas, the collection, exchange and consolidation of knowledge is promoted, supporting innovation and creativity. This also contributes to the achievement of some United Nations sustainable goals such as quality education, gender equality, innovation, decent work and economic growth.

Analytics Processes: The Journey of Data and Information towards People

Analytics processes were a fundamental element, together with the birth of a Digital Team, for the Case Company for trusting and enhancing data and information, after passing the introduction phase and consolidating of the Lean methodology. Starting from clear and defined ***processes***, the Case Company has therefore decided to internally develop an industry 4.0 platform. The previously described digital solution can smartly collect, manage, process and enhance a series of production data. Several information systems have been adopted for the production area, commercial area, supply chain.

Concerning the organizational aspects of the processes, however, the original digital solution is worthy of further study:

To make sure that technology works in the factory, one of the keys that, at least in our experience, we have found successful is "simplicity": if a technology is not simple, it is heavy, it engages the work, it does not enhance it, but precisely weighs it down, if the operators use it, it is because they are obliged against their will. (Interviewee 2)

The improvement and speed achieved in the production processes are due to the ease of use of the application, connected directly to devices such as smartwatches, mobile phones and tablets to send and receive data in real-time. Therefore, the original digital solution was created in collaboration with one of the world's largest producers of electronic devices, because of the availability of technologies as well as for the extremely collaborative approach.

Specifically, the monitors guarantee a 24-hour operation to reach the right people at the right time, removing the need to physically go to the plants: For example, based on the Production Manager requests in terms of information on the number of produced and wasted pieces, and more generally on the production trend, a *smart signage* solution for the control and analysis of flows has been installed along the production lines. The aim of this system can be summarized in the increasement of the systems' efficiency, and the satisfaction and serenity of the operator. For the same reasons, the [name of a system], a smartwatch that allows you to "take production with you" has been used. Indeed, it was considered the best solution to manage alarms and information systems related to machines. Some of the main functions are: 1) Display error codes and problems on the line; 2) Real-time notice to managers; and 3) Answer calls.

Greater reactivity becomes, thus, certainly one of the main results.

The four main technologies among the nine identified by Boston Consulting Group (2015) that concern the main analytics processes in the Case Company include:

1. **Augmented Reality**: more precisely, [name of the technology] in the quality control phase helps to visualize products without disassembling them, bringing less waste and more speed. Moreover [name of another technology] is also added to form, collaborate, interact, and make stand up meetings. Multimedia content, interaction with production systems and typical functions of a blackboard can be easily used by everyone as thanks to smartphones.
2. **Internet of things:** with the interconnection between the physical world and data, the original digital solution enables the creation and use of a real "Digital Twin" of the factory and machinery.
3. **Big Data and Analytics**: briefly summarizing what has been said, with the original digital solution the raw data are detected, processed and those of competence visualize them. Actually, within the Case Company, the staff mainly works with "Small Data", millions of data from various sources, but related only to the aspects considered strictly important and relevant for the Case Company.
4. **Cloud Computing**: as explained above, the digital solution adopted by the Case Company is available both on the company's local servers and On Cloud.

Within the wide range of rampant disruptive technologies, the original software house is the ally of *simplicity* and *fluidity* in the Case Company and for all its customers; however, once again, people are at the center of the process while the data and information move towards them.

Governance and Organizational Structure

Following the order given to the elements of the CSPG framework, *governance* is finally discussed as the source of the determination of the company's objectives, values, and culture, i.e., the guide for the design of the other elements already presented.

To have an idea of the level of complexity of the governance and the organizational structure chosen, it is necessary to recall what was anticipated about the 2019 events. Given the birth of a new business division, it is possible to imagine a divisional organizational chart where the business units are the already mentioned two lines (components or household appliances and digital solutions for companies). However, it is not a divisional organizational model in the most basic form (distinct business units, each with its own functions) since most business functions such as marketing, administration & finance, human resources, or IT are transversal: This refers to an organizational model with corporate divisions that carry out in a centralized way the activities subtracted from the specific divisions. It means that they share a unitary "vision", not for individual businesses. The central management, therefore, has a primary responsibility concerning their function and a contributory one concerning the two lines of business.

Finally, information about some of the preliminary parameters in the design of governance during a digital evolution path can be food for thought on *governance* itself:

- Ensuring the achievement of valid decisions in the long term: the Case Company is currently studying new products that in the near future will form a complete package of components. As emerged from the company documentation, "tomorrow is lived today: Anticipating customer needs with new projects has always been a sort of creed".
- Ensuring that investments in analytics generate value: Considering that 8% of revenues are invested in Research, Development, and Innovation, tangible results are not surprising. An overall improvement in production facilities (+ 10% OEE), an average improvement in machine performance (+ 10%) and an increase in products produced after one year (+ 300,000).
- Guarantee protection and security of data and products, compliance with criteria of responsibility and transparency: Confidentiality and current regulations are fully respected:

We are, since the legislation was introduced, compliant with the GDPR, every company contact person and every office has signed a confidentiality agreement for the data in its possession used daily. It is all information that we know how to manage, how to keep (Interviewee 1)

As for the products, moreover, the Case Company is ISO 9001 certified: In 2018 the surveillance visited to confirm the certification that guarantees the level of the quality system and reliability. In addition, once again, the innovative capacity of the group stands out since it is focused on the control of production processes and at the same time on customer satisfaction.

DISCUSSION AND CONCLUSION

By introducing a theoretical approach and a related analysis, this study tries to give simple answers to the main features, opportunities, and risks that are characterizing the current digital revolution. All the Industry 4.0 phenomena are also very close to everyone's daily reality, but the results regarding their role in organizations make this study particularly insightful for both scholars and businesses. Furthermore, the analysis of a notable Italian entrepreneurial reality could be seen as a set of practical suggestions and guidelines since it has been demonstrated that Italian SMEs have the potential to face the Industry 4.0 revolution with confidence and a proactive approach.

The phenomenon of Big Data is so important that the related discussion has also paved the way for other major organizational results of Industry 4.0. This could seem to have an impact on business processes and therefore more at the operational level. Consequences need actually to be evaluated also from an organizational point of view in any type of company. Indeed, through the study of the innovations that emerged over the years regarding data, information, and technologies, an increase in the "visibility of information" has been obtained as a result: extended to more operational levels the possibility of accessing company information, as well as the ability to understand and exploit them, the role of big data is also revolutionizing some decision-making processes and, reasonably, organizational design.

The opportunities offered by the Industry 4.0 revolution are seized only if, in the overall economic context and especially in the company, a *cultural change* occurs. This change is realized when the company questions its way of operating, and considers the time needed and projects itself simultaneously to the future: to survive in the current economic and social context, the only solution is to react. Indeed, talking about market leaders, it is crucial to be directly proactive, respecting the necessary times and efforts. Through the analysis of the so-called "path" of digitization of the analyzed company, the veracity of what has been theoretically exposed has emerged in practice. Accordingly, building a data culture is a long-term process. As a result, Big Data Analytics, Artificial Intelligence, and the other technologies can be defined "mainstream", but there is still a long way to go (Bean, 2021).

From a more technical point of view, at the base of the revolution of every business *process*, there is the availability of new technologies and new skills: Automation is now typical of the company reality, but the impact of digital is not only revealed in production methods, but also in new organizational forms. Thus, contrary to what can be immediately associated with technology and automation, in the analysis conducted the centrality of the *person* clearly stands out. As mentioned, the skills of the same people in the company are affected by the digital revolution; in particular, the new 4.0 organizations require both extremely specialized and technical skills as well as increasingly transversal skills also in the digital field. It would seem, therefore, that today and increasingly in the near future, every job requires, in addition to traditional skills, specific tasks, also a digital and relational completion. Putting together the considerations regarding staff and information technology, two almost opposite answers were given: on the one hand the power of *leaders* to better control the work of workers through connection and analysis tools (i.e., smartwatches) and, on the other hand, the greater staff engagement. Indeed, it is ensured by the data available at all levels of the company, which give employees greater autonomy, flexibility, satisfaction, and serenity in successful cases. Considering these two elements, it is possible, therefore, to notice a changed coordination of tasks and roles in the company. However, it must be specified that all organizations that pursue success through the famous ambidexterity rise the level of complexity in the organizational structure and, consequently, in the role of *governance*. In addition to being a guide of values and culture, the analytics governance might have to redefine the company's corporate objectives as well as coordinate them synergistically: the distinction into two autonomous business lines, which took place in the analyzed company as a fundamental step in its digital evolution path, is undoubtedly an excellent example.

The main implication of this study refers to the possibilities offered by digital technologies, and how they can be incorporated into the organizational design. Thus, it enriches the findings of many pre-existing studies proposing that adoption of technologies might need different organizational designs (Shaba et al., 2019) with the finding that adoption of technologies might need also diverse dimensions of organizational design. Scholars, practitioners, as well as policy makers, need to consider it.

REFERENCES

Adams, W. C. (2015). Conducting Semi-Structured Interviews. In K. E. Newcomer, H. P. Hatry, & J. S. Wholey (Eds.), *Handbook of Practical Program Evaluation* (pp. 492–505). John Wiley & Sons, Inc. doi:10.1002/9781119171386.ch19

Bean, R. (2021, February 5). Why Is It So Hard to Become a Data-Driven Company? *Harvard Business Review*. https://hbr.org/2021/02/why-is-it-so-hard-to-become-a-data-driven-company

Boston Consulting Group. (2020, August 19). *Industry 4.0: The Future of Productivity and Growth in Manufacturing Industries*. BCG Global. https://www.bcg.com/publications/2015/engineered_products_project_business_industry_4_future_productivity_growth_manufacturing_industries

Bousdekis, A., & Mentzas, G. (2021). Enterprise Integration and Interoperability for Big Data-Driven Processes in the Frame of Industry 4.0. *Frontiers in Big Data, 4*. https://www.frontiersin.org/article/10.3389/fdata.2021.644651

Burton, R. M., Mastrangelo, D., & Salvador, F. (2014). Introduction. *Journal of Organization Design, 3*(1), 1–1. doi:10.7146/jod.16855 PMID:24343643

Butt, J. (2020). A Conceptual Framework to Support Digital Transformation in Manufacturing Using an Integrated Business Process Management Approach. *Designs, 4*(3), 17. doi:10.3390/designs4030017

Cucciniello, M., Lapsley, I., Nasi, G., & Pagliari, C. (2015). Understanding key factors affecting electronic medical record implementation: A sociotechnical approach. *BMC Health Services Research, 15*(1), 268. doi:10.118612913-015-0928-7 PMID:26184405

Daft, R. L. (2021). *Organizzazione aziendale* (R. C. D. Nacamulli & L. Quaratino, Eds.). Maggioli.

De Mauro, A., Greco, M., Grimaldi, M., & Ritala, P. (2018). Human resources for Big Data professions: A systematic classification of job roles and required skill sets. *Information Processing & Management, 54*(5), 807–817. doi:10.1016/j.ipm.2017.05.004

Deloitte. (2015). *Industry 4.0—Challenges and Solutions for the Digital Transformation and Use of Exponential Technologies*. Study of Deloitte Consulting. https://www2.deloitte.com/content/dam/Deloitte/ch/Documents/manufacturing/ch-enmanufacturing-industry-4-0-24102014

Garzoni, A., De Turi, I., Secundo, G., & Del Vecchio, P. (2020). Fostering digital transformation of SMEs: A four levels approach. *Management Decision, 58*(8), 1543–1562. doi:10.1108/MD-07-2019-0939

Grossman, R., & Siegel, K. (2014). *Organizational Models for Big Data and Analytics* (*SSRN* Scholarly Paper ID 2458909). Social Science Research Network. doi:10.7146/jod.9799

Javaid, M., Haleem, A., Singh, R. P., & Suman, R. (2021). Substantial capabilities of robotics in enhancing industry 4.0 implementation. *Cognitive Robotics, 1*, 58–75. doi:10.1016/j.cogr.2021.06.001

Kotter, J. P. (2014, April 24). Accelerate: Building Strategic Agility for a Faster-Moving World. *Harvard Business Review*. https://hbr.org/2014/04/accelerate-building-strategic-agility-for-a-faster-moving-world

Li, Y., Dai, J., & Cui, L. (2020). The impact of digital technologies on economic and environmental performance in the context of industry 4.0: A moderated mediation model. *International Journal of Production Economics, 229*, 107777. doi:10.1016/j.ijpe.2020.107777

Liu, Z., Xie, K., Li, L., & Chen, Y. (2020). A paradigm of safety management in Industry 4.0. *Systems Research and Behavioral Science, 37*(4), 632–645. doi:10.1002res.2706

Llopis-Albert, C., Rubio, F., & Valero, F. (2021). Impact of digital transformation on the automotive industry. *Technological Forecasting and Social Change, 162*, 120343. doi:10.1016/j.techfore.2020.120343 PMID:33052150

Loebbecke, C., & Picot, A. (2015). Reflections on societal and business model transformation arising from digitization and big data analytics. *The Journal of Strategic Information Systems, 24*(3), 149–157. doi:10.1016/j.jsis.2015.08.002

Maimone, F. (2022). Organizing for Industry 4.0. In *Lecture Notes in Information Systems and Organization* (pp. 1–20). Springer. https://ideas.repec.org/h/spr/lnichp/978-3-030-83321-3_1.html

Mikalef, P., Pappas, I. O., Pavlou, P. A., & Krogstie, J. (2017). *Big Data Analytics and Business Value. Information and Management Call for Papers*. Available at: https://www.journals.elsevier.com/ information-and-management/call-for-papers

Parmentola, A., Tutore, I., & Costagliola Di Fiore, M. (2020). Environmental Side of Fourth Industrial Revolution: The Positive and Negative Effects of I4.0 Technologies. In C. M. Hussain & P. Di Sia (Eds.), *Handbook of Smart Materials, Technologies, and Devices: Applications of Industry 4.0* (pp. 1–31). Springer International Publishing. doi:10.1007/978-3-030-58675-1_84-1

Ritchie, J., Lewis, J., & McNaughton Nicholls, C. (2013). *Qualitative Research Practice*. SAGE Publications.

Shaba, E., Guerci, M., Gilardi, S., & Bartezzaghi, E. (2019). *Industry 4.0 technologies and organizational design - Evidence from 15 Italian cases*. Studi Organizzativi. doi:10.3280/SO2019-001001

Sheng, J., Amankwah-Amoah, J., Khan, Z., & Wang, X. (2021). COVID-19 Pandemic in the New Era of Big Data Analytics: Methodological Innovations and Future Research Directions. *British Journal of Management, 32*(4), 1164–1183. doi:10.1111/1467-8551.12441

Silvestri, L., Forcina, A., Introna, V., Santolamazza, A., & Cesarotti, V. (2020). Maintenance transformation through Industry 4.0 technologies: A systematic literature review. *Computers in Industry, 123*, 103335. doi:10.1016/j.compind.2020.103335

Venier, F. (2017). *Digital transformation and organizational capacity. Italian companies and the challenge of change* [Trasformazione digitale e capacità organizzativa. Le aziende italiane e la sfida del cambiamento]. EUT Edizioni Università di Trieste. https://www.openstarts.units.it/handle/10077/19885

World Economic Forum. (2019). *Fourth Industrial Revolution: Beacons of Technology and Innovation in Manufacturing*. World Economic Forum. https://www.weforum.org/whitepapers/fourth-industrial-revolution-beacons-of-technology-and-innovation-in-manufacturing/

Zolotová, I., Papcun, P., Kajáti, E., Miškuf, M., & Mocnej, J. (2020). Smart and cognitive solutions for Operator 4.0: Laboratory H-CPPS case studies. *Computers & Industrial Engineering, 139*, 105471. doi:10.1016/j.cie.2018.10.032

Chapter 4
Toward a Digital Technology Perspective of Entrepreneurship:
The Case of Small-Medium Enterprises in Lebanon

Khodor Shatila
IProCares International Research Center, Lebanon

Suha Jalloul
Lebanese American University, Lebanon

ABSTRACT

New digital technology has revolutionized the uncertainty inherent in entrepreneurial processes, results, and the methods for coping with such delay. This has sparked discussion on digital entrepreneurship and the relationship between digital technology and entrepreneurship. The survey was distributed online using Google Forms between January 2022 and February 2022. The target population for the study included entrepreneurs and young graduates in Lebanon. The survey was administered in English, considered the second language used in Lebanon. Additionally, the sample used for this study is 270 employees (N=270). Many entrepreneurs' lives and jobs are now affected by technological advancements. People aren't sure how it's going to turn out, but one thing is for sure: it's going to provide something fresh and challenging. It must be a worldwide effort, engaging all stakeholders, including politicians, business leaders, educators, and public members. With these improvements in Lebanon, the whole production, management, and governance systems will be transformed.

DOI: 10.4018/978-1-6684-4265-4.ch004

INTRODUCTION

New digital technology has revolutionized the uncertainty inherent in entrepreneurial processes, results and the methods for coping with such delay. This has sparked discussion on digital entrepreneurship and the relationship between digital technology and entrepreneurship, according to Gerrikagoitia et al. (2019). An explicit conceptualizing of notions connected to digital technology is needed to understand the two significant consequences of this research: less restricted entrepreneurial processes and outputs and a less specified location for entrepreneurial activity. This digital technology perspective's potential and usefulness might be articulated by considering how it can build on and expand existing ideas of entrepreneurialism (Rippa & Secundo, 2019).

Today's digital technologies pervade every private and public enterprise, from social media to business analytics to the Internet of Things to big data, sophisticated manufacturing to 3D printing, and cloud computing. While the phenomena of digital technology's influence on academic entrepreneurship have been studied in general, it has not been adequately addressed to the best knowledge. This study provides a new addition to the era of Digital Entrepreneurship to address this need. There are four components to the proposed framework for analyzing digital entrepreneurship: the reasons for using digital technologies for entrepreneurship (why), new forms of digital entrepreneurialism (what), and the individuals and organizations involved in achieving the goal of entrepreneurship (who), all of which are based on quantitative methods (how) (Li et al., 2020).

SIGNICANCE OF THE STUDY

The digital industrial revolution, known as Industry 4.0, brings about the current Fourth Industrial Revolution. Integration of intelligent equipment and systems and modifications in production processes to boost efficiency and provide the option of flexible alterations is referred to as Industry 4.0. People's work and personal lives are being impacted by various trends and phenomena, all of which affect how businesses operate. These include the increasing and widespread use of cutting-edge technological solutions and the economic networking that impacts the growth of various communication forms, global competitiveness, and employee mobility, according to Douglas & Prentice (2019). Combined with a constantly changing professional environment, these patterns provide new possibilities and problems for businesses. What was formerly the realm of a slew of market participants will be supplied by a single player in the future. In the business-to-business (B2B) and the business-to-consumer (B2C) arenas, trends will be driven by customer expectations and experiences, which can revolutionize practically any industry.

Over the next several years, corporations will have to rethink their business models and strategy in light of new consumer ecosystems rather than their old market rivals. A wide range of new business models, including open business models, may be created utilizing open innovation and new ideas in business. These enterprise goods and operations models may be restructured (Gupta & Chaudhry, 2019; Jun et al., 2019). A competitive advantage based on the rules of Industry 4.0 may be built upon these models. Technological advancements and solutions implemented in modern businesses lead to shifts in management paradigms and the need for new business models to maintain a balance between autonomous (intelligent) technology advancements, remote communication systems, and societally recognized values. Understanding consumer demands is a critical differentiator in the Fourth Industrial Revolution. It allows companies to gain a competitive advantage by proactively taking advantage of new possibilities, challenges, and difficulties. When it came to the absence of business models for companies operating in Industry 4.0, it was discovered that there was a research hole in the form, foundation, and sources of competitive advantage. This research aimed to identify the pillars of open business models in the Industry 4.0 environment, which will serve as a foundation for these models.

DIGITAL TRANSFORMATION SUCCESS UNDER INDUSTRY 4.0:

A Strategic Guideline for Manufacturing SMEs

Digital entrepreneurship (D.E.) is of interest to academic study, commercial practice, and governmental policies aimed at promoting this phenomenon because of its beneficial effects on job creation and economic development. Using a viewpoint that focuses on how digital entrepreneurs generate digital value by obtaining, processing, and disseminating digital information. Ko (2019) describe essential critical ideas and briefly map out current research. Research on digital entrepreneurship (D.E.) may be improved by adopting a micro-level approach that complements the recent research on D.E. that focuses on the systemic level of digital entrepreneurship ecosystems and the digital platforms economy (Ghobakhloo & Iranmanesh, 2021; Sahut et al., 2021). There are four key D.E. research streams: digital business models, the digital entrepreneurship process and establishment of start-ups for new digital businesses; D.E. in digital platforms; and entrepreneurship ecosystems. New collaborative and social dynamics offered by digital technologies enhance knowledge exchange and facilitate opportunity identification in the same way as traditional D.E. frameworks.

New digital technology has revolutionized the uncertainty inherent in entrepreneurial processes and results and the methods for coping with such uncertainty. This has sparked discussion on digital entrepreneurship and the relationship between digital technology and entrepreneurship. An explicit conceptualizing of notions connected to digital technology is needed to understand the two significant consequences of this research: less restricted entrepreneurial processes and performance and a less specified location for entrepreneurial activity. This digital technology perspective's potential and usefulness might be articulated by considering how it can build on and expand existing ideas of entrepreneurialism, according to Sahut et al. (2021).

It is becoming more critical for industrial players to understand how they may profit from new technologies like Industry 4.0 (I4.0), a term used to describe the fourth industrial revolution (Ben Jabeur et al., 2021; Nguyen et al., 2021). Using a multidisciplinary approach drawn from Business Model (BM) Innovation and Entrepreneurship disciplines, this study creates an agile framework for developing and accessing digital entrepenreuerhsip. Replicable processes based on tools and techniques from various domains may bridge the cross-disciplinary gaps inherent in the new industrial environment and generate models based on industry stakeholders' real-world knowledge and experience. Stress Testing on our created models, we're able to pinpoint potential dangers and the resulting consequences. In addition to the process itself, this study suggests several archetypes and four more B.M.s, each with stress elements and the influence of those stress factors. It is the goal of this article to give industrial stakeholders some essential tools and roadmaps to test current models further and construct new ones, all to develop a profitable and sustainable innovative manufacturing environment (Ghobakhloo & Iranmanesh, 2021)

The Impact of Technological Infrastructure on Digital Entrepreneurship

There has been a lot of interest in Industry 4.0 technologies, including the Internet of Things (IoT), cloud computing, big data and analytics. Using information processing theory, Yi et al (2019) look at the impact of Industry 4.0's new digital technologies on economic and environmental performance. Digital supply chain platforms and environmental dynamism have been presented and analyzed using a survey of Chinese manufacturing enterprises to examine the impact of these two factors, according to Li et al. (2020). According to the findings, a high degree of environmental dynamism enhances digital technologies' mediating impacts on economic and environmental performance. With this research, better understand how digital technologies impact performance and get management insight into promoting economic sustainability and ecological sustainability in the age of Industry 4.0, according to Gerrikagoitia et al. (2019).

The innovation system relies heavily on digital entrepreneurship. It influences the many levels and aspects of the innovation system by altering the broader business system's structure, goals, and networking methods. Digital technologies may provide new commercial possibilities, but they may also be disruptive and create new weaknesses in the innovation system. We did a comprehensive literature study to acquire a thorough grasp of the hybrid digital entrepreneurship idea and its significance in transforming the innovation system. For the first time, essential categories of digital entrepreneurship have been identified and vary from other business forms.

The three core dimensions of the innovation system (the entrepreneur, the entrepreneurial process, and the digitalization of organizational management processes) are analyzed to identify the determinants of digital entrepreneurship, which include, for example, behavioural, competence, and mentality patterns, as well as personal outcomes and consequences of entrepreneurial activity (Poddar et al., 2019; Ye et al., 2019). Research on the interrelationships between entrepreneurial structures in innovation systems and the broader socioeconomic system would benefit greatly from a systematization of the current literature. To fully grasp this, further study in methodological, substantive, and theoretical disciplines is required (Oh et al., 2022)

Indirectly, increased digitalization adds to economic growth by fostering entrepreneurship. In several E.U. nations and areas, digitization varies widely according to those countries and regions' economic development, infrastructure, and educational systems. As a result of these disparities, specific nations and areas have more entrepreneurial activity than others and a more significant role for entrepreneurship in economic development, according to Kreuzer et al. (2022).

To expand the number of digital entrepreneurs in these locations, it is required to establish digital infrastructure and a competitive digital business environment. Access to dependable broadband Internet infrastructures remains crucial in many regions. This issue must be addressed first and foremost to allow prospective entrepreneurs to establish businesses and benefit from them through internet transactions. A dynamic and competitive digital business environment and the growth of highly competitive entrepreneurs in the online services and development of digital apps are essential (Von Briel et al., 2021; Zahra, 2021). To further promote creative entrepreneurship, fostering a culture of innovation and entrepreneurship is critical. All levels of the educational system must address this via official and informal courses, inspiration and exchange programs, and training in entrepreneurship and big-picture visions. Additional financial incentives for innovation are also required to inspire the next generation of inventive entrepreneurs. In addition, the legal and regulatory framework should be strengthened, notably in property rights and decreasing government bureaucracy, since this may stimulate entrepreneurial activity growth.

Scientific and Technological Development and Impact on Digital Entrepreneurship

Through the creation and deployment of cutting-edge technological solutions, open innovation is a critical component in hastening the digitization of the healthcare industry. Open and collaborative innovation in the digital age: fostering sincere, digital cooperation. With digitally enabled open collaboration, these creative techniques draw on and incorporate many sources of information. However, this early stage of innovation is difficult for business practitioners and innovators since the notion is ethereal, qualitative, and lacks facts (Park et al., 2019; Poddar et al., 2019). Many established businesses now routinely use open innovation as a strategy. They depend not only on internal corporate expertise to innovate; they also encourage information from outside the organization.

Because the line separating enterprises from their immediate intellectual surroundings is porous, businesses may acquire new information. Customers, vendors, and institutions may all provide vital information for innovation. Start-ups confront unique hurdles, yet they may still benefit from open innovation. It is rare to form solid strategic alliances because they lack intangible (such as technological expertise) and financial resources. Open innovation is a driving force for emerging companies, particularly at three levels: firm creation, technology development, and technology commercialization. According to the findings, start-up companies can use various relationships with various network partners to propel the development and commercialization of innovation (Garcez et al., 2022; Ji et al., 2021).

Such linkages may vary from casual networking ties to official partnerships, such as R&D collaborations with universities and established corporations. Start-ups benefit from all types of relationships that promote innovation, but synergetic partnerships like R&D collaborations with universities and established firms create the most opportunities for innovation. Recent research shows that innovation outcomes are achieved when multiple external partners are linked and knowledge flows increase, especially in uncertain environments (Anderson & Gaddefors, 2016; Park et al., 2019).

Toward the conclusion of the twentieth century, digitalization processes spurred the move from closed innovation techniques to open innovation models. In an increasingly digital age, open innovation has become a fundamental driver of entrepreneurship, allowing for lower research expenses, more risk-sharing, and more rapid commercialization of new ideas throughout the globe. Many industries, including health care, information technology (I.T.), and academic entrepreneurship, have seen success with open innovation during the last several years.

Your company's internal innovation process will be sped up by opening up, allowing you to take benefit of the expertise of others inside the organization while allowing others to exploit your knowledge in their industry (inside out). Making yourself more vulnerable may help you come up with new ideas for solving problems and generating even more information. A wide range of issues may benefit from this integrated approach; however, those with a greater degree of complexity are the most likely (Garcez et al., 2022; Steininger et al., 2022) to benefit from it. The more complex a problem becomes, the more a company must share its expertise to find a solution. The healthcare industry relies on openness to save time, particularly in a pandemic. Even in a worldwide epidemic, transparency and open innovation may save lives. Open innovation techniques should be considered by digital entrepreneurs interested in solving large-scale challenges and influencing complicated ecosystems (such as the healthcare industry).

Technological Capability and Impact on Digital Entrepreneurship

Even though many people feel we live in a time marked by paradox because the future is so unclear, entrepreneurs may still benefit from several new technologies that are now being developed or already in use. Entrepreneurs may get a competitive advantage by anticipating and utilizing breakthrough technology in the future. Another aspect of the E.U.'s Horizon 2020 plan is fostering interdisciplinary partnerships on future technologies to launch new European research and innovation ecosystems, including so-called future and emerging technology (FET). There is no doubt that new and developing technologies are challenging to understand and deploy (Kašperová, 2021; Trongtorsak et al., 2021). A strong strategic focus and the capacity to innovate using technologies now unavailable to the general public are required to implement them. Other elements must be considered to reap the benefits of technology in economic and social realms. A technology's full potential cannot be achieved just by creating it; instead, it must be widely distributed, assimilated, and put to use. An overview prepared by (Abubakre et al., 2021) demonstrates how FETs like artificial intelligence and quantum technologies can alter our future and how they might impact the various SDGs.

Even though it may seem strange, quantum technologies are already widely used in computers, data networks, and most medical imaging modalities. This is because quantum physics concepts are used in many components, such as transistors, diodes, and lasers. Quantum technologies from the first generation began as research endeavours and have now been integrated into an array of ICTs and daily gadgets that we all use today. It's been over a century since Central Europeans invented quantum physics, and now that knowledge is opening doors for new businesses. The second quantum revolution is usually seen as following the digital transformation in the twenty-first century. Measurement equipment with more accuracy increased data security, and high-performance computers and satellites are just a few of the many places where this influence may be felt (Kašperová, 2021; Welter et al., 2019).

Technology based on quantum principles is essential for using the quantum world's unique physical laws. The notion of blended reality is another example of a potentially transformative FET. Despite the generally held belief that gaming is an unhealthy (or at the very least, not health-positive) pastime, many Health and Exergames employ virtual or augmented reality to encourage active living and exercise. It's commonly accepted as a suitable alternative for fitness in virtual reality, such as Beat Saber, which utilizes the technology to reach people at home, inspire them, and encourage them to exercise (Dowin Kennedy, 2021; Wierenga, 2020). Integrated video conferencing allows customers to work out and receive lessons together using innovative fitness equipment under the supervision of remote trainers. Exercise in virtual reality is possible with other programs, such as Supernatural. It's possible to utilize many of these technologies now, but it's only a matter of time until Blended Realities become commonplace.

SAMPLE

The survey was distributed online using google forms between January 2022 and February 2022. The target population for the study included entrepreneurs and young graduates in Lebanon. The survey was administered in English, considered the second language used in Lebanon. Additionally, the sample used for this study is 270 employees (N=270). The following sections discuss the different instruments used to measure the study's variables.

Instruments

The first section included a consent form that provides the choice for respondents whether to answer the questionnaire or not and reassures that the identity of the respondents will remain anonymous as a part of maintaining research ethics and confidentiality.

The purpose of the questionnaire was to examine the impact of the Industry 4.0 Revolution on digital entrepreneurship and on creating a better economy. Three pillars will be used to measure Industry 4.0 Revolution: technological infrastructure, technological development, and Technological Development.

Table 1. Gender

Gender					
		Frequency	**Percent**	**Valid Percent**	**Cumulative Percent**
Valid	Female	180	66.7	66.7	66.7
	Male	90	33.3	33.3	100.0
	Total	270	100.0	100.0	

It is important to note that the survey consisted of six sections. After the consent form, the second part included ten demographic questions with gender, age, marital status, level of education, years of experience, and whether the respondent is the primary provider for their family.

The third part measured technological infrastructure using 17 questions adopted from (Tasavori et al., 2018). Respondents rated the technological infrastructure activity on a 6-point Likert scale, where answers ranged between 0 (Never) to 6 (Always).

Moreover, the fourth section of the questionnaire concerned the Technological Development scale. The scale was adopted from (Senyard et al., 2014). Participants were asked to answer six questions using a 5-point scale ranging from 1 (Never) to 5 (Always).

The fifth part of the survey included a nine-item scale to measure Technological Development adopted (Ratten & Welpe, 2011). Participants rated the items on a 6-point Likert scale ranging from 0 (Never) to 6 (Everyday).

The sixth part of the survey included three items to measure economic growth and job opportunities created throughout Industry 4.0 and was adopted (Lüthy & Steyaert, 2019). The items were measured using a 5-point Likert scale ranging from 1 (Strongly Disagree) to 5 (Strongly Agree).

Descriptive Statistics

According to the above table, 180 of the respondents were females, and 90 of the respondents were males.

According to the above table, the age of 9 respondents was between 20-29, and 153 were between 20-29 years.

However, 72 of the respondents were between 30-39 years, and 36 were between 20-49 years.

According to the above table, 108 of the respondents have a graduation level where 135 of the respondents have a post-graduation level, and 27 have a secondary level.

Table 2. Age

Age					
		Frequency	Percent	Valid Percent	Cumulative Percent
Valid	20-29	9	3.3	3.3	3.3
	20-29 years	153	56.7	56.7	60.0
	30-39 years	72	26.7	26.7	86.7
	40-49 years	36	13.3	13.3	100.0
	Total	270	100.0	100.0	

Table 3. Education

Education					
		Frequency	Percent	Valid Percent	Cumulative Percent
Valid	Graduation	108	40.0	40.0	40.0
	Post -graduation	135	50.0	50.0	90.0
	Secondary	27	10.0	10.0	100.0
	Total	270	100.0	100.0	

Table 4. Regression Analysis

			Estimate	S.E.	C.R.	P
Digital Entrepreneurship	<---	Technological Developments	.262	.077	3.414	.002
Digital Entrepreneurship	<---	Technological Capability	.699	.095	7.342	.001
Digital Entrepreneurship	<---	Technological Infrastructure	.496	.069	7.158	.013
Global New Opportunities	<---	Digital Entrepreneurship	.355	.077	4.606	.013
New Market Opportunities	<---	Digital Entrepreneurship	.415	.078	5.336	.011
Current Market Opportunities	<---	Digital Entrepreneurship	.486	.075	6.491	.018

Figure 1. Path analysis

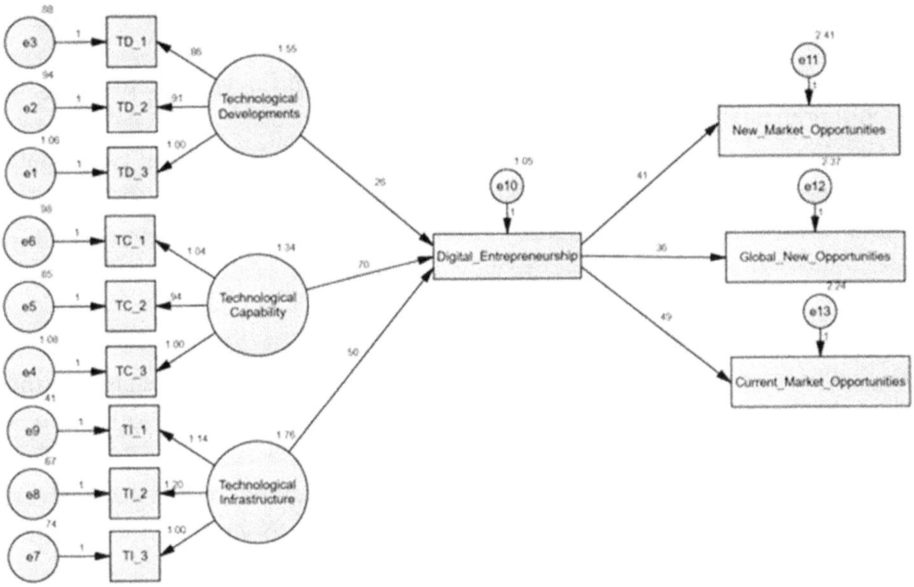

Regression Weights

Referring to the above table, it can be noted that there is a significant relationship between technological developments (P =0.002 < 0.05), (C.R = 3.414 > 2) and Estimate (0.262), technological capability (P =0.001 < 0.05), (C.R = 7.342 > 2) and Estimate (0.699), technological infrastructure (P =0.013 < 0.05), (C.R = 7.158 > 2) and Estimate (0.496), this means that there is a direct significant positive relationship between technological developments, technological capability, technological infrastructure and digital entrepreneurship.

However, it can be noted also that there is a significant relationship between digital entrepreneurship and Global New Opportunities since (P =0.013 < 0.05), (C.R = 0.077 > 2) and Estimate (0.355), and New Market Opportunities (P =0.011 < 0.05), (C.R = 5.336 > 2) and Estimate (0.415), and Current Market Opportunities (P =0.013 < 0.018), (C.R = 6.491 > 2) and Estimate (0.486), this means that there is a direct significant positive relationship between digital entrepreneurship and Global New Opportunities, New Market Opportunities and Current Market Opportunities.

The above path analysis was conducted to test the relationship between technological developments, technological Capability, technological infrastructure, and digital entrepreneurship and to study the relationship between digital entrepreneurship and how it can create new market opportunities, global opportunities and current market opportunities. However, the following can be interpreted:

- Digital Entrepreneurship = 0.262 Technological Developments + 0.699 Technological Capability + 0.496 Technological Infrastructure, and by that the following can be concluded:
- For every one-unit increase in technological developments, digital entrepreneurship tends to increase by 26.2 units
- For every one-unit increase in technological Capability, digital entrepreneurship tends to increase by 69.9 units
- For every one-unit increase in technological infrastructure, digital entrepreneurship tends to increase by 49.6 units

However, it also can be noted that:

Digital Entrepreneurship = 0.355 Global New Opportunities, which means that for every one-unit increase in digital entrepreneurship, the chance for creating Global New Opportunities will increase by 35.5 units.

Digital Entrepreneurship = 0.415 New Market Opportunities means that for every one-unit increase in digital entrepreneurship, the chance for creating New Market opportunities will increase by 41.5 units.

At last, Digital Entrepreneurship = 0.486 Current Market Opportunities, which means that for every one-unit increase in digital entrepreneurship, the current market opportunities' chance will increase by 48.6 units.

DISCUSSION

Many entrepreneurs' lives and jobs are now affected by technological advancements. People aren't sure how it will turn out, but one thing is for sure: it's going to provide something fresh and challenging. It must be a worldwide effort, engaging all stakeholders, including politicians, business leaders, educators, and public members. IR 4.0's stated goal is to bring Lebanese manufacturing up to date. Rather than being a low-cost manufacturing nation, the country aims to become a high-value competitor globally.

With these improvements in Lebanon, the whole production, management, and governance systems will be transformed. The industrial revolution has impacted businesses in Lebanon. As a start, the four primary impacts of IR 4.0 on enterprises are customers' expectations, product enhancements, collaborative innovation, and organizational structures. To keep up with these changes, businesses must adapt to the increasing openness and new consumer behaviour patterns. By generating an expectation for enhanced personalization, this IR 4.0 will revolutionize the way organizations connect with their consumers. Companies, for example, may now provide consumers with digital samples of their items so they can purchase customized versions. As a result, businesses in Lebanon are being forced to rethink and adapt their new product creation, marketing, and delivery methods. Data input and telemarketing have mainly been automated in recent years, resulting in a significant change in the workforce.

High-level employment requiring pattern recognition and cognitive non-routine work might be eliminated due to technological improvements. By eliminating job classification-based hiring practices, the revolution will free up firms to focus on activities that call for graduates with diverse abilities, such as creativity, emotional intelligence, and interpersonal communication. On the other hand, employers must adapt their recruiting procedures to meet the needs of their various roles. As a result, employment will be divided into low-skilled and high-skilled ones. Because of this, there will be an increase in the level of societal tensions. As a result of this industrial revolution, there will be a rising need for highly trained graduates, while the demand for graduates with less education and lesser skills will diminish. To use industry 4.0 tools, Lebanese graduates must have a basic understanding of technology.

Another factor that might hinder the industrial revolution is a lack of standards and technology. Consider the banking and financial services industry. Digital banks and FinTech firms are reshaping or disrupting both of them. Fintech might represent a challenge to conventional banking in the new IR4.0 age. Though a cashless society will be implemented in Lebanon by 2022, the country is now going in that direction.

Electronic payments have been introduced to Lebanon's banking and payment sector. The most used payment instruments, including credit, charge and debit cards, have been affected the most. Aside from that, V.R. has been around for a while, especially in the gaming industry, but it has recently gained traction thanks to technological advancements. However, several architectural projects in Malaysia still use 2D drawings and mock-ups to show their ideas. As V.R. technology develops, people must adapt to this new method since it will allow them to see everything in 3D.

For Lebanon's future productivity growth to be sustainable, it will largely depend on Lebanese graduates applying the advanced knowledge and technology associated with the revolution. Lebanese entrepreneurs must recognize that their changing environment directly impacts their operations. Job Prospects for Recent Graduates in the Fourth Industrial Revolution As soon as feasible after graduation, students should be allowed to work in a real-world setting. This is critical since it will broaden their view of current business trends and developments.

Graduates are often referred to be the foundation of our nation. In this age of IR 4.0, when kids are appropriately directed and are concerned about their future, they will be equipped with the information necessary to compete and survive. As a result, the 4C elements/skills must be included in our education system. 4Cs: critical thinking and problem solving, cooperation, creativity, and communication. Graduates must strengthen their problem-solving abilities in light of the increasing use of technology. They expect to take charge of the analytics, as is their knowledge of improving output on the shop floor.

With the advent of Industry 4.0, recent college grads have more options than ever. It is possible for graduates with IR 4.0 advancements and the Internet of Things to explore new career and entrepreneurship options. Cybersecurity analysts are in high demand in super-intelligent civilizations because they utilise advanced technology. Cyber-attacks, such as phishing, network assaults, and other distributed denial-of-service attacks, are dealt with by cyber-security experts. Investing in safe encryption of information, sensors, networks, and others becomes vital when firms decide to go digital. Installing firewalls, detecting threats, creating security policies, and monitoring and overcoming security breaches are some of the methods cybersecurity analysts use to secure the online data of their firms or organizations. Secondly, graduates may become IoT developers and inventors. IR 4.0 needs innovation, which means strong demand for innovators. Graduates might request funding for their initiatives to generate new items in a shorter period. Crowdfunding has become an increasingly popular method of raising money for projects. Recent college grads may turn to crowdfund sites like GoFundMe, IndieGoGo, and Kickstarter to get their creative ideas off the ground, where friends, family, and even strangers can donate cash.

Third, graduates might become online retail consigners with companies both online and off. Graduates may help clients make product and service selections by tailoring their offerings to their specific needs. Drop shippers may learn how to advertise other people's goods while promoting their own. On top of all these benefits, graduates can work with businesses and people alike to generate engaging and informative posts on social media platforms such as Instagram, Twitter, and Facebook to promote their goods and services. Having a social media manager may help firms or individuals build a favourable image of their clientele by employing excellent content and communication managed social media managers on social media platforms. Businesses and people with social media managers will build successful connections and brand images by efficiently and effectively promoting their goods and services. Aside from that, graduates may work as freelance copywriters and editors for existing firms or start-ups looking to boost their social media marketing efforts online.

Recent graduates might ask their current clients for suggestions to expand their consumer base. The grads can implement a referral award scheme to encourage their customers to recommend their services to others. They might start utilizing their blogs and social media profiles as portfolios. You can become a powerful social media influencer if you're a recent college grad. Marketers increasingly rely on social media influencers to help them reach potential clients. Authenticity may be included in graduates' lifestyle branding, and they can become trustworthy sources for the businesses they advocate. Social media influencers use social media accounts like Twitter, Facebook, YouTube, and Instagram to help their followers make educated purchase choices about products. Brands use social media influencers to communicate directly with their customers. For example, being a YouTube star may be a profitable career path for recent college grads.

In this day and age, YouTube stars have more significant influence than conventional superstars because of the pervasiveness of social media, particularly video sharing. Cooking, property management, parking, teaching and photography are just a few living skills viewers are interested in learning. From the number of people who watch their videos, YouTube celebrities benefit. The YouTube phenomenon results from narcissism, participation, self-interest, and emotions of connectedness, all of which contribute to the phenomenon. In addition, firms need digital strategy specialists with considerable data abilities to help them understand how to combine winning business strategies with digital technology while effectively using data mining tools and algorithms. Many businesses are ill-prepared for the emergence of IR 4.0 and a technologically advanced society. To thrive in IR 4.0, organizations must retrain their present workforce and implement a continuous learning culture. Graduates may fill in the need for highly-skilled IR 4.0 by providing high-value and innovative services. To sum it all up, recent college grads may take advantage of the burgeoning sharing economies that include anything from jewellery rentals to workspaces to clothing swaps to carpooling to sports equipment rentals to technology lending services to parking spots and bike-sharing to errand running. Customers and investors that want to upend existing company structures favour business strategies based on sharing.

FUTURE RESEARCH AND CONTRIBUTIONS

Venture plays a vital role in the growth of the local economy and the community's expectations for daily conveniences. Businesspeople engage the local network, the provinces, and the national financial system by doing their best for their companies. Contrary to job seekers, business visionaries create jobs by employing both their skills and the surrounding community, increasing their own company's strength. As their organizations grow, so does the local network's way of life. They bring in local assets and other businesses by conducting their business movement, allowing them to join their inventory network, and shifting money to local networks. Digital firms use different business models and full use of digital technologies to pursue their goods and services and their marketing and distribution efforts. The business environment is changing, business practices are changing, and new forms of entrepreneurial activities are being created due to advances in digitization and information and communication technology. Digital growth in Lebanon is in its infancy compared to launching a new business. With the proper use of the latest technology, small companies have a tremendous chance to grow their businesses and, therefore, their local communities. The Lebanese Government should develop a digital entrepreneurship policy framework to assist the development of digital entrepreneurship in Lebanon. These pillars are:

Digital Knowledge Base and ICT Market: There is public and private sector support for forming new firms and the growth of existing ones that embrace technology. The spread of digital innovation knowledge is promoted. The ICT industry's role is to spread and commercialize innovative services and ideas.

Digital Business Environment: A favorable legislative environment makes running a digital business easy, market entrance is enabled, and there is an active and dynamic supply and demand for digital technology. Due to enhanced ICT infrastructure, digital marketplaces have become more accessible and trustworthy.

Access to Finance: Entrepreneurs in the digital sector now have easier access to capital to help them start, develop, and prosper their businesses. Digital ventures may benefit from novel funding arrangements that supplement traditional lending methods.

Digital Skills and e-Leadership: People with the knowledge and skills necessary to increase company efficiency and create innovative new business models based on digital technology would benefit from a supportive educational system that makes the most of the new possibilities ICT development presents. As a result, company owners and CEOs have improved their e-competence and are better prepared to foster expansion and globalization.

A company's ability to compete depends on its ability to keep up with the rapid pace of change in the business environment and incorporate new technologies into its business models, both of which innovation inevitably brings. There will be a decline in intensity and even exhaustion for those who do not adapt to the digital environment. Digitalization is essential for local progress and strengthening our overall economy; we must argue the need to use these technological business advancements in this way.

Business enterprise writing has been made more dynamic and fluid by progress's emotional and liquid boundaries. Innovative methods result from the progressive and nonlinear approaches promoted by advanced artefacts and phases. As a result of the digitization of entrepreneurship operations, the boundaries between the different stages of the pioneering process have been more clearly defined, and the number of obstacles to growth has been reduced. This is why past D.E. research has not focused on the apparent proof of entrepreneurial stages but on how business visionaries can scale their thoughts into feasible organizations while utilizing computerized innovations to support opportunity recognition, creativity, approval and testing of ideas and plans of compelling actions. D.E. As a result of this investigation, it was possible to identify three previously unknown systems that promote rapid scaling: (1) information-driven activity, (2) instantaneous discharge, and (3) rapid change. Additionally, the study found that commercial enterprise success is intricately linked to the actions of many business visionaries and is assisted both within and between phases.

The transition to IR 4.0 will be difficult. Using I.T. in certain firms means that things can be done fast and efficiently. Graduates from Lebanon may pursue virtual entrepreneurship as it allows them to start firms that can link them with individuals from all sides of life worldwide. Virtual entrepreneurship has made it easier for graduates to create their own enterprises and no longer need to rely on government or private sector employment. As a result of their virtual enterprises, they may also be able to employ others. As a result, the unemployment rate for recent graduates will drop.

REFERENCES

Abubakre, M., Faik, I., & Mkansi, M. (2021). Digital entrepreneurship and indigenous value systems: An Ubuntu perspective. *Information Systems Journal, 31*(6), 838–862. doi:10.1111/isj.12343

Anderson, A. R., & Gaddefors, J. (2016). Entrepreneurship as a community phenomenon; reconnecting meanings and place. *International Journal of Entrepreneurship and Small Business, 28*(4), 504–518. doi:10.1504/IJESB.2016.077576

ben Jabeur, S., Mefteh-Wali, S., & Carmona, P. (2021). The impact of institutional and macroeconomic conditions on aggregate business bankruptcy. *Structural Change and Economic Dynamics, 59*, 108–119. doi:10.1016/j.strueco.2021.08.010

Douglas, E., & Prentice, C. (2019). Innovation and profit motivations for social entrepreneurship: A fuzzy-set analysis. *Journal of Business Research, 99*, 69–79. https://doi.org/10.1016/J.JBUSRES.2019.02.031

Dowin Kennedy, E. (2021). Creating community: The process of entrepreneurial community building for civic wealth creation. *Entrepreneurship and Regional Development, 33*(9–10), 816–836. https://doi.org/10.1080/08985626.2021.1964612

Garcez, A., Silva, R., & Franco, M. (2022). Digital transformation shaping structural pillars for academic entrepreneurship: A framework proposal and research agenda. *Education and Information Technologies, 27*(1), 1159–1182. https://doi.org/10.1007/s10639-021-10638-5

Gerrikagoitia, J. K., Unamuno, G., Urkia, E., & Serna, A. (2019). Digital manufacturing platforms in the Industry 4.0 from private and public perspectives. *Applied Sciences (Switzerland), 9*(14). doi:10.3390/APP9142934

Ghobakhloo, M., & Iranmanesh, M. (2021). Digital transformation success under Industry 4.0: A strategic guideline for manufacturing SMEs. *Journal of Manufacturing Technology Management, 32*(8), 1533–1556. https://doi.org/10.1108/JMTM-11-2020-0455

Gupta, J., & Chaudhry, S. (2019). Mind the tail, or risk to fail. *Journal of Business Research, 99*, 167–185. https://doi.org/10.1016/j.jbusres.2019.02.037

Ji, X., Wang, K., Xu, H., & Li, M. (2021). Has digital financial inclusion narrowed the urban-rural income gap: The role of entrepreneurship in China. *Sustainability (Switzerland), 13*(15). doi:10.3390/su13158292

Jun, S. Y., Kim, K. H., & Park, H. K. (2019). The effect of the preorder strategy on consumers' product choice: The moderating role of product experience and payment timing. *Journal of Business Research, 99*, 80–86. https://doi.org/10.1016/j.jbusres.2019.02.024

Kašperová, E. (2021). Impairment (in)visibility and stigma: How disabled entrepreneurs gain legitimacy in mainstream and disability markets. *Entrepreneurship and Regional Development, 33*(9–10), 894–919. https://doi.org/10.1080/08985626.2021.1974101

Ko, E. (2019). Bridging Asia and the world: Global platform for the Interface between marketing and management. *Journal of Business Research, 99*, 350–353. https://doi.org/10.1016/J.JBUSRES.2018.12.061

Kreuzer, T., Lindenthal, A.-K., Oberländer, A. M., & Röglinger, M. (2022). The Effects of Digital Technology on Opportunity Recognition. *Business & Information Systems Engineering*. doi:10.1007/s12599-021-00733-9

Li, Y., Dai, J., & Cui, L. (2020). The impact of digital technologies on economic and environmental performance in the context of industry 4.0: A moderated mediation model. *International Journal of Production Economics, 229*. doi:10.1016/J.IJPE.2020.107777

Lüthy, C., & Steyaert, C. (2019). The onto-politics of entrepreneurial experimentation: Re-reading Hans-Jörg Rheinberger's understanding of 'experimental systems.'. *Entrepreneurship and Regional Development, 31*(7–8), 652–668. https://doi.org/10.1080/08985626.2019.1596360

Nguyen, C. P., Nguyen, B., Duy Tung, B., & Dinh Su, T. (2021). Economic complexity and entrepreneurship density: A nonlinear effect study. *Technological Forecasting and Social Change, 173*. doi:10.1016/j.techfore.2021.121107

Oh, K., Kho, H., Choi, Y., & Lee, S. (2022). Determinants for Successful Digital Transformation. *Sustainability (Switzerland), 14*(3). doi:10.3390/su14031215

Park, M. S., Shin, J. K., & Ju, Y. (2019). Attachment styles and electronic word of mouth (e-WOM) adoption on social networking sites. *Journal of Business Research, 99*, 398–404. https://doi.org/10.1016/J.JBUSRES.2017.09.020

Poddar, A., Banerjee, S., & Sridhar, K. (2019). False advertising or slander? Using location based tweets to assess online rating-reliability. *Journal of Business Research, 99*, 390–397. https://doi.org/10.1016/J.JBUSRES.2017.08.030

Ratten, V., & Welpe, I. M. (2011). Special issue: Community-based, social and societal entrepreneurship. *Entrepreneurship and Regional Development, 23*(5–6), 283–286. https://doi.org/10.1080/08985626.2011.580159

Rippa, P., & Secundo, G. (2019). Digital academic entrepreneurship: The potential of digital technologies on academic entrepreneurship. *Technological Forecasting and Social Change, 146*, 900–911. https://doi.org/10.1016/J.TECHFORE.2018.07.013

Sahut, J. M., Iandoli, L., & Teulon, F. (2021). The age of digital entrepreneurship. *Small Business Economics, 56*(3), 1159–1169. https://doi.org/10.1007/S11187-019-00260-8

Senyard, J., Baker, T., Steffens, P., & Davidsson, P. (2014). Bricolage as a path to innovativeness for resource-constrained new firms. *Journal of Product Innovation Management, 31*(2), 211–230. https://doi.org/10.1111/JPIM.12091

Steininger, D. M., Kathryn Brohman, M., & Block, J. H. (2022). Digital Entrepreneurship: What is New if Anything? *Business & Information Systems Engineering*. doi:10.1007/s12599-021-00741-9

Tasavori, M., Kwong, C., & Pruthi, S. (2018). Resource bricolage and growth of product and market scope in social enterprises. *Entrepreneurship and Regional Development, 30*(3–4), 336–361. https://doi.org/10.1080/08985626.2017.1413775

Trongtorsak, S., Saraubon, K., & Nilsook, P. (2021). Collaborative Experiential Learning Process for Enhancing Digital Entrepreneurship. *Higher Education Studies, 11*(1), 137. doi:10.5539/hes.v11n1p137 von Briel, F., Recker, J., Selander, L., Jarvenpaa, S. L., Hukal, P., Yoo, Y., Lehmann, J., Chan, Y., Rothe, H., Alpar, P., Fürstenau, D., & Wurm, B. (2021). Researching digital entrepreneurship: Current issues and suggestions for future directions. *Communications of the Association for Information Systems*, *48*, 284–304. https://doi.org/10.17705/1CAIS.04833

Welter, F., Baker, T., & Wirsching, K. (2019). Three waves and counting: The rising tide of contextualization in entrepreneurship research. *Small Business Economics*, *52*(2), 319–330. https://doi.org/10.1007/S11187-018-0094-5

Wierenga, M. (2020). Uncovering the scaling of innovations developed by grassroots entrepreneurs in low-income settings. *Entrepreneurship and Regional Development*, *32*(1–2), 63–90. https://doi.org/10.1080/08985626.2019.1640478

Ye, B. H., Barreda, A. A., Okumus, F., & Nusair, K. (2019). Website interactivity and brand development of online travel agencies in China: The moderating role of age. *Journal of Business Research*, *99*, 382–389. https://doi.org/10.1016/J.JBUSRES.2017.09.046

Yi, J., Lee, Y., & Kim, S. H. (2019). Determinants of growth and decline in mobile game diffusion. *Journal of Business Research*, *99*, 363–372. https://doi.org/10.1016/J.JBUSRES.2017.09.045

Zahra, S. A. (2021). International entrepreneurship in the post Covid world. *Journal of World Business*, *56*(1). https://doi.org/10.1016/j.jwb.2020.101143

Chapter 5 Digital Technology for Institutional Investors in the Environment of Industry 4.0

Olga V. Khmyz
MGIMO University, Russia

ABSTRACT

The chapter analyzes the main applications of digital technologies by institutional investors in the context of Industry 4.0 and developing amid global challenges (i.e., the COVID-19 pandemic). First of all, these are big data analysis; blockchain technologies; artificial intelligence; cybersecurity; robotization of financial, investment, and business processes; chatbots; mobile financial services; and cloud technologies. Among the digital technologies designed to assist investment, there are digital portfolio managers and robo-advisers, as well as specialist software for investment portfolios, personalized and aggregated financial and banking services, digital payments, risk assessment, RegTech, etc. The track record of institutional digitalization will help to streamline the operation of institutional investors and will enable them to determine more clearly the directions of developing and adjusting their economic policy in the context of Industry 4.0 and the nascent transition to Industry 5.0, thereby increasing their competitiveness and sustainability.

INTRODUCTION

Institutional investors, representing the most important class of subjects of today's economy (national, for almost all countries, and globally) and the most active participants in the global financial market, are actively involved in the digitalization

DOI: 10.4018/978-1-6684-4265-4.ch005

processes at the national and global levels, following the innovations and trends of Industry 4.0. More and more digital technologies are being developed at the initiative or with the direct participation of institutional investors, considering the preferences of professional market participants and the demands of their clients. Consequently, we can talk about institutional digitalization stimulated and led by institutional investors at different levels. Accepted by institutional investors, a variety of legally defined entities engaged in and specializing in investing in various forms on their own behalf and for their own account, as well as on behalf of and for the account of clients, now go far beyond the traditional stock market (Khmyz, 2003) and include investment companies, investment funds, pension funds, management companies, insurance companies, investment banks, investment trusts, commercial banks and companies, sovereign wealth funds and charitable foundations, depositories and custodians, savings and loan associations, and credit unions in all varieties of these main types of financial and non-financial institutions. The increasing use of digital technology by institutional investors in investment and financial activities is undeniable. Digital technology is applied by fintech companies – a new kind of institutional investors in the global market – and by trading (commercial) and depository institutions, which, in the context of Industry 4.0, are increasingly integrated, providing a range of an ever-expanding set of services. The latest digital technologies used by institutional investors include big data analytics, blockchain technology integration, artificial intelligence, cyber security, robotization of financial investment and business processes, chatbots, mobile financial services, and cloud technology. Digitalization and the accelerated expansion of ubiquitous financial innovation by institutional investors have been spurred by global lockdowns designed to limit the spread of COVID-19 in 2020–2022. These factors were the main factors that changed the behavior of consumers of goods and services, including investment. They also affected monetary relations, primarily the use of various forms of payments and means of payment, and also stimulated the further spread of cashless money. As a result, there is a global transformation of the entire global investment and financial industry. It varies from country to country in terms of intensity, but there is a general digitalization trend. Relevant changes to regulatory systems are made, existing regulations are amended, and new regulations governing the digitalization of the investment and financial sector are adopted. Many changes are carried out for the benefit of institutional investors (Johnstone-Louis et al., 2020). The demand and corresponding offerings of digital financial services by institutional investors are attracting more and more attention because they are becoming an urgent need – from emergency loans for personal financial management to government payment schemes. One of the most critical segments of the global financial market (with a share of about 25%) is payments, which are intensively digitalized (ISMG & OneSpan, 2020); with lockdowns related to COVID-19, its annual share is expected to grow nearly 11% in 2022 (Statista, 2022a). In many respects, the occurring changes are predetermined by the global trends of the world economy and the international financial market. Let us briefly analyze the main aspects, considering the specifics of institutional investors.

DIGITAL TECHNOLOGY AND FINTECH COMPANIES

Among the great variety of institutional investors actively adopting digital technologies in the context of Industry 4.0, a special place belongs to financial and technological (fintech) companies that develop and implement computer programs or other technologies to support or implement financial or banking services. Digital payments, risk assessment, credit platforms, personalized financial security, RegTech, mobile and online financial services, software for commercial lending, insurance software for insurance brokers and insurers, and other services and products are provided by fintech companies, thereby supplementing the institutions of shadow banking (Orlova & Ignatova, 2021).

The growing number of fintech companies and fintech solutions, even before the COVID-19 pandemic, is changing the landscape of financial services and the global financial architecture. Nowadays, digital transformation in the global monetary and financial system goes beyond the mass adoption of technology in financial services to become an integrated component of a successful business strategy. In an ideal scenario, the digital transformation of the investment finance industry improves customer service and employee efficiency, facilitates adherence to required deadlines and compliance with regulatory orders and directives, ensures operational profitability, and maintains a high level of competitiveness. According to Information Security Media Group (ISMG & OneSpan, 2020), even before the COVID-19 pandemic, North American investment and financial institutions prioritized providing services and products to their customers based on first-class computer hardware. The most common obstacles include lengthy and insufficiently up-to-date methods of personal identification of customers, making it difficult for financial institutions to use digital technology. In turn, the need for a sufficient degree of familiarity with digital technology is also a significant obstacle in adapting the client to digital investment and financial technology. Fintech companies actively promote their services and products, spreading them worldwide.

The field of mobile financial services is becoming an increasingly common part of everyday life. Primarily, it is any banking or digital financial institutional platform. They speed up client transactions and generally make them easier to carry out (work in this direction is ongoing). Reliability, speed, availability of loan applications, ease of account-to-account transfers, and other transactional benefits attract customers.

Nevertheless, these benefits also attract fraudsters, which leads to the introduction of stricter identification procedures, in turn flattening the main advantage of mobile services – the simplified, 24/7 access, without regard to official holidays, with minimal waiting time and ease of use. According to the Central Bank of Russia, in 2021, the bulk (80%) of fraudsters used remote access and Internet fraud; the data were recruited from social networks and messengers – the cheapest channels for phishing and social engineering (Central Bank of the Russian Federation, 2022).

Mobile banking has undoubtedly changed the field of financial and banking services. Thus, mobile applications are used primarily by fintech companies that compete with banks in providing financial services, including banking-type services. In fact, they can be third-party providers of digital financial services for banks, financial managers, or other classes of institutional investors. Banks often initiate the integration of such services and financial products and applications supplied or installed by fintech developers to avoid cross-species competition and form more competitive alliances offering customers a wider range of innovative financial services and products, including mobile. In such cases, institutional investors analyze the fintech developers willing to cooperate, select information that will be offered for analysis by external employees, and choose products or services that can be offered to clients directly, without intermediaries because the need and ways to integrate third-party services depend on the target audience and the financial factor.

For its part, fintech needs to adapt to changing conditions, adjust to them, and influence them. In the near future, more than 80% of institutional financial investors plan to continue cooperating with fintech companies because many of them (almost 90%) believe that if they do not accept fintech innovations, they will lose out to specialized fintech companies. In general, institutional investors actively explore digital assets. According to Fidelity Digital Assets, Coalition Greenwich, and Fidelity Center for Applied Technology (Neureuter, 2021), as of 2021, 70% of institutional investors were going to buy digital assets in the near future.

For their part, fintech companies also intensify the financial and investment direction of their activities, which is most demanded in today's global economy. Fintech companies must develop and implement seamless and truly working software based on accumulated digital experience. This mutual demand leads to the collaboration of established financial-technology companies, traditional institutional investors, and fintech startups. Such thoughtfully structured innovative partnerships can more effectively promote themselves in the global financial market and minimize risks. Institutional distribution networks are steadily expanding, with institutional investors gaining increasing access to pricing through spot foreign exchange operations, commodity CFDs, treasuries, and indices on specialized platforms.

As an advanced technology, fintech, along with automation and machine algorithms, has been adopted by investment and financial companies and commercial banks primarily to improve the efficiency of their services. Since the first ATMs and credit cards, fintech has considerably advanced and currently represents blockchain and digital banking. In collaboration with fintech companies, institutional investors offer online budgeting, expense tracking, and client chatbots to help navigate the industry and offer various solutions to clients' challenges, thereby facilitating digital transformation for clients. The clarity and comprehensibility of investment and financial technology begin with the simplicity and ease of perception of the (intuitive) user interface. An excessive number of additional functions can make it challenging to use the applications. Many owners of gadgets do not use the proposed applications or options due to their incomprehensibility or excessive complexity, even if they are attracted by the promised result of the resource.

Nowadays, digital institutional platforms offer a full (as of today) range of diversified services, from trading to supporting and protecting digital assets, combining traditional operational and technical advantages for institutional investors with expertise in blockchain technology. This aggregation allows institutional investors to offer a virtually new digital product.

Blockchain Technologies in the Activity of Institutional Investors

For institutional investors, blockchain technology and the digital assets associated with it are quite promising. Undoubtedly, it also has and will continue to impact institutional investors. This influence is growing, primarily due to the connection of technology with peer-to-peer (P2P) online finance platforms designed to decentralize financial and monetary relationships. For example, in 2021, bitcoin mining companies actively entered the organized securities market, listing their shares on stock exchanges (using SPACS and listing without an IPO). Blockchain technology is used in the creation of cryptocurrencies.

The main benefits of blockchain for institutional investors include cheaper cross-border transactions, accuracy, and speed. Other benefits of blockchain include the accuracy and speed of credit documentation, increased efficiency of the verification process to protect against fraud, facilitation of mutual settlements and clearing, and increased efficiency and transparency of smart contracts, including when providing trade finance, etc. Blockchain trading technology is already quite mature, with spot liquidity provided by special post-trade applications available to multiple custodians at once, meaning that the key requirements of institutional investors and their clients are already being met.

The use of blockchain technology in credit processing, payments and settlements, and escrow is intensifying. Blockchain-based technology is also increasingly involved in streamlining the mechanism and procedures for regulating institutional investors.

As a result, there is an increasing interest in RegTech, which optimizes regulatory compliance, prevents and allows avoiding violations of prudential regulations.

The digitalization of many services of institutional investors and the debugging of digital asset transfer technologies, primarily safe custody, have shown investors the safety of book-entry securities and other financial assets, as well as digital investment (in its basic aspects). Many investors (and their clients) rightly feared the mistransfer or deliberate misappropriation of other people's digital investment and financial assets, or just plain glitches. Institutional custodians have been quite successful in coping with this problem, and technology has advanced. It also contributed to the growth of institutional investors' profits.

Blockchain technology is embedded in the investment and analytical process, aimed at maximizing returns with already available data, systematized into blocks. An overview of the most and least used assets, the regional structure of investors and issuers, as well as the operations and applications used. This allows optimizing the product line of investment and financial services, the most demanded and attracting clients, as well as facilitating their work and maximizing the return on investment for each asset. Thus, embedded analytics has proven its advantages (see the next paragraph for details). In this aspect, the question of the users' freedom of control over their assets and access to their management is important. On the one hand, autonomy shifts part of the investment risk from the institutional investor to its client. On the other hand, it leads to a decrease in the institutional investor's income, up to creating assets for individual use on-demand, which can distort the product line. On the other hand, when this asset becomes obsolete, it can easily be taken out of circulation because, along with the changing product mix, the consumer landscape is also changing, so the investor needs to have continuous access to a significant and ever-expanding set of services through one platform. It is not uncommon for consumers of investment and financial services to choose consistent products based on their investment experience and practice with a given institutional investor.

Potential customers who have moved into the online or virtual investment-financial space during the COVID-19 pandemic can be attracted by a willingness to customize the product according to customer demand, personalize the product as a digital asset, and personalize the remote assistant. However, we should not forget that poorly developed virtual assistants can interfere with investment (and work in general), for example, blocking the content or preventing its viewing. Advanced DAM systems seem quite capable of functioning as a central investment management platform, storing assets and giving users a degree of freedom of control, providing sophisticated clients with the confidence to get the assets they need.

As for cryptocurrencies and crypto assets, until a while ago, digital financial assets were a new asset class. However, nowadays, they encompass a broad spectrum familiar to almost all investors, from stablecoins to digital tokens. During the COVID-19 pandemic, interest and demand for such assets grew rapidly, as did their exchange rates. For 2020, the cumulative growth was 300% (Statista, 2022b), primarily due to the growing popularity of cryptocurrencies, the traditional interest in the new asset and its possibilities, the growth of the currency rate. This growth is also determined by many factors, which can be grouped into structural, technological, and geopolitical from the perspective of institutional investors. Notably, the problems with bitcoin storage led to the emergence and growth of demand for other digital assets, causing their variety. For certain types of institutional investors, such as endowments and pension funds, it is criterionally important to balance the risks of high returns when using a new type of financial instrument because bitcoin and other cryptocurrencies are still characterized by an additional level of risk associated with a sufficient complexity of technology, increased market volatility, and lack of certainty in their regulatory framework, including at the supranational level and currency and exchange rate fluctuations, which constrains many investors.

Asian institutional investors show the greatest favoring of crypto-assets in their and clients' investment portfolios. In Europe, the attitude is slightly lower – 77% of institutional investors support the inclusion of cryptocurrencies in the investment portfolio. Only 69% of institutional investors note the importance of crypto assets in the US (Neureuter, 2021). Apparently, regional affiliation is not the only factor in classifying the demand for crypto assets by institutional investors. Age is an equally important criterion because the more conservative and experienced investors have more difficulty adapting to the mechanisms of digitalization than the more tech-savvy and younger investors. Investors who grew up with gadgets are more receptive to the investment and financial potential of financial and technological innovation, including blockchain technology, which underpins many cryptocurrencies. In contrast, long-time and more experienced investors are slower to transform valuation tools and other mechanisms, often trying to value digital instruments in inappropriate and outdated ways. Thus, the fundamental analysis applied to cryptocurrencies does not give results at all.

However, institutional investors are deservedly wary of the crypto-world. The main constraints include price volatility and the lack of transparency and inaccessibility to traditional analysis to calculate the real value of cryptocurrencies and detect and prevent market manipulation. A considerable deterrent is the cryptocurrency competition between the governments of different countries. So far, the bulk of cryptocurrencies is not included in the official monetary circulation. Nevertheless, if any of the world's leading countries introduce a national cryptocurrency with the appropriate rights, the situation in the global cryptocurrency market may change. For example, in Japan, it is allowed to accept bitcoins to pay taxes; El Salvador has ranked cryptocurrency as a legal payment instrument. In mid-2021, China banned the sale and mining of bitcoins, which made Kazakhstan the second largest producer of cryptocurrency globally (Russia is in third place). In January 2022, the People's Bank of China released a mobile cryptocurrency wallet to use the digital yuan at the Olympics. By the eve of the Olympics 2022, the application for this cryptocurrency wallet had been downloaded more than 30 million times.

Institutional investors buy crypto assets, primarily expanding direct ownership of cryptocurrencies, stocks of cryptoindustry companies, and other digital investment products (Neureuter, 2021). Integrated platforms (e.g., Fidelity Investment's digital asset division, integrated with Standard Chartered Zodia Custody and TP ICAP) cover a diverse client base, combining trading infrastructure capabilities for digital assets with oversight functionality and meeting the minimum market standards of traditional markets. On the other hand, not all institutional investors are yet unequivocally optimistic about investing in cryptocurrency. According to JP Morgan, in 2021, approximately 10% of institutional investors specialized in trading digital currencies (Irrera, 2021).

Bitcoin still gets most of the attention, but its rate is quite volatile. Nevertheless, compared to the initial stage of implementation of this cryptocurrency (2009–2010), the contrast in demand for cryptocurrencies is very noticeable. This allows many institutional investors and their clients to expand their presence in the cryptocurrency market quite aggressively – on several fronts at once, from simple acquisitions for themselves and their clients to cryptocurrency exchanges or trading desks, like Goldman Sachs (Irrera et al., 2021), and to creating own cryptocurrencies, like JPMorgan (JP Morgan, 2021). In February 2022, CME Group launched the US cryptocurrency benchmark rates, with base rates calculated in US time, making the new tool suitable for institutional risk management in addition to the existing CME CF reference rate for bitcoin and CME CF-Ether Dollar for bitcoin and Ethereum.

The variety of digital financial assets is growing as markets, for their part, adjust and evolve toward investment and financial digitalization and institutionalization. New varieties (and qualities) of digital investment and financial assets often confuse regulators. For example, the classification of such assets into existing nomenclature groups (or it is necessary to create new or separate subgroups) caused long discussions, while many digital assets have several criterion properties at once. Regulatory inconsistencies have hampered the investment process involving such assets.

An optimizing solution was offered by institutional investors responding to existing demand. Smart solutions – trusts of cryptocurrency derivative – were proposed based on smart contracts. The risks of these innovative instruments are similar to those existing on the underlying assets, with a clear and compliant mechanism. Therefore, the intense demand for cryptocurrency ETFs, which provide access to cryptocurrencies rather than direct ownership, is not surprising. For their part, regulators also adjust to the requirements of time and the market (albeit with a certain lag); rules and requirements for digital assets and cryptocurrencies are clarified (Bank for International Settlements, 2015). The USA approves the use of stablecoins in the settlements of savings institutions and financial transactions of federal banks (Office of the Comptroller of the Currency, 2021).

Global trends in the global economy have also had an impact on accelerating the widespread adoption of digital assets. "The era of low-interest rates" encouraged institutional and private investors to seek and develop new investment and financial opportunities to maximize returns (Khmyz, 2021). With the relaxation of requirements for retail investing, free funds could flow into the crypto market, stimulating the growth of cryptocurrency rates and demand for their varieties. Institutional investors have also responded to this, doing their part. In this case, we should not forget about the previously noted high volatility of crypto-assets and currencies. Many trends are still new and insufficiently established to be predicted with sufficient probability (even with machine learning). As such, non-fungible tokens (NFT) can generate income because they have the intrinsic value of cryptographic assets with blockchain certificates. One of the first was the NFTs of works of art. Tokenized varieties of stocks, bonds, and other major securities can also be a step in the evolution of financial instruments and financial markets capable of lowering costs, speeding up operations, and optimizing the investment and financial process as a whole. At the end of 2021, bitcoin futures ETFs began trading on the NASDAQ exchange. It attracted nearly $40 billion in two months and showed positive trends.

The crypto market is still young, its infrastructure is also developing, developers themselves are often new to the market, and the institutional needs are often not established. The digital asset market is full of opportunities, obstacles, and even pitfalls. To realize the full potential and ensure a more successful implementation of digital assets, businesses, investors, regulators, and infrastructure providers must work together. As time passes and the crypto market develops, trends will become more established, regulation will become more normative, the characteristics of the assets will be classified, and monetary digitalization will continue to evolve, including toward sustainability (green cryptocurrency mining based on green energy sources).

A variety of digital currencies offer the opportunity to take advantage of digital assets, one of the most important of which is blockchain payment for transactions. Institutional investors take advantage of these opportunities to maximize income. Recently, digital currency projects have intensified in the direction of digital currencies of central banks (Boar et al., 2020).

Due to the success of cryptocurrencies and other digital instrumental innovations, more and more institutional investors are interested in digital assets, seeking diversity in the expanding digital space. About 50% of hedge funds are interested in digital assets, with about 30% of them working with blockchain and about 20% with cryptocurrencies (Neureuter, 2021). Many investors see blockchain as a fundamental technology with the potential to change the global financial world. Others see a digital future without this technology (D'Ankonia, 2017).

Digital investment and financial instruments, like any new asset, are evolving and will undoubtedly adapt and change, as will investment financial technology.

Digital Technologies in the Investment Process

Tracking and maintaining investment accounts of clients has always been a challenge, especially in economies with a developed financial market like the US financial market, where investors often have one or more individual retirement accounts, employers open 401(k) plans for their employees, savings are accumulated in a matching savings account, health savings contributions (on HSAs) are also accumulated, and taxable accounts are also opened. As a result, one client of an institutional investor may have dozens of such accounts, creating overlapping accounts. Managing multi-accounts requires a more thorough approach, tracking multi-scale performance and write-offs. Therefore, it is recommended to use specialized applications and management software – from a free financial dashboard to a professional robo-advisor of the fourth generation. Specialized advisors charge higher management fees (0.4% on average), while broader ETFs charge less than 0.1% due to diversification.

Built-in investment analytics are increasingly influencing investment decisions. The danger lies in the coverage of the data serving as the basis for the decision; it is also open to the question of their sufficiency (and reliability) to maximize the investment return. Therefore, the digital coordination of investment projects so far comes down exactly to bringing together, i.e., ensuring team interaction and calculating indicators. The next stage is to develop proposals and work out and decide on the most appropriate one.

One of the most apparent manifestations of digital artificial intelligence technologies in the practice of institutional investors is robo-advising in the banking system and the financial market. In the investment sector, it is used to compile a specialized investment portfolio considering the preferences and requests of a particular client. It should be noted that some of the accumulated professional experience is lost because not all financial market professionals with long experience agree to make it publicly available.

Individualized automated investment portfolio functions online, using the mechanism of automatic reinvestment (Chiang et al., 2005). This mechanism was developed in the 20th century. Nowadays, it is based on the advice of artificial intelligence, not the human financial manager, who cannot make investment decisions as quickly in today's conditions of superfast formation of information signals. At the initial (or subsequent) stages, the client fills out special questionnaires, by the results of which (considering personalized actions on gadgets) client investment and financial "virtual portrait" with calculated indicators (from the disposable income of various types to the appetite for risk) is formed. As robo-advisors improve, so do machine recommendations.

In the post-crisis years of 2008–2009, the first generation of robo-advisors was created in the USA, aimed at facilitating the actions of asset managers by reducing the intensity of their workload. The investment scheme (plan) was developed by the appropriate investment manager, and the artificial intelligence performed auxiliary functions, rebalancing the portfolio in time. In fact, robo-advisors of the second generation were still a hybrid form of investment interaction because the manager still distributed the financial resources, and the portfolio was configured independently (Abraham et al., 2019).

The simplest robots track personalized investments while users link their accounts (including pension accounts) to the platform, including investment, current, and card accounts. A robo-advisor aggregates the received financial data and analyzes the client's financial situation and potential investment opportunities. The effectiveness of investments already made is also verified. Appropriate investment instruments are offered, usually classified on a fiscal basis, considering the available information (including the client's investment preferences). Adjustment of the offered investment products and services is carried out considering the actually received income and its comparison with the benchmarks. Such investment and financial services – spending and portfolio performance tracking – present fairly straightforward platforms.

More specialized robo-advisors usually focus on pension investments and offer a typical or more complex pension plan for the client (usually based on investment reliability) based on the existing client profile and information on available assets, linked accounts, and expenditure data. Such plans provide an opportunity to integrate income-impacting events (e.g., social security programs) and plan for pre-retirement savings or large-scale expenses over time. A robot advisor will recommend an effective tax rate and tie planned expenditures and revenues to life expectancy and inflation rates, as well as other macro and microeconomic indicators. Upon request, it calculates several retirement options, for example, depending on the level of anticipated income and expenses at which the disposable investment and financial portfolio will be able to meet the laid down goals, with cash flow calculations provided.

In such platforms, it is important to have a built-in analyzer of commissions by type of investment. It calculates the total amount of fees (current and future) and calculates its impact on client portfolio returns up to the date of retirement. If the date changes, the calculated values are automatically recalculated. Such robo-advisors also offer investment checkups; the service compares the current distribution of investments by instrument with the recommended ones based on the developed alternative plan and their historical and forecasting performance, including profitability and risk.

Robotic investment and financial advisors also offer varieties of retirement savings analysis based on pension fund cash flow data (with retained client access to investments). Such automated advisors are more sophisticated, capable of predicting the future cash flows of a retirement portfolio after the client's retirement (based on available data and assumed (estimated) numbers), considering social security payments and minimum pension distribution requirements for tax-deferred retirement accounts. As a result, annual pension expenditures can be adjusted for inflationary trends because the information is presented on a year-by-year basis, considering large-scale and contingent expenditures.

Other varieties of automated portfolio managers use other approaches; for example, the investor must upload to the system each investment, and the panel offers an analysis of data on each investment, tracks the current price, dynamics, rate fluctuations, and share in the portfolio, as well as calculates the effectiveness of the entire portfolio, its historical returns, and conducts its comparison with the benchmark selected by the investor.

It is necessary to note the built-in function of detailed analysis of the distribution of portfolio assets and its instrumental investment style box broken down by region and sector of the economy. It also calculates the weighted average portfolio expense ratio and the weight of an individual investment in the portfolio, which is important for clients of mutual funds or those resorting to index investing.

The ongoing processes of digitalization at the global level have led to the creation of third- and fourth-generation robo-advisers, which have actually automated the investment process. Based on the given general investment rules, they form algorithmic recommendations for the portfolio. Advanced investment artificial intelligence is self-learning, allowing experts to make optimistic estimates. Forecasts for the US robo-advisory market reach $5–$7 trillion in 2026 (for comparison, this figure equaled $100 billion in 2016) (Orbis Research, 2020). Simultaneously, this does not mean that simpler robo-advisors have ceased to exist.

In general, the choice of an investment robo-advisor seems to be quite challenging. The main criteria are financial (commissions and fees) and functionality. However, there are other indicators – depending on client requests and the type of investor (his or her profile). Specialized analysts track the effectiveness of robo-advisors (and their products) and give them ratings based on metrics such as management and operational fees, degree of transparency, financial planning capabilities, availability of human advice, minimum account size requirements, overall portfolio performance, client experience, etc.

However, almost all advanced robo-advisors offer a diversified portfolio of low-cost ETFs. Almost all advanced robo-advisors offer taxable investments or retirement products with preferential (deferred) taxation, while a more sophisticated investor may intend to use a different investment account, such as a 529, which is an option offered by a limited number of advisors. However, work is underway to expand the product line, and more and more robo-advisors offer investments using custodial brokerage accounts with greater investment opportunities.

Institutional investors also offer software that tracks and analyzes portfolios based on investment activity and account transactions rather than specialized applications. It provides information about each investment, its rating in categories, and other benefits of automated investment portfolio management with the ability to set a target asset allocation and compare it to the actual – at the individual security, account, and entire portfolio level. The main disadvantage of this form of investment interaction is that the investor must understand the user interface.

If investors are not attracted to online tools or special programs, one can create an electronic portfolio spreadsheet, even on well-known search engines, to track one's investments. There are many possibilities – from manual entry of portfolio data to automatic updating. Nevertheless, this method is more suitable for allocation corrections, i.e., portfolio rebalancing.

Big data technologies have become indispensable in the investment activities of financial and non-financial institutions, i.e., all-encompassing. Institutional investors, primarily non-bank institutions and, more recently, depository institutions, use machine learning to improve the efficiency of data processing and the development of investment and analytical decisions. Big data helps banks and other institutional investors serve their customers more efficiently and expand their client base by tailoring services based on the information collected about customers. Eventually, despite the current lack of technology, the usage mechanism will be tweaked to attract more investment and other financial resources and improve the working environment for customers and employees.

Institutional investors already use machine learning to develop marketing campaigns to attract clients. It is designed to identify the most attractive investment and financial services and the relevant target groups based on data about the reasons for choosing a particular financial site, the choice of the transition page, and the service in demand. It appears that the analysis of consumer attitudes in conjunction with machine learning will have an increasing impact on institutional investors and the supply of financial services in the future. Currently, vast amounts of disparate data, ranging from financial reporting documents and other commercial documentation to blogs, posts on social media, video transcripts, and photos, are covered and processed. This data is sorted and systematized, and, on its basis, a personalized (individualized) customer profile is compiled, and a more holistic picture of consumer sentiment is built. With machine learning, it becomes easier to influence them, i.e., to actually control them. This can have a determining influence on the development of investment and, in general, on the dynamics of financial markets.

Despite the constraints (most notably price volatility, lack of transparency, and inaccessibility to traditional analytics), global challenges, and related concerns, institutional investors are increasingly incorporating digital assets into their portfolios. Nowadays, 80% of institutional investors are positive about digital assets and place their funds and funds of their clients in them. Moreover, institutional investors expect to receive more investment and financial services in digital form. They plan to expand access to electronic trading platforms, big data analytics, and digital asset markets in general. This implies an increase in the security of digital assets and the security of digital financial instruments. According to Fidelity Digital Assets, Coalition Greenwich, and Fidelity Center for Applied Technology (Neureuter, 2021), as of 2021, 70% of global institutional investors view digital assets positively and are going to invest in them or just buy them in the future. Of 1100 global institutional investors included in the sample, more than 60% will devote a portion of their portfolio to digital assets in the next five years.

On average, in mid-2021, 52% of institutional investors were already using digital assets for the USA, Europe, and Asia. The number of US institutional investors who have already included digital assets in their portfolios increased to 33% (compared to 27% in 2020), indicating a generally positive perception of digital assets even in more conservative markets. Fidelity Digital Assets, Coalition Greenwich, and Fidelity Center for Applied Technology (Neureuter, 2021) estimate that, if successful, digital assets have the potential to become mainstream by 2026.

Digital Technologies in Asset Management by Institutional Investors

Even before the COVID-19 pandemic, digitalization processes affected investment and financial asset management, and digital asset management emerged. In the pandemic, digital asset management developed as well. More and more institutional investors use the advances of digitalization to simplify the process of financial engineering. To attract clients, institutional investors try to combine ease of access, reliability of creation and setup, and storage of assets. One must not lag behind technological progress; one must keep up with it, or better yet, overtake it.

Artificial intelligence automates many processes, including decision-making, selecting investment objects, and managing digital assets. To improve their effectiveness, they need to be constantly improved because the wrong investment decision, especially when accelerated, just as fast generates risks and, accordingly, scales the likely losses. Another advantage of artificial intelligence is the rapid personalization, including reporting requested by individual investors – institutional clients. Also, the use of artificial intelligence by institutional investors is aimed at improving security and detecting and preventing fraud, which is not always successfully performed so far.

Artificial intelligence brings significant changes to the investment and financial industry as a whole, offering many innovations and replacing an outdated form of investment and financial management. For example, bots or partially automated asset managers are being increasingly applied, and their algorithms become more and more sophisticated, aided by machine learning. It is necessary to improve programs to calculate investment opportunities, optimize the selection of relevant lending institutions, suitable interest rates, and other key indicators, and develop customized client software, especially for VIPs.

The positive effects of introducing artificial intelligence into the digital asset management practices of institutional investors most often include expanded data coverage because the aggregation and analysis of multiple indicators and factors help study them, find new patterns, and identify new trends (or generate them), creating new patterns faster than a human can do. Also, using technical analysis (which has long been given to machines) and fundamental analysis (its transfer into artificial intelligence has not yet been completed), it is possible to predict the dynamics of the whole market or a specific financial instrument and, with a certain degree of probability, forecast possible development of events. There are also associated risks, primarily ethical ones (Sanders, 2021).

Moreover, robotic investment choices are still not optimal; the competition from a human personal investment manager (investment advisor) is high because a professional with market sense often shows better investment results than an insufficiently programmed automaton. Machine learning is working on this problem. However, it still relies more on prior experience than on intuition. This approach will work if the market situation repeats. In this case, robots can quickly make and implement a sufficiently correct management decision. However, automated investment managers simplify financial planning and improve the accuracy of institutional investors' asset management operations. Rather than building processes based on technology, we are talking about embedding technology into processes and minimal restructuring of existing and already working infrastructure.

With the accelerated accumulation, processing, and analysis of big data, institutional investors can more quickly and accurately identify market trends, optimize their management and intra-institutional financial processes, and minimize risk in the management of their own assets and assets of their clients.

Big data also contributes to the current practice of asset management by institutional investors. In terms of spending on big data (IDC, 2021), institutional investors (e.g., commercial banks using big data for business intelligence) lead the way. They track ATM cash withdrawals, credit card transactions, and payment and credit metrics; the real data on these indicators appear to be critical for improving the efficiency of financial products and processes and enables more informed and practice-related management decisions, which leads to better investor performance and greater competitiveness.

Big data also helps institutional investors develop a more comprehensive investment and financial client profile, which allows more carefully selecting investment and financial products for clients from among the offerings, improving the quality and efficiency of asset management, and developing and distributing more client-focused investment and financial products while offering these services in real-time. Thus, niche mobile products are offered to different target classes of individual and corporate investors, including non-profit sectors. It should be noted that there used to be families of funds that provided the opportunity to transfer investments.

Institutional chatbots facilitate the automation of simple tasks such as creating a new account or electronic money transfer and are also aimed at reducing costs, which has already been successfully proven in practice. That is why the world's leading institutional investors, such as (JP Morgan, n.d.) and (Bank of America, n.d.) use artificial intelligence to optimize customer service. With artificial intelligence, banking-type institutional investors are generally making mobile banking easier, and it has become a 24/7 service, which is highly demanded by customers who travel to different countries and regions or are just young, with a particular rhythm of life.

As the system and machine learning improve, artificial intelligence is already able to understand prudential norms, which improves the quality of asset management. For example, IBM's Watson cognitive system (Pizzicoli, 2018) recognizes requirements under the Financial Instruments Directive (European Parliament and the Council of Europe, 2014) and relevant information provisions of other regulations.

Apparently, the massive adoption of artificial intelligence by institutional investors is primarily driven by the financial factor – lower costs – and the cumulative amount of such savings will exceed $440 billion by 2023 (Phaneuf, 2022).

Through SaaS (software-as-a-service), a cloud computing system, Regtech's regulatory technology assists institutional investors in managing assets and understanding their investment costs in general through a clearer and faster regulatory compliance and tracking of regulatory innovations. Other benefits of Regtech include more effective risk management and fraud prevention, data analysis and operational and management decision making, and real-time reporting.

In case of non-compliance with the requirements of the regulatory authorities, the institutional investor will be subject to fines and other penalties, up to the revocation of the license. Due to the changing environment for institutional investors – both due to the COVID-19 pandemic and the recent global financial and economic crisis (2008–2009) – the need for Regtech services by institutional investors is increasing. So far, institutional investors have not relied heavily on Regtech. It seems promising due to creating a single dashboard for institutional investors that combines a warning function with analysis of incoming data of sufficient accuracy and high reliability, allowing users to improve interaction with regulators and save financial resources normally reserved for regulatory remarks.

The digital transformation of investment and financial services is occurring against a backdrop of changing customer expectations and increasing regulatory complexity due to the global tightening of financial regulations following the 2008–2009 global financial and economic crisis to avoid a repeat. Simultaneously, there is a tightening of competition due to the termination of some financial institutions during the crisis and the realization of significant losses by many others. These factors constantly stimulate institutional investors to update and optimize their financial products, investment services, and methods of work – both with clients and within the institutions themselves, adjusting the interaction between their own departments and within them.

Over 50% of institutional investors have already invested in digital assets by mid-2021 and will not give them up (Neureuter, 2021). Along with institutional investors who have proactively invested in such instruments, more investors expand their investment portfolios with digital instruments under the influence of the increasing digitalization processes and non-alternative situation of the COVID-19 environment.

The Impact of COVID-19 on Institutional Digitalization

Analyzing the institutional transformations of the recent pre-pandemic years, we can see that digitalization has led to greater convenience for customers in accessing financial products while increasing the diversity of choices and offerings based on accumulated practical experience. Nowadays, customers are increasingly attracted to digital financial products, drawing on their accumulated experience and the experience of institutional investors.

With the COVID-19 pandemic, the processes of investment-financial digitalization have accelerated. The main reasons for the fundamental digital shift of institutional investors, encouraging them to intensify their implementation of digital technologies, can be systematized as follows.

1. The evolution of the economy and market infrastructure in a digitalized direction.

In general, financial-type institutional investors have been relatively financially stable for quite some time. Nevertheless, the COVID-19 pandemic, following the previous global "black swan" crisis of 2008–2009, has put considerable pressure on institutional offerings. On the one hand, the global pre-premium decline in key interest rates has encouraged institutional investors to reconsider their investment and financial policies and credit institutions to reconsider their deposit and credit policies. Insurance companies are working to lower premiums and claims costs. Traditional banks are working on lowering fees and other client charges to compete with shadow banking institutions more successfully. However, before the pandemic, institutional investors introduced digital innovation sporadically as demand for it emerged.

The depth and duration of the economic downturn are, as usual, rather difficult to predict. There is no doubt that it forces institutional investors to work on minimizing and, most importantly, preventing risks, including in conditions of global uncertainty, while maintaining their capacity to work and their competitiveness. It is possible that even after the recovery of the global economy and the return of markets to growth, digitalization will continue to affect the investment and financial world because it is already quite large, and its role in the daily lives of clients and institutional investors is only increasing and will continue to increase in the foreseeable future, despite the adjustment of the global interest rate policy to a higher political interest rate, which has its impact on the global financial market.

2. The imperative introduction of mobile, remote, and online communication channels due to widespread lockdowns and demands to maintain social distance when rarely going out on the street and in public places. For example, in the USA, which traditionally lagged behind other countries in the speed of digitalization, there was an unprecedented increase in the number of mobile check deposit transactions. Notably, the main contributors to this growth were baby boomers and older citizens, who are usually more skeptical of digital innovation and slower than younger people to adopt new technologies. Goldman Sachs reported a 25% growth in the number of active users of its institutional platform in early 2020. (Deloitte, 2020).

This is directly related to the stimulation of contactless payments. The observed struggle of sellers of various goods and services for free or vacant market niches with the help of e-commerce tools has increased online purchases paid for through online applications and other similar solutions to counter the spread of infection, such as payment from a cell phone without entering PIN codes, QR codes, and digital wallets.

3. Virtualization of modes of working. Before the COVID-19 pandemic, the bulk of institutional investors provided their services to clients in person, when they came to the client's office or by phone with a personal manager (mostly for VIP clients). Transferring employees "to a remote location" has led to the need to accelerate the development and transfer of staff to the online form of work (including the special creation or acquisition of the required software and

even hardware infrastructure). Thus, Bank of America and Wells Fargo moved nearly 70% of their employees from offices to homes and created specialized workstations for operations staff for emergencies (Kline, 2021). Standard Chartered Bank increased the intensity of its virtual private network (VPN) by 600% (Deloitte, 2020). The transition was also facilitated by disruptions in the provision of financial services caused by COVID-19, including in digital form. Many financial companies decided to retain these ways of serving clients even after the pandemic lockdowns, optimizing the model of remote investment-financial interaction, including in case of repeated lockdowns and for meeting the needs of clients who had appreciated the benefits of this type of cooperation and are going to use it in the future.

These digitalization changes have and will undoubtedly continue to have an impact on investment and financial decision-making by institutional investors of all kinds and levels because the COVD-19 pandemic has changed the competitiveness of investment and financial institutions and affected their number and performance, moving much from physical offices to remote service and online solutions, which, in turn, requires forcing the implementation of an improved IT infrastructure requiring significant financial investments, the appropriate technological support, and the necessary degree of automation to meet the needs of institutional investors and the demands of their clients. The clients of institutional investors are getting younger. Due to the COVID-19 pandemic, the number of older clients (tending to be more conservative) tends to decrease. The younger generation uses gadgets more intensively and has a more positive perception of digitalization. The number of working firms has decreased. Even small fintech companies can be at risk despite the specific financing models they develop due to their small size and limited access to big data compared to larger companies.

In 2020, the fall of the world economy from the COVID-19 related crisis exceeded 5% (World Bank, 2022a). Simultaneously, the degree of digitalization has increased – the economic transformation associated with the lockdowns has intensified the widespread adoption of digital financial services. As already noted, even before the COVID-19 pandemic, digital transformation was among the priorities of the global economy and then became an indispensable tool for the short- and medium-term post-pandemic recovery. According to the World Bank estimates (World Bank, 2022b), in 2023, the growth rate of the global economy will slow to 2.3% in developed countries due to COVID-19, but the size of the global financial sector can grow in the coming years because the OECD promotes digital financial services to stimulate a post-pandemic recovery (Shruti, 2022). That is why financial digitalization and partnerships with fintech are supported by nearly 50% of American banks and 60% of credit unions, which estimate the global financial sector at $26.5

Figure 1. CAGR DX-technology investments
Source: Compiled by the author based on (IDC, 2021)

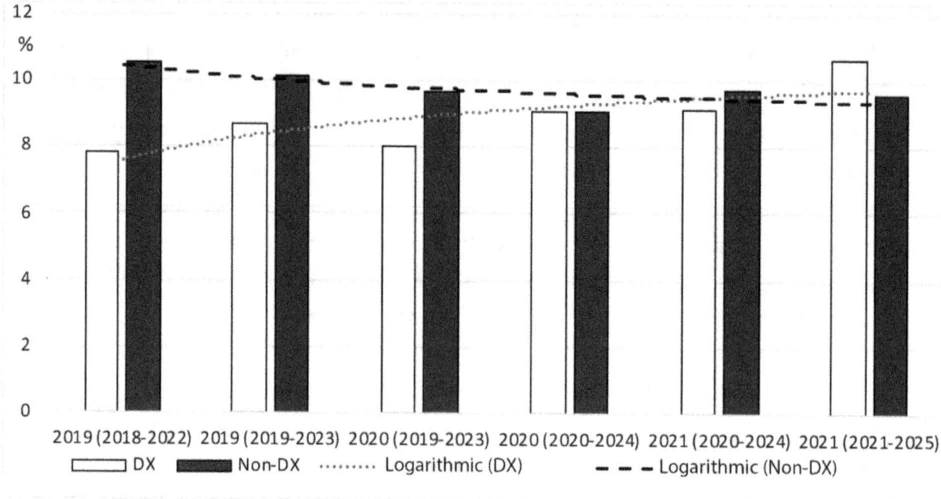

trillion in 2022 (ISMG & OneSpan, 2020). The new (remote) work environment is becoming increasingly in demand in a world of an incessant pandemic. Therefore, interest in digital technology is not diminishing. In 2020, 40% of market participants accelerated the digitalization of their activities in general and the transition to the cloud in particular (MariaDB, 2022).

Using data from International Data Corporation (IDC, 2021), we obtained estimates of the rate of three-year average annual growth of Compound annual growth rate (CAGR) and calculated a five-year forecast of returns on investment in digital technology (Figure 1), which demonstrates the high potential for returns on digital investment technology, almost three times higher than the average market level. In this regard, it is noteworthy that with equal opportunities at entry, it is digital investment and financial products that have received a strong boost in 2020 under the influence of COVID, which stimulates the transition to them. In subsequent years, there is likely to be a slowdown in the rate of growth associated with the scale of investment and the lengthening of its duration (as we emerge from the transition period).

Institutional investors believe that the main reasons for the increase in investments in digital financial assets are low correlation with the prices of other assets and high growth potential. The acceleration of digitalization and adoption of digital assets is evidenced by the Fidelity surveys (Neureuter, 2021), which form the basis of five-year projections. Despite the predicted growth of digitalization of financial processes worldwide, the USA lags far behind the Asian region and Europe. However, the increase in digitalization and the degree of use of digital assets is observed almost all over the world. As already noted, the catalyst of these changes was the COVID-19 pandemic and related monetary and fiscal measures. The increased interest of institutional investors in digital assets and technologies is also due to the evolutionary and growing complexity of investment and financial products of the global financial market and the formation of ecosystems of financial institutions, i.e., the institutionalization of digital assets.

The main obstacles are persistent (and inherent) price volatility and difficulty assessing value due to the lack of a base and the fear of manipulation. The constraints of the past, such as institutional complexity and insufficient market infrastructure, are no longer obstacles because investors have already formed an understanding of digital technologies and assets (including based on their own experience), and virtually all institutional investors are already trained in digital assets and have adopted them as an investment tool.

The most positive sentiment about digital assets and crypto assets is observed in Asia. Nevertheless, more and more institutional investors from other parts of the world are turning to digital assets, and their share is growing rapidly. Investors seek protection in cryptocurrencies against global risks (Jiang et al., 2021). For example, only two-thirds of European institutional investors included digital assets in their portfolios in 2020; in 2021, their share exceeded 75%. The share of US institutional investors also increased over the same period but only by 5% (being a little under 70%). First of all, this growth was ensured by appropriate custodial services that increase the security of digital assets in general. In 2021, e-commerce services were offered by 63% and data analytics over 55%, with a focus on the activities of US institutional investors (Neureuter, 2021)

Institutional investors monitor new economic-financial and social trends, test concepts, develop investment-financial products and ideas for them, create scalable solutions, work to improve operational efficiency, and anticipate their clients' needs and demands.

CONCLUSION

To summarize, we can note that, in general, the digitalization of the investment and financial sector is almost the same as in other sectors of the economy. Nevertheless, it is more intense and has a greater impact on the global economy, primarily because of the special place of the financial market and financial system in the current world. Digitalization has become integral to the investment and financial business, and even small companies are increasingly adopting its achievements. Individuals are not left out either.

More and more institutional investors of non-banking and banking types are introducing the latest technologies, including fintech, artificial intelligence, blockchain, and other technologies, into their operations and products to increase their competitiveness (or at least maintain it at an acceptable level), stimulate business growth, and attract customers. Above all, with digital technology, institutional investors seek to protect the interests of their clients in a post-pandemic economy, not just to maximize profits. The activity of representatives of traditional types of institutional investors in the global digital market has grown so much (following the representatives of new varieties) that institutional investors are beginning to influence the structure of the market for digital assets.

According to experts (Bray, 2022), the market for digital financial assets has been created with a focus on affluent individuals and retail investors, which is not quite possible to agree with because the bulk of today's financial products are designed for the mass customer who is not too picky about personal service (Bowles, 2019), while more affluent customers require more attention and usually count on a personal approach rather than mass-retail. Such a situation could rather refer to the crypto market, which, indeed, institutional investors entered somewhat later than speculators-individuals. According to Greenwich Coalition (Neureuter, 2021), among the participants of the crypto market, there are more and more institutional investors, who are, being usually professional market participants, act as traders or have significant amounts of financial resources, i.e., can determine the directions of supply and demand.

At the initial stage of the formation of the crypto market, various participants tried to offer first-class services for monitoring, analyzing, and calculating, as well as for storing cryptoassets. In turn, nowadays, almost all types of activities, up to trading platforms, are covered by institutional investors. Physical delivery instruments, virtual financial instruments, spots, and futures fall within the area of influence of institutional investors. Thus, 61% of institutional investors already work with ETFs. In the search for an acceptable level of liquidity, there is a transition from the quotation request mechanism to order books and streaming prices. Fully decentralized exchanges have also been created, offering innovative trading methods and management mechanisms that can compete with traditional broker-dealers and even alternative trading systems. Consequently, the new stage of digitalization will be largely predetermined by the perception of a variety of assets by market participants and the actions of regulators to ensure market stability, investor protection, and new technologies. The most promising areas for institutional investors are blockchain, Regtech, digital financial engineering, and green institutionalization because more and more institutional investors are taking care of the environment in light of global climate change. It is quite clear that these digital technologies can and are already changing the game's rules in the global financial system in Industry 4.0.

REFERENCES

Abraham, F., Schmukler, S. L., & Tessada, J. (2019, February). *Robo-advisors: Investing through machines.* Retrieved January 11, 2022, from https://documents1.worldbank.org/curated/en/275041551196836758/pdf/Robo-Advisors-Investing-through-Machines.pdf

Bank for International Settlements. (2015, November). *Digital currencies.* Retrieved January 12, 2022, from https://www.bis.org/cpmi/publ/d137.pdf

Bank of America. (n.d.). *Innovative technology that's personal.* Retrieved February 19, 2022, from https://about.bankofamerica.com/en/our-company/client-centered-technology

Boar, C., Holden, H., & Wadsworth, A. (2020). *Impending arrival – A sequel to the survey on central bank digital currency.* BIS Paper No. 107. Basel, Switzerland: Bank for International Settlements. Retrieved January 11, 2022, from https://www.bis.org/publ/bppdf/bispap107.pdf

Bowles, N. (2019, March 23). Human Contact in now a luxury good. *New York Times.* Retrieved January 11, 2022, from https://www.nytimes.com/2019/03/23/sunday-review/human-contact-luxury-screens.html

Bray, W. (2022, January 10). *Institutional investors begin to influence digital asset market structure.* Retrieved January 11, 2022, from https://www.thetradenews.com/institutional-investors-begin-to-influence-digital-asset-market-structure/

Central Bank of the Russian Federation. (2022, February 16). *Almost 2,700 illegal companies and financial pyramids identified by the Bank of Russia in 2021.* Retrieved February 19, 2022, from https://www.cbr.ru/press/event/?id=12695

Chiang, K., Frankfurter, G., & Kosedag, A. (2005). Exploratory analyses of dividend reinvestment plans and some comparisons. *International Review of Financial Analysis, 14*(5), 570–586. doi:10.1016/j.irfa.2004.10.020

D'Ankonia, F. (2017, November 2). Future of Digital currency may not involve blockchains. *Cointelegraph.* Retrieved January 12, 2022, from https://cointelegraph.com/news/future-of-digital-currency-may-not-involve-blockchains

Deloitte. (2020). *Realizing the digital promise.* Retrieved January 11, 2022, from https://www2.deloitte.com/content/dam/Deloitte/global/Documents/Financial-Services/gx-fsi-realizing-the-digital-promise-covid-19-catalyzes-and-accelerates-transformation.pdf

European Parliament and the Council of the European. (2014). *Directive 2014/65/EU of the of 15 May 2014 on markets in financial instruments and amending Directive 2002/92/EC and Directive 2011/61/EU.* Retrieved February 19, 2022, from https://eur-lex.europa.eu/legal-content/EN/TXT/?uri=CELEX%3A02014L0065-20220101

IDC. (2021, August 17). *Global spending on big data and analytics solutions will reach $215.7 billion in 2021, According to a new IDC spending guide.* Retrieved February 19, 2022, from https://www.idc.com/getdoc.jsp?containerId=prUS48165721

Irrera, A. (2021, July 20). *Most institutional investors expect to buy digital assets, study finds.* Retrieved February 19, 2022, from https://www.reuters.com/business/most-institutional-investors-expect-buy-digital-assets-study-finds-2021-07-20/

Irrera, A., Withers, I., & White, L. (2021, March 02). *Goldman Sachs restarts cryptocurrency desk amid bitcoin boom.* Retrieved February 19, 2022, from https://www.reuters.com/article/us-crypto-currency-goldman-sachs-exclusi-idUSKCN2AT390

ISMG & OneSpan. (2020). *The state of digital account opening transformation.* Princeton, NJ: ISMG. Retrieved January 11, 2022, from https://www.onespan.com/sites/default/files/2020-03/OneSpan-AnalystReport-ISMG-The-State-of-Digital-Account-Opening-Transformation.pdf

Jiang, Y., Wu, L., Tian, G., & Nie, H. (2021). Do cryptocurrencies hedge against EPU and the equity market volatility during COVID-19? *Journal of International Financial Markets, Institutions and Money*, *72*, 101324. doi:10.1016/j.intfin.2021.101324

Johnstone-Louis, M., Kustin, B., Mayer, C., Stroehle, J., & Wang, B. (2020). Business in times of crisis. *Oxford Review of Economic Policy*, *36*(SI1), 242–255. doi:10.1093/oxrep/graa021

Khmyz, O. V. (2003). Institutional investors on the securities market. *Voprosy Ekonomiki*, *8*(8), 95–101. doi:10.32609/0042-8736-2003-8-95-101

Khmyz, O. V. (2021). Unconventional directions of monetary regulation in a turbulent global economy. *Ekonomika. Nalogi. Pravo*, *14*(5), 31-38.

Kline, A. (2021, July 16). Wells Fargo tells employees to return to work in two waves this fall. *American Banker*. Retrieved January 11, 2022, from https://www.americanbanker.com/news/wells-fargo-tells-employees-to-return-to-work-in-two-waves-this-fall

Maria, D. B. (2022). *Survey: Cloud adoption statistics.* Retrieved February 13, 2022, from https://mariadb.com/survey/cloud-global/

Morgan, J. P. (2021, February 1). *J.P. Morgan creates digital coin for payments.* Retrieved February 19, 2022, from https://www.jpmorgan.com/solutions/cib/news/digital-coin-payments

Morgan, J. P. (n.d.). *Artificial intelligence research.* Retrieved February 19, 2022, from https://www.jpmorgan.com/technology/artificial-intelligence/initiatives

Neureuter, J. (2021, September). *The institutional investor digital assets study.* Retrieved February 13, 2022, from https://www.fidelitydigitalassets.com/bin-public/060_www_fidelity_com/documents/FDAS/2021-digital-asset-study.pdf

Office of the Comptroller of the Currency. (2021, January 4). *Federally chartered banks and thrifts may participate in independent node verification networks and use stablecoins for payment activities.* Retrieved February 19, 2022, from https://www.occ.gov/news-issuances/news-releases/2021/nr-occ-2021-2.html

Orbis Research. (2020, Mar 18). *Global robo advisory market size, status and forecast 2020–2026.* Retrieved January 11, 2022, from https://www.orbisresearch.com/reports/index/global-robo-advisory-market-size-status-and-forecast-2020-2026?utm_source=puja

Orlova, N. L., & Ignatova, O. V. (Eds.). (2021). International economic relations in modern conditions: Development guidelines. Scientific World.

Phaneuf, A. (2022, February 8). *Artificial intelligence in financial services: Applications and benefits of AI in finance.* Retrieved February 19, 2022, from https://www.businessinsider.com/ai-in-finance

Pizzicoli, M. (2018). *AI concierge built on IBM Watson transforms a bank's service desk.* Retrieved January 18, 2022, from https://www.ibm.com/blogs/cloud-computing/2018/12/21/creval-alfredo-concierge-ibm-watson/

Sanders, T. (2021). Testing the Black Box: Institutional investors, risk disclosure, and ethical AI. *Philosophy & Technology*, *34*(S1), 105–109. doi:10.100713347-020-00409-4

Shruti, I. (2022). *Harnessing digital financial inclusion under the G20 Digital Economy Agenda 2023.* Retrieved February 19, 2022, from https://www.orfonline.org/expert-speak/g20-digital-economy-agenda-2023/

Statista. (2022a). *Digital payments.* Retrieved February 08, 2022, from https://www.statista.com/outlook/dmo/fintech/digital-payments/worldwide#transaction-value

Statista. (2022b). *Overall cryptocurrency market capitalization per week from July 2010 to February 2022 (in billion US dollars).* Retrieved February 08, 2022, from https://www.statista.com/statistics/730876/cryptocurrency-maket-value/

World Bank. (2022a). *Global economic prospect*. The World Bank.

World Bank. (2022b, January 11). *Global Growth to Slow through 2023, Adding to Risk of 'Hard Landing' in Developing Economies.* Retrieved January 18, 2022, from https://www.worldbank.org/en/news/press-release/2022/01/11/global-recovery-economics-debt-commodity-inequality

Chapter 6
Corporate Reporting Modernization in the Digital Economy

Larisa V. Shmarova
https://orcid.org/0000-0002-1936-6446
MGIMO University, Russia

Irina O. Ignatova
https://orcid.org/0000-0002-5397-8657
MGIMO University, Russia

ABSTRACT

Currently, digital technologies are being widely introduced in various areas, which results in the transformation of numerous processes around the globe, including the system of accounting and report formation. The compilation of reporting in electronic format is an integral part of digital transformation. It is crucial to note that in the contemporary world, the users of reporting make new requests: it is no longer enough for them to have exclusively financial data presented in traditional statements. As a result, the practice of applying the new model of public reporting—integrated reporting—is becoming increasingly common. The research aims to identify tendencies in the development of corporate reporting in the era of digitalization and analyze the structure of a company's reporting that best corresponds to the information demands of stakeholders. The research characterizes the fundamental concepts and guiding principles of integrated reporting and reveals its main elements and indicators. Special attention is paid to the analysis of the concept of an enterprise's six capitals.

DOI: 10.4018/978-1-6684-4265-4.ch006

INTRODUCTION

In the contemporary world, digital transformation affects a wide range of industries. Digital technologies are increasingly penetrating business, including the preparation and publication of corporate reports. The formation of corporate reports in electronic form is becoming a topical matter. The IAS Board takes an active part in promoting digital reporting. This body set up the project called “IFRS Taxonomy,” within which the guide to preparing corporate reports in electronic format is issued annually. Furthermore, in the era of digitalization of the economy, stakeholders are increasingly demanding information disclosed in corporate reports. To make economically rational decisions, they need not only data on the organization’s performance but also information on its plans for future development. As a result, the new model of corporate reporting – integrated reporting – is getting increasingly demanded and common. Integrated reporting harmoniously combines financial indicators and non-financial information.

Currently, integrated reporting is the most effective way to provide data on a company’s business model. It is intended to eliminate existing informational and analytical constraints of traditional financial reporting and meet the practical requirements of the users of the information on the organization’s activity (Janshanlo & Kogut, 2020).

Integrated reporting is a single document that presents transparent and reliable data on the company’s strategic development plans, its corporate management system, economic indicators, and information on the enterprise’s social and environmental responsibility (Kuzmenko & Abrosimova, 2014).

As for the main feature of integrated reporting, it aims to analyze the company’s past performance and evaluate prospects for its development and growth in certain key areas (Gerasimova, 2013). Integrated reporting reflects information that enables financial capital providers to assess the company’s value most fully and accurately in the 21st century.

Fundamental changes that occur under the conditions of digitalization concern the composition of information in corporate reports and the ways of its presentation. These shifts undoubtedly demand scholarly elaboration, analysis, and systematization, which determine the relevance of the selected research topic.

The research aims to identify tendencies in the development of corporate reports in the era of the digital economy, reveal peculiarities of integrated reporting, and analyze its structural elements. To achieve the set goal, the following tasks are defined:

- To analyze conditions for the transformation of corporate reporting at the present stage;
- To determine the range of the users of integrated reporting and their interests;

- To disclose the essence of the fundamental concepts of integrated reporting;
- To categorize the capital used by an enterprise;
- To characterize the guiding principles of integrated reporting generation;
- To reveal the critical elements of integrated reporting;
- To define the composition of the indicators of integrated reporting.

METHOD

During the research, the authors applied two types of general scientific methods: empirical (the study of scientific literature and regulatory legal acts, the systematization of materials, description, and comparison) and theoretical (the analysis of schemes and comparable data presented in the form of tables, the generalization and formalization of the obtained results, synthesis, detailing, abstraction, induction, deduction, systems approach, and chronological analysis).

The information base of this research was laws and regulations on accounting and financial report generation, the International Integrated Reporting Framework, educational and methodical literature, scientific articles in specialized periodicals, and other topical information sources by Russian and foreign authors.

RESULTS

In the era of digital transformation, companies are dynamically developing, which increases the complexity of business models. The environment in which economic entities function is substantially changing as well. As a result of such tendencies, financial reporting is no longer a sufficient source of information on an enterprise's operation (Luzganova et al., 2020). This is due to the fact that financial statements contain data on conducted business operations and reflect only the current business situation. Nowadays, the users of corporate reports have an increasing need for information on the future development of the company in the medium and long run. This data should involve financial information and non-financial indicators. In the current world, the new enhanced reporting model – integrated reporting – could comply with stakeholders' demands (Malinovskaya, 2020).

The essence of integrated reporting is the combination of financial and non-financial data on an enterprise's activity which gives an idea of the organization's ability to create and preserve its value in the short and long terms (Tjahjadi et al., 2020). Integrated reporting constitutes a single document that contains information on the company's strategy, its corporate management system, and indicators characterizing economic, environmental, and social aspects of the enterprise's operation (Bolvachev et al., 2019).

According to the International Integrated Reporting Framework, the primary goal of integrated reporting is to provide the providers of financial capital with clarifications on how the company creates, preserves, or erodes its value over time (IIRC, 2013). The enterprise's value is not formed exclusively within the organization itself. It is also influenced by the nature of relations with stakeholders and external conditions. Integrated reporting aims to give stakeholders a holistic idea of the organization's current operation and prospects of its future development and growth in a number of main areas (Musipova, 2020).

Integrated reporting gives detailed information on the following:

- The company's resources that are called capitals;
- The external environment that has an impact on the enterprise;
- The organization's interaction with the external environment and the use of capitals for creating and preserving value in the future.

The range of the users of integrated reporting is extremely wide, and their requirements are various:

- Investors, creditors, shareholders, company management, and competitors who need information that allows them to evaluate the enterprise's image and its ability to create value and assess the organization's investment attractiveness (in particular, it is referred to indicators such as labor productivity, compliance with legislative regulations, and customer loyalty);
- Authorized executive authorities that require data on the economic, social, and environmental aspects of the company's operation for ensuring the sustainable use of natural resources in the country and socio-economic stability;
- Business partners that need information enabling them to determine whether their debtors can fulfill their obligations in time and comply with ethical principles;
- Company employees and trade union representatives interested in information on the future plans of management, safety and health regulations in the organization, and pay and social programs implemented in the company;
- Clients who require data on the quality of produced goods or provided services and information on the enterprise's stability, particularly when it comes to long-term relations;
- The public that is interested in various data on the organization's activity and its contribution to the national economy;

- Auditors, whose key task is to verify financial and non-financial information on the enterprise's operation contained in integrated reporting (Popadyuk & Tabakova, 2019).

Integrated reporting preparation is based on three fundamental concepts (Figure 1):

- Value creation for the organization and for others;
- The capitals;
- The process through which value is created, preserved, or eroded (IIRC, 2021).

Figure 1. Fundamental concepts of integrated reporting formation
Source: Compiled by the authors based on International Integrated Reporting Framework, January 2021 (IIRC, 2021)

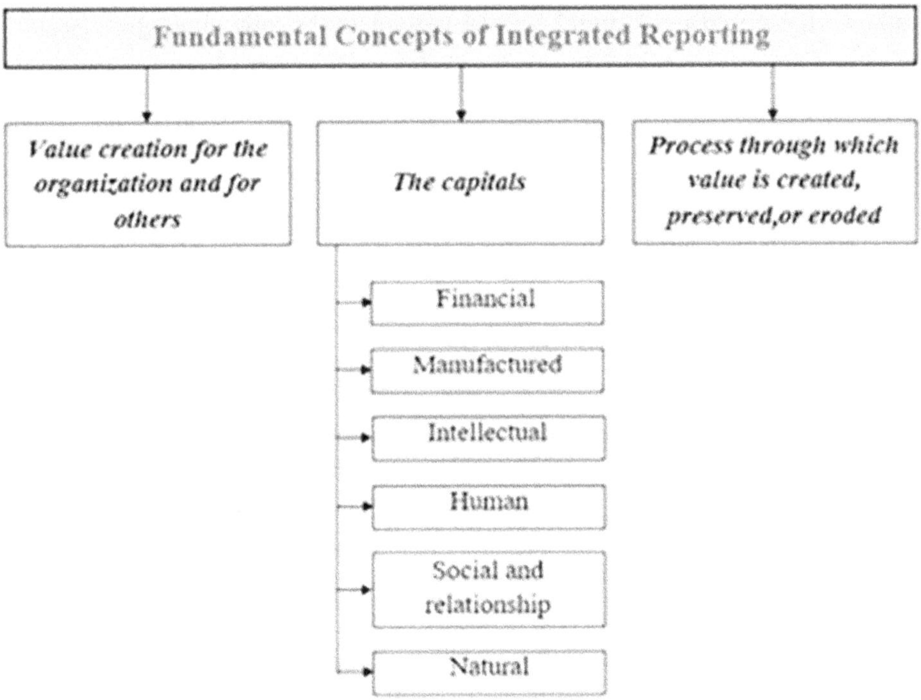

The creation of the enterprise's value in the course of business activity, its preservation, or decrease in the long-term results in a rise or reduction in the organization's capital. A company's value can be categorized into two interrelated elements: value that is created for the enterprise and gives a return on investment to financial capital providers and value that is created for the company's stakeholders and society (IIRC, 2013).

The value created for the organization is correlated with the value formed by the company for others (Figure 2). This interrelationship appears as a result of various events conducted by the enterprise and interaction with stakeholders. The nature of relations with stakeholders also has a certain impact. Thus, for instance, the value created for the company is influenced by the level of customer satisfaction, the willingness of suppliers to conclude partnership agreements, the enterprise's image, etc.

If certain activities of the organization, its interaction with stakeholders, or the nature of relations with some stakeholders impact the company's ability to form value for itself, this data is included in integrated reporting.

The organization's success and the amount of its market capitalization depend on the company's capital. According to the International Integrated Reporting Framework, a company's capital is categorized into the following types:

- Financial;
- Manufactured;
- Intellectual;
- Human;
- Social and relationship;
- Natural (IIRC, 2021).

An organization's capital constitutes the stock of value, which could increase or decrease depending on the company's performance. For example, profit leads to a rise in financial capital, and staff training contributes to an increase in human capital.

Globally, an enterprise's capital can be categorized into financial and non-financial. In turn, non-financial capital is divided into tangible and intangible (Figure 3). The main feature of financial and tangible capital implies that these capitals are under the complete control of the organization, while the company could manage intangible capital only to a certain extent (Kogdenko, 2017).

Each type of capital has its peculiarities. Financial capital is a resource for creating other capital types (Plotnikov & Azrakuliev, 2018). The part of financial capital, which is not used for forming tangible and intangible capitals, is transformed into financial assets. In compliance with the International Integrated Reporting Framework, financial capital is the pool of funds that are available to the enterprise for employing in the production of different goods and services or that come into the company by means of raising debt or equity funding, receiving grants, and doing business and making investments (IIRC, 2021).

Figure 2. The interrelationship between value created, preserved, or eroded for the organization and value created, preserved, or eroded for others
Source: Compiled by the authors based on International Integrated Reporting Framework, January 2021 (IIRC, 2021)

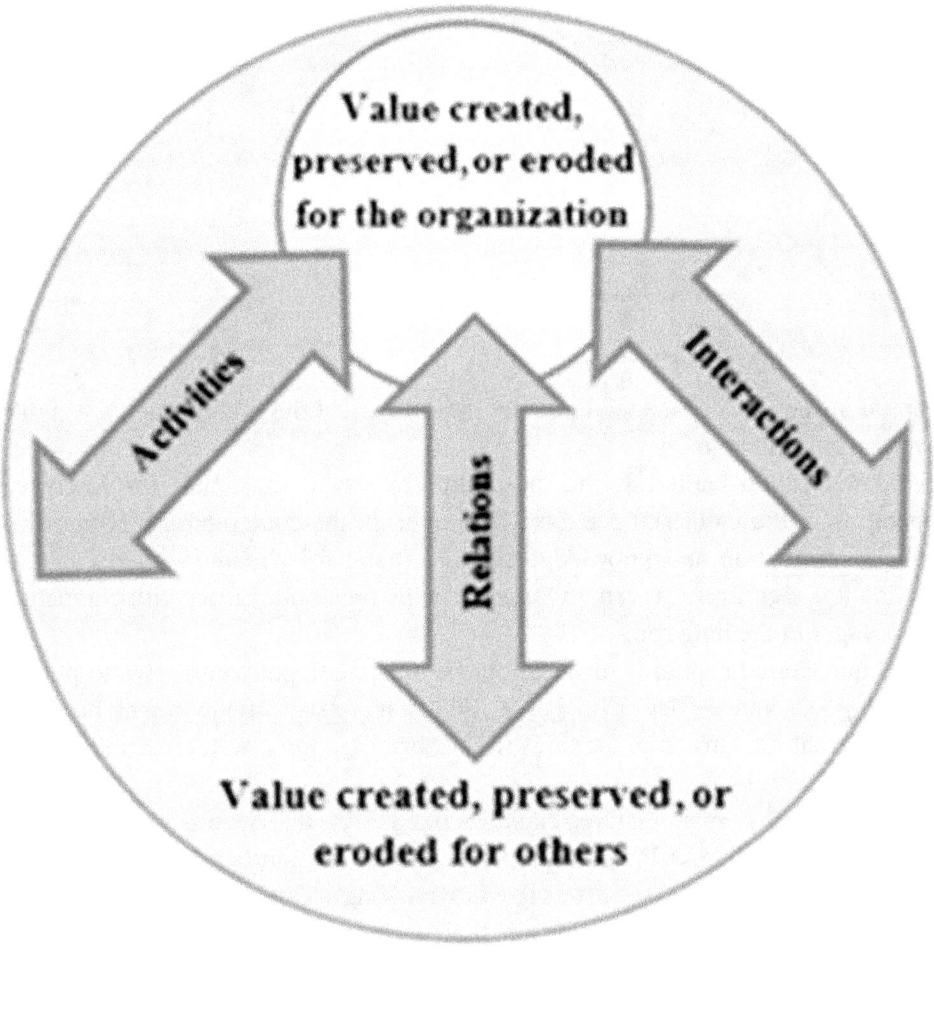

As to the fund-raising sources, financial capital is categorized into equity one and debt one. As for the purpose of use, financial capital is divided into fixed (fixed assets) and current (current assets). The main types of equity capital are contributions of the organization's owners and retained earnings. Debt capital is most commonly raised in the form of bank loans, bond loans, and capital lease.

All elements of financial capital are assessed based on financial reporting, namely a balance sheet. The structure of the sources of the enterprise's financial

Figure 3. Company capital
Source: Compiled by the authors based on (Kogdenko, 2017)

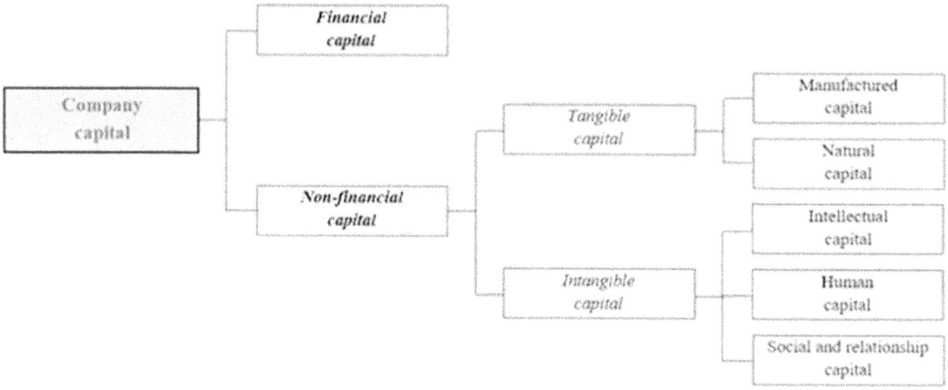

capital influences its financial position, stability, and the organization's weighted average cost of capital.

Manufactured capital is the most important type of capital for enterprises operating in the industrial economy. However, in the contemporary economy, in which information and knowledge play a crucial role, manufactured capital is getting less significant: it can no longer provide the organization with competitive advantages in the long run.

Manufactured capital is physical objects that a company possesses to produce certain goods and services (Suits et al., 2020). It consists of equipment, buildings, and different infrastructure facilities (roads, bridges, ports, water treatment plants, etc.) (IIRC, 2021).

In other words, manufactured capital is fixed assets that the organization has and construction in progress. Integrated reporting should contain data on the composition, state, and movement of fixed assets (pawning, taking a lease or leasing out, a transfer to conservation) and information on their current market price, manufacturing capacity, their utilization level, equipment operating mode, its idle time, and the amount of investments in manufactured capital. Additionally, integrated reporting should present a capital-output ratio, a labor-output ratio, an energy-output ratio, and labor mechanization and automation indicators.

The state and efficiency of utilization of fixed assets of an enterprise have an impact on its competitiveness, return on equity and capital turnover, and the company's ability to create value.

Intellectual capital is the totality of identifiable and unidentifiable intangible assets fully or partially controlled by the organization (Serebryakova, 2016). It consists of intellectual property items, including copyrights, licenses, patents, software, and organizational capital, which comprises knowledge bases and databases, corporate culture, the business mission and strategy, the enterprise's organizational and financial structures, information systems, management processes, systems of internal control and management accounting, etc. (IIRC, 2021).

Data on intellectual property is presented in financial reporting in the form of intangible assets.

The peculiarities of intellectual capital are uniqueness for a specific company, incomplete information disclosure, volatile efficiency, and a change in value. Intellectual capital is extremely hard to identify and evaluate. It is imperative to analyze their fair value when considering intellectual property items. The assessment of organizational capital, as a rule, is carried out by experts who consider the impact of organizational capital on the parameters of riskiness and effectiveness of the organization, as well as on the process of creating and implementing innovations.

While evaluating intellectual capital, the following analytical indicators are used: the share of intangible assets in the bottom-line figure of the balance sheet, the rate of their increment, and the qualitative features of organizational capital components. The main for assessing intellectual capital is the creation of technological and organizational innovations, as well as product and marketing ones.

Intellectual capital is the source of long-term competitive advantages. It promotes the development and growth of the company and the creation and preservation of its value in the future. Intellectual capital contributes to the improvement of technologies, the increase in the enterprise's efficiency, sustainability, and growth rates, and the enhancement of business processes. Moreover, it allows using financial, tangible, and labor resources in a more economical way.

Human capital is the abilities and skills of employees, their professional experience, and the willingness to implement innovations (Kashkovskaya, 2020). It consists of the orientation on the management structure of the organization and the adherence to the company's ethical standards, the ability to act in accordance with the enterprise's strategy and contribute to its development, the motivation to perform employment duties, the loyalty to the organization, and the competence to manage and cooperate (IIRC, 2021).

Human capital could be increased by means of hiring creative and highly motivated staff, creating corporate culture, and making investments in advanced professional training of employees and health maintenance.

Integrated reporting should present information on the average number of staff, the number of employees who work under civil contracts, the number of external part-time workers, and the number of employees attracted under outsourcing contracts. Besides, integrated reporting should reflect data on staff categories (managerial personnel, basic workers, specialists, and support staff), their seniority and age, educational level, the average pay in the enterprise and its differentiation, and workers' movement figures (turnover ratios for staff recruitment and staff attrition). No less important are indicators, such as creativity, motivation, job satisfaction, and staff professionalism. The final indicator in the assessment of human capital is the rate of labor productivity.

Nowadays, the role of human capital is increasing year by year due to the instability of the external environment, tougher competition, the acceleration of scientific and technological progress, and the reduction in the duration of products' life cycle. Under these conditions, employees must have a high level of qualification. What is more, they should be loyal to the organization, creative, dynamic, and can rapidly adapt to alterations.

Social and relationship capital is the company's goodwill, its relations with stakeholders, and its willingness to share information to improve individual and collective welfare. It includes the following:

- The organization's values and behavior patterns;
- The nature of relations with stakeholders, credibility, and willingness to build partnerships;
- Intangible values related to the enterprise's image and brand;
- The social license for the company's activity (IIRC, 2021).

The main component of social and relationship capital is credibility, which means that stakeholders' expectations are met. Stakeholders' confidence provides the organization with competitive advantages.

Decency and responsibility in interaction with suppliers, clients, and employees considerably contribute to creating the enterprise's social and relationship capital. Social and relationship capital increases at the expense of implementing social projects, incurring advertising expenses, improving relations with counterparts, and enhancing the structure of the client base.

Integrated reporting should reveal data on workforce stability, the organization's image, its key partners, and the duration of cooperation with them, as well as social investments (for instance, investments in culture and sports or investments in projects for the construction of social facilities) (Kogdenko & Melnik, 2014).

Currently, the evaluation of social and relationship capital is taking on particular significance because this capital substantially defines the company's value and development prospects. Social and relationship capital is formed by stable business contacts with stakeholders. It facilitates the transition from the control of the production process to the management of relations with stakeholders. Social and relationship capital contributes to the creation and preservation of the organization's value at the expense of minimizing the level of uncertainty in cooperation with counterparts, establishing trust relations with stakeholders, decreasing transaction costs in interaction with them, and exchanging information with suppliers and clients.

Natural capital has become the subject of particular attention since the 1970s. This is connected with the fact that the overuse of natural resources and environmental pollution significantly reduced development opportunities for future generations. The pursuit of maximizing profit in the short run caused the depletion of mineral resources and resulted in a decrease in the pace of economic development. An approach aimed at the long term implies natural capital accounting and its efficient use (Kogdenko, 2017).

Natural capital is the totality of renewable and non-renewable resources and natural processes that allow the company to create different goods or services and thus provide its prosperity. It consists of land, air, water, forests, and minerals, as well as biodiversity and ecosystem health (IIRC, 2021).

Integrated reporting should contain information on the enterprise's land resources, data on ultimate, probable, and possible mineral reserves (metal, fuel, and non-ore). Moreover, it has to present information on the value of natural capital and the number of years for which the organization will have enough natural resources. As analytical indicators, integrated reporting might include indicators such as the occurrence depth of natural resources, mineral output, location, composition, and properties (Kogdenko & Melnik, 2014).

The significance of natural capital in the contemporary economy is extremely high because numerous manufacturing companies cannot conduct business without the use of minerals. It is natural capital that allows many Russian enterprises to operate and create value.

The above capitals are of unequal importance for the organization. The capital which the company has in very small amounts, and which exerts only an indirect impact may not be presented in integrated reporting (IIRC, 2013).

In the course of time, the stocks of certain capitals might change. All capitals are closely interrelated. Thus, for example, training costs increase the enterprise's human capital and decrease its financial capital. In this way, financial capital transforms into a human one.

One more fundamental concept that currently underlies the preparation of integrated reporting is the process of the company's value creation (Figure 4). Conditions in which the enterprise functions are influenced by the external environment, which includes the environmental situation, economic parameters, social issues, and technological progress. Its goals, mission, and strategic vision determine the organization's prospects. People who undertake management functions are responsible for forming an appropriate supervision structure that will coordinate the actions of the staff and contribute to the creation of the company's value.

Figure 4. The process through which value is created, preserved, or eroded
Source: International Integrated Reporting Framework, January 2021 (IIRC, 2021)

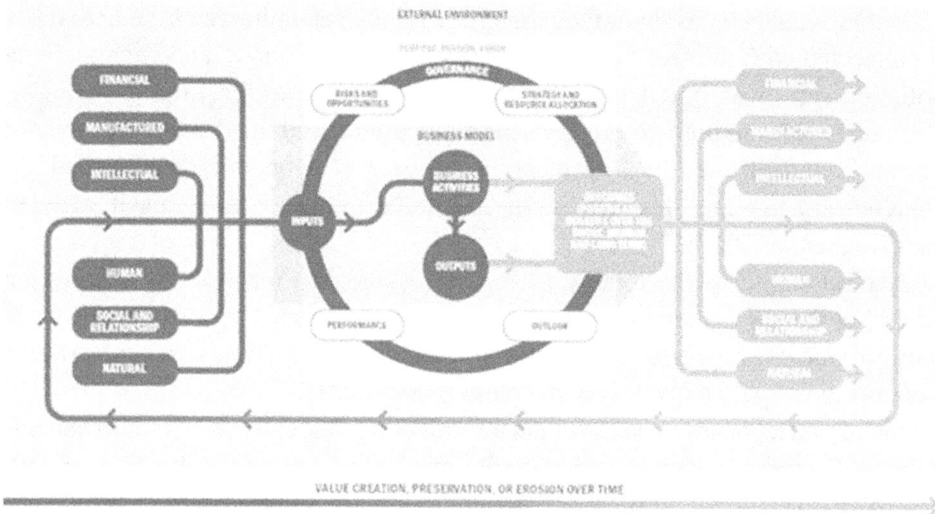

The enterprise's center is its business model based on different capitals that constitute the totality of various resources. Commercial activities result in the transformation of these resources into goods, services, or waste (IIRC, 2021). Figure 5 shows the interrelation between resources and the company's capitals.

By using all capitals in its activities, the company produces particular goods or services and gets certain results. The ability of the business model to adapt to alterations in the quality and availability of resources defines the enterprise's viability in the long run. Regular monitoring of the external environment, taking into account the organization's mission and strategic vision, helps identify the company's opportunities and risks related to its business model.

The process of value creation is volatile. The ongoing analysis of all elements of this process and their impact on each other enables making certain changes and enhancing particular aspects.

Integrated reporting is generated in accordance with guiding principles, which determine its content and the form of information presentation. These principles include the following:

- Strategic focus and future orientation;
- Connectivity of information;
- Stakeholder relations;
- Materiality;
- Conciseness;

Figure 5. Interrelations between resources and company capitals
Source: Compiled by the authors based on (Popadyuk & Tabakova, 2019)

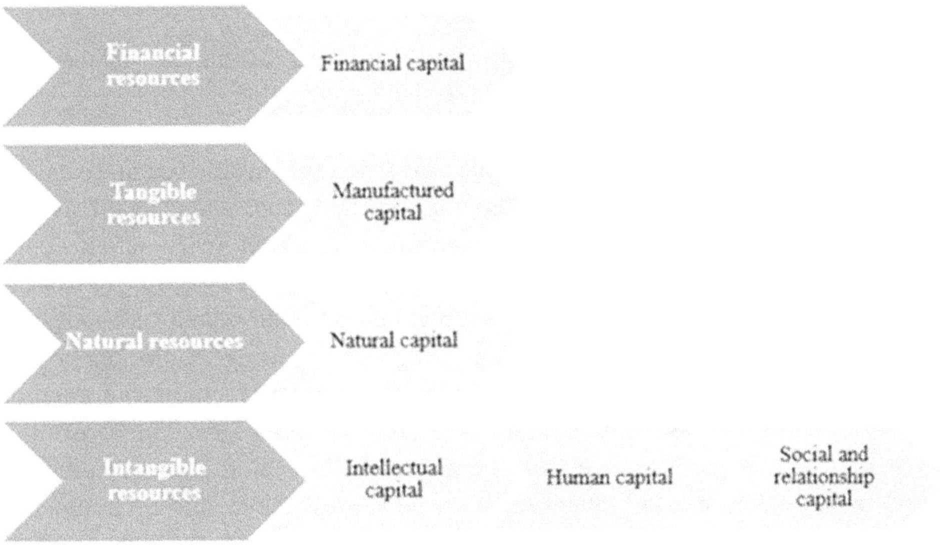

- Reliability and completeness;
- Consistency and comparability (IIRC, 2021).

Strategic focus and future orientation mean that integrated reporting should analyze the organization's strategy and present an explanation of how the strategy is consistent with the company's ability to create and preserve value in the short, medium, and long run, as well as with the use of the enterprise's capital (IIRC, 2013).

This principle implies that integrated reporting could reveal the organization's strategy, future prospects, and other information, if necessary. For instance, integrated reporting might reflect the company's important risks and opportunities or opinions of employees who perform management functions regarding particular matters.

Information connectivity means that integrated reporting should present data on all factors that define the creation of the enterprise's value, as well as on the impact they have on each other. To ensure the connectivity of information contained in integrated reporting, it is essential to promote integrated thinking in the organization.

According to the principle of data connectivity, there must be a link between:

- The elements of integrated reporting;
- The company's capitals;
- Quantitative and qualitative information;
- The past, present, and future;

- Data reflected in integrated reporting and other data provided by the enterprise to the stakeholders;
- Financial and non-financial information;
- Management data, information for the board of directors, and information presented to external parties (IIRC, 2021).

Data connectivity enhances if the integrated report is well structured and set out in an understandable language without using highly specialized terms, as well as contains convenient navigation components (e.g., cross-references and logically delimited sections). To increase information connectivity, it is possible to harness information technologies, which considerably facilitate data search and analysis.

The relations of stakeholders imply that integrated reporting should contain data on the nature of the organization's relations with stakeholders, including information on how the company takes into account their interests and information demands.

Stakeholders express their opinions concerning the factors that are crucial to them. In particular, they are interested in the economic, social, and environmental aspects of the enterprise's operation, which somehow influence the creation of the organization's value. Information obtained from stakeholders allows the company to realize how stakeholders assess the organization's value, determine and manage potential risks, identify current tendencies, and adjust the company's strategy (IIRC, 2021).

In compliance with the materiality principle, integrated reporting should reflect data on matters that might significantly impact the enterprise's ability to create value in the future.

The process of defining materiality consists of the following stages:

- The identification of the factors that can influence the creation of the organization's value;
- The evaluation of the significance of major factors based on the existing or potential impact on the creation of the company's value;
- The prioritization of important factors, depending on their significance;
- The selection of significant factors that should be reflected in integrated reporting based on professional judgment.

Materiality is determined based on the concept of the reporting boundary. This concept includes two aspects: the enterprise that compiles financial reporting and risks and opportunities that are connected with stakeholders and might have a substantial impact on the ability of the organization to create value (IIRC, 2013).

Figure 6. Integrated reporting boundary
Source: International Integrated Reporting Framework, January 2021 (IIRC, 2021)

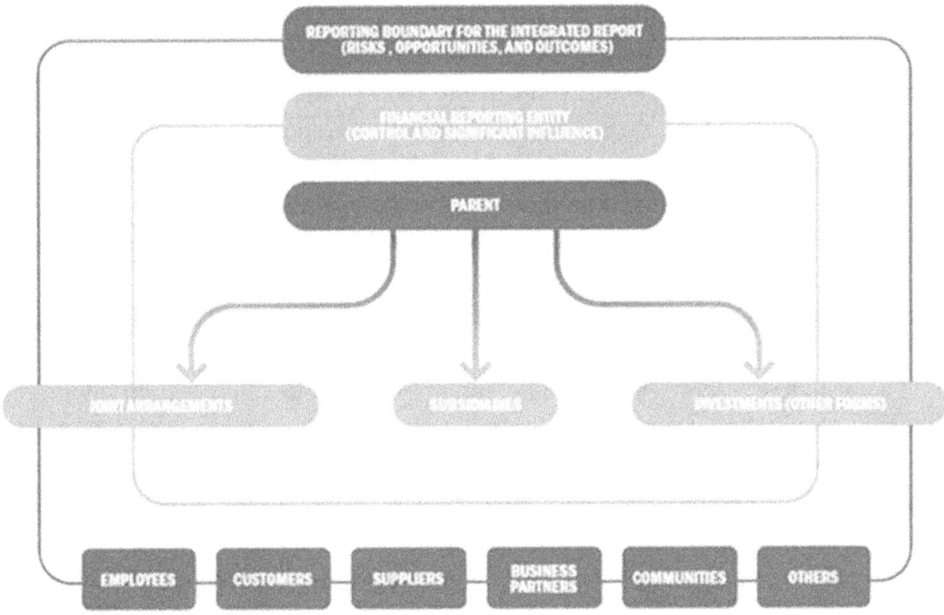

Figure 6 presents the reporting boundary. The center of the reporting boundary is the company that generates financial reporting because the providers of financial capital make investments in this enterprise and need information on it.

The principle of conciseness implies that integrated reporting should present clear and brief data on the organization's strategy, its management model, performance, and development prospects without reflecting irrelevant information (IIRC, 2021). When compiling integrated reporting, the company strives to strike a balance between conciseness and other guiding principles (this particularly concerns completeness and comparability).

According to the principle of reliability and completeness, integrated reporting should reveal positive and negative essential facts in a balanced way. Apart from that, integrated reporting should not contain material errors. Information reliability is determined by its equilibrium and accuracy. Data precision is ensured by the creation of the internal control system, conducting an internal audit, and receiving independent external assurance.

The balance of data is provided by using formats of information presentation, which allow stakeholders to make an objective assessment. The balance of data is also influenced by reflecting facts of an increase and decrease in the capital, positive and negative performance results, the enterprise's advantages and disadvantages, and the estimated figures and development prospects of the organization.

The absence of material errors does not imply that data contained in integrated reporting is absolutely accurate. This feature means that the organization has an operating control system, which reduces the risks of material misstatement to the lowest acceptable level. Furthermore, if integrated reporting contains estimated figures, this fact has to be clearly defined. In this case, integrated reporting should reflect the applied assessment methodology and constraints of this process.

To ensure information completeness, the organization must consider what aspects are presented by other enterprises in a particular industry in their reporting because certain factors might be significant for all companies of a specific industry (IIRC, 2021).

The principle of consistency and comparability implies that data in integrated reporting should be reflected in accordance with the information disclosure policy that has been used for many years. It is necessary to provide the possibility of comparing the company with other enterprises in respect of the aspects that have a considerable impact on the organization's ability to create value.

The policy of presenting data on the company's operation remains unchanged year by year. It could be corrected only if adjustments enhance the quality of information revealed in integrated reporting. If the enterprise alters the policy of presenting data, it is imperative to explain the reason for the adjustment and describe the consequences with providing a quantitative evaluation if it could be carried out in practice and is material.

The information included in integrated reporting of various organizations inevitably differs because the process of creating value is unique for each company. Nevertheless, data reflected in integrated reporting is, to a certain extent, comparable because the elements of integrated reporting of all enterprises are the same (IIRC, 2021).

The summarized substance of the guiding principles of integrated reporting is presented in Figure 7. These principles might be used individually and in aggregate. The way of their application is defined based on professional judgment. This is especially topical when one principle clearly contradicts the other (for instance, conciseness and completeness).

The fundamental concepts and guiding principles that we have considered are the basis for generating integrated reporting. They determine the procedure for its compilation and establish the criteria for information disclosure.

The preparation of integrated reporting constitutes a rather complex process involving representatives from all corporate management levels. Importantly, they interact with internal and external stakeholders.

Integrated reporting includes the following eight structural elements:

Figure 7. Content of guiding principles of integrated reporting
Source: Compiled by the authors based on International Integrated Reporting Framework, January 2021 (IIRC, 2021)

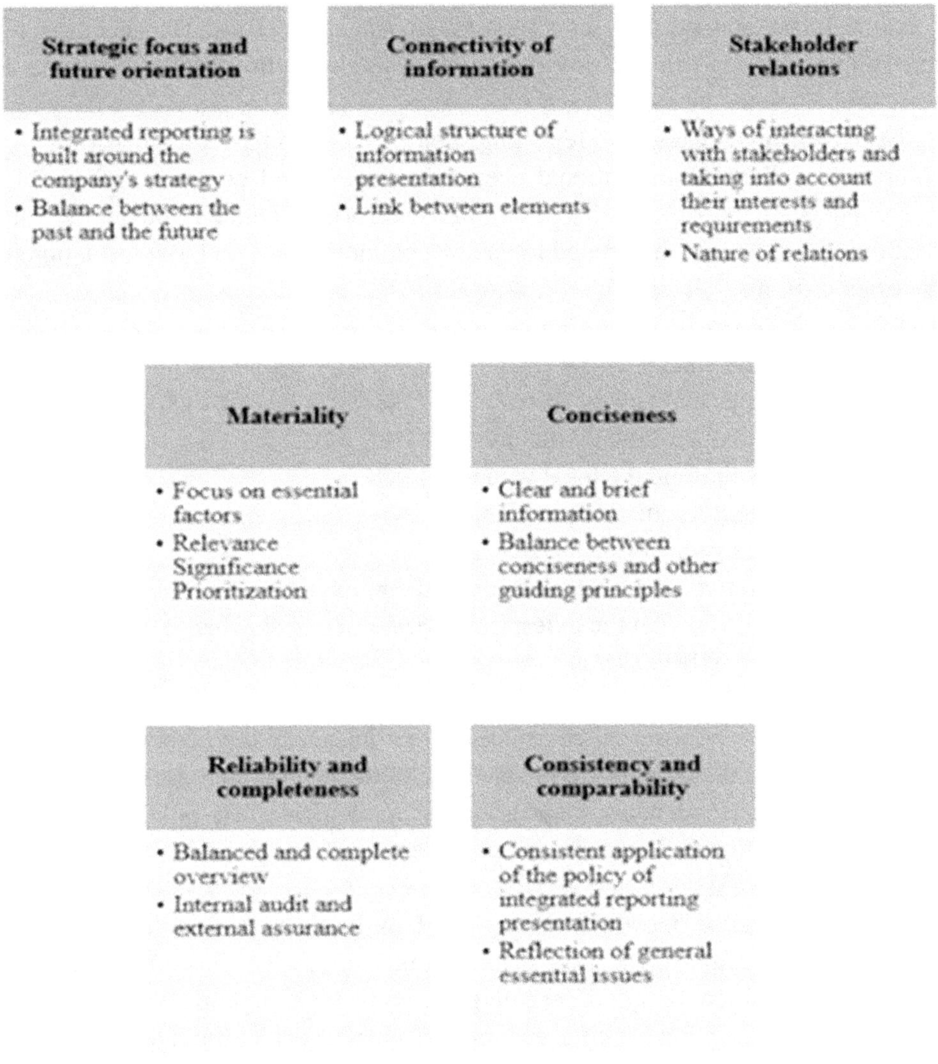

- Organizational overview and external environment;
- Governance;
- Business model;
- Risks and opportunities;
- Strategy and resource allocation;
- Performance;
- Outlook;

- Basis of preparation and presentation (IIRC, 2021).

The listed components of integrated reporting are not mutually exclusive, they are connected. The sequence of disclosing these elements is not fixed. Data in integrated reporting is reflected in the way that allows demonstrating the link between its structural components most clearly.

Each element of integrated reporting should respond to a certain question. The component called "Organizational overview and external environment" enables stakeholders to realize in what areas the enterprise operates and under what conditions it functions. Integrated reporting contains the following information on the organization:

- Mission and strategy;
- Core activities and key markets;
- Property and operational structure;
- Corporate culture and ethical values;
- Main competitors, market position;
- Place in the overall value chain;
- Key quantitative data (annual income, the number of employees, the number of countries in which the enterprise operates, etc.), its change relative to the previous year (IIRC, 2021).

The factors of the external environment that influence the company's activity and its ability to create value are the stability of the legal system, macroeconomic conditions, market tendencies, social issues, technological shifts, political situation, and environmental conditions. They could exert a direct and indirect impact on the company (IIRC, 2021).

The element called "Governance" explains how the enterprise's structure supports its ability to create value in the short, medium, and long run. This section of integrated reporting tends to contain data revealing the company's organizational structure, including the description of skills, experience, and the sociocultural diversity of the staff who perform management functions. Additionally, integrated reporting presents the procedure for making strategic decisions and creating corporate culture, as well as adopted approaches to risk management. Special attention is paid to describing the responsibility of employees performing management functions for the creation and implementation of innovations. Integrated reporting reflects the relationship between the amount of remuneration of employees who are in charge of corporate management and the organization's ability to create its value in the short, medium, and long terms (IIRC, 2013).

The section called "Business model" shows what the company's business model is. An enterprise's business model is the system within which resources transform into certain products, which is the result of the company's commercial activities aimed at achieving strategic goals and creating the company's value. An enterprise's business model includes information characterizing resources, the organization's key activities, its products (goods or services, waste, and by-products), and performance results (positive and negative, internal and external; an internal result might be the moral spirit of the staff or the enterprise's income and an external result could be the loyalty to the brand, the level of customer satisfaction, and tax payments).

Organizations operating in different market segments can use several business models in their activities. In this case, the company describes each business model and explains how they are connected (IIRC, 2021).

The component called "Risks and opportunities" gives information on the enterprise's risks and opportunities that might potentially influence its ability to create its value in the short, medium, and long terms. Besides, integrated reporting provides data on how the organization manages these risks and uses such opportunities. Risks and opportunities can be internal and external.

Integrated reporting could present the assessment of the probability of realizing risks and the severity of their consequences, as well as describe the actions that the company takes to minimize risks. Guided by the principle of materiality, enterprises tend to include in their integrated reporting the risks, which might have a significant impact on the organization's ability to create its value even if the probability of their realization is relatively low (IIRC, 2021).

The element called "Strategy and resource allocation" allows stakeholders to realize in what direction the enterprise intends to develop and how it will achieve the goals set. This section of integrated reporting usually reflects information concerning the organization's strategic goals in the short, medium, and long terms, its strategy and plans for using resources. Additionally, it reveals the procedure for evaluating achieving target indicators (IIRC, 2013).

The section called "Performance" gives data on how the organization managed to achieve the set strategic goals and presents the stocks of its capitals. Integrated reporting reveals quantitative and qualitative data on the company's performance. Apart from that, it considers the relationship between the enterprise's performance indicators in the past and present and its development prospects (IIRC, 2021).

The component called "Outlook" provides information on the difficulties and uncertainties, which the organization might face in the future during the realization of its strategy, as well as data on the consequences for the company's business model and future operation that these difficulties and uncertainties lead to. Integrated reporting reflects the enterprise's expectations for possible shifts in the external environment, the influence that these changes will have on the organization's activity, and the company's ability to cope with encountered difficulties and uncertainties (IIRC, 2021).

Integrated reporting could contain information on estimated key indicators, planned projects, projected prices for raw materials and exchange rates, and data on their impact on the enterprise's performance results and sensitivity analysis (Popadyuk & Tabakova, 2019).

The element called "Basis of preparation and presentation" explains how the organization identifies the matters to be reflected in integrated reporting and how they are quantitatively or qualitatively assessed. This section should describe the process of determining materiality, integrated reporting boundaries, and the procedure for their identification, basic methods used for the quantitative and qualitative assessment of significant factors (IIRC, 2013).

Integrated reporting is characterized by the fact that it interrelates the financial and non-financial indicators of the company's operation, which can be forecast and current. Non-financial indicators could be assessed qualitatively and quantitatively. Quantitative information enables stakeholders to analyze data for various periods and make predictions regarding their dynamics in the future. The composition of integrated reporting figures is presented in the figure (Figure 8).

Financial indicators are reflected in the enterprise's financial reporting. They describe the organization's property and financial status. The balance of assets and liabilities is revealed in the company's Balance Sheet, which is compiled as of a certain reporting date. Financial capital is determined based on the indicators of the Income Statement, Cash Flow Statement, and Capital Statement.

Financial figures presented in integrated reporting give information on the enterprise's financial position, its autonomy, and sustainability. Based on this data, potential investors evaluate the attractiveness of investments in the organization and its development prospects.

Non-financial indicators allow internal and external users to get a full idea of creating, existing, and using the company's capitals. The list of non-financial indicators that integrated reporting could contain is presented in the table (Table 1).

DISCUSSION

In terms of data coverage and the level of detail, the conducted research is unparalleled around the globe. The results obtained in the course of analytical work give a holistic view of integrated reporting, which constitutes the innovative model of corporate reporting. Based on the collected, analyzed, and systematized data, the authors come to a convincing conclusion that, in the era of the digital economy, integrated reporting best meets stakeholders' information requirements because it reveals the

Figure 8. Composition of the indicators of integrated reporting
Source: Compiled by the authors based on (Lyubishina, 2022)

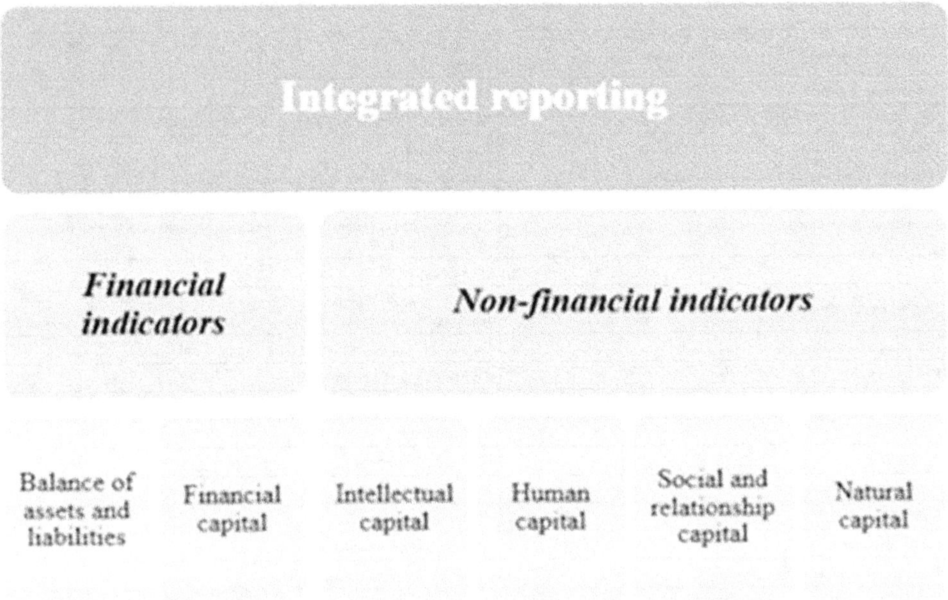

most complete and transparent information on various aspects of the enterprise's activity interesting for stakeholders and enables them to make informed decisions. This conclusion is generally consistent with the opinions of the authors of studies in the field of integrated reporting carried out previously (Bolvachev et al., 2019; Tjahjadi et al., 2020).

CONCLUSION

Thus, the implementation of integrated reporting considerably contributes to the development of corporate reporting. Integrated reporting allows getting detailed and transparent data on the organization's performance and development prospects (Kalabikhina et al., 2017). It facilitates improving the accounting system within the enterprise and takes it to a qualitatively new level.

The transition to integrated reporting is the basis of a new paradigm of management, the logical and fundamental base for the accounting system evolution. This process is due to integration and internationalization in the economy as well as stakeholders' demands for information characterizing the organization's operation. These requirements are increasing in the era of the digital economy. Integrated reporting

Table 1. Non-financial indicators of integrated reporting

Indicator	Source
Intellectual capital	
Efficiency of research and production activities	Revenue from innovative products (services), number of ongoing innovative projects
Order backlog growth	Order backlog
Ways of carrying out scientific and technological activities	Number of registered patents and certified developments
Effectiveness of innovative project development	Patent use ratio
Efficiency of infrastructure and networking	Implementation of new information technologies
Creation of new markets	Relationship between breakthrough (creation of new markets and product categories) and enhancing (development of products available on the market) projects, %
Human capital	
Number of employees	Data of the accounting information system (AIS) reflected in accounting registers
Age and gender composition	Data of the AIS directories on the company employees
Pay system	Compensation and benefit policy
Fringe benefits	Compensation and benefit policy
Labor productivity	Estimated ratio
Staff policy	Human resource policy
Employee turnover	Estimated ratio
Staff training and development activities	Staff training policy
Union activities	Collective employment agreement
Student and youth engagement	Collective employment agreement
Occupational health and safety measures	Regulations on labor protection and occupational safety
Social and relationship capital	
Customer mix and structure	Analytical data of the AIS
Supplier mix and structure	Analytical data of the AIS
Share of major suppliers	Analytical data of the AIS
Share of large clients	Analytical data of the AIS
Stability of supply	
Revenue per client	Data of the AIS reflected in accounting registers
Profit per client	Data of the AIS reflected in accounting registers
Frequency of reference in the media	Media sources
Investments in public infrastructure	Data of the AIS reflected in accounting registers
Charitable expenses	Data of the AIS reflected in accounting registers
Natural capital	
Resource consumption volume	Data of the AIS reflected in accounting registers
Water use and water disposal. Water withdrawal and consumption volume	Data of the AIS reflected in accounting registers
Level of environmental impact (waste generation, wastewater discharge, greenhouse gas emissions, soil pollution, etc.)	Data of the AIS reflected in accounting registers
Environmental cost scale and structure	Data of the AIS reflected in accounting registers
Scale and structure of payments for a negative impact on the environment	Data of the AIS reflected in accounting registers
Fines and penalties for environmental impact in damages	Data of the AIS reflected in accounting registers
Ecological properties of goods	Environmental certification
Measures taken to protect the environment	Regulations on labor protection and natural resources

Source: Compiled by the authors based on (Lyubishina, 2022)

formation aims at the company's sustainable development, the enhancement of its relations with stakeholders, and the enhancement of the organization's efficiency and investment attractiveness.

The purpose of integrated reporting is to provide investors and creditors with detailed financial and non-financial data on the enterprise's performance and prospects so that they can rationally make economic decisions with regard to the organization. Integrated reporting might be used within the company. However, it is primarily targeted at presenting transparent, reliable, and complete information to external users.

Generation of integrated reporting gives certain advantages to a range of actors, including the following:

- Enterprises – decreased cost of capital, easier entry to the international market;
- Investors, creditors, auditors, financial analysts, and counterparts – access to transparent, reliable, comparable, and complete data on the organization's financial position, performance, risks, and prospects;
- National state bodies developing accounting standards – the basis for developing national accounting standards and their convergence with international accounting principles.

The impact and importance of integrated reporting are increasing year by year. The global long-term tendency is shaping the integrated perception of reality which implies the indivisibility of the economic, social, and environmental components of the company's operation and the connectivity and mutual influence of its capitals (IIRC, 2019).

Integrated reporting reflects all significant data on the enterprise's strategy, management system, performance, and future plans. It provides information on the economic, social, and environmental aspects of the organization's activity. Integrated reporting allows assessing the efficiency of a company's operation and gives a clear idea of how it creates and preserves its value over time (Dakhaeva, 2020).

REFERENCES

Bolvachev, A. I., Kurochkina, I. P., & Novozhilova, U. V. (2019). *Integrated reporting and its information and analytical provision*. Filigran.

Dakhaeva, F. D. (2020). Integrated company reporting – Essence and features. In Education. Culture. Society (pp. 86-88). St. Petersburg, Russia: HNRI "National Development."

Gerasimova, L. N. (2013). Integrated financial report: Advantages and the Outlook in Russia. *Audit and Financial Analysis*, *4*, 33–35.

International Integrated Reporting Council (IIRC). (2013, December). *International Integrated Reporting Framework.* Retrieved January 11, 2022, from https://integratedreporting.org/wp-content/uploads/2015/03/13-12-08-THE-INTERNATIONAL-IR-FRAMEWORK-2-1.pdf

International Integrated Reporting Council (IIRC). (2019). *Building consensus towards a global system: IIRC integrated report 2019.* Retrieved January 12, 2022, from https://integratedreporting.org/integratedreport2019/download/pdf/IIRC_Integrated_Report_2019.pdf

International Integrated Reporting Council (IIRC). (2021, January). *International Integrated Reporting Framework.* Retrieved January 11, 2022, from https://www.integratedreporting.org/wp-content/uploads/2021/01/InternationalIntegratedReportingFramework.pdf

Janshanlo, R. E., & Kogut, O. Yu. (2020). Conceptual bases of formation of integrated reporting. *Central Asian Economic Review*, *1*(130), 111–123.

Kalabikhina, I. E., Dosikov, V. S., & Voloshin, D. A. (2017). The integrated reporting – The new level of transparency of modern corporate reporting. *Market Economy Problems*, *2*, 45–50.

Kashkovskaya, M. S. (2020). Reflection of six capitals in integrated reporting. In G. Yu. Gulyaev (Ed.), *Modern Scientific Research: Topical Issues, Achievements and Innovations* (pp. 163–165). Nauka i Prosveshcheniye.

Kogdenko, V. G. (2017). *Economic analysis. Analysis of integrated reporting: A textbook.* Unity-Dana.

Kogdenko, V. G., & Melnik, M. V. (2014). Integrated reporting: Formation and analysis issues. *International Accounting*, *17*(10), 2–15.

Kuzmenko, O. A., & Abrosimova, M. C. (2014). Integrated reporting is the new reporting model for Russian corporations. *Academic Bulletin*, *1*(27), 102–113.

Luzganova, A. S., Popova, A. A., & Reshetova, A. A. (2020). Increasing business transparency through the development of corporate integrated statements. In Yu. N. Akimova, M. Ya. Kreer, N. V. Ostrovskaya, & Yu. E. Putikhin (Eds.), *Management problems in public and corporate sector of the economy* (pp. 25–29). Skifiya-Print.

Lyubishina, O. A. (2022). Integrated reporting as a tool for assessing the effectiveness of the organization. *Vectoreconomy*, *12*(30), 13.

Malinovskaya, N. V. (2020). *Integrated reporting: A textbook.* KnoRus.

Musipova, L. K. (2020). Integrated reporting: Need for composition and prospects for development. *Bulletin of Russian University of Cooperation*, *2*(40), 84–87.

Plotnikov, V. S., & Azrakuliev, Z. M. (2018). The concept of productive capital in business model accounting and integrated reporting. *International Accounting*, *21*(1), 4–16. doi:10.24891/ia.21.1.4

Popadyuk, I. F., & Tabakova, M. V. (2019). *Integrated reporting: A textbook.* St. Petersburg, Russia: SPbSUE Publishing.

Serebryakova, T. Yu. (2016). Integrated accounting and reporting: Institutional approach. *Accounting. Analysis. Auditing*, *2*, 24–33.

Suits, V. P., Horin, A. N., & Sheremet, A. D. (2020). *Comprehensive analysis and audit of integrated reporting on sustainable development companies.* INFRA-M. doi:10.12737/1072676

Tjahjadi, B., Harymawan, I., & Warsidi, N. S. (2020). Implementation of integrated reporting: A cross-countries' study. *Entrepreneurship and Sustainability Issues*, *7*(4), 2832–2850. doi:10.9770/jesi.2020.7.4(17)

Chapter 7
Corporate Governance Digitalization Trends

Sergei B. Zainullin
RUDN University, Russia

Olga A. Zainullina
Synergy University, Russia

ABSTRACT

The digitalization processes of the economy and business cannot bypass an important sphere of management – corporate governance. The coronavirus pandemic has spurred the transition of corporate procedures to the digital environment. Almost all corporate events of the boards of directors and general meetings of shareholders have moved to a remote or online format. Public online platforms and proprietary electronic platforms are actively used for corporate events of shareholders, board of directors and management board, inspectors, and auditors. Simultaneously, the introduction of corporate procedures and communication into the digital environment brings advantages associated with saving time, money on business trips, higher efficiency of events, and the convenience of fixing decisions. Assessing the opportunities and threats of digitalization trends makes it necessary to balance the combination of digital and non-digital approaches to corporate governance procedures.

INTRODUCTION

The paper aims to find out how the methods of corporate governance are changing now together with regulation in Russia and abroad. On the one hand, this analysis will enable corporations to assess the potential threats to their security from the

DOI: 10.4018/978-1-6684-4265-4.ch007

regulator, which may impose significant penalties for violations in the corporate information disclosure, corporate reporting, and stock exchanges, which may carry out the procedure for removing the company's shares and bonds from trading. On the other hand, following new trends in corporate governance is a powerful PR tool that increases the loyalty of internal and external stakeholders – from investors to customers and consumers.

Simultaneously, digitalization can be find out as the most actively developing trend, both as an independent trend and as a trend accompanying trends towards achieving sustainable development goals, ESG investment, and increasing the transparency of information disclosure.

METHODOLOGICAL FRAMEWORK

The active introduction of digital technologies in corporate governance began in 2014.

The recommendation of the Corporate Governance Code indicates the following areas of digitalization.

In the field of exercising the rights of shareholders Central Bank of the Russian Federation (2014): "29. Companies with a large number of shareholders are recommended to use telecommunication means to provide shareholders with remote access to the general meeting (e.g., broadcast the general meeting of shareholders on the company's website on the Internet, use video conferencing).

In the field of activity of the Board of Directors: "160. It is also recommended to provide members of the board of directors who are absent at the meeting venue with the opportunity to participate in the discussion of agenda items and voting remotely – via conference and video conferencing."

According to paragraph 4 of Guidelines for organizing the work of the Board of Directors in a joint-stock company, approved in 2013 by the Rosimushestvo, the meetings of the Board of Directors held in the teleconferencing mode, when using telephone and other communications, are meetings held in person (Federal Agency for State Property Management, 2013).

Thus, we can conclude that the Russian regulations that establish corporate governance standards for state-owned companies and joint-stock companies equate teleconferences as a type of joint attendance at in-person events of the Board of Directors recommended the widespread use of them in corporate practice. The same situation for General Meetings of Shareholders too.

The reasons for this recommendation are apparent:

- Greater coverage of participants in a corporate event;

- Reduction of costs for participation in a corporate event, especially for minority shareholders who are not covered for the costs of travel, accommodation, and loss of working time;
- Consequently, the practice of introducing electronic means of communication contributed to a better implementation of the rights of shareholders.

Digitalization in corporate governance contributes to implementing the following corporate governance principles defined by the Russian Corporate Governance Code.

1.1. The corporation needs to establish an equal and fair treatment of all shareholders so that shareholders can exercise the right to manage the company:

 1.1.1. Corporations need to make sure that the shareholders have the most favorable opportunities to participate in the general meeting, to express their opinion on issues.

  1.1.5. Each shareholder of a corporation, regardless of how many shares he has, has the right to vote in the most simple and convenient way.

  1.1.6. In a corporation, there should be such a voting procedure that all shareholders at the meeting can express their opinion and ask questions.

1.3. Corporate governance needs to create a level playing field for all shareholders including small shareholders and foreign shareholders.

2.7. The board of directors must ensure the efficient operation of the board of directors..

The Bank of Russia presented its plans in the "Overview of corporate governance practices in Russian public companies in 2020" published at the end of 2021 (Central Bank of the Russian Federation. (2021a).

According to the plans announced by the Bank of Russia, in 2020–2021, work to implement measures aimed at improving corporate governance was carried out in accordance with the "Main Directions for the Development of the Financial Market of the Russian Federation for the period 2019–2021" and the action plan "Transformation of the business climate" (direction "Improving corporate governance"), approved by order of the Government of the Russian Federation No. 1723-r (July 2, 2020) (Government of the Russian Federation, 2020).

According to the activities aimed at preventing the spread of COVID-19, Federal Law No. 17-FZ was adopted, which determines the possibility of holding general meetings (annual) of shareholders in 2021 in absentia (Russian Federation, 2021).

Many corporations have become holding general shareholder meetings via videoconferencing

To make better disclosure by public joint-stock companies of non-financial, the Bank of Russia has developed recommendations aimed at defining uniform approaches to the disclosure of non-financial information on the accounting by public joint-stock companies of ESG factors and related risks and opportunities, as well as information on the impact of public joint-stock companies on the outside world - the environment (including climate), the social sphere and the economy Central Bank of the Russian Federation. (2021b).:

Principle II. Shareholder rights, equal treatment of all shareholders, and key ownership functions.

This Principle contains the following clarifications from the OECD (2015).

A. Key shareholder rights should include the right to:

4) voting at general meetings of shareholders.

C. Shareholders should be given the right to participate and vote at general meetings

Shareholders need to receive all information about the regulations

General Meetings of Shareholders:

2) The processes and procedures of general meetings of shareholders must respect equal rights

all shareholders. Voting procedures should not create difficulties or increase the cost of voting.

5) Shareholders must be able to vote directly in person or without personal presence, and votes cast in person and without personal presence must have equal force.

6) Barriers to cross-border voting need to be removed.

The implementation of digital technologies in voting procedures makes participation in them easier and cheaper and equalizes the opportunity for all shareholders to vote in corporate procedures, including those shareholders who are outside the voting region or even abroad.

International initiatives are represented by several overviews.

The OECD has published a report on The Future of Corporate Governance in Capital Markets after the COVID-19 crisis, which provides an overview of the measures taken by G20 governments in response to the COVID-19 pandemic, as well as an overview of changes in national legislation on associated with the COVID-19 pandemic (OECD, 2021).

The Global Reporting Initiative (GRI) (GRI overview of global ESG disclosure trends(2020)) has released the fifth edition of its overview of global ESG disclosure trends covering 84 countries and 614 sustainability reporting requirements, updated three sustainability reporting standards (tax, health and safety, water and wastewater), as well as guidance on disclosure of information in relation to the UN Sustainable Development Goals in accordance with the provisions enshrined in the GRI standards..

Guidance of the Sustainable Development Goals to the GRI standards has been introduced to make it even easier for organizations to report their efforts in support of the UN Sustainable Development Goals (SDGs) using the most widely used sustainability reporting standards – the GRI Standards.

A new version of the document Linking the SDGs and GRI Standards has been published. This resource provides a breakdown of the targets for each of the 17 SDGs and shows how they correlate with the disclosures in the GRI Standards, including the latest published versions.

The communication document complements broader GRI support to help companies communicate their impact on sustainability. These include a toolkit for integrating SDGs into reporting and examples of SDG reporting from different countries.

"The GRI standards allow companies to integrate SDG reporting into their sustainability reports, and this revised guidance helps them make those links clearly and consistently.

The SDGs address the most pressing sustainability issues in our world. Thus, it is critical that the contributions of the private sector be recognized and understood. That is why GRI continues to work with partners and reporting entities to ensure the transparency needed to support the real trends of the SDGs."

GRI standards also require the disclosure of reports in digital form.

The four-year SDG Reporting Action Platform, led by GRI and the UN Global Compact, has successfully engaged companies and strengthened their capacity. GRI then launches the Business Leaders Forum to bring companies and key stakeholders together to use the power of corporate reporting to drive action towards the SDGs.

Target 6 of SDG-12 requires all countries to encourage companies to adopt sustainable business practices and include sustainability data in their corporate reporting.

DISCUSSION

Many researchers note the problems associated with the digitalization of corporate procedures.

In particular, I. V. Romanova and T. M. Lavrik note the need for additional regulatory regulation of corporate procedures by the state (Romanova & Lavrik, 2021).

Y. N. Moseykin and his co-authors note that "the openness of information systems is a weakness, as it increases the risk of leakage of innovative knowledge and developments, and is also a 'target for their own or targeted acquisition' (about 80%

of attackers are full-time employees of large companies)" (Moseykin, Semenovich & Chernyaev, 2020).

P. A. Levchaev and B. Khezazna note that today's management technologies in all areas are becoming digital, which increases management efficiency (Levchaev & Khezazna, 2021).

Simultaneously, the main problems are the possibility of information leakage, issues of identification of participants in corporate procedures and events.

L. B. Boldareva notes that one of the general goals of digitalization and "digital government" is to optimize communications, information exchange, and reporting between corporations and authorities (Boldareva, 2020).

I. V. Romanova and T. M. Lavrik also noted that the charters of corporations provide for the tools of using digital technologies during general meetings of shareholders, and also, in connection with their use, increase the share of local meetings in relation to absentee ones (Romanova & Lavrik, 2021).

From the position of the Bank of Russia, and the Federal Agency for State Property Management, holding general meetings of shareholders and meetings of directors locally is the best practice because it allows participants to participate in the discussion of agenda items actively, openly express opinions, and ask necessary questions.

RESULTS

The following innovations were established in Russia (Table 1):

In Russia, the disclosure of non-financial reporting and information about beneficial owners is implemented in practice in the form of electronic documents posted on companies' official websites.

Regarding the USA, 19 innovations have been established. We consider the following key innovations (Table 2):

In the USA, the disclosure of non-financial reporting, ESG reporting, the internal regulations and policies of companies are used in the form of electronic documents posted on the official resources of companies.

With regard to Germany, ten innovations have been established. We consider the following key innovations (Table 3):

In Germany, the disclosure of non-financial reporting on the goals of the SDGs and CSR is implemented in the form of electronic documents posted on the official internet resources of companies.

In Japan, 19 innovations were established. We consider the following key innovations (Table 4):

Table 1. Innovations in corporate governance in Russia

No.	Type of innovation	Mandatory/Voluntary	Content
1	Draft Federal Law on Public Non-Financial Reporting	Mandatory	The obligation to disclose non-financial reporting has been established, covering: • For state corporations; • For state-owned companies; • For public companies; • For state unitary enterprises with a turnover/value of assets over RUB 10 billion • For business entities with a turnover/ value of assets over 10 billion rubles • For business companies that are in the lists of stock exchanges.
2	Regulations of Bank of Russia "On the disclosure of information by issuers of securities" (Dec. 30, 2014 No. 454-P)	Mandatory	In general, entities are required to disclose the following information: • Information about the issue (additional issue) of securities; • Information presented in the form of a securities prospectus; • Financial statements and consolidated ones of the issuer; • Companies Quarterly reports; • Information about material facts of the companys activity; • Other information about the fulfillment by the issuer of its obligations and the exercise of rights under the placed securities (placed securities).
3	Federal Law "On amending the law on combating the legalization of proceeds from crime and the Code of Administrative Offenses of the Russian Federation" (No. 215-FZ)	Mandatory	All Russian joint-stock companies and LLC are required to collect and annually update information on their beneficial owners and store this information.
	Decree of the Government of the Russian Federation No. 03-849 / r	Mandatory	Amendments are being made to Decree of the Federal Commission for the Securities Market 03-849/r of 2003 on the presentation of information in annual compliance reports on compliance with the Corporate Governance Code.
	Directive of the Government of the Russian Federation 1710-13	Mandatory	It requires government representatives on the boards of directors of Russia's 22 largest state-owned companies to consider regular publication of non-financial reports, including disclosures on sustainability and environmental responsibility, at board meetings.

Prepared by authors based on the Overview of Global ESG Disclosure Trends

Table 2. Innovations in US corporate governance

No.	Type of innovation	Mandatory/Voluntary	Content
1	SEC Regulation S-K Amendment: Wage Ratio Disclosure Rule	Mandatory	The rule requires SEC to disclose to their trustees the median annual total compensation of all employees (other than the CEO) and the ratio of the median to the annual total CEO compensation.
2	Charitable Corporation Legislation	Mandatory	This state legislation permits the formation of charitable corporations. A charitable corporation is a traditional corporation with modified commitments to higher standards of purpose, accountability, and transparency. Charitable corporations (1) have a corporate goal of making a material positive impact on society and the environment The law has been passed in 31 states and introduced in at least seven states.
3	NASDAQ ESG 2.0 Reporting Guide – A Companion Resource for Companies	Voluntary	The guidance highlights the importance of ESG reporting as beneficial to individual companies and investors while emphasizing the need to consider the impact on bottom-line results and improve/harmonize management practices. The guidance is based on the SSE model guide, but includes 30 ESG metrics to track and disclose company performance on ESG issues. GRI is referenced in all metrics as a source/ reference that companies can refer to for more information on ESG disclosures.
4	NYSE Corporate Governance Rules Section 3 Corporate Responsibility	Mandatory	The rules require that corporations must adapt a code of business conduct and ethics for directors, and other officers.
5	Securities and Exchange Commission Guidelines for Climate Change Disclosures	Mandatory	The guidance highlights the following areas as examples of where climate change may lead to disclosuress.
6	ESG Disclosure Facilitation Act of 2021	Mandatory	Subsection 2(a) of this bill amends section 14 of the Securities Exchange Act of 1934 by adding a new subsection (k). The new subsection (k) will require issuers who hold registered securities or who file annual returns to disclose in any powers of attorney or AGM consent materials: a clear description of the ESG relationship; indicators and long-term business strategy of the issuer; and a description of any process the issuer uses to find out the impact of these ESG metrics on its long-term business strategy.

Prepared by authors based on the Overview of Global ESG Disclosure Trends

Table 3. Innovations in corporate governance in Germany

No.	Type of innovation	Mandatory/ Voluntary	Content
1	National Strategy for CSR (Action Plan) – of the German Federal Government	Voluntary	The goal of the Action Plan is to strengthen the CSR of enterprises and government bodies and to attract even more small and SMEs to CSR. The strategy also envisages that individual federal ministries, acting as models and pacemakers in the Sphere of SCR, will issue CSR reports that are in line with international reporting systems and principles such as GRI and UNGC.
2	Deutsche Börse AG Best Practice Guide for Sustainability Reporting	Voluntary	The CSR Action Plan is based on the positions of the National CSR Forum, which advises and assists the German government on its policies to promote corporate social responsibility. The recommendations have been drafted in collaboration with representatives of prominent issuers and investors from the Issuer Markets Advisory Committee (IMAC), Deutsche Börse AG's capital markets advisory committee. They are also supported by biggest corporations and Asset Management (German Association for Financial Analysis and Asset Management, DVFA
3	National Action Plan for the Implementation of the UN Guiding Principles on Business and Human Rights	Voluntary	The Action Plan is intended to launch the process of creating a roadmap for the practical execution of the Guiding Principles. It includes procedures for investigating human rights violations, measures and mechanisms to verify compliance with human rights standards, transparent reporting, and a complaint procedure.
4	Transposition of the EU directive: Act implementing the CSR directive	Mandatory	The draft emphasizes the need for corporationss to be judged on more than just financial information, making information on social, environmental, and human rights mandatory issues for establishing communication channels with their internal and external stakeholders.
5	Supply Chain Corporate Due Diligence Act	Mandatory	The company's due diligence obligations under the Supply Chain Law include analyzing human rights risks, taking steps to prevent and mitigate human rights violations, and establishing complaint mechanisms. Additionally, companies will be required to report on their due diligence activities. As a first step, the Law will apply and establish due diligence obligations for companies with more than 3000 employees, including employees posted abroad. The law also applies to German subsidiaries of foreign companies. From January 1, 2024, companies employing more than 1000 people will have to comply with new obligations.

Prepared by authors based on the Overview of Global ESG Disclosure Trends

The disclosure of non-financial reporting in Japan – on the conditions of the SDGs, climate, ESG indicators, and CSR – is used in the form of electronic documents

Table 4. Innovations in corporate governance in Japan

No.	Type of innovation	Mandatory/ Voluntary	Content
1	Principles of financial action towards a sustainable society	Voluntary	It sets a specific standard that financial institutions must follow according to human rights. ."
2	Principles for Responsible Institutional Investors	Voluntary	This guidance sets out principles that are considered beneficial to institutional investors who conduct themselves as responsible institutional investors in carrying out their management responsibilities with due regard to their clients, beneficiaries, and the investor companies. "Management Responsibilities" refers to the responsibilities of institutional investors to enhance the medium- and long-term investment returns for their clients and beneficiaries (including ultimate beneficiaries; the same applies hereinafter) by improving and driving the corporate value and sustainability of the investee companies, growth through constructive interaction or focused dialogue based on deep knowledge of companies and their business environment.
3	Japanese Corporate Governance Code for Sustainable Corporate Growth and Enhancement of Corporate Value in the Medium to Long Term (Draft Revised)	Voluntary	It states that companies must go beyond what is required of them in disclosure rules, including non-financial information such as business strategies and business matters, risk, and governance. Japan's Corporate Governance Code (2021) requires companies listed on the TSE Prime Market (Tokyo Stock Exchange) to make advisory disclosures. There is no single ESG reporting structure mandated for companies not registered there, although corporations are required to disclose their sustainability initiatives.
4	Upcoming Mandatory Climate Disclosures	Mandatory	"The Japan Financial Services Agency (FSA) has announced that it intends to make climate disclosure mandatory for major Japanese companies with the recommendations TCF) first."
5	Guidance on Comprehensive Corporate Disclosure and Dialogues between Companies and Investors to Co-Create Value	Mandatory	The guide provides a basic structure consisting of the following points. The guiding principles described in each paragraph should be used by corporations in accordance with their strategies and goals. 1. Value (which gives companies the basic principles for deciding their future directions and strategies, such as corporate philosophy and vision); 2. Business models (structures in which companies can deliver value to customers and society through their business and drive results towards sustainable corporate growth); 3. Sustainability/growth (material elements to ensure the sustainability of business models and maintain the growth potential of companies, such as ESG factors and potential risks); 4. Strategies (retaining and investing in management resources, intangible assets, etc. that maintain the competitive advantages of companies and optimize their business portfolio); 5. Performance and KPIs (Key Performance Indicators) (financial and non-financial KPIs to assess the financial performance of companies and achieve their strategies); 6. Management

Prepared by authors based on the Overview of Global ESG Disclosure Trends

posted on the official internet resources of companies.

An important factor influencing the digitalization of corporate procedures was the COVID-19 pandemic and its associated restrictions:

- Quarantines;
- Lockdowns;
- A ban on mass events;
- Mandatory remote work mode;
- Other sanitary restrictions.

The above measures significantly hampered the face-to-face format of holding corporate events, and changes in the legislation even made it possible to postpone the maximum dates for holding annual shareholders meetings in 2020 from June 30 to September 30 because the period of the lockdown.

In practice, in 2020–2021, most meetings of the Board of Directors were held; only one of them was held in-person offline format during the period of local weakening of anti-epidemic measures, and it was caused by the election of a state representative to the Board of Directors of the company with state participation and a desire to get to know the company and its management better.

The rest of the face-to-face meetings were held in the format of video conferences via Zoom, Teams, and similar platforms.

The advantages of video conferencing systems for corporate events are that they allow:

- Identifying the participant by face;
- Identifying the participant by identity documents;
- Conducting automatic registration of participants;
- Conducting automatic video recording of the event;
- Exchanging messages, documents, and draft decisions among the participants.

The next direction of digitalization in corporate governance can be called the creation of a fully digital environment in corporate governance.

As best practices, we can consider the introduction of a digital environment in corporate governance for corporations with state participation by the Federal Agency for State Property Management, which acts as a shareholder in state-owned companies.

A special type of corporate governance in Russia is the management of companies with state participation.

The principles of Corporate Governance in the Public Sector are as follows Federal Agency for State Property Management (n.d.):

1. Openness.

   a. Development of a methodological framework and consulting support for companies; Interaction with professional communities.
2. Transparency.
   a. Formation of the composition of by the Commissions for the selection of professional directors and independent experts? CEO;
      i. Improving communication tools between the Federal Agency for State Property Management, state-owned companies, and other participants. Interaction system of the Federal Agency for State Property Management (n.d.) through OpenCorp; Interaction through The Interdepartmental Portal
3. Predictability.
   a. Improving the corporate governance of governmental joint-stock companies with unified methodological recommendations
      i. Carrying out a unified strategy and dividend policy in governmental companies. Strategic planning in state-owned companies (approval of strategies, long-term development programs (LDP), systems of KPIs, etc.)

State interests are represented immediately by two authorities: Federal Agency for State Property Management. (acting as a shareholder at general meetings of shareholders) and authority, which is the supervising agency (making key decisions under the Directives of the governmental).

The digital implementation of these principles is the Interdepartmental Portal of the Federal Agency for State Property Management.

The Interdepartmental Portal Federal Agency for State Property Management (n.d.) is a single information space for all members in the processes of state government.

Participants of the Interdepartmental Portal of the Federal Agency for State Property Management (n.d.): are:

Federal Agency for State Property Management:, its employees;

- Supervising federal executive authority, its employees;
- Company, by creating a personal account (LC);
- Employees who have access to its personal account;
- CEO of the Company, through its own personal account;
- Members of the Board of Directors, through their own personal account;
- Members of the Audit Commission of the Company, through their own personal account;
- Candidates for the position of CEO, the Board of Directors, e Audit Commission through their own cabinet;

The level of access is different, the lowest level of access is given to candidates who have access to the main information of the company, its reporting, the maximum level is given to the General Director through the Personal Account of the company, members of the Board of Directors and the RC, who have access to reporting and corporate procedures. Employees of the Federal Agency for State Property Management (n.d.) also have full access.

In addition to the multi-level access system, data is protected by two-factor authorization through a login/password and through an EDS issued by an accredited certification center.

The following actions are available through the Interdepartmental Portal of the Federal Agency for State Property Management (n.d.):

- To get the information;
- To form the Board of Directors, the Audit Commission, and CEO;
- To submit applications for members of the Board ;
- To participate in corporate events of the Board, the Audit Commission, and General Meetings of Shareholders, initiate, distribute materials, conduct voting, and draw up minutes;
- To form reports of the company, members of the Board of Directors, the Audit Commission to the shareholders.

The procedures carried out are carried out through the Interdepartmental Portal, with the exception of the in-person meeting of the Qualification Selection Commission, which is attended by the heads of the Federal Agency for State Property Management, which oversees the federal executive authorities and representatives of professional associations.

There are three types of members of the Board of Directors elected to the Board of Directors of companies with state participation.

Classification of members of the Board of Directors is as follows:

- A civil officer (an employee of the supervising federal executive authority or the Federal Agency for State Property Management) who is obliged to vote in accordance with the directives of the Federal Agency for State Property Management, combines membership in the Board of Directors with public service and is not entitled to receive any remuneration from the company.
- A professional attorney who has entered into an agreement with the Federal Agency for State Property Management is obliged to vote in accordance with the directives of Federal Agency for State Property Management, combines membership in the Board of Directors with other activities, and is entitled to receive remuneration from the company.

- An independent director who has entered into an agreement with the Federal Agency for State Property Management is not required to vote in accordance with the directives of the Federal Agency for State Property Management, combines membership in the Board with other activities, and is entitled to receive remuneration from the company.

CONCLUSION

The study showed that the main trends of modern corporate governance regulation in countries such as the USA, Germany, Japan, Russia, despite local differences, generally have common directions. These areas are implementation of the UN Sustainable Development Goals, implementation of the ESG principles, environmental agenda, social responsibility of business, increased transparency of corporate governance, and public disclosure of non-financial reporting.

Analyzing the use of digital technologies in corporate governance in Russia, we can conclude that despite the potential threats from the use of digital technologies associated with unauthorized access to corporate governance systems, information leakage, in general, digital technologies are a positive aspect of the development of management technologies.

Digital technologies simplify and reduce the cost of access to corporate procedures, reflected in both Russian and international standards – the exercise of shareholder rights.

They also contribute to the more active participation of members of the Board of Directors and the Audit Commission in corporate procedures, which contributes to make better the quality of management.

ACKNOWLEDGMENT

The publication was made with the support of the RUDN University Strategic Academic Leadership Program and Synergy University.

REFERENCES

Boldareva, L. B. (2020). Communication between government and business entities and challenges of creation of "digital government.". *Event Management*, *3*(1), 75–85. doi:10.26425/2658-3445-2020-1-75-85

Central Bank of the Russian Federation. (2014). Information letter "On the Corporate Governance Code" (April 10, 2014 No. 06-52/2463). Bank of Russia.

Central Bank of the Russian Federation. (2021a). *Review of corporate governance practices in Russian public companies based on the results of 2020.* Moscow, Russia: Bank of Russia. Retrieved January 12, 2021, from https://cbr.ru/Collection/Collection/File/39590/Review_corp_3011021.pdf

Central Bank of the Russian Federation. (2021b). Information letter "On recommendations for disclosing non-financial information by public joint-stock companies related to the activities of such companies" (July 12, 2021 No. IN-06-28/49). Bank of Russia.

Federal Agency for State Property Management. (2013). *Guidelines for organizing the work of the Board of directors in a Joint-Stock Company*. Author.

Federal Agency for State Property Management. (n.d.). *Interdepartmental portal for state property management.* Retrieved February 18, 2022, from https://mp.rosim.ru/web/guest/portal

Government of the Russian Federation. (2020). Action plan "Transformation of the business climate" (direction "Improvement of corporate governance") (approved by the order No. 1723-r of July 2, 2020). Author.

GRI overview of global ESG disclosure trends. (2020). *Sustainability reporting instruments worldwide*. https://www.carrotsandsticks.net/

Levchaev, P. A., & Khezazna, B. (2021). Features of the strategic activities of corporations in the digital economy. *Finance and Management, 1*, 12-60. doi:10.25136/2409-7802.2021.1.30823

Moseykin, Yu. N., Semenovich, V. S., & Chernyaev, M. V. (2020). *National economy: Textbook*. RUDN University.

OECD. (2015). *G20/OECD Corporate governance principles.* Paris, France: OECD Publishing. doi:10.1787/9789264236882-en

OECD. (2021). *The future of corporate governance in capital markets after the COVID-19 crisis: Report.* Paris, France: OECD Publishing. doi:10.1787/efb2013c-en

Romanova, I. V., & Lavrik, T. M. (2021). Application of digital technologies in the sphere of corporate relations. *Law: History and Modernity, 2*(15), 137-142. doi:10.17277/pravo.2021.02

Russian Federation. (2021). Federal Law "On amendments to the Federal law 'On international companies and international funds' and on the suspension of certain provisions of the Federal law 'On joint-stock companies" and the Federal law 'On limited liability companies'" (February 24, 2021 No. 17-FZ). Author.

Chapter 8
Investment Attractiveness of "Young" Companies in the Context of Global Changes Associated With the New Industrial Revolution

Ekaterina Yu. Voronova
MGIMO University, Russia

Yulia A. Lukina
MGIMO University, Russia

ABSTRACT

Many factors act as criteria for assessing investment attractiveness, including the digitalization of business processes within companies and the introduction of innovative technologies to optimize the activities of an enterprise. The research purpose is to assess the volume of investments attracted by "young" companies through the use of advanced digital and information technologies, as well as to determine an integrated approach to activities aimed at developing the digitalization of the leading sectors of the economy. The theoretical basis of the research is the work of experts studying the impact of digitalization on attracting investment in the face of global economic uncertainty. The methodological basis of the study consists of the methods of statistical analysis of expert evaluation. As a result of the study, the authors have revealed the beneficial effect of digital technologies on the volume of attracted funding sources.

DOI: 10.4018/978-1-6684-4265-4.ch008

INTRODUCTION

At each stage of its formation, humanity is developing at an ever-increasing pace. Nowadays, the global community is already on the threshold of a new industrial revolution (Industry 4.0). The changes associated with society's transition to a new stage of development are global in nature and are reflected in all areas, from everyday life to the global economy.

Many companies are already actively using new technologies to optimize business processes, which, in turn, affects the investment attractiveness of these companies. The most important trend of Industry 4.0 in the context of business processes is the development of technology platforms based on which supply and demand are combined. This approach is somewhat revolutionary and breaks down the idea of the existing structure in the economy. In today's reality, the idea of what is more valuable to the business is changing the platform for transactions or the underlying asset. Nowadays, the world's largest corporations (e.g., Facebook, Uber, Airbnb, and Amazon) are not the primary owners of the benefits they offer. For example, Uber does not own vehicles but operates thousands of transportation services, and Amazon is not a publisher but sells thousands of books daily. Thus, the activities of the largest companies are reduced to providing a virtual space in which the buyer and seller function and supply and demand meet.

A characteristic feature of companies that earn through the creation of virtual platforms is the scalability of their activities; that is, the activities of companies are not limited by production capacity or the time factor. Many offers can be placed on virtual platforms that operate 24/7. This feature of today's companies is reflected in the primary market trends. Thus, the average "life expectancy" of companies included in the S&P 500 rating for the period of the existence of the index has decreased significantly. In the 1920s, the figure reached 60 years; in 1965, the average age of companies decreased to 32 years; in 2020, the value was just over 21 years (Statista, 2021). There is a clear downward trend in the life expectancy of companies used to calculate the US stock index S&P 500; according to analysts, the indicator will continue to decline in the 2020s (Statista, 2021). Companies started to grow and multiply their capital much faster; it took Facebook six years to reach annual revenues of one billion dollars, while Google – only five years.

Considering the rapid development of "young" companies, this research will focus on such companies. A kind of indicator of the company's maturity is its entry into the stock market when it becomes an object of close attention of investors, and each of its actions can lead to the rise or fall of the shares. Thus, "young" companies are companies that launched their IPOs during the COVID-19 pandemic under global economic uncertainty. At the initial public offering stage, companies try to present themselves to potential investors in the most advantageous way. It is noteworthy that in their presentations to investors, companies pay special attention to advanced technologies used in business processes. In other words, company executives believe that leveraging Industry 4.0 megatrends can increase the investment appeal of their stock.

Thus, rapidly developing technology is reflected in economic processes. The use of high technology increases the company's efficiency and positively affects its reputation.

METHODOLOGY

Industry 4.0 involves the digitalization and integration of technological, manufacturing, and business processes vertically across the enterprise, from product development and procurement to production, logistics, and service in operation. Nowadays, information technology is actively implemented in companies. In other words, the transition to a new technological revolution can already be considered quite real. Thus, given the urgent nature of the Industry 4.0 phenomenon, a study of the impact of information technology on companies' operations is extremely relevant.

The research aims to identify the interdependence between the factor of investment attractiveness and the company's technological development. The research should assess whether "young" companies using Industry 4.0 megatrends for optimizing their operations are more interesting and, therefore, attract more investment than companies that neglect cutting-edge technologies. Additionally, the authors define a comprehensive approach of measures to develop the digitalization of the leading sectors of the economy.

In accordance with the research goal, the authors have formulated the following objectives. First, Industry 4.0 is no longer something distant and ghostly; we already see certain changes that inevitably affect our lives. At this stage, it would be critical to assess the role of Industry 4.0 and its megatrends for leading companies and the economy as a whole. Second, since the research object is "young" companies that have just entered the stock market during the COVID-19 pandemic, it would be useful to consider how actively these companies use the information and digital technology and how this affects the course of their IPO. Third, it is necessary to formulate what trends will prevail in the current decade, what technologies of the future are currently implemented in companies, and how this will affect their productivity. Fourth, the research would be useful to highlight a set of measures aimed at the further development and implementation of technology in individual companies and individual sectors of the economy.

The research is based on the scientific works of Russian and foreign scientists who study the impact of information and digital technologies of Industry 4.0 on the investment attractiveness of companies. The methodological basis of the research consists of the methods of comparative analysis, comparison of dynamic series, and the method of expert evaluation. During the research, the authors used the official statistics of stock exchanges and data presented in the statements of companies and their official websites.

The conducted research is of scientific novelty because most experts assess the impact of Industry 4.0 on certain sectors of the economy, and the use of digitalization elements is regarded as a factor that increases the investment attractiveness of the industry. Fewer researchers looked at the role of information and digital technology in the context of companies, and only in this paper, the research object was just companies but a narrow group of companies that conducted IPOs in the context of adverse real economy dynamics and global economic uncertainty.

RESULTS

The fourth industrial revolution is a natural stage in the development of human society. In the 19th century, the transition to the first industrial revolution, Industry 1.0, was marked by the creation of the steam engine and machine production, which greatly expanded human production capabilities at that stage of development and set the stage for subsequent technological advances (Machkour & Abriane, 2020). The second industrial revolution was triggered by the creation and use of the electric motor at the end of the 19th century, which enabled the transition to mass production in the 20th century. At the stage of the third industrial revolution, the automation of production and the introduction of information technology ensured the further development of society. The most important elements of Industry 3.0 were computers, software, telecommunications, fiber optics, and information services. The processes of calculation automation and the development of cybernetic systems allowed creating digital information processing.

Nowadays, in the realities of the 21st century, developed countries are already on the threshold of the fourth industrial revolution, which implies the introduction of full penetration of the Internet and artificial intelligence at all stages of economic processes (Machkour & Abriane, 2020). In other words, Industry 4.0 involves the transition to the digital economy of all nations, which will change the entire world, not just the most developed countries. A key difference in Industry 4.0 will be its ubiquity, with elements of the digital economy expected to spread across the globe, accompanied by increasing levels of education and scientific development. Thus, throughout human history, the transition to the new industrial revolution has been associated with changes in production and the economy. At the present stage, Industry 4.0 will significantly impact the economy; the digital economy will be the most significant product of the fourth industrial revolution. Digitalization of the economy implies not only the introduction of technologies capable of processing big data but also changing existing business models for online users.

Industry 4.0 megatrends include artificial intelligence (AI), robotics, big data, Internet of Things (IoT), 3D printing, nanotechnology, biotechnology, quantum computing, and energy storage. Artificial intelligence (AI) is foremost among all the above megatrends. AI can be considered the quintessence of the fourth industrial revolution. Nowadays, many companies use some elements of Industry 4.0 in their activities. During the work, the authors will consider megatrends that are most widely used by "young" companies that have entered the stock market.

In recent years, despite the unfavorable situation in the real economy (Mazumder & Saha, 2021), the stock market has shown very positive dynamics, as evidenced by the active growth of stock indices, including DJI, S&P 500, NASDAQ, and others. The Dow Jones Industrial Average (DJIA) fell 6400 points in just four trading days (Mazur et al., 2021). However, already in April, stock indices began to grow actively and maintained a positive trend for a long time; in February 2022, there was a certain decrease in indices against the background of political instability.

The growth of stock markets can be explained by the attempts of governments represented by the Central Banks to keep the economy from serious collapses during the COVID-19 pandemic. As part of the stimulative economic policy, key interest rates have been reduced to zero or have taken a negative value at all. The governments of many developed countries launched large-scale quantitative easing programs and actively engaged in purchasing assets. In this regard, investors who had free money started to look for higher-yielding instruments on stock exchanges against the background of falling rates on bank deposits.

Against the background of the expanding stock market, the management of many companies regarded the period of the global pandemic as the best time for an IPO. Figure 1 shows the dynamics of the global IPO market from 2000 to 2021. the number of IPOs held in 2021 is a record for the analyzed period (Go, 2021). The period from 2008 to 2009, when the global financial crisis broke out, was the least successful in the context of IPO. Notably, the crisis caused by the COVID-19 pandemic has had exactly the opposite effect on the stock market because of the policies of maintaining the economy in crisis by the countries (Kumar & Kumara, 2021; Smales, 2021). It should be noted that not all scholars consider the impact of the COVID-19 pandemic on the IPO market in a positive way, guided by the indicator of information uncertainty (Bai & Chen, 2021).

The number of companies that had IPOs during the COVID-19 pandemic is extremely high. The most large-scale and high-profile IPOs of the period of global economic uncertainty are those presented in Table 1. The table shows nine companies that conducted an IPO from 2020 to 2021; the companies are very different from each

Figure 1. Dynamics of the global IPO market in the period from 2000 to 2021
Source: Compiled by the authors based on (Levy, 2020)

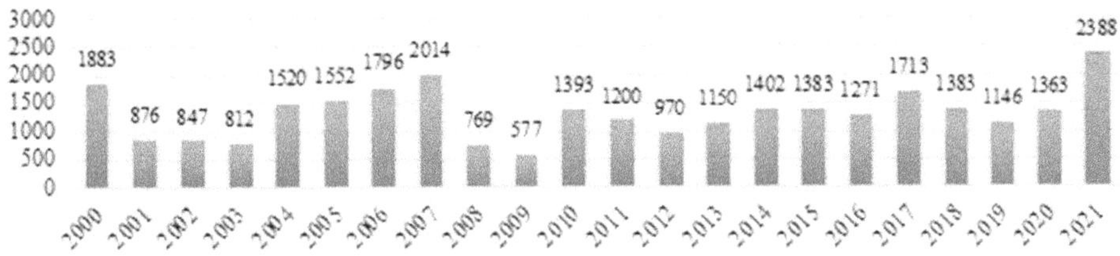

other in terms of scope of activity. The most popular were placements of American companies. However, there was also interest in placements of Coupang Inc. from South Korea, Didi Global Inc. from China, and Ozon and Fix Price from Russia.

At the marketing stage, in the context of the initial public offering, the company develops a presentation of its business, which displays the main advantages of the business model. In today's realities, company management at the Road Show stage focuses on key performance indicators, profitability, solvency, and other aspects that are not directly related to financial potential. Thus, investors increasingly consider the ESG rating when choosing investment objects or consider the company's image and the specifics of its activities. For example, fewer investors are interested in tobacco companies.

Another aspect of companies that attracts the attention of investors is their technological potential and the implementation of advanced information and digital technologies in business processes. Table 2 shows the main megatrends of the fourth industrial revolution used by "young" companies. It is noteworthy that among the companies that have attracted great interest in the stock market, only one company is engaged in the production of goods; the rest are mainly platforms providing services online, which once again emphasizes that in today's environment, it is more valuable to own a platform than an underlying asset.

Airbnb allows renting an apartment anywhere in the world. It actively introduces information technology. Thus, the company uses the technology of artificial intelligence. Using artificial intelligence technology, the company analyzes tenants' social networks for signs of mental illness, including narcissism, Machiavellianism, and psychopathy. Thus, the company can assess the risks of each booking. Currently, it is difficult to judge how effective the system is. Nevertheless, according to the company's management, the introduction of such technology will help save landlords' property. Additionally, in the IPO prospectus, the company states that its future development will involve the introduction of blockchain and augmented reality technologies and continue to use artificial intelligence. Nevertheless, company

Table 1. Companies that conducted IPO during the global economic uncertainty caused by the COVID-19 pandemic

Company	Country	Date of IPO	Exchange	Offering price	Volume of attracted funds
Airbnb	USA	December 9, 2020	NASDAQ	$68	$3.7 bln.
Coupang Inc.	South Korea	March 11, 2021	NYSE	$35	$4.6 bln.
Didi Global Inc.	China	June 30, 2021	NYSE	$14	$4.4 bln.
DoorDash	USA	December 8, 2020	NYSE	$102	$3.4 bln.
Fix Price	Russia	March 10, 2020	London Stock Exchange, MOEX	$9.75	$1.74 bln.
Ozon	Russia	November 24, 2020	NASDAQ	$30 (2277 rubles as of the placement date)	$990 mln.
Palantir	USA	September 30, 2020	NYSE	$7.5	$2.75 bln.
Rivian Automotive Inc.	USA	November 10, 2021	NASDAQ	$78	$11.9 bln.
Robinhood Markets Inc.	USA	July 29, 2021	NASDAQ	$38	$2.1 bln.
Snowflake	USA	September 15, 2020	NYSE	$120	$3.9 bln.

Source: Compiled by the authors

management reports that these initiatives can be extremely costly and, therefore, unprofitable. Still, the company is willing to take the risk and optimize its operations through costly new technologies. Investors gave a very high evaluation of the company at the IPO stage. The company attracted about $3.7 billion, making this initial public offering one of the largest placements among US technology companies.

Another American company DoorDash, engaged in food delivery, is also actively using artificial intelligence to optimize the delivery process. The fundamental task of DoorDash is to ensure the interaction of the three parties: restaurants, couriers, and consumers based on one platform. To maximize the optimization of interaction, the company uses various methods of artificial intelligence and machine learning, which allow making optimal decisions for each order. As a result, the company has significantly increased efficiency: delivery time has decreased, couriers receive more tips and can fulfill more orders, which leads to an increase in wages, and the partner restaurants can significantly increase revenues. Thus, the use of advanced technology has not only proven to be a benefit to the platform's key users but has helped to enhance DoorDash's reputation in the eyes of consumers and, subsequently, in the eyes of potential investors. The quality service of DoorDash has become one of the factors of the company's investment attractiveness.

Table 2. Megatrends of Industry 4.0 applied by "young" companies to their production processes

Company	Company's area of activity	Megatrends of Industry 4.0
Airbnb	Short term housing rental (online platform)	• Using artificial intelligence to analyze Airbnb tenants; • Preparation for the use of augmented reality and blockchain
Coupang Inc.	E-commerce, retail (online platform)	Artificial intelligence, cloud computing, and machine learning to optimize logistics and procurement processes
Didi Global Inc.	Taxi, carsharing, and ridesharing aggregator (online platform)	• Improvements in security technology and protection of personal data; • Prediction algorithms and trip optimization; • Autonomous driving and V2X technologies
DoorDash	Food delivery (online platform)	Using artificial intelligence to optimize logistics processes
Fix Price	Retail trade (discounter)	Automated system of goods accounting and control (Set Mark Centrum)
Ozon	E-commerce, retail (online platform)	• Developing robots for use in warehouses and delivering goods to customers; • Using artificial intelligence for targeting advertising; • Automation of pricing, technical support, and procurement.
Palantir	Development of data analysis software	The company is a leader in artificial intelligence and big data analytics
Rivian Automotive Inc.	Electric car production	Creation of smart batteries
Robinhood Markets Inc.	FinTech, financial services in the stock market (online platform)	"I Know First" prediction algorithm (using artificial intelligence to determine the most effective investment strategy)
Snowflake	Data storage based on cloud computing	Development of cloud technology

Source Compiled by the authors

Palantir Technologies is one of the most influential and expensive startups. The IPO of this company aroused considerable interest among investors in the stock market primarily because of the specifics of the company's activities and its key customers. Palantir creates software that allows analyzing, managing, and protecting big data. The company's developments can prevent fraud, financial fraud, and even terrorism. The company's key customers are US intelligence agencies; with the software developed by Palantir, they can analyze phone records, photos, financial transactions, and other elements. The company's role in US security and counterterrorism provided a significant influx of investment at the IPO stage.

Robinhood Markets Inc. is the company that changed the online broker industry. Advantageous conditions for stock trading, user-friendly interface, and "I Know First" prediction algorithm allowed the company to become the largest provider of brokerage services in the American market. Nowadays, the company accounts for about 26% of the market (Kremer, 2020). Additionally, the COVID-19 pandemic and its accompanying restrictions have had a favorable impact on the development of FinTech; many financial transactions began to be carried out independently by the user in a mobile app (Fu & Mishra, 2020). Platform users increased their capital by using the company's patented "I Know First" algorithm. The algorithm is based on artificial intelligence, which calculates the best investment strategy in the context of global economic uncertainty, allowing investors to make better and more informed decisions. Robinhood Markets Inc. raised over $2.1 billion in its IPO in July 2021, which is very significant.

The company Snowflake plays a special role in the context of Industry 4.0 because it focuses on building a platform to support machine learning and data processing applications based on artificial intelligence. In other words, Snowflake allows other market players to create machine learning algorithms and implement AI, with Snowflake taking control of the integration and associated costs. The company's IPO in 2020 was one of the most successful, with the market valuing the company at $3.9 billion, making Snowflake's IPO the fifth-largest initial public offering among US technology companies. The largest IPOs of technology companies on the US stock market include Facebook (May 2012 – $16 bln.), Uber (May 2019 – $8.1 bln.), Agere Systems (March 2001 – $4.1 bln.), Snap (March 2017 – $3.9 bln.), Snowflake (September 2020 – $3.9 bln.), Airbnb (December 2020 – $3.7 bln.), and Doordash (December 2020 – $3.4 bln.) (Levy, 2020). Notably, the largest IPOs include three companies that conducted IPO in 2020 at a time of global economic uncertainty caused by the global COVID-19 pandemic. The cited statistics allow making two key assumptions about the dynamics of the technology market in the future. First, the number of companies whose main tool for increasing profits will be information and digital technology will continue to grow. Second, investors' interest in such companies will also maintain an upward trend in the new economic reality.

The only company involved in manufacturing activities in this research is Rivian Automotive Inc. This company is a manufacturer of electric cars. Like the other companies featured in this research, it is looking to incorporate Industry 4.0 elements into its products to make them more competitive in the market and attract the customers' attention. At this stage, the company is working on an artificial intelligence battery system that will improve performance and allow the battery to last three times longer. IPO of Rivian Automotive Inc. was the largest initial public offering of 2021; the company was valued at a record $11.9 billion.

This research primarily looked at US-based companies. However, these companies are not the only ones using advanced technology in their operations. Coupang Inc., one of South Korea's largest e-commerce marketers, managed to significantly improve the efficiency of business processes within the company through the use of artificial intelligence technology. The company's patented algorithms determine literally every step of the business: the purchase of goods, storage and delivery of goods, the best way to pack the goods, and the delivery route. Such technology allows the company to deliver millions of items in less than a day. Coupang Inc. is the e-commerce company of the future, and its innovation component is one of the key factors that made it an attractive investment at the time of its listing on the NYSE. The IPO of Coupang Inc. became the largest IPO of an Asian company on the US stock market since Alibaba's IPO in 2014.

Chinese cab aggregator Didi Global Inc. uses advanced information technology in three main business areas. First, the company uses advanced technology to ensure the physical safety of passengers and drivers, putting the protection of the personal data of application users as one of the main priorities. Second, algorithms based on artificial intelligence allow optimizing trips and make it possible to predict the dynamics of demand for cabs, which allows for an effective pricing policy. Third, the company seeks to introduce autonomous driving and V2X technologies. Didi Global Inc. develops computer vision and HD mapping technologies within these projects and already tests a fleet of autonomous vehicles in China and the US. Like Coupang, Didi Global chose the NYSE for its initial public offering, probably to expand the geography of investors and attract foreign capital. The company of Chinese origin was able to attract about $4.4 billion.

We would like to pay special attention to the Russian companies included on the list – OZON and Fix Price. Russian companies began to massively implement artificial intelligence in business processes because the introduction of information technology increased business competitiveness. According to recent estimates, more than half of the largest companies in Russia transform their business processes to meet current realities. Companies that ignore new trends can lose their position in the market. OZON is Russia's largest e-commerce company. Artificial intelligence helps the company strengthen its position as a market leader. Using AI, the company optimized purchasing, pricing, and technical support, evaluated the existing pickup points network, and robotized warehouses. At this stage, the company has developed an automated system to recommend products for purchase; the recommendation is sent to users of the application via e-mail, and the click-through rate (CTR) has increased by 10% compared to the value of targeting mailing performed by people. Better targeting allowed the company to significantly increased its gross revenue. During the initial public offering, OZON attracted about 990 million dollars, which is a very decent indicator for a Russian company.

Goods of the company Fix Price are very popular among Russian consumers; the brand has earned a reputation as a network that sells goods at the best prices. Nowadays, Fix Price provides a wide variety of products, but the company plans to expand the range of products, which necessitates the automation of accounting and control processes. The retail chain Fix Price has launched a pilot project Set Mark Centrum to control labeled goods. The introduction of Set Mark Centrum provides a wide range of opportunities. This system allows for determining the compliance of goods with labeling requirements, preventing errors of cashiers and sale of uncertified goods and counterfeit, leveling out provocations of competitors, and detecting unscrupulous suppliers of products. The system maintains strict records of goods by unique labeling; it blocks the sale of goods that have not been put on record, eliminates the re-sale of the same product, and does not allow the return of products purchased in other retailers. Thus, the system allows for optimizing the control mechanisms of labeled goods and preventing possible fraud schemes in the field of sales. Additionally, it should be noted that Fix Price, originally created as a network of Brick-and-Mortar stores, today, guided by global trends, has created an application for smartphones, which allows customers to shop online. A key driver for the mass creation and development of shopping apps by major retailers has been the global pandemic, which has severely limited people's ability to move freely. In such circumstances, many companies were forced to resort to the creation of online platforms and arrange the delivery of their products to keep market share and maintain consumer loyalty to the brand.

In the midst of the COVID-19 pandemic, Fix Price held an initial public offering that raised more than $1740 million; it was the most successful IPO in the Russian market in 2020. However, the company has not managed to maintain its initial success; the stock has shown a steady decline since the IPO. An especially strong decline in value was observed in February 2022. Like the shares of other Russian companies, the shares of Fix Price saw a significant drop in price against the background of geopolitical instability. Analysts' forecasts for Fix Price and other companies in the Russian stock market remain positive. Nevertheless, it is impossible to predict the stock market dynamics with great accuracy at this stage. It should be noted that the position of Fix Price on the Russian market only strengthened because the crisis conditions may serve as a particular incentive to attract interest to the retailer of low prices.

Thus, looking at the nine "young" companies whose IPOs took place amid the global pandemic, we can conclude that all of them have won the favor of investors because of the use of Industry 4.0 megatrends in their activities. The introduction of artificial intelligence, machine learning, and cloud computing allows for running operations as efficiently as possible and improving brand image, which, in turn, has a favorable effect on the flow of investment. The innovativeness of companies cannot be considered the only factor ensuring.

Nowadays, artificial intelligence plays a leading role in the development of companies. Regardless of the field of activity, companies actively introduce AI to improve efficiency. There are many possible ways to use this technology: creating algorithms to predict the dynamics of the stock market, finding the best delivery or transportation route, creating targeted advertising offers, determining the most effective way to package goods, and many others. Additionally, Industry 4.0 megatrends make it easier for companies to handle unforeseen disruptions and external shocks and cope with their contingencies in the face of global economic uncertainty (Cugno et al., 2022). The introduction of advanced technology is a benefit for the companies and consumers, who can now get their order more quickly or identify which stocks will be more profitable to invest in. Artificial intelligence products have evolved from sci-fi abstractions to everyday reality.

The importance of digital and information technology in the context of economic and social development is apparent to corporate management and government officials. According to some current research, Industry 4.0 tools can help stop the COVID-19 pandemic by detecting and diagnosing coronavirus infections (Javaid et al., 2020). In some countries, such as Russia, government agencies are developing a set of measures aimed at further developing and implementing technology. The authorities adhere to this strategy because they regard digitalization as an effective tool for attracting foreign and domestic investment. For many world leaders, the role of artificial intelligence in the development of society and national economies is paramount in today's realities. In the near future, the well-being of society will directly depend on the digitalization of the economy.

Due to the paramount importance of digitalization, governments in more than 60 countries have issued AI strategies and provided a greater influx of public investment in the industry. Countries that seek to increase their AI capacity and that have developed roadmaps include the USA, China, the UAE, Saudi Arabia, Qatar, Germany, France, the UK, the EU, and others. Nowadays, the leaders of the artificial intelligence market are the USA and China, which account for 42% and 23% of technology startups in quantitative terms in artificial intelligence or 38% and 48% in financial terms, respectively. The US AI market is leading in key areas such as algorithms and chips. To maintain the positive development trend, the US authorities introduce several initiatives, including National Artificial Intelligence (AI) Initiative Act, National Robotics Initiative 3.0, and others. The US market has a clear advantage in technological innovation and is currently far superior to the PRC market. The AI market in China has great potential and has more support from government agencies. The main areas of investment in the country are applied research, including finance, security structures, and the Internet. According to the analysts' forecasts, the AI sector in China is steadily growing and constantly expanding.

Some countries create separate ministries specializing in the implementation and development of advanced Industry 4.0 technologies. However, stimulating the development of AI is not limited to the political plane because universities of artificial intelligence are created in different parts of the world. The emergence of such educational institutions confirms the importance of advanced technology in today's realities and the need for highly qualified personnel in the global AI market.

At the current stage, the Russian AI market cannot be called the most developed; it is significantly inferior to its competitors in size and volume of attracted investments. However, the government is taking decisive steps to increase the investment appeal of the IT industry. The initial stage in the development of the IT industry in Russia can be considered 2015, when ABBYY, a company specializing in information processing and business process analysis, created Compreno, a technology that allows analyzing, translating, and searching texts in foreign languages. It should be noted that certain developments in robotics and artificial intelligence were made before 2015. However, the last ten years were the most breakthrough for the Russian AI market, as well as for the world. In 2016, the gradual development of the industry continued; this year saw two key events. First, the founder of ABBYY, David Yang, launches Findo, a smart search engine, in the USA. A unique feature of this search engine is its ability to recognize speech and search for the requested information on the Internet, cloud, or local files. Second, Yandex used advanced technology to create three products at once: Search, Zen, and Audience. At this stage, the company was actively working on implementing neural networks to take search engines to the next level. Zen technology allows personalizing the information search process while considering the user's interests. The Yandex.Audience service allowed optimizing targeting ads using AI technology to find a target audience.

The volume of the Russian artificial intelligence and machine learning market was about $700 million in 2017; the main market drivers at the time were the financial sector, industry, and retail. The number of cases of application of artificial intelligence in the world and Russia has increased several times. Thus, in 2015, 17 projects in the field of AI were announced; in 2017, the number of projects has increased to 74 (Tadviser, 2021a). According to the TADVISER research, the main reasons for introducing advanced technologies into business processes is the desire of companies to reduce costs (72%), improve the quality of their products or services (68%), increase labor productivity (56%), provide a competitive advantage in the market (52%), and improve communication with customers (40%). (Tadviser, 2021b). In 2017, personal assistant technology began to actively develop: Yandex developed its voice assistant Alice and American e-commerce company Amazon improved the functionality of Echo and Alexa.

In 2018, the Russian AI market reached $2 billion; at this stage, AI technology has become the most discussed among domestic businesses. This year was marked by a tremendous growth in the number of digital platforms and mobile applications based on AI and neural networks, with advanced technologies beginning to be applied to new sectors of the economy. The largest representatives of Russian business began to implement AI to optimize business processes; such companies include Sberbank, Rostelecom, MTS, Megafon, VkusVill, Gazprom Neft, MVideo, MMK, Yandex, and others. The range of possibilities opened by AI and machine learning technologies is extremely wide. Gazprom Neft processes data while drilling wells. VkusWill created a bot to help customers. Rostelecom uses AI in HR at the stage of selecting candidates for vacancies in the company. Sberbank has implemented the Jet Detective anti-fraud system. It should also be noted that the issue of information security has become extremely urgent; there is a need to improve the quality and technology to protect users' personal data.

Interest in artificial intelligence technology grew even stronger in 2019, with Russian companies investing $172.5 million in the industry, with a similar figure in European countries already reaching $2 billion. Most active investors in advanced technology were companies in the financial sector (41%); manufacturing companies accounted for about 16% of the total investment; the contribution of retail chains was 14%, and state-owned enterprises invested 6% (Tadviser, 2021a).

Additionally, in 2019, artificial intelligence, for the first time, became an object of state standardization in Russia. The Federal Agency for Technical Regulation and Metrology approved two state standards in the field of AI: GOST R 58776-2019 and GOST R 58777-2019. The technical committee for AI standardization was also established. This committee is in charge of the normative and technical regulation of the technology.

However, the most significant event for the development of AI was the approval of the "National strategy for the development of artificial intelligence for the period up to 2030" by the President of the Russian Federation. The main goal of this strategy is to ensure the growth of welfare and quality of life of its population, guarantee national security and the rule of law, and achieve sustainable competitiveness in the Russian economy, including a leading position in the field of artificial intelligence (Presidential Executive Office, 2019). The strategy implies a set of measures to develop high-tech industries in Russia. So far, two stimulus packages for the industry have been developed. These measures aim to create favorable conditions for IT companies in Russia and increase domestic demand for services of domestic companies. It is still difficult to unequivocally assess the impact of such a policy; conclusions about the effectiveness of business incentives can be made after several years.

Despite the global crisis caused by the COVID-19 pandemic, the artificial intelligence market in Russia has continued to expand, reaching $291 million in 2020. Spending on the use of AI technology in government and commercial organizations increased by 22.4% compared to the same value in 2019. In the face of the restrictions aimed at combating the spread of the virus, advanced technology to reduce the number of people involved in business processes has become a real solution for companies. Organizations that started investing in AI in advance increased the flow of cash into the field, and those companies that neglected technological advances in their operations were forced to upgrade and digitalize as a matter of urgency, otherwise, they could lose market share and customers.

During the crisis year, the volume of investment in the field of AI for the country was about 3 billion rubles, which is not such a significant indicator against the background of similar values in other countries. For example, in 2020, the amount of investment in the development of AI technology in the USA was $6 billion; this figure was 150 times higher than investment in AI in Russia, while the GDP of the analyzed countries differed 14 times in favor of the USA. The People's Republic of China was more impressive in terms of investment, investing over $14.3 billion in the development of AI, which is 350 times higher than in Russia; the gap in investment volumes is enormous, while the volume of Chinese GDP is ten times higher than Russia's GDP. It is noteworthy that even in the conditions of global economic instability, countries do not stop investing in the development of information technology, which emphasizes the importance of this industry for particular countries. Additionally, it should be noted that the most expedient strategy for Russia would be to increase the amount of government investment in the industry, as the market leaders are doing today. It is also necessary to ensure the investment attractiveness of the industry to stimulate the inflow of private investment.

AI technology in health care has become especially significant in the context of the COVID-19 pandemic (Fortune Business Insights, 2021). Automation of diagnostic and patient communication processes has greatly increased the efficiency of the health care system, which was under tremendous pressure during this difficult period. In 2020, a solid foundation was laid for the future accelerated adoption of digital and information technology in the healthcare industry.

Additionally, a legal concept for regulating artificial intelligence and robotics was developed in 2020. By 2024, the legal framework for information and digital technology will be created based on the created concept.

In 2021, as the global economy gradually recovered from the crisis, there were several significant developments in the field of AI and robotics. First, federal ministries and agencies of the Russian Federation started implementing AI technology in their activities. Thus, representatives of the Ministry of Sports came up with the initiative to digitize sports awards. Second, the President of Russia instructed developers of AI technology to provide access to impersonal state databases. The monopoly on data is a factor restraining the development of the industry and preventing the establishment of a competitive environment. The president's order has already begun to be enforced in January 2022, and preparations are underway to make data public for the development of AI in some government agencies, including the Federal Tax Service, Rosstat, Rosreestr, etc.

Nowadays, the most relevant news in the field of digitalization of the economy is the launch of testing of the Russian state digital currency (digital ruble) in 2022. The banks involved in testing the digital ruble have already successfully conducted a full cycle of operations with this currency. The creation of a digital currency platform opens up new opportunities for businesses, government agencies, and citizens. This innovation will reduce the costs of entrepreneurs and create conditions for the development and introduction of innovative projects. In the context of public administration, there will be a new tool for public targeted funding and control of tax and other revenues. Individuals will be able to make free and fast transfers throughout Russia (Central Bank of the Russian Federation, 2022).

Thus, countries strive to support the development of digital and information technology in their territory because digitalization can be a factor that stimulates the active development of the economy and society. Nowadays, the USA and China are generally recognized as market leaders; other countries are also building up their AI capabilities, but they are far behind the established leaders. The idea of introducing artificial intelligence has already become ubiquitous. Nowadays, the spirit of Industry 4.0 is promoted not only at the state level when developing development strategies but also within certain companies from various industries. The scale of the Russian AI market is significantly inferior to the leaders. Nevertheless, the country's authorities carry out a set of measures to stimulate the IT industry. Presidential Decree No. 490 (October 10, 2019) set a clear goal for market representatives and government officials. After adopting this decree, the development and improvement of information technology have officially become one of the country's priorities. Nowadays, Russia has an ambitious goal, like many other countries in the world, it wants to strengthen its position and expand its influence in the AI market. However, significant resources and a competent development strategy are required to put these plans into practice.

Industry 4.0 currently generates tremendous interest from government officials and the commercial sector. This excitement around information technology, in particular artificial intelligence, allows us to make a positive prediction about the further development of the market and its growth prospects. Experts expect the market to grow at a compound annual growth rate of 42.2% in 2020–2027 (Mamontov, 2020), which is a very impressive figure. If the projected growth rate is maintained, by 2027, the size of the global AI market will be about $667 billion (Mamontov, 2020). Such growth rates appear to be possible due to a wide range of advanced technologies. For example, the automotive industry has the potential to develop and implement uncrewed driving and augmented reality, something that Didi Global Inc. is actively engaged in. In health care, there are also opportunities to expand the impact of high-tech, such as the digitization of genetic material for laboratory tests. There are many uses for artificial intelligence in other industries as well, such as retail, wholesale, finance, and all kinds of services.

Companies of various sizes (MNCs, small and medium-sized businesses), organizational forms (public and private), and statuses (young, established in the market) adopt AI technologies and machine learning to optimize their business processes. The introduction of technology and optimization allows companies to achieve their main goal – profit at a minimal cost. The factors driving the demand for technology in the coming future will include significant growth of 5G users, cloud computing, databases, and so on (Fortune Business Insights, 2021). The global public is striving to become part of the new digital era and Industry 4.0 and enjoy all benefits of information technology.

CONCLUSION AND RECOMMENDATIONS

Nowadays, we are witnessing the birth of a new industrial revolution, as earlier stages of development would entail a radical transformation of the economy and industry. The role of Industry 4.0 for companies and the economy cannot be overestimated. Major megatrends, including artificial intelligence and machine learning, allowed companies to increase the efficiency of business processes significantly.

This research examined nine companies whose IPOs have caused the greatest excitement among investors in the stock market. It is noteworthy that all reviewed companies use advanced technology, which allows them to strengthen a positive image in the eyes of consumers and investors. In other words, the use of information and digital technology can ensure investment attractiveness at the IPO stage.

Technology is developing rapidly, with innovations that could only have been dreamed of yesterday. According to the authors, in the current decade, the rapid pace of development of information and digital technology will continue; the leading role will be played by artificial intelligence, which will find more new applications. Companies will have to constantly improve and optimize business processes because their efficiency will directly depend on competitiveness. Neglecting the introduction of advanced technology, companies risk losing their market position in the near future.

Many countries, realizing the importance of digital transformation and information technology for the national economy and society, try to stimulate the development of the IT industry and AI technology in their territory. For example, the government of the Russian Federation, as well as many other developed countries, introduced a set of measures aimed at the further development and implementation of technology in particular companies and specific sectors of the economy. There is significant growth potential in the industry due to the wide range of possible applications of advanced technologies in various industries and the realization of the importance of digitalization by company executives after the crisis caused by the global COVID-19 pandemic.

REFERENCES

Bai, A. S., & Chen, M. (2021). Did the COVID-19 pandemic (really) positively impact the IPO Market? An Analysis of information uncertainty. *Finance Research Letters, 102372*. Advance online publication. doi:10.1016/j.frl.2021.102372

Central Bank of the Russian Federation. (2022, 15 February). *Digital ruble: Start of testing*. Retrieved March 27, 2022, from https://www.cbr.ru/eng/press/event/?id=12692

Cugno, M., Castagnoli, R., Büchi, G., & Pini, M. (2022). Industry 4.0 and production recovery in the covid era. *Technovation, 114*, 102443. doi:10.1016/j.technovation.2021.102443

Fortune Business Insights. (2021). *Artificial intelligence (AI) market size, share & COVID-19 impact analysis, by component (hardware, software, and services), by technology (computer vision, machine learning, natural language processing, and others), by deployment (cloud, on-premises), by industry (healthcare, retail, IT & telecom, BFSI, automotive, advertising & media, manufacturing, and others), and regional forecast, 2021–2028.* Retrieved March 27, 2022, from https://www.fortunebusinessinsights.com/industry-reports/artificial-intelligence-market-100114

Fu, J., & Mishra, M. (2020). Fintech in the time of COVID-19: Technological adoption during crises. *Journal of Financial Intermediation, 50*, 100945. doi:10.1016/j.jfi.2021.100945

Go, P. (2021). *Global IPO has record-breaking 2021, prepare for headwinds in 2022*. Ernst & Young Global Limited. Retrieved February 18, 2022, from https://www.ey.com/en_gl/ipo/trends

Javaid, M., Haleem, A., Vaishya, R., Bahl, S., Suman, R., & Vaish, A. (2020). Industry 4.0 technologies and their applications in fighting COVID-19 pandemic. *Diabetes & Metabolic Syndrome, 14*(4), 419–422. doi:10.1016/j.dsx.2020.04.032 PMID:32344370

Kremer, J. (2020, June 21). Identifying the best stocks on Robinhood using AI. *I Know First*. Retrieved March 01, 2022, from https://iknowfirst.com/identifying-the-best-stocks-on-robinhood-using-ai

Kumar, M. P., & Kumara, N. V. M. (2021). Market capitalization: Pre and post COVID-19 analysis. *Materials Today: Proceedings*, *37*(2), 2553–2557. doi:10.1016/j.matpr.2020.08.493 PMID:33052307

Levy, A. (2020, December 12). Three of the 10 biggest tech IPOs have happened in 2020 – including two in the last week. *CNBC*. Retrieved March 01, 2022, from https://www.cnbc.com/amp/2020/12/12/10-biggest-tech-ipos-ever-three-in-2020-two-last-week.html

Machkour, B., & Abriane, A. (2020). Industry 4.0 and its Implications for the Financial Sector. *Procedia Computer Science*, *177*, 496–502. doi:10.1016/j.procs.2020.10.068

Mamontov, A. (2020). Industries of the future. Investing in artificial intelligence. *BCS Express*. Retrieved March 27, 2022, from https://bcs-express.ru/novosti-i-analitika/industrii-budushchego-investitsii-v-iskusstvennyi-intellekt

Mazumder, S., & Saha, P. (2021). COVID-19: Fear of pandemic and short-term IPO performance. *Finance Research Letters*, *43*, 101977. doi:10.1016/j.frl.2021.101977 PMID:33613130

Mazur, M., Dang, M., & Vega, M. (2021). COVID-19 and the march 2020 stock market crash. Evidence from S&P1500. *Finance Research Letters*, *38*, 101690. doi:10.1016/j.frl.2020.101690 PMID:32837377

Presidential Executive Office. (2019). *Decree "On the development of artificial intelligence in the Russian Federation" (together with the "National strategy for the development of artificial intelligence for the period up to 2030")* (October 10, 2019 No. 490). Retrieved March 27, 2022, from http://www.consultant.ru/document/cons_doc_LAW_335184/1f32224a00901db9cf44793e9a5e35567a4212c7/

Smales, L. A. (2021). Investor attention and global market returns during the COVID-19 crisis. *International Review of Financial Analysis*, *73*, 101616. doi:10.1016/j.irfa.2020.101616

Statista. (2021). *Average company lifespan on Standard and Poor's 500 Index from 1965 to 2030, in years*. Retrieved February 18, 2022, from https://tinyurl.com/mw24zkw2

Tadviser. (2021a). *Artificial intelligence (Russian market)*. Retrieved March 27, 2022, from https://www.tadviser.ru/index.php/

Tadviser. (2021b). *Artificial intelligence (World market).* Retrieved March 27, 2022, from https://www.tadviser.ru/index.php/Статья:Искусственный_интеллект_(мировой_рынок)

Chapter 9
Digitalization of Infrastructure Development Based on the Use of Public-Private Partnership Mechanisms:
Is Russia in Trend?

Oleg V. Ivanov
MGIMO University, Russia

ABSTRACT

The author considers the digitalization of infrastructure policy at the global and national levels as an important tool for providing quality infrastructure and promoting sustainable development. The specifics of the author's approach to problems of digitalization of infrastructure development based on the use of public-private partnership mechanisms consists of a combination of "vertical" (analysis of digital and platform solutions in the field of infrastructure investment) and "horizontal" (research of sectoral spectrum of the use of information technologies in the infrastructure of public-private partnership projects) analysis. The author analyses the international experience of developing digital and platform solutions in the field of infrastructure investments. The latest approaches to the development and improvement of the infrastructure complex in the Russian Federation are analyzed. Suggestions and recommendations on ways to further improve the infrastructure complex in Russia based on digitalization and the active use of public-private partnership mechanisms are made.

DOI: 10.4018/978-1-6684-4265-4.ch009

INTRODUCTION

Infrastructure is an essential component of a market economy. It ensures the reproductive process and directly affects the quality of peoples' lives. It is a driver of economic growth, having a powerful multiplier effect on many sectors of the economy. Numerous studies confirm close correlations between the state of infrastructure and its impact on various socio-economic processes in society. According to the IMF estimates, an increase in annual budget expenditures on infrastructure in OECD countries by 1% of GDP reduces the number of unemployed by 0.11% in the short term and by 0.35% in the long term (Abiad et al., 2015). McKinsey experts claim that an increase in annual total infrastructure investments by 1% of GDP will create 3.4 million new jobs in India, 1.5 million jobs in the USA, and 1.3 million jobs in Brazil (Woetzel et al., 2016). The World Bank estimates that reducing infrastructure gaps in sub-Saharan Africa to the level of countries such as Germany and the UK (less than 0.5% of GDP) could lead to annual growth of their GDP by 2.6% (World Bank, 2017).

The impact of infrastructure on the economy is ambiguous. On the one hand, it is an engine of growth and well-being. On the other, it is a source of negative impact on society and the environment. About 60% of greenhouse gases emitted into the atmosphere are the result of the construction and operation of infrastructure, while buildings consume more than 30% of the world's natural resources (UNEP, 2021).

The latter circumstance leads to increased attention to the topic of the quality and sustainability of infrastructure and its ability to meet new challenges – the growth of social problems, including the problem of inclusivity, an increase in anthropogenic pressure on the environment and its pollution, climate change, pandemics, etc.

For Russia, the issues of development and improvement of the infrastructure complex occupy a special place due to the extraordinary geographical features of the country and the low quality of public infrastructure. The country's leaders emphasize the need to accelerate the modernization of infrastructure and note that "the growth of infrastructure investments is a long-term priority of the country's economic policy" (Presidential Executive Office, 2021). Meanwhile, leading Russian experts agree that despite some progress in recent years, in general, the infrastructural "status quo" remains in the regions of Russia (InfraONE Research, 2021). Russia's positions in the world rankings of digital development are quite modest; in terms of business digitalization, Russia is noticeably lagging behind the leading countries (Shuisky, 2020).

METHODOLOGY

Over the past decade, several concepts and doctrines related to the concepts of "sustainable infrastructure," "quality infrastructure," responsible investment," etc. have become widespread in economic science and practice (Ivanov & Shamanina, 2021). Despite all differences in new concepts and approaches, they have a "common denominator": to achieve the quality and sustainability of facilities, maximum synergy can be achieved only through an integrated approach that considers the environmental, social, and economic aspects of infrastructure (Ministry of Finance of the Russian Federation, 2019).

Digitalization has been a distinct trend of global infrastructure development in recent years. Process innovations provide an opportunity to promptly disseminate information, reduce or save costs for preparing and launching infrastructure projects, and contribute to improving the quality of projects and building effective interaction between participants in the infrastructure ecosystem (Tsenzharik et al., 2021). With this in mind, the author considers the digitalization of infrastructure policy at the global and national levels as an important tool for providing quality infrastructure and promoting sustainable development. The specifics of the author's approach to problems of digitalization of infrastructure development based on the use of public-private partnership mechanisms consists of a combination of "vertical" (analysis of digital and platform solutions in the field of infrastructure investment) and "horizontal" (research of sectoral spectrum of the use of information technologies in the infrastructure of public-private partnership projects) analysis.

RESULTS

Digital and Platform Solutions in the Field of Infrastructure Investments

One of the notable phenomena of the last decade in the infrastructure track is the active development of digital platform solutions at the international and national levels with a wide range of functionality necessary to provide comprehensive support to infrastructure projects.

Digital infrastructure platforms solve the following main tasks. Globally, it assists governments in developing and implementing infrastructure policy, providing a platform for exchanging experience and best practices, and supplying information to potential investors with project databases. At the national level, digital products support the development of the infrastructure market, transmitting signals to politicians and raising awareness of business and the public, as well as creating a virtual market for services and know-how related to infrastructure. Many countries already use digital platforms to improve the quality of investment projects' preparation and build effective interaction between participants in the infrastructure investment market.

Nowadays, large international digital products have been created and are successfully functioning, contributing to the global development of infrastructure. Each of them has exceptional characteristics and purpose. The most representative of them are described below.

The largest database is the World Bank's database on private-public partnership (PPP) projects. It contains information on more than 8400 infrastructure projects with a total value of over $2 trillion, implemented in 137 countries. The database is available for free access. Users can visualize this data using a set of interactive tools, including maps, graphs, and charts (World Bank, n.d.).

Global Infrastructure Hub (Global Infrastructure Center) is a G20 initiative that offers a large group of digital products to support local policies and investments in lighthouse infrastructure (Global Infrastructure Hub, n.d.), including the following:

- *Reports on global investor surveys* allow investors to take a fresh look at the changing infrastructure markets;
- *InfraCompass* is a tool for exploring the country's capabilities to implement infrastructure projects. It covers the indicators and capacity of 56 countries to implement infrastructure projects, identify priority reforms and accurately identify best practices in infrastructure management;
- *Global Infrastructure Outlook* – aims to forecast infrastructure investment needs and gaps around the world. The country-by-country needs for global investments in electricity, water, communications, and transport have been identified for the next two decades.
- *PPP Risk Allocation Tool* is a guide to typical risk allocation in PPP transactions. This tool provides a set of annotated risk allocation matrices for PPP transactions in the sectors of transport, energy, water supply, and waste disposal. The PPP risk-sharing tool should be used to provide additional recommendations to countries wishing to develop a program of PPP operations acceptable to banks.
- *Global Infrastructure Project Pipeline* is a comprehensive project database connected to the databases of national and multilateral development banks to help potential investors find projects. As a free digital platform, it allows governments to promote public infrastructure projects *in a global network of investors.*
- *Project Preparation Reference Tool* offers useful assistance to policymakers and practitioners in their quest to improve project preparation methods and their capacity to prepare high-quality infrastructure projects based on the

G20 Principles at the stage of infrastructure project preparation. The tool is designed to help solve problems faced by governments at an early stage of project preparation by providing recommendations and lessons learned in an enabling environment for project preparation, project financing preparation, infrastructure planning, and project prioritization; project feasibility study, review, and approval; and project communication.

SIF SOURCE platform is a multilateral platform for creating quality infrastructure. It is funded by multilateral development banks, including the World Bank, ADB, EBRD, EIB, and IDB. Sustainable Infrastructure Foundation (SIF), a non-profit Swiss foundation headquartered in Geneva, coordinates the provision of the SOURCE platform. In the context of the activities of the G20, the foundation performs the following functions:

- Providing a standardized and comprehensive map of the aspects that need to be considered when developing a quality infrastructure;
- Providing project managers at the relevant stage of the decision-making process with tools, reference materials, and best practices of multilateral development banks;
- Controlling whether projects meet intended results and benefits during the implementation period;
- Collecting structured and standardized project data on a global scale to assess the effectiveness of projects compared to standards and benchmarks.

Nowadays, SIF SOURCE helps manage more than 260 projects in 50 countries, works in 9 languages, and is used by more than 2600 users (SIF, n.d.).

National products, as a rule, offer data adapted to the rules and practices of a particular country. Their primary mission is to promote market growth and attract investment. Currently, we are witnessing the rapid evolution of domestic databases into fully functional digital ecosystems consisting of several functional modules that include: pipeline and database of current infrastructure and PPP projects; characteristics of infrastructure management and measures of state support; expert platform and "Facebook" of market participants; interactive analytical and other tools. According to the G20 survey, seven countries use databases of infrastructure projects, and some countries have already switched to the introduction of integrated infrastructure platforms, with Canada, Mexico, and Russia becoming pioneers of transformation.

National digital products for the creation of electronic trade and logistics platforms in the PPP format have been launched in Japan (NACCS, n.d.), the Republic of Korea (Ministry of Trade, Industry, and Energy, n.d.), Malaysia, Thailand, and Singapore.

One of the reasons why the authorities choose the PPP format for their creation is the higher efficiency of operation and maintenance by a private partner. Thus, according to the TradeXchange concession project in Singapore, which involves the development of a universal platform for collecting, storing, and exchanging trade and logistics information between government agencies and the private sector, and its 10-year operation by a private partner, the authorities and the private partner shared the expenses. The state has assumed the costs of developing and further maintaining, that is, a capital grant and a conceded fee. The investor also invested in the development and operation of the system. TradeXchange was the first project aimed at software development (Singapore Customs, n.d.).

In world practices, there are PPP projects in the field of e-government, in particular, related to creating a "single window" for the provision of public services. They often include the supply of equipment and the development of specialized software. As a rule, such projects are implemented in non-traditional "quasi" PPP formats, including operator contracts, long-term lease agreements, Build-Operate-Transfer (BOT) contracts, and their variations. The examples of such successful PPP projects are as follows:

- Bangalore project in India. The goal is to create urban centers to provide public services for businesses and the public in the "One-Stop-Shop" format, i.e., obtaining the required services in one visit. The public partner transfers the equipped space in the form of a service center, and the private partner is responsible for integration, computer, and software. During the first five years of operation of the system, more than 40 million transactions were carried out (Bangalore One Services, n.d.);
- New Brunswick initiative in the Canadian province of New Brunswick. The project aims to combine various public services in a "single window" with the possibility of obtaining them through the website. Under the long-term lease agreement, the private partner created all necessary infrastructure for the provision of public services, and the government assumed the functions of the operator and started to pay for the lease of the relevant facilities (Service New Brunswick, n.d.).

ROSINFRA Infrastructure Project Support platform

Since 2019, Russia has been operating a unique digital solution for the preparation and implementation of infrastructure projects – the ROSINFRA platform. To launch the platform, the National PPP Center digitized project data, analytical materials, experience, and competencies accumulated over ten years of its activity. The mission of the platform is to overcome such inherent obstacles of the Russian infrastructure market as the lack of experience of public and private entities, difficulties and high cost of attracting qualified specialists, and the lack of comprehensive data reflecting the current state and trends of infrastructure development and the PPP market. ROSINFRA's design logic aims to facilitate effective interaction between the parties in infrastructure investment projects. Its products and services that are based on various databases form a single digital solution.

The core of ROSINFRA is a database of infrastructure projects and organizations involved in their implementation, which currently contains information about almost 4000 ongoing projects and 1400 project initiatives. Over 5700 market participants are already working with the platform as registered users. More than 70 industry experts support ongoing projects and project initiatives.

As an accelerator of design solutions, expert competencies, and financial instruments, the ROSINFRA platform performs the following:

- Provides up-to-date information about the PPP market and trends in law enforcement practice;
- Provides access to regularly updated data on planned and ongoing projects;
- Provides the expertise necessary to launch projects;
- Assists in the preparation of projects and attracting investments;
- Improves the quality of project development by attracting leading market experts;
- Provides search and attraction of potential investors and partners to implement projects.

In 2020, VEB.RF state corporation and the National PPP Center have launched a program to support public-private partnerships in the regions. Within its framework, the subjects of the Russian Federation receive consulting assistance in the development of infrastructure based on PPP principles and, together with experts, develop and apply measures to launch promising PPP initiatives. By September 2021, 75 regions and 12 cities joined the program, which sent 766 project initiatives with a total investment of 1.4 trillion rubles for consideration.

In 2021, the Digital Project Office service was launched on the ROSINFRA platform, which allows regional and municipal authorities to work together online to launch investment projects, including with the involvement of external experts, investors, and financing organizations. ROSINFRA platform allows building partnerships with foreign countries and international organizations interested in the development of similar digital platforms.

PPP Projects in the Field of Information and Communication Technologies (ICT)

Due to the combination of innovative business solutions with far-sighted government policies in the framework of PPP, ICT is now introduced into many spheres of public life. Nowadays, according to the World Bank, there are about 525 PPP projects in the field of ICT in the world that are at different stages of implementation. The total volume of investments in these projects is estimated at $119.3 billion (World Bank, 1990-2021). According to the World Bank, the ICT sector ranks fourth in the world in the number of PPP projects. The volume of investments in PPP projects in ICT also lags behind the same indicator in such sectors as electricity and roads. This is primarily due to the fact that, as a rule, the creation of IT facilities and systems is much less capital-intensive and does not require significant financial investments for the construction or reconstruction of real estate. However, it should be borne in mind that PPP in the field of information technology began to develop much later than in traditional industries.

PPP projects in ICT can be classified into two main types. The first type covers projects related to traditional infrastructure, which includes these elements. As a rule, these usually include projects for the construction of social facilities with "digital solutions" for organizing the process of providing services, integrated IT systems on highways, digitalization of public transport ("smart" stops, automated toll collection, etc.), housing and communal services with accounting systems, etc. The second type includes the so-called "technological" projects, which often do not have a link to the traditional infrastructure. Within the framework of such projects, broadband communication lines and state information systems are being created, the transfer of public services into digital format is being implemented, urban communications (Wi-Fi Internet, navigation) are being developed, and aerial photography (cadastral registration) is being carried out for tax collection and control over the targeted use of land plots.

The primary catalyst for the digitalization of the economy is urbanization. Cities are the centers of gravity of business activity. Numerous companies, together with a large number of residents, form a request for "smart" solutions. In general, the development of cities and the strengthening of their role is due to the increasing attention paid in the world to improve the quality of the urban environment, which is impossible without a corresponding improvement in infrastructure. The urban population accounts for about 55% of the world's population (4.2 billion people); by 2050, it is expected that about 70% of people will live in cities (World Bank, 2020). Cities account for more than 80% of global GDP. Simultaneously, in cities, a number of problems are particularly acute, including socio-economic inequality and poverty, inconsistency with the principles of sustainable development, and the need to adapt to global climate change. At the same time, there are not enough funds for the implementation of these projects – according to the World Bank, the global need for investment in urban infrastructure is estimated at $4.5–5.4 trillion per year (World Bank & GFDRR, 2015)

Digital technologies are rapidly introduced into urban infrastructure. Across the globe, smart city technology spending was $80 billion in 2016 (Maddox, 2018), reached $410 billion in 2020, and is set to double to $820.7 billion by 2025 (Vuppuluri, 2020).

The main driving factor in the digitalization of cities is the need to improve the efficiency of urban management and the implementation of investment projects. In particular, advanced technologies are in demand to automate and improve the efficiency of management systems of utility and energy infrastructure.

Over the past decade, one of the leading directions of urban development has been implementing the "smart city" concept. The urbanization of the late 20th caused a significant increase in the number of megacities associated with an increase in the number of problems for their residents: from environmental to administrative problems. Significant funds are invested in creating the infrastructure of "smart" cities in many countries of the world. According to Deloitte estimates, more than 1000 pilot projects of smart cities are being implemented in the world, more than half of which are in China (Deloitte, n.d.). A report from the National League of Cities shows that US cities are incubators for new technology, and a sharing economy is a major part of the plan for many municipalities. It should be noted that 66% of cities report that they are investing in smart city technology, and 25% of those without any smart city systems are exploring how to implement it (National League of Cities, 2017).

PPP in the IT sector of Russia

The development of public-private partnerships in information technology in Russia can be divided into two stages: before and after the adoption of Federal Law No. 173-FZ of 2018, according to which IT objects became independent objects of concession and PPP agreements. This decision meant a significant breakthrough because it significantly expanded the boundaries of the use of PPP tools. The objects of PPP agreements can now be programs for electronic computers, information systems, including state information systems (GIS), databases, websites on the Internet or other information and telecommunication networks, data processing centers, and other IT facilities and property that are technologically interconnected.

Simultaneously, the project does not have to be purely "informational": the object of the agreement can be mixed and have a clear industry orientation. For example, a project may simultaneously include the construction/modernization of immovable objects to provide educational or medical services (preschools, schools, hospitals, laboratories, etc.) and the creation of information systems, platforms, websites, and other IT facilities for this infrastructure.

The adoption of new legislation has given an additional impetus to the development of PPP projects in the field of ICT. Today, infrastructure projects using digital technologies are being actively implemented in Russia, and the PPP market in the field of IT infrastructure is steadily growing. According to the ROSINFRA platform, 42 projects worth 278 billion rubles are being implemented in the country, of which 98% are private investments (National PPP Center & VEB.RF, 2021).

As a rule, these projects are associated with the development of urban infrastructure – these are automated systems of integrated road safety (photo-video recording of violations, weight and size control), automated lighting systems of the road network (lighting in cities and on regional highways), systems for the organization and operation of parking space, automated traffic management systems (traffic lights, monitoring systems, etc.), and "smart stops" and information systems on public transport (including for fee collection).

Two major projects that are currently being implemented can be considered a landmark for the digitalization of infrastructure in the country.

The first project, "Platon," is a concession project to create and operate a toll collection system to compensate for damage caused to highways by vehicles weighing more than 12 tons. The total cost of the project is 29 billion rubles. By the end of 2021, more than 685 thousand Russian and foreign cargo carriers have registered more than 1.5 million trucks in the system. Over six years of operation, the state budget received more than 166 billion rubles. All collected funds go to the road fund of the Russian Federation, from where they are then directed to the construction and repair of highways as well as to the implementation of PPP projects (Platon, 2021).

The second is a PPP project that has no analogs in the world to create a system of digital marking and tracing of goods ("Honest Mark" project), designed to control the passage of goods from manufacturers and importers through consumer retail networks or, in other words, a control system for counterfeit goods. The total investment of the private partner in the project, following the PPP agreement, will amount to about 220 billion rubles over 15 years. The payback period of the project is at least seven years. At this stage, the agreement includes 13 commodity groups: fur products, dairy and tobacco products, medicines, perfumes and eau de toilette, tires, five categories of light industry goods, shoes, cameras, and flashlights (Rosinfra, 2019). A complex and expensive technological mechanism must be implemented entirely at the expense of a private partner without using federal budget funds. It is expected that the implementation of the project will have a great socio-economic effect: the share of counterfeit products in the markets will decrease by 50%–60%, the collection of excise taxes will increase by 20%–40% in 1–2 years (ATDC, 2019).

In recent years, improving the quality of urban infrastructure has increasingly promoted to the forefront of infrastructure priorities in Russia. Russia has an even higher proportion of people living in cities than the rest of the world – 3/4 of the population, or 109.5 million people, of which 33.6 million people live in the 15 largest cities of the country. The latter reflects the peculiarity of "Russian urbanization," which consists of the fact that the population migrates mainly not from rural areas to cities but from small towns to larger ones (InfraONE Research, 2020).

In the long term, the growth trend of the urban population and, in particular, the population of the largest agglomerations will continue. The pressure on the transport system will increase in cities, the need for social services will grow, and the issues of environmental degradation will become more acute. This means that the demand for "smart" solutions in all areas – from highways to medicine – will increase, as will the need for their financing.

VEB.RF state corporation actively implements a program to support the development of an advanced urban economy, which focuses on 100 of the country's largest cities (VEB.RF, 2021a). The urgency of these problems is due to the state of the urban environment: residents of 72 out of 118 cities considered in the Index of Quality of Life in Russian cities have expressed their dissatisfaction with the quality of life (VEB.RF, 2021b). Four Russian cities got into the top 20 of the international rating of urban traffic intensity for 2020; Moscow turned out to be the absolute leader of the list (TomTom, 2021). These facts reflect the importance of the development of urban infrastructure. In Russia, annual investments in urban infrastructure amount to an average of 1.5 trillion rubles, while 2.5 trillion is necessary. Annually, only about 200 billion rubles are invested in urban infrastructure on PPP principles (National PPP Center & VEB.RF, 2021).

Since 2018, the Federal project "Smart City" has been implemented in Russia within the framework of two National projects "Housing and Urban Environment" and "Digital Economy." The project involves the introduction of energy-efficient lighting and automated systems in the urban environment and intelligent public and environmental safety systems. To implement this federal project, PPP projects have been launched in many Russian regions, including the following (National PPP Center, 2018):

- Project for the creation of a photo-video recording system in St. Petersburg worth 10.1 billion rubles, which is the largest in terms of attracted investments among all PPP projects for "smart cities";
- Project for the creation and operation of traffic safety control in the Moscow Region worth 4.9 billion rubles,
- Project for creating a cashless passenger fare system in the Moscow Region worth 3.4 billion rubles, etc.

The practice of digitalization of the educational environment is spreading. A PPP project in the field of education – a project to create, implement, and ensure the functioning of a unified information system for accounting and monitoring of educational achievements of schoolchildren is being implemented in the Moscow Region. Rostelecom PJSC acts as a private partner. The information portal created within the framework of the project covers almost 1500 schools with 776500 students and 56000 teachers throughout the Moscow Region. In the first two years after the introduction of the system, more than 80% of schools in the region have abandoned paper journals and diaries.

CONCLUSION AND RECOMMENDATIONS

The role of information technologies in the economy is increasing globally. The dependence on "smart" solutions of a wide range of sectors of the infrastructure complex – transport, healthcare, education, and urban economy – is also increasing.

For Russia, the IT industry is traditionally private. According to expert estimates, the state invests no more than 10% of total investments in the Russian market (InfraONE Research, 2020). This creates objective opportunities for combining the efforts of the state and private business to cover the state's "digital needs" for infrastructure in the PPP format.

The inclusion of IT facilities in the Russian PPP legislation has expanded the scope of its application. It is also important that now concessions and PPP agreements can be concluded not only in relation to property but also the results of intellectual activity.

In general, there are grounds for concluding that Russia's efforts to digitalize the development of the infrastructure complex using PPP mechanisms are in line with key trends in the global infrastructure market. A technological and, in many ways, a unique digital platform for supporting infrastructure projects has been created. This platform allowed making a "digital leap" in the field of supporting the development of the infrastructure complex. The digital project office launched on the platform for the preparation of PPP projects is unprecedented and uses the maximum public-private partnership opportunities. Currently, the digital project office is already actively working on several dozen projects in the field of housing and communal services, school education, landscaping, solid waste treatment, IT, public transport, and healthcare. Interested investors and financing organizations have already been involved in several projects.

Gradually, a new direction of cooperation between the state and business is gaining momentum – partnership in the field of IT, which covers a wide range of infrastructure sectors – from traffic control to school education.

Despite significant progress in the developing digitalization of the infrastructure of PPP in Russia, there are still problems and bottlenecks, including the following:

- The legislation regulating concluding concession and PPP agreements in IT requires further refinement. The subject composition of the partnership raises many questions. Unlike other sectors, municipalities cannot be public partners in PPP projects in the field of IT. However, as practice shows, municipalities express a special interest in implementing IT projects. This legislative restriction is a significant deterrent to the digitalization process at the local level. There are also restrictions on the participation of foreign investors in the launch of IT projects.
- Several problems hamper the launch of IT projects in the Russian regions. These problems include the generally low level of development of the telecommunications sector. The lack of the necessary infrastructure "framework" for implementing most IT initiatives (broadband Internet access, developed mobile and landline communications, etc.) does not allow implementing projects for storing large amounts of data, their transmission and processing, as well as use in other industries, including related ones. The development of PPP in the IT sector in the regions is hindered by the low level of competence of the authorities to work with projects at the "zero stage." In most regions, the dominant form of interaction between the state and business in the field of infrastructure IT is the conventional state procurements. In the current economic situation and the logic of the IT market development, it is necessary to gradually move away from conventional forms to a more complex "infrastructure partnership," a broader application of PPP mechanisms – concession agreements, PPP agreements, long-term contracts based on the principles of LCC, creation of SPV, which were previously not very actively used in IT.
- The "sore" issue for the emerging niche is the "legal immaturity" of the issues of monetization of projects in the industry. The market has not yet formed a sufficient understanding of what IT projects could be launched under concessions and PPPs, as well as how they could pay off if private investment is attracted to them. The authorities, mainly regional ones, have difficulties estimating the costs of creating IT objects (the results of intellectual activity and services for their creation). One of the ways to solve the problem with the payback of projects could be the possibility of subsidizing and financing digital PPP projects by analogy with the recently adopted government program to stimulate the construction of educational facilities throughout the country.

- Many digital projects are platform solutions. It is still unclear whether they can become objects of concessions and PPP agreements and how the authorities will interact with each other if such projects turn out to be multifunctional – related to various industries.

It seems that eliminating the above bottlenecks will increase the investment attractiveness of the industry and realize the objective opportunities that this new and promising direction provides. According to the almost unanimous assessment of Russian experts, the potential volume of the domestic IT market is huge, and the degree of its saturation is still low. Among the promising projects of the very near future are projects in transport telematics (creation of a federal automated system of weight and size control, creation of a system for monitoring the transit of sanctioned goods through Russia, large regional projects – the creation of an automated system of weight and size control in St. Petersburg and "smart stops" in Novosibirsk and Voronezh).

The approval by the Ministry of Construction of the Smart City project standard, which involves the introduction of intelligent systems in urban management, transport, housing, energy, public safety, solid waste management, and environmental control, opens up broad prospects. The authorities plan to introduce the standard in cities with a population of more than 100 thousand people and regional centers with a smaller population. According to our estimate, 171 cities fall under the first requirement, and eight more regional capitals fall under the second. In total, 76.5 million people, or 52.1% of the country's population, live in these 179 territories (InfraONE Research, 2020). Solving these tasks would also be a significant contribution to achieving the Sustainable Development Goals.

REFERENCES

Abiad, A., Furceri, D., & Topalova, P. (2015, May). *The macroeconomic effects of public investment: Evidence from advanced economies*. IMF Working Paper. Retrieved February 12, 2021, from https://www.imf.org/external/pubs/ft/wp/2015/wp1595.pdf

Advanced Technology Development Center (ATDC). (2019). *Labeling and traceability: A brief overview of the PPP project*. ATDC.

Bangalore One Services. (n.d.). *Official website*. Retrieved February 12, 2021, from https://www.e-challan.com/2015/01/bangalore-one-services.html

Deloitte. (n.d.). *Super smart city: Happier society with higher quality*. Retrieved February 12, 2021, from https://www2.deloitte.com/cn/en/pages/public-sector/articles/super-smart-city.html

Global Infrastructure Hub. (n.d.). *Official website*. Retrieved February 12, 2021, from https://www.gihub.org

Infra O. N. E. Research. (2020, March). *Investments in infrastructure. Information Technologies*. Retrieved February 12, 2021, from https://infraone.ru/sites/default/files/analitika/2020/investicii_v_infrastrukturu_informacionnye_tekhnologii_infraone_research.pdf

Infra O. N. E. Research. (2021, October 26). *Infrastructure of Russia: Development Index 2021*. Retrieved February 12, 2021, from https://infraoneresearch.ru/u5usp7/m2r7v0?s1qtyk=1r5i77

Ivanov, O. V., & Shamanina, E. A. (2021). PPP as a tool to achieve Sustainable Development Goals and implement the concept of "Quality infrastructure investments.". In E. B. Zavyalova & E. G. Popkova (Eds.), *Industry 4.0. Exploring the consequences of climate change* (pp. 309–322). Palgrave MacMillan. doi:10.1007/978-3-030-75405-1_28

Maddox, T. (2018, July 16). *Smart cities: A cheat sheet*. Retrieved February 12, 2021, from https://www.techrepublic.com/article/smart-cities-the-smart-persons-guide/

Ministry of Finance of the Russian Federation. (2019). *G20 Principles for quality infrastructure investment*. Retrieved February 12, 2021, from https://minfin.gov.ru/ru/document/?id_4=129246-printsipy_g20_po_investitsiyam_v_kachestvennuyu_infrastrukturu

Ministry of Trade, Industry, and Energy. (n.d.). *uTradeHub*. Retrieved February 12, 2021, from https://www.utradehub.or.kr/porgw/index.jsp?_locale=en&sso=ok

National P. P. P. Center. (2018). Review of the practice of using public-private partnership mechanisms to create the infrastructure of "smart cities." National PPP Center.

National P. P. P. Center & VEB.RF. (2021, September). *Investments in infrastructure and PPP. Analytical review 2021*. Retrieved February 12, 2021, from https://pppcenter.ru/upload/iblock/312/312a2ad6182866e21407990ab0bb16a2.pdf

National League of Cities. (2017). *Cities and the innovation economy: perceptions of local leaders*. Retrieved February 12, 2021, from https://www.nlc.org/resource/cities-and-innovation-economy-perceptions-of-local-leaders

Nippon Automated Cargo and Port Consolidated System (NACCS). (n.d.). *Official website.* Retrieved February 12, 2021, from https://www.naccs.jp/e/

Platon. (2021, November 18). *More than 685 thousand truckers and logistics companies registered in the state system "Platon."* Retrieved February 12, 2021, from https://platon.ru/ru/без-рубрики/18-11-2021/13238

Presidential Executive Office. (2021, November 30). *Russia calling! Investment forum.* Retrieved February 12, 2021, from http://kremlin.ru/events/president/news/67241

ROSINFRA. (2019, June 7). *The first PPP agreement in the field of IT has been signed in Russia.* Retrieved February 12, 2021, from https://rosinfra-awards.ru/press/2019-06-07-3.html

Service New Brunswick. (n.d.). *Official website.* Retrieved February 12, 2021, from https://www2.snb.ca/content/snb/en.html

Shuisky, V. P. (2020). Digitalization of the Russian economy: Achievements and prospects. *Bulletin of the Institute of Economics of the Russian Academy of Sciences, 6*, 158–169. doi:10.24411/2073-6487-2020-10076

Singapore Customs. (n.d.). *TradeXchange.* Retrieved February 12, 2021, from https://unece.org/fileadmin/DAM/cefact/single_window/sw_cases/Download/Singapore.pdf

Sustainable Infrastructure Foundation (SIF). (n.d.). *Multilateral platform for sustainable infrastructure.* Retrieved February 12, 2021, from https://public.sif-source.org/

TomTom. (2021). *Traffic index ranking, 2021.* Retrieved February 12, 2021, from https://www.tomtom.com/en_gb/traffic-index/ranking/

Tsenzharik, M. K., Arenkov, I. A., Steshenko, V. I., & Ivanova, D. V. (Eds.). (2021). *Business Management in the Digital Economy: Collection of abstracts of speeches Fourth International Conference.* St. Petersburg, Russia: St. Petersburg State University of Industrial Technologies and Design.

UNEP. (2021, February 24). *Integrated approaches in Action: A Companion to the International Good Practice Principles for Sustainable Infrastructure.* Retrieved February 12, 2021, from https://www.unep.org/resources/publication/integrated-approaches-action-companion-international-good-practice-principles

VEB.RF. (2021a). *Urban economy.* Retrieved February 12, 2021, from https://вэб.рф/biznesu/finansirovaniye-proyektov/gorodskaja-ekonomika/

VEB.RF. (2021b). *City life index.* Retrieved February 12, 2021, from https://www.pwc.ru/ru/publications/assets/indeks-kachestva-zhizni/indeks-kachestva-zhizni.pdf

Vuppuluri, P. (2020, December 3). Investing in innovation: The rise of the smart city. *Forbes.* Retrieved February 12, 2021, from https://www.forbes.com/sites/forbesfinancecouncil/2020/12/03/investing-in-innovation-the-rise-of-the-smart-city/?sh=40a03ce75ba6

Woetzel, J., Garemo, N., Mischke, J., Hjerpe, M., & Palter, R. (2016, June 14). *Bridging global infrastructure gaps: Report.* McKinsey Global Institute. Retrieved February 12, 2021, from https://www.mckinsey.com/business-functions/operations/our-insights/bridging-global-infrastructure-gaps

World Bank. (2017, April). *Why We Need to Close the Infrastructure Gap in Sub-Saharan Africa.* Retrieved February 12, 2021, from https://www.worldbank.org/en/region/afr/publication/why-we-need-to-close-the-infrastructure-gap-in-sub-saharan-africa

World Bank. (2020, April 20). *Urban development overview.* Retrieved February 12, 2021, from https://www.worldbank.org/en/topic/urbandevelopment/overview#1

World Bank. (1990-2021). *Private participation in infrastructure: ICT.* Retrieved February 12, 2021, from https://ppi.worldbank.org/en/snapshots/sector/ict

World Bank. (n.d.). *Private participation in infrastructure.* Retrieved February 12, 2021, from https://ppi.worldbank.org/en/ppi

World Bank & GFDRR. (2015). *Investing in urban resilience: Protecting and promoting development in a changing world.* Retrieved February 12, 2021, from https://www.gfdrr.org/sites/default/files/publication/Investing%20in%20Urban%20Resilience%20Final.pdf

Chapter 10
The Role of Management of Innovations in the Digital Transformation Age

Alexander I. Voinov
MGIMO University, Russia & Russian State Academy of Intellectual Property (RGAIS), Russia

Mikhail V. Rybin
MGIMO University, Russia

Evgeny P. Torkanovskiy
https://orcid.org/0000-0001-6391-9872
Institute of Economics of the Russian Academy of Sciences, Russia

ABSTRACT

The extremely important role of innovation management in the digital transformation age determines the relevance of this research. The development of the theory of innovation, which began in the first half of the 20th century, has gained numerous apologists and antagonists. However, the process of evolution of innovative views in the society of the cyber industries is being further updated. The research aims to consider the prospects of information systems in knowledge management in the search for new resources for the growth of the real sector of the economy and, in particular, through the organization of the process of commercial use of intellectual property objects in industrial production in the period of digital transformation. The following research tasks are set: to determine contemporary methodological approaches in innovation management, to identify new opportunities for the growth of the real sector due to the use of the strategy of intellectual capital management, to consider specific trends for bringing knowledge-intensive products to the market in branches 4.0.

DOI: 10.4018/978-1-6684-4265-4.ch010

INTRODUCTION

A distinctive feature of the current state of the world economy is the extremely important role of innovation management in the period of digital transformation. Innovations a posteriori is the creation of new knowledge or a previously unknown combination of existing knowledge, embodied in new products or technological chains, and influencing the cyclical nature of economic development in a global context. Innovative industrial production reveals the essence of the economic content of technology as an object of commodity-money relations: cost, separability from its developers, and the possibility of digitization, transfer, commercialization, and capitalization. Large periods of K-waves include alternating phases of relatively high and relatively low economic growth rates.

As opposed to novelties of the early 20th century, contemporary innovations are much more radical, digital in nature. As a result, the process of their dissemination is much faster and affects a much larger number of sectors of the world economy, thereby increasing their knowledge intensity. Classical innovations represent an original view of a previously known approach, the effective application of a new invention or discovery in economics and other fields. Exploring the theoretical aspects of the definition of "innovations," we can say that this is a certain result of innovation activity – the activity of creating, mastering, and distributing products. For its implementation, companies need a permanent innovation development, symbolizing "the totality of relations arising in the course of purposeful improvement of the economic efficiency and competitiveness of the company based on innovations" (Kotter et al., 2021). Since the 1980s, innovation in national economic models has been an innovative type of development, focused on synthesizing scientific and technical knowledge, breakthrough technologies, and efficient and competitive business. Therefore, the current stage in the digital society of post-industries is often called the "innovation economy" or "knowledge economy."

The research subject is the definition of "innovations" in the discourse of the evolution of the cybersocium, influencing the approaches of management of innovations to the order parameters.

The research object is the technological branches of the world economy, as well as their innovative products, digitalized and commercialized through the development of innovation management methods.

A research objective is to consider the prospects of information systems in knowledge management in the search for new resources for the growth of the real sector of the economy and, in particular, through the organization of the process of commercial use of intellectual property objects in industrial production in the period of digital transformation. Research problems include the analysis of innovative development of branches of the economy in the discourse of the digital society paradigm. The authors also formed the theoretical and methodological essentials of research: system approach to the studied object and subject; scientific publications of foreign and domestic scholars based on problems of implementation of the industry 4.0 improvements; the materials of international scientific conferences and seminars related to problems of global technosphere development.

MATERIALS AND METHODS

Several scientific methods, such as descriptive analysis, factor analysis, synthesis, comparative analysis, and systemic approach, were adapted in accordance with the research objective. The institutional analysis allows us to describe the market architecture of the newest innovative products. The research used statistical data of Lux Research (CORDIS) and USPTO to show the tendencies of high-tech developments for the combined analysis of related dimensions of the national markets' dynamics, spending budgets, and the number of patents on nanotechnology. Given the integrated nature of nanotechnology patents that involve several fields of knowledge and industries and the absence of specific nanotechnology markers, the authors were obliged to undertake in-depth research of patents to discriminate nanotechnology patents from others.

Innovation Imperative

In the second half of the 19th century, the American engineer Frederick Taylor introduced the concept of "scientific management." According to his worldview, scientific management is a means to save labor by forming effective management mechanisms in production and introducing rational labor techniques into the practice of training workers. The typical periodization for K-waves (Kondratiev waves) that describe large innovative cycles of industrial production is 50 years with an acceptable deviation of 10 years (from 40 to 60 years). Such cycles consist of alternating phases of relatively high and relatively low economic growth rates. N. D. Kondratiev identified four empirical patterns in the development of large cycles. These patterns are described by the so-called infra-trajectories, which show what part of the potential "market niche" for a certain macro-technology has already been mastered, what part of the way in the development of the industry in question has already been passed, and in what phase of the natural cycle it is located.

Understanding these issues is extremely important because economic, scientific, technological, educational, and innovation policies in different countries directly depend on the development phase of the considered industries. The definition of "technological structure" introduced by political economists is one of the fundamentals in innovation management methodology and is certainly associated with K-waves. The theory defines five historical structures (digital solutions are conceptualized in the fourth structure) and two promising ones – the sixth and seventh, where fundamental scientific knowledge underlying the genesis of basic technologies is distinguished.

Another key concept of "innovations" was introduced into scientific circulation by the Austrian economist Joseph Schumpeter as a measurement applied in the inculcation and use of new types of consumer goods, production and transport vehicles, markets, and organizational forms in the industry. According to his views, innovation is a complex and differentiated activity with many interacting components located in the middle of the production process. However, this statement does not seem to be indisputable in recent decades. There is an increasing tendency to shift innovative thinking and innovation to the research and development (R&D) stage and to use technology foresight models to set global trends in the development of the technosphere and ensure total strategic dominance in priority industries. Along with this, the founder of the theory of innovative economic development introduced two new concepts – "adaptive behavior" and "creative behavior." The first concept is currently directly related to the digital transformation of society (Siggelkow & Terwiesch, 2019). It is associated with the adaptive type of enterprise management in the conditions of constantly changing organizational resources and the influence of various external and internal factors. The second concept is associated with the development of creative thinking and behavior of people based on the use of a combination of resources for creative purposes, the creation of innovations, and the promotion of new ideas. Schumpeter considered the waves of innovative development discrete in time, calling "clusters" (bundles) those periods in which there is a surge of innovations. In a review of his book "Business Cycles," Simon Kuznets also recognized the discreteness of scientific and technological revolutions.

Ideas on the role of entrepreneurship in the innovation process and the discreteness of innovations over time have been further developed in the works of many contemporary foreign researchers. In particular, the definition given by the famous American management specialist Peter Drucker indicates that innovation is a special tool for entrepreneurs, a means by which they use change as a chance for different types of business or services. The German "patriarch of innovations," Gerhard Mensch, drew theoretical parallels between the rate of economic growth and the cyclical nature of basic innovations. In his work "Technological Stalemate: Innovations overcome depression," he assessed the relationship of novelties with the market environment. According to the concept proposed by G. Mensch, technical and socio-organizational changes are internal factors in the development of the economy, which is characterized by the instability of the cycles of conjuncture: boom – recession – depression – recovery. Market cycles do not exist by themselves; they are primarily determined by innovation dynamics or innovation atrophy, respectively. In Mensch's understanding, innovation is the commercial application of scientific discoveries. Nowadays, the scientist's ideas have partially gone beyond the boundaries of economic theory and have become practical tools for high-tech cyber industries, where the innovation process can be represented in the following phases: basic research, applied research, demand forecasting, development and design, production, positioning, and sales.

The English scientist Brian Twiss considered innovation as a process in which an invention or idea acquires its economic content. Michal Kalecki, a Polish macro-level researcher, noted that within the limits of the commodity circulation cycle, it is possible to ensure constant economic growth, but the "main impulses" that cause changes in the system of conditions can lead the economy out of cyclical development and make it "jumpy" in the long term. Innovation is also one of these impulses. According to the scientist, innovations stimulate economic development, reducing the duration of economic downturns and lengthening periods of booms in the long term. The intensification of scientific and technological progress and the formation of *industry 4.0* and *the digital society 5.0* continued the evolution of classical political economic thought (Torkanovskiy, 2021). The generation of innovations occurs in the natural cycle of development of macro-technology, consisting of three stages:

- The formation of fundamental and experimental science, ideas that can be put into practice, training, and organization of R&D;
- The creation of technologies, rapid improvement of products, production, and the beginning of the realization of the opening opportunities;
- Diffusion of emerging innovations into the existing technosphere and economic system" (Rybin & Voinov, 2020).

Simultaneously, the spread of the converging interdisciplinary paradigm of NanoBioInfoCognito (NBIC) technologies actualizes the problems of prolonging the global innovation imperative, preserving only the environment and human civilization. In turn, Francis Fukuyama is inclined to consider it as a problem of the post-human future. In contemporary research, there is a tendency to merge social technologies with NBIC-technologies (NBICS). In this regard, NBICS-convergences are discussed as a basis for social progress (Spohrer, 2002), representing the concept of managing the development of the technosphere, a project for improving human capabilities based on the methodology of self-development and complexity. In the holistic paradigm, the individual can integrate into the evolutionary process, making the process acquire a new complexity. Thus, one of the goals of the Santa Fe Institute's long-term search is to turn the discovery of complexity into a method of knowing complexity.

The Western European innovator and researcher Alfred Kleinknecht argued that innovations-products are created in the depression phase and innovations-processes – in the upward stage of the longwave. According to him, innovation activity should be considered a key factor that causes dynamic changes of a large wave character in the economy and society (Kleinknecht, 1987, 2020). Until recently, economic theory assigned 30–45 years to the natural cycle of macro-technology development. On the other hand, the Fourier theorem shows the probability of any function on a certain segment being decomposed into the sum of periodic (cyclic) functions. In this case, if we consider the world economy over the past 250 years, it is not entirely excluded that there are also 20–30 years among these cycles. The skepticism of some researchers is due to the fact that when choosing, for example, a slightly different segment, the cycles may turn out differently.

In this regard, the supporters of the theory of cyclical innovation waves can give a sufficiently convincing sociological and even economic explanation of how the development of technologies occurs in the historical and temporal context, which leads to the start of the next cycle and allows the theory of technocenosis. In the last decade, focusing on the field of breakthrough technologies, it is impossible not to consider the theory of American scientists L. G. Badalyan and V. F. Kryvorotov, answering a very relevant question – which period from the past is closest to the situation of the current economic downturn with ongoing globalization, weakening centers of power, and rapidly growing former outsider countries. According to this theory, which is not falsified in general terms but lies as one of the methodological foundations of the scientific activity of the Institute of Complexity in Santa Fe, understanding the past, strategic forecasting (Choi et al., 2018; Islam et al., 2020) requires a comprehensive and systemic analysis of technocenoses, including the developed and used territory, the main energy sources, applied economic technologies and management systems, characteristics of "human capital" that is a key from the point of view of survival and development in certain natural and climatic conditions.

Practical Aspects

Until recently, researchers identified four relatively independent innovation management approaches to order parameters: factor approach, functional concept, and system and situational approaches. In the period of digital transformation, it is necessary to add to these theoretical approaches a fifth approach – the cybernetic concept.

The factor approach is a cornerstone in developing the economic mode of production due to the achievements of science and technology. The leading factors of production potential are R&D, which is provided with human capital (professional personnel), scientific equipment, intangible assets (information funds), and material and technical base.

A functional concept is a set of business administration functions and ways of making managerial decisions in activities that influence innovation.

The system approach considers innovative business as a complex organized system that consists of a complex of mutually dependent elements focused on achieving specific development goals, considering the static state of a plurality of internal and external factors that affect the final management decision.

At the turn of the 1990s, the situational approach became widespread, where the situation was already understood as a set of values of factors that influence the functioning of a business, an innovative project in a designated period. Some experts believe that the situational approach synthesizes the advantages of each of the above methods for specific decisions of the manager.

Cybernetic concept – the connection of the subconscious with consciousness occurs in each case of perception of phenomena and processes of the world surrounding the individual. Understanding this statement is especially important when studying and designing a complex, dissipative, and dynamically developing system, in which the main factors of its existence are the irreversibility and uncertainty of the future. Here, the methodology of complexity theory at the stage of the shift of the digital techno-economic paradigm of the fifth structure is almost the only tool that allows us to classify by means "the components of the subconscious sample," dynamically compare real processes due to their metrics and typology, and form a scientific representation within the interpretations of well-known scientific schools.

In the last few decades, the world economic dynamics have been presented as an uneven and uncertain process of evolution of social reproduction based on the intensification of scientific and technological progress (STP). The current non-linear development of STP has created prerequisites for the internationalization and digitization of macro-technologies of production, which actualize competition in the international markets of goods, services, patents, licenses, and know-how through the prism of intellectual capital management. The focus of management's efforts not only on digitalization but on the transformation of the business of digital companies and real sector companies in various industries is also extremely important. The accent should be made on changing the business strategy in the current market conditions, meeting new customer needs, increasing the efficiency of business processes, and ensuring the economic feasibility of novelties.

For example, the German company "SAP SE" (System Analysis and Software Development) and its product SAP Knowledge Management – a knowledge management platform that provides the processing of unstructured information. It can transform this information into organized arrays of knowledge available to the staff. Such information can be stored on web servers, computer files, or in document management systems. The strategy of intellectual capital management includes the systemic exchange of knowledge, its acquisition, structuring, storage, and application for indirect and timely distribution. Releases of digital technologies "SAP SE" include an ERP-system (Enterprise Resource Planning), which expands the functions of administration of internal and external resources of the enterprise, forming a single information space of input, processed and received information about its activities. The combination of SAP ERP options allows entrepreneurs to design a logistics system that meets the current requirements of technologies and stages of promoting innovative products to the market. This system includes any number of consumers of the company's products. Monitoring and tracking of operations performed in individual segments of the logistics system ensure full transparency of business processes related to the management of material flows.

The adapted SAP BI (SAP Business Intelligence) system also allows entrepreneurs to implement strategic analysis of the data array and support the management decision-making process within the company. SAP BI is designed to provide access and processing of information contained in various systems or databases of enterprises, as well as its generalization. Any information systems, accounting and financial software, specialized industry solutions, and local resources can serve as sources in this case. Together with SAP BI, SAP BO (SAP Business Objects) system is applied. Built in the system, individual dashboards, based on flash technology, process special requests and reports and perform analysis, focusing on the segment of business users. The unified SAP BO interface for accessing data sets and the familiar terminology in the markets when formulating an analytical query open up opportunities for conducting an independent non-standard search in the environment of online subscribers of the software product.

The work of innovation managers with the results of intellectual activity is the backbone component of the contemporary *strategy of entrepreneurship 4.0.* Through the commercial use of intellectual property, surplus value is maximized, new markets for high-tech products are won, excess profits are guaranteed, mergers and acquisitions are made, cross-industry partnerships are entered into, licensing agreements are signed, and venture projects are invested. In this case, the approach to the organization of the process (B. Guo & J. Guo, 2011) of commercial use of the results of intellectual activity in industrial production is based on the assessment of the probable commercial benefits for a certain estimated period (Figure 1).

DISCUSSION

1. The adsorption of technological novelties on a global scale, which forms the core of the technological order, is impossible without the participation of

Figure 1. The work of innovation managers on the selection of intellectual activity results in the context of Industry 4.0
Source: Compiled by the authors and based on (Voinov & Lomakina, 2022)

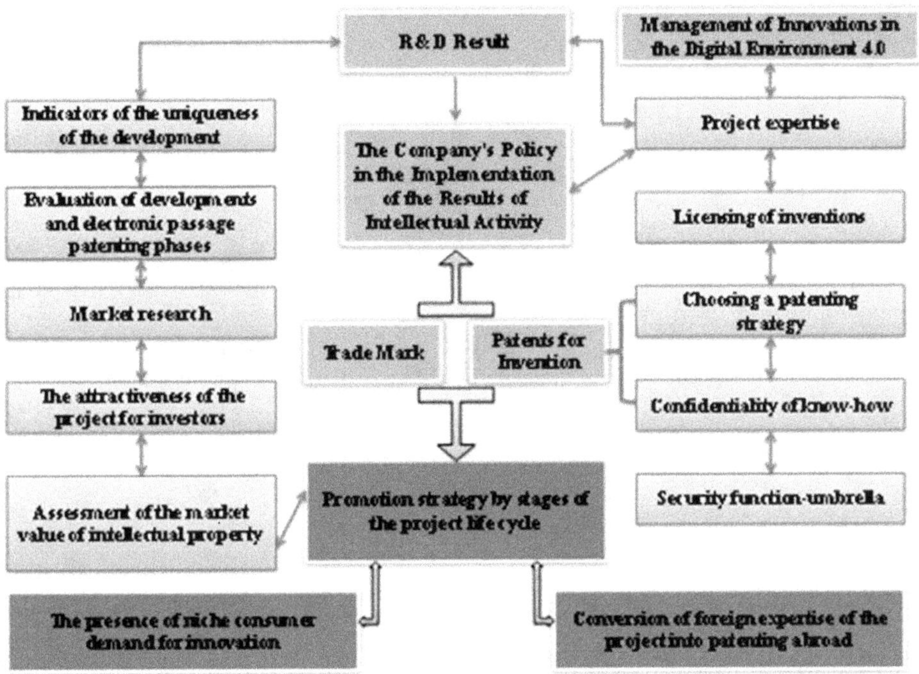

international communities of innovators. Thus, the Program (Strategy) for developing the Chinese nano industry (Voinov, 2015; Cheng et al., 2019) allocated $5.4 billion to the national market of nanoproducts in 2005; by 2015, it was planned to increase this figure to $144.8 billion.

In 2015–2018, smartphone sales just in the country territory reached around 1.725 billion. According to the American Patent and Trademark Office (USPTO) statistics, up to two-thirds of patents accounted for the share of Chinese nanotech manufacturers (Chou et al., 2011), included in the four world flagship countries of the number of nanotechnology patents in 2021. The global network structure has developed, among other things, around the Institute for Complexity, whose primary purpose is to participate in the design of the future of human civilization, analyzing direct and indirect influences that can change the situation in a predictable cybernetic direction in years and decades to come. The program of technological and socio-cultural transition of the European Union to the society of industry 4.0 and

Figure 2. Calculations of the potential global volume of nanotechnology patents received by countries.
Source: Compiled by the authors based on their own calculations and (Voinov et al., 2022)

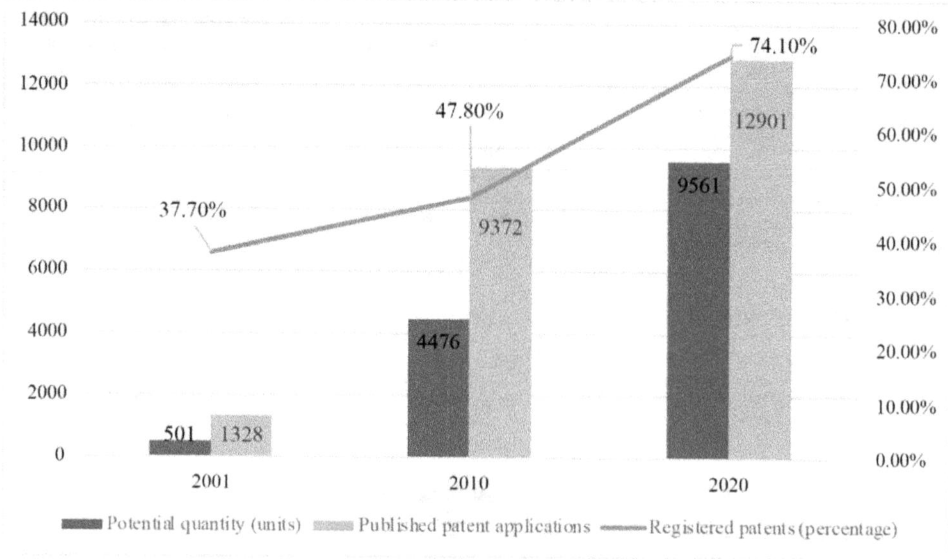

the factories of the future "Next generation" assumes a total amount of funding of €1.8 trillion. As a result, new technologies may appear at the top of the cycle but do not fit into the ascending technological trends already set by the global innovation communities. Accumulated breakthrough developments begin to "shoot" at the bottom when these trends turn out to be downward. For example, a special place in the implementation of the new UK industry strategy is occupied by the activities of "catapult" or "launch" national innovation centers (Catapults Centers) aimed at accelerating the commercialization of technologies of the sixth technological structure (Rybin et al., 2020).

Nanotechnology patents, which conceptually influence the formation of the core of the technological order, are the determining factor for the digital society (Voinov, 2014). If in 2001, according to the statistics of the USPTO and the authors' calculations, the global volume of nanotechnology patents received by countries was 501 units with 1328 published patent applications (37.7% registered), then this figure increased to 4476 and 9372 (47.8% registered) in 2010 and to 9561 and 12901 (74.1% registered) by the end of 2020 (Figure 2).

2. It is necessary to note such an updated method of commercialization of developments as "venture booms." On average, the global venture cycle takes about a decade. However, these cycles have decreased under the influence

of long-term trends of globalization, internationalization, and digitation of macro-technologies of production, which have intensified competition in the world markets of innovation-rich goods, services, patents, and licenses. The recovery of the American economy, which lasted from 2004 to 2007 and after 2010, also affected the public market. In 2000, the Taiwanese company "Semiconductor Manufacturing International Corp." (SMIC) held an IPO worth $1.8 billion, which was a historic high at the time. The previous record belonged to telecommunications company "Corvis," which, in 2000, almost at the very top of the market, conducted an IPO that slightly exceeded $1 billion. These highs continued their update – "Google" ($23 billion in 2004), "Twitter" ($24 billion in 2013), and "Alibaba" ($238 billion in 2014). Narrative changes in the discourse of the evolution of the cybersocium can be traced in the core of the first venture boom of the 1960s (microelectronics), during the boom of the 1970s–1980s (personal computers), the 1990s (the Internet and digital technologies), and the mid-2000s (Internet resources and online applications). Segments of the venture capital boom, which began in 2012 and peaked in 2018, include online services, e-commerce, and fintech. For example, in China, the total value of companies promoting online payment platforms exceeded 1.6 trillion yuan by the end of 2018. However, in the USA, the most attractive segments for investment in 2020 were IT companies ($11.2 billion, which is $0.6 billion more than in 2019) and biotechnologies and the pharmaceutical industry ($5.7 billion, which is $0.8 billion more than in 2019) (Ksiazkiewicz, 2017; Statista, 2021). What will be the basis for the next global innovation breakthrough? If we make forecasts, then the drivers of the next decade are undoubtedly metamaterials and nanobioelectronics, the singularity, gene therapy and nanobiomedicine, factories of the future, "green" and uncrewed automotive industry. Thus, despite the background of the COVID-19 pandemic, the period from 2019 to 2025 may be a favorable moment for aggressive technological investments in breakthrough companies. By many signs, the most experienced venture capitalists have already chosen startups that fit into the techno-economic paradigm of the sixth structure (Voinov et al., 2022).

3. During the proliferation of digital solutions, technology analysts coined the term "skunk workshops," which in the international innovation business refers to "breakout groups" working remotely and freelance on conceptual projects to make something fundamentally new or solve intractable problems. Foreign workshops of multinational corporations have been updated under quarantine restrictions. They specialize in high-tech software products in the initial stages, where the basic technology is created, which is brought to the final product by internal structural divisions. Technology transfer centers in corporations

exchange information materials and form digitized knowledge bases in their scientific fields. The products and technologies elaborated by the workshops are transmitted via feedback to the relevant enterprises. On the other hand, the fact that companies in the high-tech sector are included in international networks of venture acceleration increases the chances of success. It substantively multiplies their ability to extract maximum commercial benefits from the vast network communities of innovators that have acquired the status of virtual ones (JETRO, 2004).

CONCLUSION

In the last few decades, the world economic dynamics have been presented as an uneven and uncertain process of evolution of social reproduction based on the intensification of scientific and technological progress. Continuing to study the breadth of the definition of "innovations," we can state that in the discourse of the evolution of cyber society, it is a certain result of the projected multiplication of innovation activity. In the almost traditional activity of creating, mastering, and distributing innovations, NBICS-convergences, digitalization of industry 4.0 productions, additive 3D and 4D models of factories of the future, and the complexity of thinking are conceptualized. However, the understanding of digital transformation is much broader. It goes beyond the boundaries of not so much the unfolding global processes of digitalization of production but rather the mass introduction of ICT developments into the personal space of an individual. The difference between the design of the future (cybernetic concept) is that the prevailing method of analysis and synthesis considers the static states of complex systems, and the methodology of complexity theory considers the accumulated set of analyses and syntheses as a dynamic recursive series. The smooth functioning of the mechanisms of the digital economic paradigm is ensured by the effective management of the innovation process, where the increased activity of researchers and entrepreneurs is observed in the high-tech sector. At the junction of the fifth and sixth structures, it includes the production of semiconductor and electronic matrix components, micro-devices, aerospace equipment, computer, office and telecommunications equipment, products of low-tonnage chemistry, medicinal substances, and the creation of fundamentally new branches of knowledge and manufacturing industries, in particular, genetic engineering, bio- and nanotechnology, artificial intelligence. According to experts, high-tech products sold on global markets are generally based on the use of 50–55 macro-technologies, among which converging nanotechnologies currently occupy a special place. Nanotechnology patents, conceptually influencing the formation of the core of the technological order, are a determining factor for the digital society.

Industries with the digitalization of production, which intensively use this factor and play a leading role in the spread of new technological essentials, are carrier industries. Nanotechnologization of the global industrial space in the medium term can provide revenue from the sale of nanoproducts in the amount of up to $6–6.5 trillion. Simultaneously, there is an overall qualitative improvement in the number of published patent applications for subject nanoblasts. In this dynamic, the methods and trends set by international forecasting centers become increasingly noticeable. The adsorption of technological novelties on a global scale, which intensifies the formation of the core of the technological structure, is impossible without the participation of international communities of innovators. In this context, NBICS-convergences are more often discussed as a basis for social progress, representing the concept of managing the sustainable development of the technosphere, a project to improve the individual's potentiality based on the methodology of self-development and complexity.

According to empirical observations, the resulting economic effect from the use of knowledge management platforms (protection of critical volumes of knowledge, improving employee skills, increasing business capitalization by structuring intangible assets, expanding the route of opportunities for commercialization of the results of intellectual activity) increases up to 1.5 times. Information resources and accumulated knowledge become the foundation of digital technological development. Intellectual capital and advanced technologies associated with the applications of information systems determine the growth rate of the world economy. In particular, the SAP ERP solution combines comprehensive, scalable, and efficient high-tech business management software and a flexible operating platform based on open innovations 4.0. This platform allows entrepreneurs to integrate SAP product solutions with systems from other manufacturers, not excluding product licensing and SaaS software, and get increasing returns from the regular exchange.

The development and launch of innovative products that embody the results of intellectual activity require the most effort, cost, and time when bringing a knowledge-intensive product to market is the key to the success of the business as a whole. For the gradual promotion of the product, a systemic analysis of markets and the selection of commercially significant technologies is necessary. This cycle is completed faster and better due to the introduction of digital technologies. The market, covered by the third platform of the IT giants of e-commerce, cannot wait for products endowed with additional consumer properties to fill their niche. The speed of their appearance has substantively magnified (from 3 years in the early 2000s to several weeks by the 2020s), which requires manufacturers to offer a much larger number of variable solutions at the stages of "seed" and "startup." The spread of 5G and 6G networks, connected control centers, and the Internet of Things makes it relevant to have a flexible perception of digital innovations, the presence of creative behavior, and "turquoise" thinking in the team (school, college, university, work, and social activities). In the new "transparent world" of cyber industries, issues of marketing and product availability to the end customer are the prerogative of future releases of information and telecommunications technologies, artificial neural networks, and corporate ecosystems. However, the digital transformation of the company cannot be limited only to the modernization of its IT component and business virtualization. This leads to irrational and irresponsible investments, opening for implementation of clearly irrelevant projects, which ultimately imposes a special responsibility and significance on the effective management of innovative activities in companies in the context of the ongoing digital transformation of society.

REFERENCES

Cheng, Y., Liu, Y., Fan, W., Yan, Z., & Ye, X. (2019). Triple helix on globalization: A case study of the China International Nanotech Innovation Cluster. *Information Development, 35*(2), 272–289. doi:10.1177/0266666917743050

Choi, H., Shin, J., & Hwang, W.-S. (2018). Two faces of scientific knowledge in the external technology search process. *Technological Forecasting and Social Change, 133*, 41–50. doi:10.1016/j.techfore.2018.02.020

Chou, T., Ching, C., Fan, S., & Chang, J. (2011). Global linkages, the Chinese high-tech community and industrial cluster development: The semiconductor industry in Wuxi, Jingsu. *Urban Studies (Edinburgh, Scotland), 48*(14), 3019–3042. doi:10.1177/0042098010396237

Guo, B., & Guo, J.-J. (2011). Patterns of technological learning within the knowledge systems of industrial clusters in emerging economies: Evidence from China. *Technovation, 31*(2-3), 87–104. doi:10.1016/j.technovation.2010.10.006

Islam, N., Gyoshev, S., & Amona, D. (2020). External complexities in discontinuous innovation-based R&D projects: Analysis of inter-firm collaborative partnerships that lead to abundance. *Technological Forecasting and Social Change, 155*, 119303. doi:10.1016/j.techfore.2018.05.014

Japan External Trade Organization (JETRO). (2004, June). *Stimulation of regional clusters and international exchange (International Comparative Survey for Virtualization of the Japanese Economy)*. Tokyo, Japan: JETRO.

Kleinknecht, A. (1987). *Innovation patterns in crisis and prosperity. Schumpeter's long cycle reconsidered* (1st ed.). Palgrave Macmillan.

Kleinknecht, A. (2020). The (negative) impact of supply-side labour market reforms on productivity. An overview of the evidence. *Cambridge Journal of Economics, 44*(2), 445–464. doi:10.1093/cje/bez068

Kotter, J. P., Brown, T., Martin, R. L., & Rigby, D. K. (2021). *HBR's 10 must reads on change management* (Vol. 2). Harvard Business Review Press.

Ksiazkiewicz, R. (2017, March 23). *Useful Stats: Share of US venture capital activity and per capita investment by state, 2010–2016.* Retrieved April 15, 2020, from https://ssti.org/blog/useful-stats-share-us-venture-capital-activity-and-capita-investment-state-2010-2016

Rybin, M. V., & Voinov, A. I. (2020). Theoretical aspects and development of innovation management methods. *Economic Sciences, 185*, 37–43. doi:10.14451/1.185.37

Siggelkow, N., & Terwiesch, C. (2019, May-June). The age of continuous connection. *Harvard Business Review*. Retrieved January 19, 2020, from https://hbr.org/2019/05/the-age-of-continuous-connection

Spohrer, J. (2002). NBICs (nano-bio-info-cogno-socio) convergence to improve human performance: Opportunities and challenges. In M. C. Roco & W. S. Bainbridge (Eds.), *Converging technologies for improving human performance* (pp. 101–116). Edvard Press.

Statista. (2021). *The amount of venture capital investments in the US by branches for the 4th quarter of 2020*. Retrieved March 18, 2021, from https://www.statista.com/statistics/277506/venture-caputal-investment-in-the-united-states-by-sector/

Torkanovskiy, E. (2021). National competitiveness in the era of industry 4.0 and new individual freedoms. *World Futures*, *77*(2), 137–153. doi:10.1080/02604027.2020.1755213

Voinov, A. I. (2014). Evolution of the concept of "nanotechnology.". *Izobretatelstvo, 14*(11), 35–39.

Voinov, A. I. (2015). China's national science and technology policy. *Birzha intellektual'noj sobstvennosti, 3*, 38-41.

Voinov, A. I., & Lomakina, O. B. (2022). Nanotechnologization – the determining factor of the VI technostructure of the world economy. In T. M. Isachenko & L. S. Revenko (Eds.), *A new paradigm for the development of international economic relations: Challenges and prospects for Russia* (pp. 129–137). MGIMO University.

Chapter 11
Digitalization as a Factor in Improving the Competitiveness of the National Economy:
Opportunities and Prospects for the Agro-Industrial Complex of the Russian Federation

Vera A. Tikhomirova
https://orcid.org/0000-0002-4510-4319
FSBI "Agroexport", Russia

ABSTRACT

The need for the transition of the Russian agro-industrial complex to a qualitatively new level of technological development, which fully meets the current challenges and contradictions, has become more apparent. The research presents a review of the most promising innovative technologies of agro-industrial production, the introduction of which in the Russian AIC will increase the competitiveness of Russian food on the foreign market, positively affect the efficiency of environmental management, and reduce anthropogenic risks. The consideration of the advanced foreign experience in improving the sustainability of national food systems through the use of innovations in the resource provision of food production, expanding the use of remote channels of sale of food products, digitalization of customs procedures, and monitoring the safety and quality of goods in the implementation of export-import operations allowed the author to identify the most pressing areas of the Russian economy and propose a set of measures that can be used during the creation of a national food ecosystem.

DOI: 10.4018/978-1-6684-4265-4.ch011

INTRODUCTION

The global transformations caused by the permanent instability of the epidemiological situation in various regions of the world and, consequently, the disruption of world economic relations have brought humanity to the threshold of a new technological mode of international economic relations. In particular, the effects of the COVID-19 pandemic highlighted the need to modernize national agricultural and food production and distribution systems.

It is widely known that the development of the global food industry is characterized by heterogeneity and is correlated from country to country depending on the level of economic development. Having come a long way in its evolution, from traditional farming to the "biotechnological revolution" and "high-precision agriculture," agricultural production has now entered a new stage of scientific and technological development, which involves a large-scale digitalization of the value-added process and cross-border trade mechanisms (Funabashi, 2018).

The requirement implemented by several major players in the world food market for complete traceability of production chains and logistics of imported products, accompanied by increasingly clear prospects for the introduction of total electronic document management, stimulates the process of exporting food far beyond the traditional models of foreign economic activity and e-commerce to a qualitatively new technological format, the general principles of which are currently being formulated (European Commission, n.d.; General Administration of Customs of the People's Republic of China [GACC], 2021).

Humankind has accumulated a vast body of scientific research on the digitalization of virtually every aspect of food production (Gindele & Doluschitz, 2018; Lovchikova & Alpatov, 2020). However, it should be noted that the subject matter of the vast majority of works in this area mainly refers to the area of innovative technological support of the highest possible level of production of these products with minimal resource costs to reduce the anthropogenic impact on the ecosystem and refers to the segment of the national economy.

Simultaneously, the current realities of cross-border trade imply an increasing degree of "transparency" of the production cycles of goods at all stages of value-added formation and the entire range of logistics processes up to the arrival to the final consumer (European Commission, n.d.). This fact, together with the increasing practice of restricting imports of goods that do not meet the host country's geographical indications, quality and type of used raw materials, safety, and other criteria (GACC, 2021), encourages countries to modernize domestic policies to support exports of national agro-industrial enterprises in the international market and involves strengthening the cooperation of the business community with government agencies.

When considering possible ways to improve the competitiveness of Russian food products, the author proposes to identify two complementary blocks, which involve the digitalization, on the one hand, of production processes, and, on the other hand, the activities associated with the cross-border promotion of national products.

Given the above, the research aims to identify the most promising areas for innovation for the Russian economy through studying the best international practices in the digitalization of national food systems, the implementation of which will increase the sustainability of the food system of Russia and contribute to the competitiveness of Russian-made food in foreign markets.

To achieve this goal, the author set and consistently solved the following problems:

- To analyze the best practices of advanced economies in the digitalization of the national food system;
- To identify the most promising innovative technologies for the production of agricultural raw materials and food products;
- Based on the study of Russian and foreign academic literature, to identify factors that impede the effectiveness of national agricultural production through the introduction of innovative technologies and management methods;
- To define a set of measures necessary for the successful digitalization of Russian agriculture;
- To propose a version of the concept of digitalization of the Russian agro-industrial complex.

The theoretical basis of the research includes the following normative legal documents, analytical materials, and data:

- Analytical studies and forecasts of international organizations (FAO and OECD);
- State regulations governing the digitalization of agriculture;
- Russian regulatory framework for digitalization of agriculture;
- Materials from the world's leading consulting agencies and forecasting centers;
- Scientific articles and other materials from databases such as ISI Web of Knowledge, Scopus, RSCI, etc.;
- Data from customs statistics ITC Trade Map, Statista Business Data Platform.

The methodological basis of the research is the economic-prognostic method, systemic and comparative analysis, and the method of strategic planning (SWOT analysis). The data obtained as a result of the research was visualized using the calculation and constructive and graphical methods of scientific knowledge.

Thus, the design of this research implies a comprehensive review of the most relevant areas of digitalization of food production, followed by clarification of the most promising technologies for the current level of development of the Russian agro-industrial complex. Next, by identifying reference points of the current export-import policy and state programs of the leading players in the world market of agricultural raw materials and food products, the author proposes possible scenarios for modernization of the Russian food system and foreign economic policy.

Possible methodological limitations of this research include the lack of freely available sufficient empirical data on the studied issues.

The proposed research design fully meets the goals and objectives set by the author. It has a high degree of practical relevance because, in the context of current realities, the harmonious development of processes of value-added food products and their distribution channels can lay a solid foundation for improving the marketing of food produced in Russia, providing a high degree of competitiveness compared with similar products.

BACKGROUND

Nowadays, the foreign academic literature has accumulated a large body of theoretical and applied scientific research on the problems of transition to a new technological mode of agriculture. Western authors predominantly prefer to consider possible ways of digitalization of agriculture through the lens of technology, namely the introduction of high-tech data collection devices (Lytos et al., 2020), robotization of the industry, and the application of artificial intelligence and the Internet of Things (Moysiadis et al., 2020; Gindele et al., 2018).

When considering the foreign scientific base on the studied subject, it is necessary to take into account the fact that the high level of automation of agricultural production in developed countries has led to a shift in most scientific research from the already implemented technologies of "precision farming" (Zhang & Kovacs, 2012) to innovative development of "smart farming" (Jawad et al., 2017).

With regard to Russian realities, the vast majority of researchers in assessing the possible effectiveness of the introduction of advanced foreign technologies of agro-industrial production in the Russian agricultural sector conclude that, on the one hand, the level of technological and material support of enterprises in the sector is not consistent with these goals (Paptsov et al., 2019) and, on the other hand, on the insufficient level of professional competence of employees in the sector (Shelkovnikov et al., 2019).

The results of a systemic analysis of the theoretical framework of the research showed a deep degree of scientific understanding formed by Russian authors of the vast majority of the main theoretical and practical aspects of digitalization of agriculture, as well as the possible consequences of the introduction of this technological paradigm (Arkhipov et al., 2019; Konovalenko et al., 2020; Pyzhikova & Ozerova, 2018).

However, the issue of digitalization of the agro-industrial sector of the country through the development and implementation of a nationwide digital infrastructure, which would include agricultural production, the food industry, and related industries, has not yet received sufficient attention from the scientific community and requires further development. This direction is good because it has all chances to become one of the most effective approaches to the harmonious and gradual introduction of advanced food production technologies (which are now actively developing abroad) in the Russian agro-industrial complex.

The obtained data confirm the hypothesis of this research and proceed to the presentation of its most significant results.

THE ROLE OF DIGITALIZATION IN ENHANCING THE COMPETITIVENESS OF THE NATIONAL ECONOMY (Using THE AGRo-INDUSTRIAL SECTOR AS AN EXAMPLE)

Global Market of Digital Agricultural Technology

The unprecedented concentration of scientific potential in the field of improving the efficiency of production processes observed in recent decades has led to an avalanche growth of promising scientific developments and technologies of digitalization of the agricultural sector, which, in the Western scientific literature, were called digital agricultural technology (Digital AgTech).

In a broad sense, these innovative agricultural technologies are a set of high-tech digital techniques for crop, livestock, and aquaculture production to improve the economic efficiency of production, which are implemented with the requirements of sustainable environmental management and environmental safety (AgFunder, 2017).

Due to the highly dynamic emergence of this segment of the global economy, the scientific community currently has no generally accepted approach to quantify the size of the global market for digital agro-technology. Accordingly, the information field on the studied issue is saturated with a large array of approaches to quantitative assessment, which vary greatly due to the differentiation of the data set under study and the calculation methods used (Research Informatic, 2021; Statista, n.d.; GlobeNewswire, 2021). It should be noted that all analytical reports reviewed in

Figure 1. Global digital agricultural technology market forecast, 2020–2027 ($ billion)
Source: Compiled by the author based on (Research Informatic, 2021)

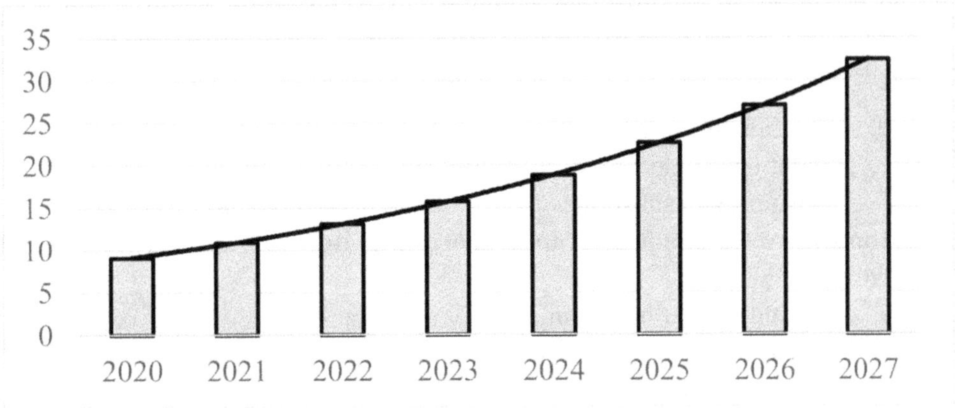

this research predict an upward trend in the digitalization of agricultural production in all regions of the world.

When describing the current size of the global market for digital agricultural technology, the author is guided by the results of a study conducted in 2021 by one of the US leading analytical agencies – Research Informatic. The methodology of the used study involves the broadest array of data under consideration. According to the results of this study, as of 2020, the global market for digital agricultural technology was $9.11 billion. It is expected to reach $32.5 billion by 2027 at a compound annual growth rate of 19.9% (Figure 1).

The analysis of the regulatory framework and materials of international organizations and the world's leading analytical agencies showed that the main directions of implementation of innovative technologies in agricultural production are as follows:

1. **Technological support for high-precision agriculture**:
   a. Remote monitoring systems for agricultural assets and natural-climatic conditions.
   b. Software for processing accumulated data to ensure the most efficient management of natural and industrial resources.
2. **High-tech crop production**:
   a. Development of highly productive genetics of agricultural plants that are resistant to adverse climatic conditions and weather events.
   b. Innovative greenhouse crop production.
   c. Hydroponics.
   d. Aeroponics.

3. **High-tech production of animal and alternative proteins**:
    a. Technologies for sustainable and resource-efficient forage production.
    b. Development of highly productive species of farm animals, birds, and aquaculture.
    c. Disease prevention systems for farm animals, birds, and aquaculture.
    d. Artificially cultured meat.
    e. Plant-based meat protein substitutes.
    f. Meat protein substitutes from alternative ingredients.
4. **Innovative technologies of food processing, delivery, and sale to the end consumer**:
    a. Digital marketing channels for agri-food products.
    b. Remote customs clearance of export-import operations.
    c. Contactless high-precision logistics and transshipment systems.
    d. Technologies that ensure traceability of agricultural commodities and food value chains.
    e. Ensuring the monitoring of the safety of agri-food products.
    f. Development of a recipe for innovative food products.
5. **Related technologies**:
    a. Irrigation and water management technologies.
    b. Products and technologies to improve soil fertility.
    c. Innovative ways to protect biodiversity.
    d. Robotic contactless techniques.

The given list of innovative technologies of agricultural production, depending on the ultimate goal of implementation of activities in this area, can be divided into the following categories:

- Commercial projects to develop and implement digital solutions in the production process of innovative food products.
- Public-private partnership aimed at collecting, accumulating, and analyzing data that maximally covers the process of food production and environmental management, necessary for forecasting and making informed management decisions.

The growth of new innovative digital technologies is mainly due to the activities of agricultural start-ups that attract more and more investments for their development every year because of the projected high profitability (AgFunder, 2017).

On the other hand, national governments are increasingly interested in accumulating a wide range of agricultural data (OECD, 2019). This trend is caused by current challenges and contradictions that require government agencies to monitor the state of the national food system in real-time to develop a balanced and most appropriate policy for the national interest and make highly accurate forecasts of further economic development.

At the time of this research, pioneers in the development of national programs for the practical application of advanced technologies and methods of digitalization of food production were such developed economies as the EU (digital platform RECAP), the USA (databases ECHO, EnviroAtlas, etc.), Japan (national platform for agricultural data exchange "WAGRI"), and New Zealand (national program "Our Land and Water").

Summarizing the experience of digital transformation of agriculture in the above countries, we can say that cloud-based digital technologies for precision farming are currently the most widespread. These technologies are implemented through the accumulation of a wide range of data on the actual state of natural resources and enterprises of the sector, with subsequent transfer of part of the collected information to the authorized public authorities (OECD, 2019; United States Environmental Protection Agency, n.d.-a, n.d.-b; Ministry of Agriculture, Forestry and Fisheries of Japan, n.d.).

Together with the accumulation of data on the development of agriculture, several commercial technological trends have been formalized, including promising agricultural technologies such as hydroponics, aeroponics, robotization of the agricultural sector, production of cultured meat and alternative animal and plant proteins, and the selection of highly productive farm animals and plants through genetic engineering (Tikhomirova, 2021).

Of the above list, innovative crop production based on hydroponics technology is the most widespread (at the time of this research). This innovation allows growing agricultural plants in an artificial environment without the use of soils based on mineral nutrient solutions in the sand, gravel, or liquid. The relatively low capacity of natural resources allows this technology to be successfully implemented in regions with a shortage of agricultural land and freshwater. According to UN studies, plants grown in hydroponic systems give 20%–25% higher yields than in traditional farming (United Nations, 2017).

Simultaneously, the large-scale introduction of this technology to crop production is hindered by the high cost of the final product due to high energy costs. Accordingly, the commercial introduction of hydroponics may be of interest to independent energy countries with high levels of economic development and scarcity of fresh water and land suitable for sustainable agriculture.

In 2020, the world's leading analytical agencies valued the global hydroponics market at $9.5 billion. This figure is expected to reach $16.2 billion by 2025 at an average annual growth rate of 11.3% (Figure 2).

Figure 2. Global hydroponics market forecast 2021–2025 ($ mln.)
Source: Compiled by the author based on (Markets and Markets, 2021)

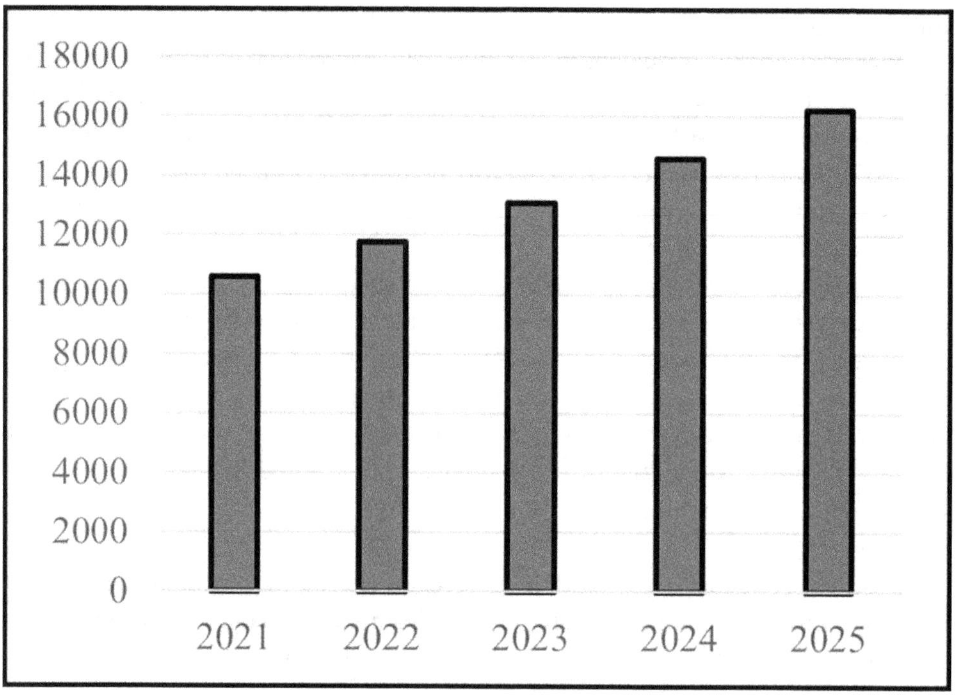

The vegetable meat substitutes sector also shows positive dynamics against the background of the transformation of consumer habits in developed countries, whose policies involve implementing measures to prevent global climate change by reducing the emission of methane into the atmosphere (Figure 3). One of the main advantages of meat substitutes from plant protein is the high price competitiveness compared to the products of the traditional livestock sector. Additionally, this food product is aimed at a wide range of people who do not eat animal proteins. The most promising areas in this field are the production of vegetable substitutes for red meat and poultry meat from soybeans and peas (Markets and Markets, 2020).

According to leading industry analysts, the volume of the global market for meat product substitutes from raw materials of plant origin in value terms amounted to $4.3 billion by the end of 2020. By 2025, this figure is expected to reach $8.3 billion, at an average annual growth rate of 14% (Markets and Markets, 2020).

Another promising area of high-tech meat production is the production of laboratory-grown cultured meat. The primary advantages of this model of animal protein production are environmental friendliness and the low consumption of non-renewable or slowly replenishable natural resources. In the future, this approach can

Figure 3. Global vegetable meat market forecast 2021–2025 ($ mln.)
Source: Compiled by the author based on (Markets and Markets, 2020)

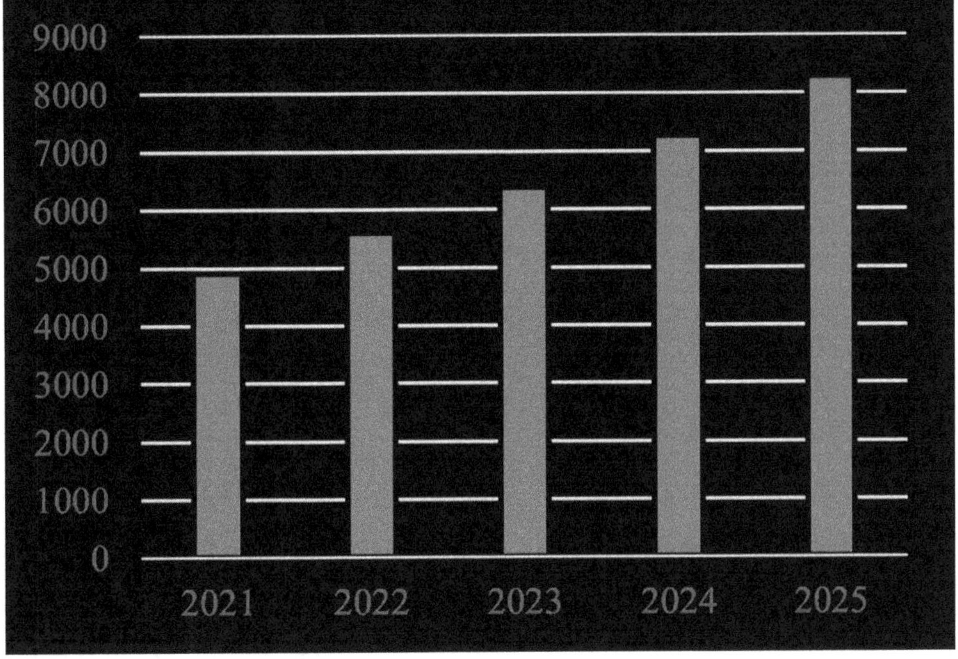

serve as an effective alternative to traditional forms of livestock farming in regions where, in accordance with objective circumstances, the arrangement of traditional livestock farms is difficult.

Nowadays, the global cultured meat industry is at the beginning of its formation process. However, the great prospects for the large-scale introduction of this technology and its possible potential in achieving food security at the national and global levels are already evident. In terms of value, the global cultured meat market is expected to reach only a modest $1.6 million this year. However, as the production process is streamlined, it will become cheaper and, by 2025, at an average annual growth rate of 95.8%, its total value will rise to $41.6 million. By 2030, it will grow to $41.6 million with the potential to grow to $2.8 billion (Figure 4).

Innovation is also actively developing in the production of feed for livestock, poultry, and aquaculture. Over the past year, the enormous jump in world corn and soybean prices was one of the drivers of world food prices; it also increased the economic costs of national food systems dependent on feed imports.

The search for alternatives to traditional crops, the use of which in the formulation of feed would be comparable in terms of performance indicators of the final product

Figure 4. Global cultured meat market growth forecast, 2021–2025 ($ mln.)
Source: Compiled by the author based on (Allied Market Research, 2021)

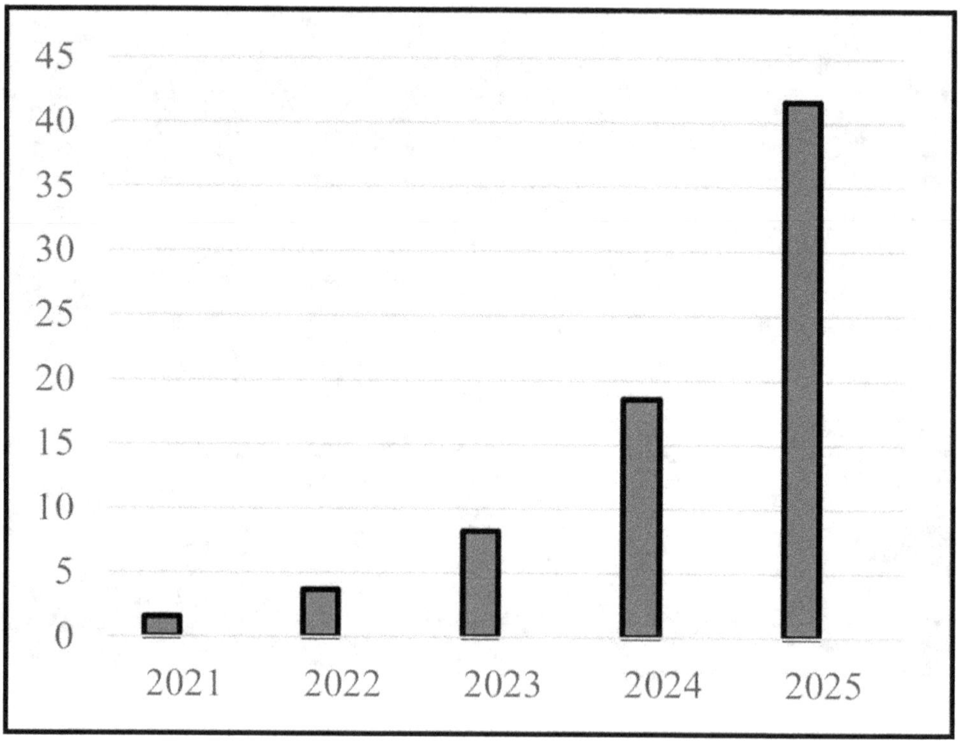

and would not have an additional economic burden, is one of the most important directions of scientific thought in today's agriculture.

Nowadays, according to analysts, one of the most promising technologies in this area is the use of alternative proteins derived from the processing of edible insects in the formulation of feed for the needs of livestock, poultry, and aquaculture. This approach is characterized by low production costs. It can be implemented as one of the stages of food waste processing.

As of 2020, the market for alternative protein for feed production exceeded $2.6 billion in value terms. The market is projected to reach $3.5 billion by 2025 at an average annual growth rate of 7% (Figure 5). Further development of the alternative protein industry will be driven by the growing global demand for food due to the increasing global population (Global market insights, 2021).

The technologies of innovative agro-industrial production considered in this research are highly promising and are designed to optimize the functioning of the global food system in light of the expected global climate change (FAO, 2020). Concerning the agro-industrial complex of the Russian Federation, this experience

Figure 5. Forecast for global market growth of alternative proteins for feed production 2021–2025 ($ mln.)
Source: Compiled by the author based on (Global Market Insights, 2021)

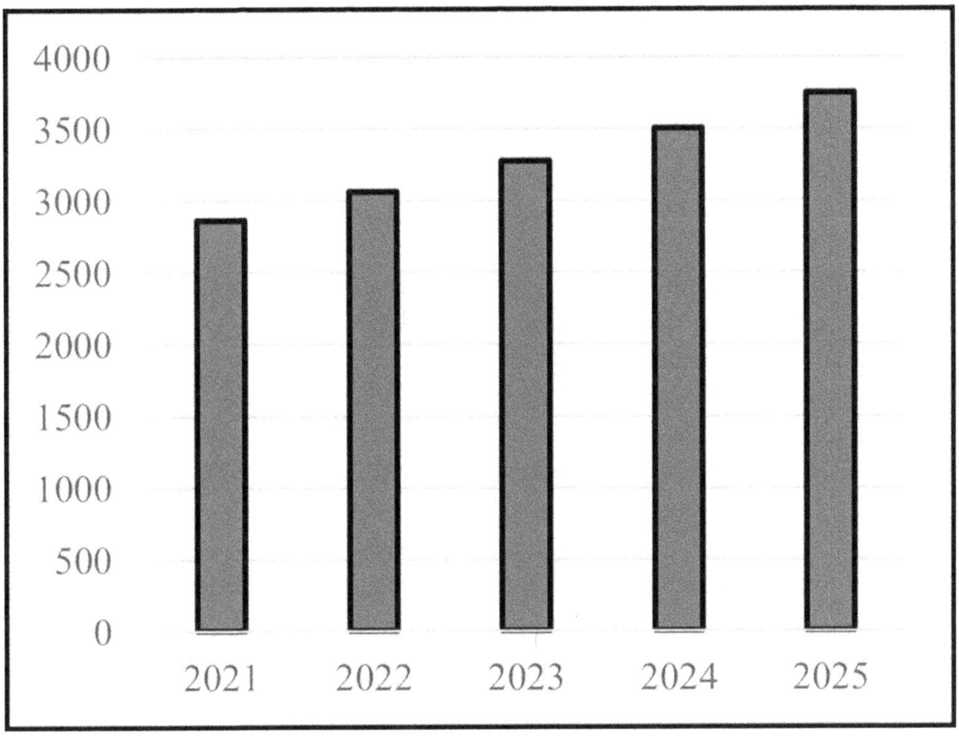

may be of interest as one of the possible directions of the state strategy in the economic integration of Siberia and the Far East. Realization of access to a wide range of economically affordable food in the northern regions of the country will have a positive impact on the inflow of labor resources, which, in turn, will allow fully developing the economic potential of these territories against the background of the expected reduction in permafrost (Demeter, 2021).

International Experience in Digitalization of National Food Systems and Improving Their Competitiveness

It should be noted that the global trend towards digitalization of production and distribution processes of agricultural and food products was largely inspired by the global crisis of cross-border trade and logistics of goods, which destabilized the turnover of agricultural and food products in the spring of 2020.

The lack of guarantees of access to supplies of strategic categories of food, plant seeds, breeding animals, birds, and other reproductive fauna, fertilizers, veterinary drugs, and related goods became an important stimulus for the development of national strategies for import substitution with goods necessary to form the added value of key food products, the shortage of which is associated with a significant threat to a stable food supply. (Tikhomirova, 2019).

As a result, during the COVID-19 pandemic, the political course for the implementation of the maximum possible import substitution of agricultural raw materials, food, and other goods necessary for agricultural production in various interpretations was repeatedly voiced by officials of Russia, Japan, China, the Republic of Korea, Vietnam, Thailand, India, Indonesia, Malaysia, Sri Lanka, the Philippines, European countries, Africa, and Latin America (Agroexport, n.d.). Thus, virtually every international actor has begun to develop policy documentation on the transformation of the national food system toward food security in the face of global uncertainty.

Considering the world experience in improving the stability of national food systems in the context of the digitalization of national economies, the author has made several conclusions, which are described below.

First, total self-sufficiency in the entire list of necessary food products is difficult to achieve and requires significant government funding, quality planning, and staging, which is not always achievable even for developed economies. Next, the author briefly considers the extremes of this process, using Sri Lanka and Japan as an example, which, as island states, are highly dependent on food imports.

The internal political situation in Sri Lanka in 2021 and the limited economic access to some food products and agricultural chemicals prompted the country's leadership to transform the national agro-industrial complex in the direction of a total greening of food production and a ban on the application of chemical fertilizers in agricultural soils to implement a strategy for specifying the country on the production of exclusively organic food with high competitive advantages in the global market (RFI, 2021).

It should be noted that this project for the development of agricultural production did not consider several important aspects of the national economy. The implementation of this project eventually led to an imbalance of mechanisms for providing food to the population and, consequently, a significant reduction in the country's export potential.

When developing forecasts of agricultural production, no account was taken of the objective condition of the lands involved in agricultural production, the fertility of the vast majority of which has been substantially degraded. A breakneck transition to organic agricultural production led to a total decrease in crop yields, which was difficult to compensate for by higher prices of export products due to high price competition, distance from high-margin markets for these products, and the rising cost of freight. Thus, the pursuit of near-total self-sufficiency has been a destabilizing factor, further undermining Sri Lanka's economy (RFI, 2021).

In contrast, another island nation in the region, Japan, which has a developed economy compared to Sri Lanka, has adopted a more moderate plan to increase the sustainability of the industry and has focused on increasing the efficiency of production of only the most promising categories of food for sale in domestic and foreign markets, namely aquatic resources, wagyu beef, and traditional alcoholic and tonic beverages (The Japan Agricultural News, 2022).

Due to objective circumstances, until recently, the agro-industrial sector of Japan has been the most problematic sector of the national economy in terms of increasing productivity; it provided only a small share of the country's GDP. A lack of self-sufficiency in agricultural and food products, labor shortages, and the low level of competitiveness of manufactured products compared to imported counterparts were a traditional obstacle to attracting investment in this area (Eurasian Economic Commission, 2017).

In the wake of the COVID-19 pandemic, widespread disruptions in food chains and cross-border commodity logistics have prompted Japanese leaders to rethink the role and importance of the country's agri-food sector in ensuring national security. The supercycle of prices for agricultural raw materials, energy resources, chemicals, and medicines used in food production, established after the global lockdown, also greatly contributed to the transformation of the national economic paradigm.

The application by Japanese farmers of the wide range of innovative digital technologies described above has contributed to overcoming a significant number of obstacles to the large-scale establishment of national agricultural production. As a result, the undernourished Asian nation managed to increase its self-sufficiency in some basic food categories and develop a significant export turnover. Thus, the total volume of national exports of agroforestry and livestock products was estimated at \$5.07 billion in 2010, while in 2021, this figure increased by a record 41.5% and reached a historical maximum of \$8.67 billion (South China Morning Post, 2022).

Accordingly, we can state that a clear definition of the country's specification in the world food market, the key competitive advantages of the production, and the introduction of innovative digital technologies, in combination, allow achieving much greater progress in improving the sustainability of the national food system than populism, not backed by the necessary resource support (Lovchikova et al., 2020).

Second, the widespread and poorly controlled mass epizootics of livestock and poultry over the past two years have resulted in reduced foreign exchange earnings for exporters from countries where outbreaks of these diseases have been detected and reduced access to high-yielding breeding stock to restore production.

According to the World Organization for Animal Health (OIE), of the total list of epizootics, the most devastating impact on global food production in recent years has been caused by African swine fever (ASF) and several strains of highly pathogenic avian influenza, the destructive effects of which are manifested in the countries located in both hemispheres of our planet and affected the largest exporters of high-yielding genetics of farm animals and birds (OIE, 2021a, 2021b).

In this context, the author proposes to consider the Russian experience in developing the national poultry industry. Characterized by a short payback period and relatively low cost compared to other animal proteins, the poultry industry gave the initial impetus to the development of Russian self-sufficiency in meat products, which subsequently contributed to the inclusion of Russia in the top 15 world exporters of poultry products (ITC Trade Map, n.d.).

Simultaneously, the lack of technologies in the Russian food system for self-sufficiency in high-yielding poultry breeds with hatching eggs against the backdrop of more frequent outbreaks of bird flu, including in the USA, the Netherlands, and Germany (the world's largest suppliers of these products), has put Russian farmers on the brink of payback and led to an increase in domestic prices in the segment (Poultry World, 2022).

An unprecedented increase in the degree of international uncertainty and tension stimulates Russia to think about creating a digital register of the genetic material of flora and fauna presented in the country to avoid significant losses to the domestic economy. The implementation of this project will help to make significant progress in breeding the own broodstock of highly productive farm animals and birds, which are characterized by a high degree of assimilation to Russian climatic conditions. Moreover, this project allows neutralizing possible risks of introducing restrictions on access to the genetic support of the agro-industrial complex.

Third, the global trend towards increasing requirements for the quality of imported food forces industry enterprises to increase the traceability of the value chain of exported food, which brings a new level of logistics and labeling of food products.

The driver of the digitalization of food chain production processes is the PRC's foreign economic policy. At the end of 2021, to prevent the entry of COVID-19 on food packaging, the leadership of the world's largest food importer launched a new system to ensure the safety of imported food. This system requires providing data on the place of production of the final product and the place of production of raw material from which the final product was obtained (GACC, 2021). In the medium term, this experience is expected to be adopted by other countries in the region.

Fourth, as e-commerce has reached a new level in countries worldwide, there is a growing need for a digital transformation of customs clearance of export-import operations. As of the moment of the research, the customs authorities of the PRC and some provinces of Vietnam had switched to a fully remote digital workflow

(GACC, 2021; Anh, 2022). This process is accompanied by developing a single legal framework for entrepreneurs in the ASEAN countries.

Of particular interest is the joint position of the ASEAN countries. These countries believe that digitalization focused on simplifying and algorithmizing processes for the sale of produced food through electronic marketing channels in the domestic and foreign markets can effectively combat food inflation. These countries also note that reducing the food chain will effectively reduce the margins on food and increase the income and purchasing power of the rural population.

Based on the above, the digitalization of the agro-industrial complex is currently occurring in four key areas, which are as follows:

- Creation of the state register of the genetic material of agricultural flora and fauna available in the country to use in the breeding of own seed and breeding stock, characterized by high economic efficiency indicators.
- Introduction of geographical indications and maximum traceability of value chains of produced food, which contributes to maintaining high-quality standards and forms a significant competitive advantage when exporting products.
- Introduction of a wide range of digital technologies for monitoring the health of farm animals and poultry in production processes. These technologies enable timely response and prevention of large-scale outbreaks of diseases in farm animals and poultry.
- Stimulating the growth of digital turnover of agricultural products through the development of transport infrastructure, technical support, logistics, and the organization of educational programs for the population of rural areas.

Nowadays, it is safe to predict that in the medium term, the world food system will undergo a transformation toward a change in the technological paradigm. In this case, the greatest dividends from this process will receive the countries that will manage to advance in the digitalization of production processes and the entire cycle of food production from the development of seed and breeding stock to the arrival of products to the end consumer. Simultaneously, the tightening of requirements for the safety of imported food creates new barriers to the promotion of agricultural products, the overcoming of which is possible only with the consolidation of efforts of government agencies and agribusiness.

Russia's Experience in Digitalization of the National Agro-Industrial Complex: Preliminary Assessment and Prospects

The Russian Federation has a well-developed agro-industrial complex. It is one of the world's top 20 food exporters, supplying a wide range of agricultural and food products to foreign markets (OECD, 2019). According to the departmental project "Digital agriculture" (DAM), one of the main directions of promoting the Russian agri-food sector in the medium term is "digital transformation of the industry through the introduction of innovative technologies and platform solutions to ensure a technological breakthrough in agriculture and achieve productivity growth at the 'digital' agricultural enterprises" (Gordeev et al., 2019). The implementation of DAM should be carried out based on the public-private partnership to develop and implement a unified national Internet platform of the agro-industrial complex of the Russian Federation by 2024, which will provide for the digitalization of the following areas of the national agriculture and food industry:

1. Regulation of land use and land management.
2. Ensuring traceability of agricultural products throughout the entire value chain.
3. Implementation of government support and a wide range of services through the service "personal account of the user."
4. Improving the level of professional competencies of the sector's employees.
5. Storage and distribution of information materials.
6. Collection and accumulation of industry data.
7. Implementation of agricultural and weather forecasting.

The lack of sufficient empirical data on the results of the implementation of the DAM (as of the moment of the research) does not allow carrying out a qualitative and quantitative assessment of the preliminary results of the monitoring criteria specified in the passport of the considered state program. In connection with this circumstance, the author decided to make a SWOT analysis of the possible pros and cons of the digitalization of the national food system of the Russian Federation based on the study of academic literature on the declared subject (Table 1).

Among the apparent benefits of the innovative technological transition, it is important to note that the digitalization of foreign economic activity reduces barriers for small and medium enterprises (SMEs) to carry out foreign economic activity. SMEs in China, Vietnam, and several countries in Southeast Asia have already benefited from cross-border Internet commerce. This trend has also provided a strong impetus for the ASEAN bloc to develop a unified regulatory framework governing cross-border distance sales of goods, including food.

Table 1. Swot analysis of possible prospects for digitalization of the national food system of the Russian Federation

Weaknesses	Strengths
• The need to implement an integrated intersectoral approach. • The attraction of a considerable amount of funding, including from extrabudgetary sources, is required. • Shortage of personnel with the necessary competencies and qualifications. • Low level of technical development. • • Possible reluctance of some subjects of the business community to provide commercial information to government bodies.	• Availability of a considerable amount of agricultural land and areas suitable for agricultural production in the future. • Self-sufficiency in ores of a large assortment of heavy and non-ferrous metals. • Geographical proximity to significant and promising food logistics channels.
Threats	**Opportunities**
• The risk of undermining national information security by accumulating a large array of industry and private data on a digital Internet resource. • High risk of not achieving the declared objectives due to the need for a large number of preparatory works in related sectors of the national economy necessary to implement a technological leap.	• Development of self-sufficiency in semiconductors and microcircuits necessary for the production and after-sales service of innovative equipment. • Ensuring the economic development of the country's regions and rural areas through the introduction of remote business technologies. • Digital integration of rural areas by providing access to a broadband Internet connection. • A large-scale modernization of transportation and storage chains. • Creation of new jobs in rural areas. • Reduction of the outflow of labor from the agro-industrial complex.

Source: Compiled by the author based on (Bylina et al., 2018; Tarasov et al., 2018; Akmarov et al., 2019; Pyzhikova et al., 2018)

In the context of the Russian reality, government support for the output of national agro-industrial SMEs on the external market can trigger the economic recovery of rural areas and reduce the outflow of the population to large cities. Simultaneously, to achieve a tangible effect, the public administration must commit itself to the modernization and construction of the necessary infrastructure and logistics facilities and ensure unhindered access to energy resources and broadband Internet access for the population.

With the implementation of a balanced integrated approach, the digitalization of the Russian agro-industrial complex can become a consolidating platform for the development of the country's regions, as well as for the formation of a domestic agro-industrial ecosystem, uniting the interests of agribusiness enterprises and related industries, without which the development of innovative production technologies of agricultural and food products, outlined in the first part of this research, is impossible.

In many respects, the low level of professional competence of workers in the industry is one of the obstacles to the modernization of technological support of the Russian agro-industrial complex. Robotization of the food production process, the use of AI technologies, the selection of own seed and breeding base of highly productive agricultural flora and fauna, the use of innovative technologies for the synthesis of animal and plant proteins, and the implementation of cross-border electronic commerce require the training of highly qualified personnel.

Accordingly, the organization of preferential right of access of the rural population to distance education programs, social and medical support, development and implementation of state policy in the field of professional training, and attraction of competent personnel in the national agriculture and food industry will ensure an increase in labor productivity, reduce production costs, contribute to the competitiveness of Russian-made food, and "in practice" help reduce the gap in the "quality of life" of urban and rural residents.

In addition to the apparent advantages of the considered technological structure of the agro-industrial complex, it is essential to note that without a preliminary solution to the problem of self-sufficiency in semiconductors and microchips, the creation of independent data storage servers, the development of software, and the implementation of the targets set out in the passport of the DAM not only seems difficult to achieve but are also associated with the risk of undermining Russia's national security (Ganieva & Bobrov, 2019). Overcoming dependence on imported hardware and digital technology can be an effective defense against the misuse of government monitoring data and commercial and private information.

SOLUTION

In the process of transition to a new technological formation, Russia, first and foremost, needs to focus on the development of public-private partnerships in the field of resource provision of information and communication technologies and the creation of advanced secure communication channels and documents flow.

To reach a new technological level in the domestic economy, it is necessary, using a comprehensive approach, to create a national agri-food ecosystem, which would include related industries: personnel training, production of semiconductors and microchips, development of own software and databases, and modernization and construction of necessary infrastructure. These projects must be implemented simultaneously; otherwise, the invested funds will not pay off, and the technological gap will be exacerbated. Simultaneously, achieving the highest possible efficiency of digitalization of the Russian agro-industrial complex should bring economic benefits to the country, business, and the country's population.

FUTURE RESEARCH DIRECTIONS

Today's world is in the process of transforming the economic paradigm towards a qualitatively new technological mode of the global economy, the general features of which are already taking shape. In the medium term, the trend towards cross-border digital commerce is expected to grow even further, encompassing an increasing range of goods, including food, every year. The transition to electronic customs declaration of export-import operations will significantly accelerate the turnover of goods. Simultaneously, the role of self-provision of basic equipment and competencies necessary to ensure cyber security of the national economy will increase.

CONCLUSION

Digitalization of Russian agricultural production is an objectively overdue need for a change in the technological paradigm, the implementation of which will significantly increase the competitiveness of Russian agricultural raw materials and food products on foreign markets. The introduction of innovative production and processing methods in the Russian agro-industrial complex will increase the efficiency of natural resource allocation and reduce the risks of using natural resources against the current background of global climate change.

Hydroponics, cultured meat, and alternative proteins of plant and animal origin allow optimizing the production process and reducing the differentiation in achieving a sustainable level of self-sufficiency in agricultural production between regions with significant climatic differences.

The current main obstacles to the digitalization of the Russian agro-industrial complex are as follows:

- Low level of technical equipment of industry enterprises (low level of automation and mechanization, lack of access to broadband Internet);
- Unsatisfactory level of qualifications and professional competencies of industry workers and high staff turnover;
- Lack of self-sufficiency in sensors, other technical means, and software necessary for high-precision farming;
- The need to develop an effective model to ensure the cybersecurity of monitoring data of the development of the agricultural sector.

The digitalization of the national agro-industrial complex requires a systemic approach that involves the integrated development of rural areas of the country and the conjunction of interests of the government, business, and the population on a mutually beneficial basis. Achieving this goal is only possible with the development of regulations and roadmaps detailing the totality of the elements necessary to create a national digital food ecosystem.

REFERENCES

AgFunder. (2017). *Agfunder agri-food tech: Investment report.* Retrieved December 28, 2021, from https://research.agfunder.com/2017/AgFunder-Agrifood-Tech-Investing-Report-2017.pdf

Agroexport. (n.d.). *Digests of foreign media.* Retrieved December 27, 2021, from https://aemcx.ru/media/digestino/

Akmarov, P. B., Gorbushina, N. V., & Knyazeva, O. P. (2019). Features of digital transformation in the agricultural sector of the economy. *Agricultural Education and Science*, *2*, 1–12.

Allied Market Research. (2021). *Cultured meat market: Global opportunity analysis and industry forecast 2022–2030.* Retrieved December 27, 2021, from https://www.alliedmarketresearch.com/cultured-meat-market-A06670

Anh, Q. (2022, February 21). From February enterprises importing and exporting goods through Lang Son border gate must declare through the digital platform. *Toquoc*. Retrieved February 28, 2022, from http://nhipsongkinhte.toquoc.vn/tu-21-2-doanh-nghiep-xuat-nhap-khau-hang-hoa-qua-cua-khau-lang-son-phai-khai-bao-qua-nen-tang-so-420222121031357 68.htm

Arkhipov, A. G., Kosogor, S. N., Motorin, O. A., Gorbachev, M. I., Suvorov, G. A., & Truflyak, E. V. (2019). *Digital transformation of Russian agriculture.* Moscow, Russia: Rosinformagrotech. Retrieved December 27, 2021, from https://mcx.gov.ru/upload/iblock/28f/28f56de9c3d40234dbdcbfac94787558.pdf

Bylina, S. G., Kadomtseva, M. E., & Osovin, M. N. (2018). *Informatization of the agri-food complex and rural areas of Russia: Opportunities and limitations incl. development of the digital economy.* Saratov, Russia: Saratovskiy istochnik.

Demeter. (2021). *Produce and feed: The daily challenge of a confused world.* Retrieved December 18, 2021, from https://www.clubdemeter.com/fr/le-demeter

Eurasian Economic Commission. (2017). *State support for agriculture developed and developing countries.* Retrieved December 23, 2021, from Retrieved from http://www.eurasiancommission.org/ru/act/prom_i_agroprom/dep_agroprom/sxs/Documents/Государственная%20поддержка%20сельского%20хозяйства%20в%20развитых%20и%20развивающихся%20странах%20(2017).pdf

European Commission. (n.d.). *Regulations on food and agricultural products.* Retrieved January 08, 2022, from https://ec.europa.eu/info/food-farming-fisheries/food-safety-and-quality/certification/quality-labels/quality-schemes-explained_en#geographicalindications

Food and Agriculture Organization (FAO). (2020). *World food and agriculture – Statistical yearbook, 2020.* Rome, Italy: FAO. Retrieved December 19, 2021, from https://www.fao.org/3/cb1329en/CB1329EN.pdf

Funabashi, M. (2018). Human augmentation of ecosystems: Objectives for food production and science by 2045. *NPJ Science of Food*, *2*(1), 16. doi:10.103841538-018-0026-4 PMID:31304266

Ganieva, I. A., & Bobrov, N. E. (2019). Digital platforms in Russian agriculture: The legal aspect of implementation. *Achievements of Science and Technology of the Agro-Industrial Complex*, *33*(9), 83–86. doi:10.24411/0235-2451-2019-10918

General Administration of Customs of the People's Republic of China (GACC). (2021). *Measures for the administration of import and export food safety of the People's Republic of China.* Retrieved December 27, 2021, from http://jckspj.customs.gov.cn/spj/zcfg18/bmgz91/4034487/index.html

Gindele, N., & Doluschitz, R. (2018). *"Agriculture 4.0" Germany – current state and prospects. "German-Russian Agrarian-Political Dialogue" Cooperation project of the German Federal Ministry of Food and Agriculture.* Retrieved December 25, 2021, from https://agrardialog.ru/files/prints/gindele_dolushitts_%C2%ABselskoe_hozyaystvo_4_0%C2%BB_germanii_tekushchee_sostoyanie_i_perspektivi.pdf

Global Market Insights. (2021). *Alternative protein market for animal feed application, competitive market share & forecast, 2021–2027.* Retrieved December 27, 2021, from https://www.gminsights.com/industry-analysis/alternative-protein-market-for-animal-feed

GlobeNewswire. (2021). *Smart agriculture market size globally estimated to reach USD 22.5 Bn, with 8.9% CAGR by 2026: Facts & factors.* Retrieved December 28, 2021, from https://www.globenewswire.com/news-release/2021/10/18/2315821/0/en/Smart-Agriculture-Market-Size-Globally-Estimated-to-Reach-USD-22-5-Bn-with-8-9-CAGR-by-2026-Facts-Factors.html

Gordeev, A. V., Patrushev, D. N., Lebedev, I. V., Arkhipov, A. G., Bulanov, K. A., Grebenkov, D. V., & Kosogor, S. N. (2019). *Departmental project "Digital agriculture."* Moscow, Russia: Rosinformagrotech. Retrieved December 20, 2021, from https://mcx.gov.ru/upload/iblock/900/900863fae06c026826a9ee43e124d058.pdf

Jawad, H. M., Nordin, R., Gharghan, S. K., Jawad, A. M., & Ismail, M. (2017). Energy-efficient wireless sensor networks for precision agriculture: A review. *Sensors (Basel), 17*(8), 1781. doi:10.339017081781 PMID:28771214

Konovalenko, L. Yu., Mishurov, N. P., Golubev, I. A., Nikitina, M. A., & Bredikhin, S. A. (2020). *Digital transformation of the food and processing industry: An analytical review.* Moscow, Russia: Rosinformagrotech. Retrieved December 19, 2021, from https://tinyurl.com/2mrs8tnf

Lovchikova, E. I., & Alpatov, A. V. (2020). *Diversification and specialization of agricultural production in terms of social and labor employment and the development of the digital economy.* Publishing House of Oryol State Agrarian University.

Lytos, A., Lagkas, T., Sarigiannidis, P., Zervakis, M., & Livanos, G. (2020). Towards smart farming: Systems, frameworks and exploitation of multiple sources. *Computer Networks, 172*, 107147. doi:10.1016/j.comnet.2020.107147

Markets and Markets. (2020). *Plant-based meat market: Global forecast to 2025.* Retrieved December 27, 2021, https://www.marketsandmarkets.com/Market-Reports/plant-based-meat-market-44922705.html

Markets and Markets. (2021). *Hydroponic market: Global forecast to 2026.* Retrieved December 27, 2021, from https://www.marketsandmarkets.com/Market-Reports/hydroponic-market-94055021.html

Ministry of Agriculture, Forestry, and Fisheries of Japan. (n.d.). *Efforts to realize "Smart agriculture."* Retrieved December 27, 2021, from https://www.maff.go.jp/e/policies/tech_res/smaagri/robot.html

Moysiadis, V., Sarigiannidis, P., Vitsas, V., & Khelifi, A. (2020). Smart farming in Europe. *Computer Science Review, 39*, 100345. doi:10.1016/j.cosrev.2020.100345

OECD. (2019). *Digital opportunities for better agricultural policies.* OECD Publishing. doi:10.1787/571a0812-

Paptsov, A. G., Altukhov, A. I., Kashevarov, N. I., Petrushkevich, P. M., Denisov, A. S., Rudoy, E. V., Petukhova, M. S., Kapustyanchik, S. Yu., Dobryanskaya, S. L., Potseluev, O. M., Sadokhina, T. A., Petrov, A. F., Ryumkin, S. V., Galeev, R. R., Polunin, G. A., Taran, V. V., & Sokolova, Zh. E. (2019). Forecast of scientific and technological development of the crop industry, including seed production and organic farming in Russia, in the period up to 2030. Novosibirsk, Russia: Publishing Center “Zolotoy kolos”.

Poultry World. (2022). *Russia again hit by hatching eggs shortage.* Retrieved December 27, 2021, from https://www.poultryworld.net/poultry/russia-again-hit-by-hatching-eggs-shortage/

Pyzhikova, N. I., & Ozerova, M. G. (2018). Digitization of agriculture: Advantages and problems. In N. V. Gavrilets (Ed.), *The role of agricultural science in the sustainable development of rural areas* (pp. 1138–1140). Novosibirsk State Agricultural University.

Research Informatic. (2021). *Global agtech market – growth, share, opportunities and competitive analysis, 2021–2027.* Retrieved December 27, 2021, from https://www.researchinformatic.com/reports/agtech-market-32

RFI. (2021, November 21). *Sri Lanka backtracks on chemical ban in agriculture.* Retrieved December 27, 2021, from https://www.rfi.fr/fr/asie-pacifique/20211121-le-sri-lanka-revient-sur-l-interdiction-des-produits-chimiques-dans-son-agriculture

Shelkovnikov, S. A., Kuznetsova, I. G., Petukhova, M. S., & Alekseev, A. A. (2019). Digitalization as a trend in the development of agriculture in the context of a new technological order. *Bulletin of the Transbaikal State University*, *25*(8), 119–126. doi:10.21209/2227-9245-2019-25-8-119-126

South China Morning Post. (2022). *Mainland China was top importer of Japanese food in 2021, surpassing Hong Kong and the US, with sake, scallops and whiskey in demand.* Retrieved December 27, 2021, from https://www.scmp.com/week-asia/article/3166259/mainland-china-was-top-importer-japanese-food-2021-surpassing-hong-kong.

Statista. (n.d.). *Agricultural technology (Agtech) market value worldwide from 2020 to 2025.* Retrieved December 28, 2021, from https://www.statista.com/statistics/1222528/worldwide-agricultural-technology-market-value/#statisticContainer

Tarasov, A. N., Kavardakov, V. Ya., Semenenko, I. A., & Maksutova, L. G. (2018). *Innovative and technological development of animal husbandry in the Russian Federation in the context of the industry’s transition to a bioinformatic technological structure: Theory, methodology, practice*. AzovPrint.

The Japan Agricultural News. (2022). *How will digital introduction agriculture change?* Retrieved February 08, 2021, from https://www.scmp.com/week-asia/article/3166259/mainland-china-was-top-importer-japanese-food-2021-surpassing-hong-kong

Tikhomirova, V. A. (2019). *Ensuring food security: International and Russian experience* (Dissertation of Candidate of Economic Sciences). Moscow, Russia: RUDN University.

Tikhomirova, V. A. (2021). Innovations in agro-industrial production as a driver for increasing the sustainability of national food systems. *RUDN Journal of Economics, 29*(4), 773–784. doi:10.22363/2313-2329-2021-29-4-773-784

Trade Map, I. T. C. (n.d.). *Trade statistic for international business development.* Retrieved January 08, 2022, from https://www.trademap.org/Index.aspx

United Nation. (2017, June 21). *World population projected to reach 9.8 billion in 2050, and 11.2 billion in 2100.* Retrieved December 04, 2021, from https://www.un.org/development/desa/en/news/population/world-population-prospects-2017.html

United States Environmental Protection Agency. (n.d.a). *ECHO Data Services.* Retrieved December 28, 2021, from https://echo.epa.gov/

United States Environmental Protection Agency. (n.d.b). *EnviroAtlas.* Retrieved December 28, 2021, from https://www.epa.gov/enviroatlas

World Organisation for Animal Health (OIE). (2021). *Global control of African swine fever: A GF-TADs initiative (2020–2025).* Retrieved May 19, 2021, from https://www.oie.int/fileadmin/Home/eng/Animal_Health_in_the_World/docs/pdf/ASF/ASF_GlobalInitiative_Web.pdf

World Organisation for Animal Health (OIE). (2021). *Situation reports for avian influenza.* Retrieved May 19, 2021, from https://www.oie.int/en/disease/avian-influenza/

Zhang, C., & Kovacs, J. M. (2012). The application of small unmanned aerial systems for precision agriculture: A review. *Precision Agriculture, 13*(6), 693–712. doi:10.100711119-012-9274-5

Conclusion

The Perspectives of Using Digital Technologies in Entrepreneurship in Industry 4.0 in the Age of Neo-Globalization

The use of digital technologies in entrepreneurship in Industry 4.0 is largely determined by the context. This book demonstrated that the COVID-19 pandemics and crisis had a serious impact on online business in Industry 4.0. Digital technologies for institutional investors stimulate the development of hi-tech entrepreneurship in the environment of Industry 4.0. Modernization of corporate reporting and corporate management in the digital economy facilitates the increase in the investment attractiveness of companies, including "young" companies under the conditions of global changes that are connected with a new industrial revolution.

Digitalization of the infrastructure development based on the use of the public-private partnership mechanisms is very active. The role of innovation management in the age of digital transformation grows, and digitalization becomes a factor in the increase in the national economy's competitiveness. The digital economy and digital transformation dictate a new organizational design and open new paths toward digital technologies for entrepreneurship in Industry 4.0. All successful results of the dissemination and use of digital technologies in entrepreneurship in Industry 4.0, which are mentioned in this book, were achieved in the context of an open economy and free trade in the age of total globalization.

The modern world entered a new age – neo-globalization. In this age, international trade continues developing dynamically, but becomes more segmented and selective – oriented toward the most reliable suppliers and the most stable demand. Global chains of value-added creation are transformed. World shocks of the new millennium, which include the global financial and economic crisis, the COVID-19 pandemic and crisis, and the international sanction crisis, demonstrated that unlimited and absolute freedom of international trade might reduce the resilience of the economy and entrepreneurship to crises.

Due to this, the very notion of competitiveness (including digital competitiveness) is reconsidered from the position of sustainability. In this new context of neo-globalization, the Fourth Industrial Revolution continues, and entrepreneurship of Industry 4.0 has to look for new ways of obtaining access to digital technologies and their use. This causes new research questions (RQ), which include the following:

RQ1: What contribution can the use of digital technologies in entrepreneurship in Industry 4.0 make to the increase in its resilience to crises?

RQ2: How is it possible to raise the stability of entrepreneurship in Industry 4.0 during the use of digital technologies and what role do the issues of cyber-security have in this process?

RQ3: What is the way of developing new practices of highly effective and competitive use of digital technologies in entrepreneurship in Industry 4.0 in the new global chains of value-added creation?

The above research questions form a new wide field for further research in the continuation of this book. Future scientific studies should elaborate on the prospects for using digital technologies in entrepreneurship in Industry 4.0 in the age of neo-globalization.

Elena G. Popkova
MGIMO University, Russia

Compilation of References

Abiad, A., Furceri, D., & Topalova, P. (2015, May). *The macroeconomic effects of public investment: Evidence from advanced economies.* IMF Working Paper. Retrieved February 12, 2021, from https://www.imf.org/external/pubs/ft/wp/2015/wp1595.pdf

Abraham, F., Schmukler, S. L., & Tessada, J. (2019, February). *Robo-advisors: Investing through machines.* Retrieved January 11, 2022, from https://documents1.worldbank.org/curated/en/275041551196836758/pdf/Robo-Advisors-Investing-through-Machines.pdf

Abubakre, M., Faik, I., & Mkansi, M. (2021). Digital entrepreneurship and indigenous value systems: An Ubuntu perspective. *Information Systems Journal, 31*(6), 838–862. doi:10.1111/isj.12343

Acemoglu, D., & Restrepo, P. (2019). Artificial intelligence, automation, and work. In A. Agrawal, J. Gans, & A. Goldfarb (Eds.), *The economics of artificial intelligence: An agenda* (pp. 197–236). The University of Chicago Press.

Acs, Z. J., Song, A. K., Szerb, L., Audretsch, D. B., & Komlósi, E. (2021). The evolution of the global digital platform economy: 1971-2021. *Small Business Economics, 57*(4), 1629–1659. doi:10.100711187-021-00561-x

Adams, W. C. (2015). Conducting Semi-Structured Interviews. In K. E. Newcomer, H. P. Hatry, & J. S. Wholey (Eds.), *Handbook of Practical Program Evaluation* (pp. 492–505). John Wiley & Sons, Inc. doi:10.1002/9781119171386.ch19

Advanced Technology Development Center (ATDC). (2019). *Labeling and traceability: A brief overview of the PPP project.* ATDC.

AgFunder. (2017). *Agfunder agri-food tech: Investment report.* Retrieved December 28, 2021, from https://research.agfunder.com/2017/AgFunder-Agrifood-Tech-Investing-Report-2017.pdf

Agroexport. (n.d.). *Digests of foreign media.* Retrieved December 27, 2021, from https://aemcx.ru/media/digestino/

Akmarov, P. B., Gorbushina, N. V., & Knyazeva, O. P. (2019). Features of digital transformation in the agricultural sector of the economy. *Agricultural Education and Science, 2*, 1–12.

Al-Khateeb, B. A. A. (2019). The conceptual framework for the examination of a successful digital entrepreneurship in 21st century. In K. Mezghani & W. Aloulou (Eds.), *Business transformations in the era of digitalization* (pp. 126–141). IGI Global. doi:10.4018/978-1-5225-7262-6.ch008

Allied Market Research. (2021). *Cultured meat market: Global opportunity analysis and industry forecast 2022–2030.* Retrieved December 27, 2021, from https://www.alliedmarketresearch.com/cultured-meat-market-A06670

Alsheyadi, A. (2022). Collaborative e-business efforts and firm performance. *International Journal of Productivity and Performance Management, 71*(1), 100–124. doi:10.1108/IJPPM-11-2019-0516

Anderson, A. R., & Gaddefors, J. (2016). Entrepreneurship as a community phenomenon; reconnecting meanings and place. *International Journal of Entrepreneurship and Small Business, 28*(4), 504–518. doi:10.1504/IJESB.2016.077576

Anh, Q. (2022, February 21). From February enterprises importing and exporting goods through Lang Son border gate must declare through the digital platform. *Toquoc*. Retrieved February 28, 2022, from http://nhipsongkinhte.toquoc.vn/tu-21-2-doanh-nghiep-xuat-nhap-khau-hang-hoa-qua-cua-khau-lang-son-phai-khai-bao-qua-nen-tang-so-42022212103135768.htm

Arkhipov, A. G., Kosogor, S. N., Motorin, O. A., Gorbachev, M. I., Suvorov, G. A., & Truflyak, E. V. (2019). *Digital transformation of Russian agriculture.* Moscow, Russia: Rosinformagrotech. Retrieved December 27, 2021, from https://mcx.gov.ru/upload/iblock/28f/28f56de9c3d40234dbdcbfac94787558.pdf

Astafeva, O. V., Astafyev, E. V., Khalikova, E. A., Leybert, T. B., & Osipova, I. A. (2020). XBRL reporting in the conditions of digital business transformation. In S. Ashmarina, M. Vochozka, & V. Mantulenko (Eds.), *Digital age: Chances, challenges and future* (pp. 373–381). Springer. doi:10.1007/978-3-030-27015-5_45

Bai, A. S., & Chen, M. (2021). Did the COVID-19 pandemic (really) positively impact the IPO Market? An Analysis of information uncertainty. *Finance Research Letters, 102372*. Advance online publication. doi:10.1016/j.frl.2021.102372

Bangalore One Services. (n.d.). *Official website.* Retrieved February 12, 2021, from https://www.e-challan.com/2015/01/bangalore-one-services.html

Bank for International Settlements. (2015, November). *Digital currencies.* Retrieved January 12, 2022, from https://www.bis.org/cpmi/publ/d137.pdf

Bank of America. (n.d.). *Innovative technology that's personal.* Retrieved February 19, 2022, from https://about.bankofamerica.com/en/our-company/client-centered-technology

Bean, R. (2021, February 5). Why Is It So Hard to Become a Data-Driven Company? *Harvard Business Review*. https://hbr.org/2021/02/why-is-it-so-hard-to-become-a-data-driven-company

ben Jabeur, S., Mefteh-Wali, S., & Carmona, P. (2021). The impact of institutional and macroeconomic conditions on aggregate business bankruptcy. *Structural Change and Economic Dynamics, 59*, 108–119. doi:10.1016/j.strueco.2021.08.010

Beninger, S., & Francis, J. N. P. (2022). Resources for business resilience in a COVID-19 world: A community-centric approach. *Business Horizons*, *65*(2), 227–238. doi:10.1016/j.bushor.2021.02.048

Boar, C., Holden, H., & Wadsworth, A. (2020). *Impending arrival – A sequel to the survey on central bank digital currency.* BIS Paper No. 107. Basel, Switzerland: Bank for International Settlements. Retrieved January 11, 2022, from https://www.bis.org/publ/bppdf/bispap107.pdf

Boldareva, L. B. (2020). Communication between government and business entities and challenges of creation of "digital government.". *Event Management*, *3*(1), 75–85. doi:10.26425/2658-3445-2020-1-75-85

Bolvachev, A. I., Kurochkina, I. P., & Novozhilova, U. V. (2019). *Integrated reporting and its information and analytical provision.* Filigran.

Boston Consulting Group. (2020, August 19). *Industry 4.0: The Future of Productivity and Growth in Manufacturing Industries*. BCG Global. https://www.bcg.com/publications/2015/engineered_products_project_business_industry_4_future_productivity_growth_manufacturing_industries

Boulton, C. (2021, June 24). *What is digital transformation? A necessary disruption.* CIO. https://www.cio.com/article/230425/what-is-digital-transformation-a-necessary-disruption.html

Bousdekis, A., & Mentzas, G. (2021). Enterprise Integration and Interoperability for Big Data-Driven Processes in the Frame of Industry 4.0. *Frontiers in Big Data, 4*. https://www.frontiersin.org/article/10.3389/fdata.2021.644651

Bowles, N. (2019, March 23). Human Contact in now a luxury good. *New York Times*. Retrieved January 11, 2022, from https://www.nytimes.com/2019/03/23/sunday-review/human-contact-luxury-screens.html

Bray, W. (2022, January 10). *Institutional investors begin to influence digital asset market structure.* Retrieved January 11, 2022, from https://www.thetradenews.com/institutional-investors-begin-to-influence-digital-asset-market-structure/

Burton, R. M., Mastrangelo, D., & Salvador, F. (2014). Introduction. *Journal of Organization Design*, *3*(1), 1–1. doi:10.7146/jod.16855 PMID:24343643

Butt, J. (2020). A Conceptual Framework to Support Digital Transformation in Manufacturing Using an Integrated Business Process Management Approach. *Designs*, *4*(3), 17. doi:10.3390/designs4030017

Bylina, S. G., Kadomtseva, M. E., & Osovin, M. N. (2018). *Informatization of the agri-food complex and rural areas of Russia: Opportunities and limitations incl. development of the digital economy.* Saratov, Russia: Saratovskiy istochnik.

Central Bank of the Russian Federation. (2014). Information letter "On the Corporate Governance Code" (April 10, 2014 No. 06-52/2463). Bank of Russia.

Central Bank of the Russian Federation. (2021a). *Review of corporate governance practices in Russian public companies based on the results of 2020.* Moscow, Russia: Bank of Russia. Retrieved January 12, 2021, from https://cbr.ru/Collection/Collection/File/39590/Review_corp_3011021.pdf

Central Bank of the Russian Federation. (2021b). Information letter "On recommendations for disclosing non-financial information by public joint-stock companies related to the activities of such companies" (July 12, 2021 No. IN-06-28/49). Bank of Russia.

Central Bank of the Russian Federation. (2022, 15 February). *Digital ruble: Start of testing.* Retrieved March 27, 2022, from https://www.cbr.ru/eng/press/event/?id=12692

Central Bank of the Russian Federation. (2022, February 16). *Almost 2,700 illegal companies and financial pyramids identified by the Bank of Russia in 2021.* Retrieved February 19, 2022, from https://www.cbr.ru/press/event/?id=12695

Cheng, Y., Liu, Y., Fan, W., Yan, Z., & Ye, X. (2019). Triple helix on globalization: A case study of the China International Nanotech Innovation Cluster. *Information Development, 35*(2), 272–289. doi:10.1177/0266666917743050

Chhatwani, M., Mishra, S. K., Varma, A., & Rai, H. (2022). Psychological resilience and business survival chances: A study of small firms in the USA during COVID-19. *Journal of Business Research, 142*, 277–286. doi:10.1016/j.jbusres.2021.12.048

Chiang, K., Frankfurter, G., & Kosedag, A. (2005). Exploratory analyses of dividend reinvestment plans and some comparisons. *International Review of Financial Analysis, 14*(5), 570–586. doi:10.1016/j.irfa.2004.10.020

Childs, M., Turner, T., Sneed, C., & Berry, A. (2022). A contingency theory approach to understanding small retail business continuity during COVID-19. *Family and Consumer Sciences Research Journal, 50*(3), 216–230. doi:10.1111/fcsr.12434 PMID:35600319

Choi, H., Shin, J., & Hwang, W.-S. (2018). Two faces of scientific knowledge in the external technology search process. *Technological Forecasting and Social Change, 133*, 41–50. doi:10.1016/j.techfore.2018.02.020

Chou, T., Ching, C., Fan, S., & Chang, J. (2011). Global linkages, the Chinese high-tech community and industrial cluster development: The semiconductor industry in Wuxi, Jingsu. *Urban Studies (Edinburgh, Scotland), 48*(14), 3019–3042. doi:10.1177/0042098010396237

Clauss, T., Breier, M., Kraus, S., Durst, S., & Mahto, R. V. (2022). Temporary business model innovation – SMEs' innovation response to the COVID-19 crisis. *R & D Management, 52*(2), 294–312. doi:10.1111/radm.12498

Cucciniello, M., Lapsley, I., Nasi, G., & Pagliari, C. (2015). Understanding key factors affecting electronic medical record implementation: A sociotechnical approach. *BMC Health Services Research, 15*(1), 268. doi:10.118612913-015-0928-7 PMID:26184405

Cugno, M., Castagnoli, R., Büchi, G., & Pini, M. (2022). Industry 4.0 and production recovery in the covid era. *Technovation, 114*, 102443. doi:10.1016/j.technovation.2021.102443

D'Ankonia, F. (2017, November 2). Future of Digital currency may not involve blockchains. *Cointelegraph.* Retrieved January 12, 2022, from https://cointelegraph.com/news/future-of-digital-currency-may-not-involve-blockchains

Daft, R. L. (2021). *Organizzazione aziendale* (R. C. D. Nacamulli & L. Quaratino, Eds.). Maggioli.

Dakhaeva, F. D. (2020). Integrated company reporting – Essence and features. In Education. Culture. Society (pp. 86-88). St. Petersburg, Russia: HNRI "National Development."

De Mauro, A., Greco, M., Grimaldi, M., & Ritala, P. (2018). Human resources for Big Data professions: A systematic classification of job roles and required skill sets. *Information Processing & Management*, *54*(5), 807–817. doi:10.1016/j.ipm.2017.05.004

Deloitte. (2015). *Industry 4.0—Challenges and Solutions for the Digital Transformation and Use of Exponential Technologies*. Study of Deloitte Consulting. https://www2.deloitte.com/content/dam/Deloitte/ch/Documents/manufacturing/ch-enmanufacturing-industry-4-0-24102014

Deloitte. (2020). *Realizing the digital promise.* Retrieved January 11, 2022, from https://www2.deloitte.com/content/dam/Deloitte/global/Documents/Financial-Services/gx-fsi-realizing-the-digital-promise-covid-19-catalyzes-and-accelerates-transformation.pdf

Deloitte. (n.d.). *Super smart city: Happier society with higher quality.* Retrieved February 12, 2021, from https://www2.deloitte.com/cn/en/pages/public-sector/articles/super-smart-city.html

Demeter. (2021). *Produce and feed: The daily challenge of a confused world.* Retrieved December 18, 2021, from https://www.clubdemeter.com/fr/le-demeter

Digilina, O. B., Teslenko, I. B., & Andronova, I. V. (2022). New management technologies in the context of digitalization. In E. G. Popkova (Ed.), *Imitation market modeling in digital economy: Game theoretic approaches* (pp. 333–339). Springer. doi:10.1007/978-3-030-93244-2_37

Douglas, E., & Prentice, C. (2019). Innovation and profit motivations for social entrepreneurship: A fuzzy-set analysis. *Journal of Business Research*, *99*, 69–79. https://doi.org/10.1016/J.JBUSRES.2019.02.031

Dowin Kennedy, E. (2021). Creating community: The process of entrepreneurial community building for civic wealth creation. *Entrepreneurship and Regional Development*, *33*(9–10), 816–836. https://doi.org/10.1080/08985626.2021.1964612

Engidaw, A. E. (2022). Small businesses and their challenges during COVID-19 pandemic in developing countries: In the case of Ethiopia. *Journal of Innovation and Entrepreneurship*, *11*(1), 1. doi:10.118613731-021-00191-3 PMID:35036286

Eurasian Economic Commission. (2017). *State support for agriculture developed and developing countries.* Retrieved December 23, 2021, from Retrieved from http://www.eurasiancommission.org/ru/act/prom_i_agroprom/dep_agroprom/sxs/Documents/Государственная%20поддержка%20сельского%20хозяйства%20в%20развитых%20и%20развивающихся%20странах%20(2017).pdf

European Commission. (n.d.). *Regulations on food and agricultural products.* Retrieved January 08, 2022, from https://ec.europa.eu/info/food-farming-fisheries/food-safety-and-quality/certification/quality-labels/quality-schemes-explained_en#geographicalindications

European Parliament and the Council of the European. (2014). *Directive 2014/65/EU of the of 15 May 2014 on markets in financial instruments and amending Directive 2002/92/EC and Directive 2011/61/EU.* Retrieved February 19, 2022, from https://eur-lex.europa.eu/legal-content/EN/TXT/?uri=CELEX%3A02014L0065-20220101

Faheem, M., & Butt, R. A. (2022). Big datasets of optical-wireless cyber-physical systems for optimizing manufacturing services in the Internet of things-enabled Industry 4.0. *Data in Brief*, *42*, 108026. doi:10.1016/j.dib.2022.108026 PMID:35330737

Fairlie, R., & Fossen, F. M. (2022). The early impacts of the COVID-19 pandemic on business sales. *Small Business Economics*, *58*(4), 1853–1864. doi:10.100711187-021-00479-4

Federal Agency for State Property Management. (2013). *Guidelines for organizing the work of the Board of directors in a Joint-Stock Company*. Author.

Federal Agency for State Property Management. (n.d.). *Interdepartmental portal for state property management.* Retrieved February 18, 2022, from https://mp.rosim.ru/web/guest/portal

Food and Agriculture Organization (FAO). (2020). *World food and agriculture – Statistical yearbook, 2020.* Rome, Italy: FAO. Retrieved December 19, 2021, from https://www.fao.org/3/cb1329en/CB1329EN.pdf

Fortune Business Insights. (2021). *Artificial intelligence (AI) market size, share & COVID-19 impact analysis, by component (hardware, software, and services), by technology (computer vision, machine learning, natural language processing, and others), by deployment (cloud, on-premises), by industry (healthcare, retail, IT & telecom, BFSI, automotive, advertising & media, manufacturing, and others), and regional forecast, 2021–2028.* Retrieved March 27, 2022, from https://www.fortunebusinessinsights.com/industry-reports/artificial-intelligence-market-100114

Fu, J., & Mishra, M. (2020). Fintech in the time of COVID-19: Technological adoption during crises. *Journal of Financial Intermediation*, *50*, 100945. doi:10.1016/j.jfi.2021.100945

Funabashi, M. (2018). Human augmentation of ecosystems: Objectives for food production and science by 2045. *NPJ Science of Food*, *2*(1), 16. doi:10.103841538-018-0026-4 PMID:31304266

Gadekar, R., Sarkar, B., & Gadekar, A. (2022). Investigating the relationship among Industry 4.0 drivers, adoption, risks reduction, and sustainable organizational performance in manufacturing industries: An empirical study. *Sustainable Production and Consumption*, *31*, 670–692. doi:10.1016/j.spc.2022.03.010

Ganieva, I. A., & Bobrov, N. E. (2019). Digital platforms in Russian agriculture: The legal aspect of implementation. *Achievements of Science and Technology of the Agro-Industrial Complex*, *33*(9), 83–86. doi:10.24411/0235-2451-2019-10918

Gao, J. (2022). Has COVID-19 hindered small business activities? The role of Fintech. *Economic Analysis and Policy*, *74*, 297–308. doi:10.1016/j.eap.2022.02.008

Garcez, A., Silva, R., & Franco, M. (2022). Digital transformation shaping structural pillars for academic entrepreneurship: A framework proposal and research agenda. *Education and Information Technologies*, *27*(1), 1159–1182. https://doi.org/10.1007/s10639-021-10638-5

Garzoni, A., De Turi, I., Secundo, G., & Del Vecchio, P. (2020). Fostering digital transformation of SMEs: A four levels approach. *Management Decision*, *58*(8), 1543–1562. doi:10.1108/MD-07-2019-0939

General Administration of Customs of the People's Republic of China (GACC). (2021). *Measures for the administration of import and export food safety of the People's Republic of China*. Retrieved December 27, 2021, from http://jckspj.customs.gov.cn/spj/zcfg18/bmgz91/4034487/index.html

Gerasimova, L. N. (2013). Integrated financial report: Advantages and the Outlook in Russia. *Audit and Financial Analysis*, *4*, 33–35.

Gerrikagoitia, J. K., Unamuno, G., Urkia, E., & Serna, A. (2019). Digital manufacturing platforms in the Industry 4.0 from private and public perspectives. *Applied Sciences (Switzerland), 9*(14). doi:10.3390/APP9142934

Ghobakhloo, M., & Iranmanesh, M. (2021). Digital transformation success under Industry 4.0: A strategic guideline for manufacturing SMEs. *Journal of Manufacturing Technology Management*, *32*(8), 1533–1556. https://doi.org/10.1108/JMTM-11-2020-0455

Giantari, I. G. A. K., Yasa, N. N. K., Suprasto, H. B., & Rahmayanti, P. L. D. (2022). The role of digital marketing in mediating the effect of the COVID-19 pandemic and the intensity of competition on business performance. *International Journal of Data and Network Science*, *6*(1), 217–232. doi:10.5267/j.ijdns.2021.9.006

Gindele, N., & Doluschitz, R. (2018). *"Agriculture 4.0" Germany – current state and prospects. "German-Russian Agrarian-Political Dialogue" Cooperation project of the German Federal Ministry of Food and Agriculture*. Retrieved December 25, 2021, from https://agrardialog.ru/files/prints/gindele_dolushitts_%C2%ABselskoe_hozyaystvo_4_0%C2%BB_germanii_tekushchee_sostoyanie_i_perspektivi.pdf

Global Infrastructure Hub. (n.d.). *Official website*. Retrieved February 12, 2021, from https://www.gihub.org

Global Market Insights. (2021). *Alternative protein market for animal feed application, competitive market share & forecast, 2021–2027*. Retrieved December 27, 2021, from https://www.gminsights.com/industry-analysis/alternative-protein-market-for-animal-feed

GlobeNewswire. (2021). *Smart agriculture market size globally estimated to reach USD 22.5 Bn, with 8.9% CAGR by 2026: Facts & factors*. Retrieved December 28, 2021, from https://www.globenewswire.com/news-release/2021/10/18/2315821/0/en/Smart-Agriculture-Market-Size-Globally-Estimated-to-Reach-USD-22-5-Bn-with-8-9-CAGR-by-2026-Facts-Factors.html

Go, P. (2021). *Global IPO has record-breaking 2021, prepare for headwinds in 2022.* Ernst & Young Global Limited. Retrieved February 18, 2022, from https://www.ey.com/en_gl/ipo/trends

Goldfarb, A., & Tucker, C. (2011). Online display advertising: Targeting and obtrusiveness. *Marketing Science*, *30*(3), 389–404. doi:10.1287/mksc.1100.0583

Goldfarb, A., & Tucker, C. (2012). Privacy and Innovation. *Innovation Policy and the Economy*, *12*, 65–89. doi:10.1086/663156

Goldfarb, A., & Tucker, C. (2019). Digital Economics. *Journal of Economic Literature*, *57*(1), 3–43. doi:10.1257/jel.20171452

Gómez, J., Salazar, I., & Vargas, P. (2022). Production outsourcing, technological cooperation and E-business adoption by Spanish manufacturing firms. *Journal of Engineering and Technology Management*, *63*, 101677. doi:10.1016/j.jengtecman.2022.101677

Gordeev, A. V., Patrushev, D. N., Lebedev, I. V., Arkhipov, A. G., Bulanov, K. A., Grebenkov, D. V., & Kosogor, S. N. (2019). *Departmental project "Digital agriculture."* Moscow, Russia: Rosinformagrotech. Retrieved December 20, 2021, from https://mcx.gov.ru/upload/iblock/900/900863fae06c026826a9ee43e124d058.pdf

Gorelikov, K. A., Komarov, A. V., & Bezsmertnaya, E. R. (2021). A paradigm shift in business management in the context of Industry 4.0. In E. G. Popkova & V. N. Ostrovskaya (Eds.), *Meta-scientific study of artificial intelligence* (pp. 469–476). Information Age Publishing.

Government of the Russian Federation. (2020). Action plan "Transformation of the business climate" (direction "Improvement of corporate governance") (approved by the order No. 1723-r of July 2, 2020). Author.

GRI overview of global ESG disclosure trends. (2020). *Sustainability reporting instruments worldwide.* https://www.carrotsandsticks.net/

Grossman, R., & Siegel, K. (2014). *Organizational Models for Big Data and Analytics (SSRN* Scholarly Paper ID 2458909). Social Science Research Network. doi:10.7146/jod.9799

Guckenbiehl, P., & Corral de Zubielqui, G. (2022). Start-ups' business model changes during the COVID-19 pandemic: Counteracting adversities and pursuing opportunities. *International Small Business Journal: Researching Entrepreneurship*, *40*(2), 150–177. doi:10.1177/02662426211055447 PMID:35250144

Guo, B., & Guo, J.-J. (2011). Patterns of technological learning within the knowledge systems of industrial clusters in emerging economies: Evidence from China. *Technovation*, *31*(2-3), 87–104. doi:10.1016/j.technovation.2010.10.006

Gupta, J., & Chaudhry, S. (2019). Mind the tail, or risk to fail. *Journal of Business Research*, *99*, 167–185. https://doi.org/10.1016/j.jbusres.2019.02.037

Hansson, J., Landstad, B. J., Vinberg, S., Hedlund, M., & Tjulin, Å. (2022). Small business managers and COVID-19 – The role of a sense of coherence and general resistance resources in coping with stressors. *PLoS One*, *17*(3), e0265029. doi:10.1371/journal.pone.0265029 PMID:35302995

Hussain, A., Farooq, M. U., Habib, M. S., Masood, T., & Pruncu, C. I. (2021). COVID-19 challenges: Can industry 4.0 technologies help with business continuity? *Sustainability*, *13*(21), 11971. doi:10.3390u132111971

IDC. (2021, August 17). *Global spending on big data and analytics solutions will reach $215.7 billion in 2021, According to a new IDC spending guide.* Retrieved February 19, 2022, from https://www.idc.com/getdoc.jsp?containerId=prUS48165721

IMD World Competitiveness Center. (2021). *IMD World Digital competitiveness ranking 2021.* https://www.imd.org/centers/world-competitiveness-center/rankings/world-digital-competitiveness/

IMD. (2022). *World digital competitiveness rankings 2019–2021.* Retrieved April 17, 2022, from https://www.imd.org/centers/world-competitiveness-center/rankings/world-digital-competitiveness/

Infra O. N. E. Research. (2020, March). *Investments in infrastructure. Information Technologies.* Retrieved February 12, 2021, from https://infraone.ru/sites/default/files/analitika/2020/investicii_v_infrastrukturu_informacionnye_tekhnologii_infraone_research.pdf

Infra O. N. E. Research. (2021, October 26). *Infrastructure of Russia: Development Index 2021.* Retrieved February 12, 2021, from https://infraoneresearch.ru/u5usp7/m2r7v0?s1qtyk=1r5i77

International Integrated Reporting Council (IIRC). (2013, December). *International Integrated Reporting Framework.* Retrieved January 11, 2022, from https://integratedreporting.org/wp-content/uploads/2015/03/13-12-08-THE-INTERNATIONAL-IR-FRAMEWORK-2-1.pdf

International Integrated Reporting Council (IIRC). (2019). *Building consensus towards a global system: IIRC integrated report 2019.* Retrieved January 12, 2022, from https://integratedreporting.org/integratedreport2019/download/pdf/IIRC_Integrated_Report_2019.pdf

International Integrated Reporting Council (IIRC). (2021, January). *International Integrated Reporting Framework.* Retrieved January 11, 2022, from https://www.integratedreporting.org/wp-content/uploads/2021/01/InternationalIntegratedReportingFramework.pdf

International Monetary Fund. (2022). *World Economic Outlook Database: October 2021.* Retrieved April 18, 2022, from https://www.imf.org/en/Publications/WEO/weo-database/2021/October

Irrera, A. (2021, July 20). *Most institutional investors expect to buy digital assets, study finds.* Retrieved February 19, 2022, from https://www.reuters.com/business/most-institutional-investors-expect-buy-digital-assets-study-finds-2021-07-20/

Irrera, A., Withers, I., & White, L. (2021, March 02). *Goldman Sachs restarts cryptocurrency desk amid bitcoin boom.* Retrieved February 19, 2022, from https://www.reuters.com/article/us-crypto-currency-goldman-sachs-exclusi-idUSKCN2AT390

Islam, N., Gyoshev, S., & Amona, D. (2020). External complexities in discontinuous innovation-based R&D projects: Analysis of inter-firm collaborative partnerships that lead to abundance. *Technological Forecasting and Social Change*, *155*, 119303. doi:10.1016/j.techfore.2018.05.014

ISMG & OneSpan. (2020). *The state of digital account opening transformation.* Princeton, NJ: ISMG. Retrieved January 11, 2022, from https://www.onespan.com/sites/default/files/2020-03/OneSpan-AnalystReport-ISMG-The-State-of-Digital-Account-Opening-Transformation.pdf

Ivanov, O. V., & Shamanina, E. A. (2021). PPP as a tool to achieve Sustainable Development Goals and implement the concept of "Quality infrastructure investments.". In E. B. Zavyalova & E. G. Popkova (Eds.), *Industry 4.0. Exploring the consequences of climate change* (pp. 309–322). Palgrave MacMillan. doi:10.1007/978-3-030-75405-1_28

Janshanlo, R. E., & Kogut, O. Yu. (2020). Conceptual bases of formation of integrated reporting. *Central Asian Economic Review*, *1*(130), 111–123.

Japan External Trade Organization (JETRO). (2004, June). *Stimulation of regional clusters and international exchange (International Comparative Survey for Virtualization of the Japanese Economy).* Tokyo, Japan: JETRO.

Javaid, M., Haleem, A., Singh, R. P., & Suman, R. (2021). Substantial capabilities of robotics in enhancing industry 4.0 implementation. *Cognitive Robotics*, *1*, 58–75. doi:10.1016/j.cogr.2021.06.001

Javaid, M., Haleem, A., Vaishya, R., Bahl, S., Suman, R., & Vaish, A. (2020). Industry 4.0 technologies and their applications in fighting COVID-19 pandemic. *Diabetes & Metabolic Syndrome*, *14*(4), 419–422. doi:10.1016/j.dsx.2020.04.032 PMID:32344370

Jawad, H. M., Nordin, R., Gharghan, S. K., Jawad, A. M., & Ismail, M. (2017). Energy-efficient wireless sensor networks for precision agriculture: A review. *Sensors (Basel)*, *17*(8), 1781. doi:10.339017081781 PMID:28771214

Ji, X., Wang, K., Xu, H., & Li, M. (2021). Has digital financial inclusion narrowed the urban-rural income gap: The role of entrepreneurship in China. *Sustainability (Switzerland)*, *13*(15). doi:10.3390/su13158292

Jiang, Y., Wu, L., Tian, G., & Nie, H. (2021). Do cryptocurrencies hedge against EPU and the equity market volatility during COVID-19? *Journal of International Financial Markets, Institutions and Money*, *72*, 101324. doi:10.1016/j.intfin.2021.101324

Johnstone-Louis, M., Kustin, B., Mayer, C., Stroehle, J., & Wang, B. (2020). Business in times of crisis. *Oxford Review of Economic Policy*, *36*(SI1), 242–255. doi:10.1093/oxrep/graa021

Jun, S. Y., Kim, K. H., & Park, H. K. (2019). The effect of the preorder strategy on consumers' product choice: The moderating role of product experience and payment timing. *Journal of Business Research*, *99*, 80–86. https://doi.org/10.1016/j.jbusres.2019.02.024

Kalabikhina, I. E., Dosikov, V. S., & Voloshin, D. A. (2017). The integrated reporting – The new level of transparency of modern corporate reporting. *Market Economy Problems*, *2*, 45–50.

Kane, G. C., Palmer, D., Phillips, A. N., Kiron, D., & Buckley, N. (2015). Strategy, not technology, drives digital transformation. *MIT Sloan Management Review and Deloitte University Press*, *14*, 1–25.

Kashkovskaya, M. S. (2020). Reflection of six capitals in integrated reporting. In G. Yu. Gulyaev (Ed.), *Modern Scientific Research: Topical Issues, Achievements and Innovations* (pp. 163–165). Nauka i Prosveshcheniye.

Kašperová, E. (2021). Impairment (in)visibility and stigma: How disabled entrepreneurs gain legitimacy in mainstream and disability markets. *Entrepreneurship and Regional Development*, *33*(9–10), 894–919. https://doi.org/10.1080/08985626.2021.1974101

Khmyz, O. V. (2021). Unconventional directions of monetary regulation in a turbulent global economy. *Ekonomika. Nalogi. Pravo*, *14*(5), 31-38.

Khmyz, O. V. (2003). Institutional investors on the securities market. *Voprosy Ekonomiki*, *8*(8), 95–101. doi:10.32609/0042-8736-2003-8-95-101

Kleinknecht, A. (1987). *Innovation patterns in crisis and prosperity. Schumpeter's long cycle reconsidered* (1st ed.). Palgrave Macmillan.

Kleinknecht, A. (2020). The (negative) impact of supply-side labour market reforms on productivity. An overview of the evidence. *Cambridge Journal of Economics*, *44*(2), 445–464. doi:10.1093/cje/bez068

Kline, A. (2021, July 16). Wells Fargo tells employees to return to work in two waves this fall. *American Banker*. Retrieved January 11, 2022, from https://www.americanbanker.com/news/wells-fargo-tells-employees-to-return-to-work-in-two-waves-this-fall

Ko, E. (2019). Bridging Asia and the world: Global platform for the Interface between marketing and management. *Journal of Business Research*, *99*, 350–353. https://doi.org/10.1016/J.JBUSRES.2018.12.061

Kogdenko, V. G. (2017). *Economic analysis. Analysis of integrated reporting: A textbook*. Unity-Dana.

Kogdenko, V. G., & Melnik, M. V. (2014). Integrated reporting: Formation and analysis issues. *International Accounting*, *17*(10), 2–15.

Kohli, R., & Melville, N. P. (2019). Digital innovation: A review and synthesis. *Information Systems Journal*, *29*(1), 200–223. doi:10.1111/isj.12193

Konovalenko, L. Yu., Mishurov, N. P., Golubev, I. A., Nikitina, M. A., & Bredikhin, S. A. (2020). *Digital transformation of the food and processing industry: An analytical review*. Moscow, Russia: Rosinformagrotech. Retrieved December 19, 2021, from https://tinyurl.com/2mrs8tnf

Korolev, O. G., Yankovskaya, V. V., Grazhdankina, O. A., Tkachenko, V. V., & Kuchko, S. A. (2022). Financial model of digital cooperation in business. In A. V. Bogoviz, A. E. Suglobov, A. N. Maloletko, & O. V. Kaurova (Eds.), *Cooperation and sustainable development* (pp. 175–182). Springer. doi:10.1007/978-3-030-77000-6_21

Kotter, J. P. (2014, April 24). Accelerate: Building Strategic Agility for a Faster-Moving World. *Harvard Business Review*. https://hbr.org/2014/04/accelerate-building-strategic-agility-for-a-faster-moving-world

Kotter, J. P., Brown, T., Martin, R. L., & Rigby, D. K. (2021). *HBR's 10 must reads on change management* (Vol. 2). Harvard Business Review Press.

Kraus, A., Durst, S., Ferreira, J. J., Veiga, P., Kailer, N., & Weinmann, A. (2022). Digital transformation in business and management research: An overview of the current status quo. *International Journal of Information Management*, *63*, 102466. doi:10.1016/j.ijinfomgt.2021.102466

Kremer, J. (2020, June 21). Identifying the best stocks on Robinhood using AI. *I Know First*. Retrieved March 01, 2022, from https://iknowfirst.com/identifying-the-best-stocks-on-robinhood-using-ai

Kreuzer, T., Lindenthal, A.-K., Oberländer, A. M., & Röglinger, M. (2022). The Effects of Digital Technology on Opportunity Recognition. *Business & Information Systems Engineering*. doi:10.1007/s12599-021-00733-9

Krishnakumar, S. K., Kishore, R., & Suresh, N. C. (2022). Expansive or focused attention? An exploration–exploitation perspective on e-Business systems and firm performance. *Production and Operations Management*, *31*(5), 2038–2066. Advance online publication. doi:10.1111/poms.13664

Ksiazkiewicz, R. (2017, March 23). *Useful Stats: Share of US venture capital activity and per capita investment by state, 2010–2016*. Retrieved April 15, 2020, from https://ssti.org/blog/useful-stats-share-us-venture-capital-activity-and-capita-investment-state-2010-2016

Kumaran, L. A., & Jeyachandran, H. (2022). Modelling e-business influencing factors for supply chain performance of Indian MSMEs: An ISM approach. *International Journal of Process Management and Benchmarking*, *12*(1), 28–45. doi:10.1504/IJPMB.2022.120444

Kumar, M. P., & Kumara, N. V. M. (2021). Market capitalization: Pre and post COVID-19 analysis. *Materials Today: Proceedings*, *37*(2), 2553–2557. doi:10.1016/j.matpr.2020.08.493 PMID:33052307

Kunkel, S., Matthess, M., Xue, B., & Beier, G. (2022). Industry 4.0 in sustainable supply chain collaboration: Insights from an interview study with international buying firms and Chinese suppliers in the electronics industry. *Resources, Conservation and Recycling*, *182*, 106274. doi:10.1016/j.resconrec.2022.106274

Kuzmenko, O. A., & Abrosimova, M. C. (2014). Integrated reporting is the new reporting model for Russian corporations. *Academic Bulletin*, *1*(27), 102–113.

Levchaev, P. A., & Khezazna, B. (2021). Features of the strategic activities of corporations in the digital economy. *Finance and Management, 1*, 12-60. doi:10.25136/2409-7802.2021.1.30823

Levy, A. (2020, December 12). Three of the 10 biggest tech IPOs have happened in 2020 – including two in the last week. *CNBC*. Retrieved March 01, 2022, from https://www.cnbc.com/amp/2020/12/12/10-biggest-tech-ipos-ever-three-in-2020-two-last-week.html

Li, Y., Dai, J., & Cui, L. (2020). The impact of digital technologies on economic and environmental performance in the context of industry 4.0: A moderated mediation model. *International Journal of Production Economics, 229*. doi:10.1016/J.IJPE.2020.107777

Li, F. (2020). Leading digital transformation: Three emerging approaches for managing the transition. *International Journal of Operations & Production Management, 40*(6), 809–817. doi:10.1108/IJOPM-04-2020-0202

Liu, Z., Sampaio, P., Pishchulov, G., Mehandjiev, N., Cisneros-Cabrera, S., Schirrmann, A., Jiru, F., & Bnouhanna, N. (2022). The architectural design and implementation of a digital platform for Industry 4.0 SME collaboration. *Computers in Industry, 138*, 103623. doi:10.1016/j.compind.2022.103623

Liu, Z., Xie, K., Li, L., & Chen, Y. (2020). A paradigm of safety management in Industry 4.0. *Systems Research and Behavioral Science, 37*(4), 632–645. doi:10.1002res.2706

Li, Y., Dai, J., & Cui, L. (2020). The impact of digital technologies on economic and environmental performance in the context of industry 4.0: A moderated mediation model. *International Journal of Production Economics, 229*, 107777. doi:10.1016/j.ijpe.2020.107777

Llopis-Albert, C., Rubio, F., & Valero, F. (2021). Impact of digital transformation on the automotive industry. *Technological Forecasting and Social Change, 162*, 120343. doi:10.1016/j.techfore.2020.120343 PMID:33052150

Loebbecke, C., & Picot, A. (2015). Reflections on societal and business model transformation arising from digitization and big data analytics. *The Journal of Strategic Information Systems, 24*(3), 149–157. doi:10.1016/j.jsis.2015.08.002

Lovchikova, E. I., & Alpatov, A. V. (2020). *Diversification and specialization of agricultural production in terms of social and labor employment and the development of the digital economy*. Publishing House of Oryol State Agrarian University.

Lusch, R. F., & Nambisan, S. (2015). Service innovation: A service-dominant logic perspective. *Management Information Systems Quarterly, 39*(1), 155–175. doi:10.25300/MISQ/2015/39.1.07

Lüthy, C., & Steyaert, C. (2019). The onto-politics of entrepreneurial experimentation: Re-reading Hans-Jörg Rheinberger's understanding of 'experimental systems.'. *Entrepreneurship and Regional Development, 31*(7–8), 652–668. https://doi.org/10.1080/08985626.2019.1596360

Luzganova, A. S., Popova, A. A., & Reshetova, A. A. (2020). Increasing business transparency through the development of corporate integrated statements. In Yu. N. Akimova, M. Ya. Kreer, N. V. Ostrovskaya, & Yu. E. Putikhin (Eds.), *Management problems in public and corporate sector of the economy* (pp. 25–29). Skifiya-Print.

Lytos, A., Lagkas, T., Sarigiannidis, P., Zervakis, M., & Livanos, G. (2020). Towards smart farming: Systems, frameworks and exploitation of multiple sources. *Computer Networks*, *172*, 107147. doi:10.1016/j.comnet.2020.107147

Lyubishina, O. A. (2022). Integrated reporting as a tool for assessing the effectiveness of the organization. *Vectoreconomy*, *12*(30), 13.

Machkour, B., & Abriane, A. (2020). Industry 4.0 and its Implications for the Financial Sector. *Procedia Computer Science*, *177*, 496–502. doi:10.1016/j.procs.2020.10.068

Maddox, T. (2018, July 16). *Smart cities: A cheat sheet.* Retrieved February 12, 2021, from https://www.techrepublic.com/article/smart-cities-the-smart-persons-guide/

Maimone, F. (2022). Organizing for Industry 4.0. In *Lecture Notes in Information Systems and Organization* (pp. 1–20). Springer. https://ideas.repec.org/h/spr/lnichp/978-3-030-83321-3_1.html

Malinovskaya, N. V. (2020). *Integrated reporting: A textbook.* KnoRus.

Mamontov, A. (2020). Industries of the future. Investing in artificial intelligence. *BCS Express.* Retrieved March 27, 2022, from https://bcs-express.ru/novosti-i-analitika/industrii-budushchego-investitsii-v-iskusstvennyi-intellekt

Margherita, E. G., & Braccini, A. M. (2021). Managing industry 4.0 automation for fair ethical business development: A single case study. *Technological Forecasting and Social Change*, *172*, 121048. doi:10.1016/j.techfore.2021.121048

Maria, D. B. (2022). *Survey: Cloud adoption statistics.* Retrieved February 13, 2022, from https://mariadb.com/survey/cloud-global/

Markets and Markets. (2020). *Plant-based meat market: Global forecast to 2025.* Retrieved December 27, 2021, https://www.marketsandmarkets.com/Market-Reports/plant-based-meat-market-44922705.html

Markets and Markets. (2021). *Hydroponic market: Global forecast to 2026.* Retrieved December 27, 2021, from https://www.marketsandmarkets.com/Market-Reports/hydroponic-market-94055021.html

Martin, K. (2018). The penalty for privacy violations: How privacy violations impact trust online. *Journal of Business Research*, *82*, 103–116. doi:10.1016/j.jbusres.2017.08.034

Mazumder, S., & Saha, P. (2021). COVID-19: Fear of pandemic and short-term IPO performance. *Finance Research Letters*, *43*, 101977. doi:10.1016/j.frl.2021.101977 PMID:33613130

Mazur, M., Dang, M., & Vega, M. (2021). COVID-19 and the march 2020 stock market crash. Evidence from S&P1500. *Finance Research Letters*, *38*, 101690. doi:10.1016/j.frl.2020.101690 PMID:32837377

Mei, S., Yuan, M., Cui, J., Dong, S., & Zhao, J. (2022). Machinery condition monitoring in the era of industry 4.0: A relative degree of contribution feature selection and deep residual network combined approach. *Computers & Industrial Engineering*, *168*, 108129. doi:10.1016/j.cie.2022.108129

Meyer, B. H., Prescott, B., & Sheng, X. S. (2022). The impact of the COVID-19 pandemic on business expectations. *International Journal of Forecasting*, *38*(2), 529–544. doi:10.1016/j.ijforecast.2021.02.009 PMID:35185229

Mikalef, P., Pappas, I. O., Pavlou, P. A., & Krogstie, J. (2017). *Big Data Analytics and Business Value. Information and Management Call for Papers*. Available at: https://www.journals.elsevier.com/ information-and-management/call-for-papers

Ministry of Agriculture, Forestry, and Fisheries of Japan. (n.d.). *Efforts to realize "Smart agriculture."* Retrieved December 27, 2021, from https://www.maff.go.jp/e/policies/tech_res/smaagri/robot.html

Ministry of Finance of the Russian Federation. (2019). *G20 Principles for quality infrastructure investment.* Retrieved February 12, 2021, from https://minfin.gov.ru/ru/document/?id_4=129246-printsipy_g20_po_investitsiyam_v_kachestvennuyu_infrastrukturu

Ministry of Trade, Industry, and Energy. (n.d.). *uTradeHub*. Retrieved February 12, 2021, from https://www.utradehub.or.kr/porgw/index.jsp?_locale=en&sso=ok

Morgan, J. P. (2021, February 1). *J.P. Morgan creates digital coin for payments.* Retrieved February 19, 2022, from https://www.jpmorgan.com/solutions/cib/news/digital-coin-payments

Morgan, J. P. (n.d.). *Artificial intelligence research.* Retrieved February 19, 2022, from https://www.jpmorgan.com/technology/artificial-intelligence/initiatives

Moseykin, Yu. N., Semenovich, V. S., & Chernyaev, M. V. (2020). *National economy: Textbook.* RUDN University.

Moysiadis, V., Sarigiannidis, P., Vitsas, V., & Khelifi, A. (2020). Smart farming in Europe. *Computer Science Review*, *39*, 100345. doi:10.1016/j.cosrev.2020.100345

Musipova, L. K. (2020). Integrated reporting: Need for composition and prospects for development. *Bulletin of Russian University of Cooperation*, *2*(40), 84–87.

Mutingi, M. (2018). Towards a customer-centric framework for evaluation of E-health service quality. In N. Gwangwava & M. Mutingi (Eds.), *E-manufacturing and e-service strategies in contemporary organizations* (pp. 199–218). IGI Global. doi:10.4018/978-1-5225-3628-4.ch008

Nambisan, S., Wright, M., & Feldman, M. (2019). The digital transformation of innovation and entrepreneurship: Progress, challenges and key themes. *Research Policy*, *48*(8), 103773. doi:10.1016/j.respol.2019.03.018

National League of Cities. (2017). *Cities and the innovation economy: perceptions of local leaders*. Retrieved February 12, 2021, from https://www.nlc.org/resource/cities-and-innovation-economy-perceptions-of-local-leaders

National P. P. P. Center & VEB.RF. (2021, September). *Investments in infrastructure and PPP. Analytical review 2021*. Retrieved February 12, 2021, from https://pppcenter.ru/upload/iblock/312/312a2ad6182866e21407990ab0bb16a2.pdf

National P. P. P. Center. (2018). Review of the practice of using public-private partnership mechanisms to create the infrastructure of "smart cities." National PPP Center.

Neureuter, J. (2021, September). *The institutional investor digital assets study*. Retrieved February 13, 2022, from https://www.fidelitydigitalassets.com/bin-public/060_www_fidelity_com/documents/FDAS/2021-digital-asset-study.pdf

Nguyen, C. P., Nguyen, B., Duy Tung, B., & Dinh Su, T. (2021). Economic complexity and entrepreneurship density: A nonlinear effect study. *Technological Forecasting and Social Change*, *173*. doi:10.1016/j.techfore.2021.121107

Nguyen, L. T. M., & Hoang Dinh, P. (2021). Ex-ante risk management and financial stability during the COVID-19 pandemic: A study of Vietnamese firms. *China Finance Review International*, *11*(3), 349–371. doi:10.1108/CFRI-12-2020-0177

Niemczyk, J., Trzaska, R., Wilczyński, M., & Borowski, K. (2021). Business models 4.0 using network effects: Case study of the cyfrowy polsat group. *Sustainability*, *13*(21), 11570. doi:10.3390u132111570

Nippon Automated Cargo and Port Consolidated System (NACCS). (n.d.). *Official website*. Retrieved February 12, 2021, from https://www.naccs.jp/e/

OECD. (2015). *G20/OECD Corporate governance principles*. Paris, France: OECD Publishing. doi:10.1787/9789264236882-en

OECD. (2019). *Digital opportunities for better agricultural policies*. OECD Publishing. doi:10.1787/571a0812-

OECD. (2021). *The future of corporate governance in capital markets after the COVID-19 crisis: Report*. Paris, France: OECD Publishing. doi:10.1787/efb2013c-en

Office of the Comptroller of the Currency. (2021, January 4). *Federally chartered banks and thrifts may participate in independent node verification networks and use stablecoins for payment activities*. Retrieved February 19, 2022, from https://www.occ.gov/news-issuances/news-releases/2021/nr-occ-2021-2.html

Oh, K., Kho, H., Choi, Y., & Lee, S. (2022). Determinants for Successful Digital Transformation. *Sustainability (Switzerland), 14*(3). doi:10.3390/su14031215

Orbis Research. (2020, Mar 18). *Global robo advisory market size, status and forecast 2020–2026.* Retrieved January 11, 2022, from https://www.orbisresearch.com/reports/index/global-robo-advisory-market-size-status-and-forecast-2020-2026?utm_source=puja

Orlova, N. L., & Ignatova, O. V. (Eds.). (2021). International economic relations in modern conditions: Development guidelines. Scientific World.

Osipov, V. S., Larionova, E. I., Sigarev, A. V., & Mishchenko, V. V. (2021). The key types of economic activities in the pleasure economy in the context of developing countries' transition to Industry 4.0. *International Journal of Trade and Global Markets, 14*(4-5), 413–422. doi:10.1504/IJTGM.2021.116739

Paptsov, A. G., Altukhov, A. I., Kashevarov, N. I., Petrushkevich, P. M., Denisov, A. S., Rudoy, E. V., Petukhova, M. S., Kapustyanchik, S. Yu., Dobryanskaya, S. L., Potseluev, O. M., Sadokhina, T. A., Petrov, A. F., Ryumkin, S. V., Galeev, R. R., Polunin, G. A., Taran, V. V., & Sokolova, Zh. E. (2019). Forecast of scientific and technological development of the crop industry, including seed production and organic farming in Russia, in the period up to 2030. Novosibirsk, Russia: Publishing Center "Zolotoy kolos".

Park, M. S., Shin, J. K., & Ju, Y. (2019). Attachment styles and electronic word of mouth (e-WOM) adoption on social networking sites. *Journal of Business Research, 99*, 398–404. https://doi.org/10.1016/J.JBUSRES.2017.09.020

Parmentola, A., Tutore, I., & Costagliola Di Fiore, M. (2020). Environmental Side of Fourth Industrial Revolution: The Positive and Negative Effects of I4.0 Technologies. In C. M. Hussain & P. Di Sia (Eds.), *Handbook of Smart Materials, Technologies, and Devices: Applications of Industry 4.0* (pp. 1–31). Springer International Publishing. doi:10.1007/978-3-030-58675-1_84-1

Pashentsev, D. A., & Antonova, N. V. (2022). Ensuring economical resilience in the conditions of developing penetrative (digital) technologies: Mechanisms for Protecting Rights and Legitimate Interests of Economic Subjects. In A. O. Inshakova & E. E. Frolova (Eds.), *The transformation of social relationships in Industry 4.0: Economic security and legal prevention* (pp. 75–84). Information Age Publishing.

Patel, D., Goyal, S., & Agarwal, R. (2018). E-commerce business model. In G. Sreedhar (Ed.), *Improving E-commerce web applications through business intelligence techniques* (pp. 110–129). IGI Global. doi:10.4018/978-1-5225-3646-8.ch005

Peñarroya-Farell, M., & Miralles, F. (2022). Business model adaptation to the COVID-19 crisis: Strategic response of the Spanish cultural and creative firms. *Journal of Open Innovation, 8*(1), 39. doi:10.3390/joitmc8010039

Phaneuf, A. (2022, February 8). *Artificial intelligence in financial services: Applications and benefits of AI in finance.* Retrieved February 19, 2022, from https://www.businessinsider.com/ai-in-finance

Pizzicoli, M. (2018). *AI concierge built on IBM Watson transforms a bank's service desk.* Retrieved January 18, 2022, from https://www.ibm.com/blogs/cloud-computing/2018/12/21/creval-alfredo-concierge-ibm-watson/

Platon. (2021, November 18). *More than 685 thousand truckers and logistics companies registered in the state system "Platon."* Retrieved February 12, 2021, from https://platon.ru/ru/без-рубрики/18-11-2021/13238

Plotnikov, V. S., & Azrakuliev, Z. M. (2018). The concept of productive capital in business model accounting and integrated reporting. *International Accounting, 21*(1), 4–16. doi:10.24891/ia.21.1.4

Poddar, A., Banerjee, S., & Sridhar, K. (2019). False advertising or slander? Using location based tweets to assess online rating-reliability. *Journal of Business Research, 99*, 390–397. https://doi.org/10.1016/J.JBUSRES.2017.08.030

Popadyuk, I. F., & Tabakova, M. V. (2019). *Integrated reporting: A textbook.* St. Petersburg, Russia: SPbSUE Publishing.

Popkova, E. G., De Bernardi, P., Tyurina, Y. G., & Sergi, B. S. (2022). A theory of digital technology advancement to address the grand challenges of sustainable development. *Technology in Society, 68*, 101831. doi:10.1016/j.techsoc.2021.101831

Popkova, E. G., Inshakova, A. O., & Sergi, B. S. (2021c). Venture capital and Industry 4.0: The G7's versus BRICS' experience. *Thunderbird International Business Review, 63*(6), 765–777. doi:10.1002/tie.22235

Popkova, E. G., Krivtsov, A. I., & Bogoviz, A. V. (2021). Digital economy in the 21st century: An introduction to the institutional approach. In E. G. Popkova, A. I. Krivtsov, & A. V. Bogoviz (Eds.), *The institutional foundations of the digital economy in the 21st century* (pp. ix–xi). De Gruyter. doi:10.1515/9783110651768-203

Popkova, E. G., & Sergi, B. S. (2021). Digital public health: Automation based on new datasets and the Internet of Things. *Socio-Economic Planning Sciences.* Advance online publication. doi:10.1016/j.seps.2021.101039

Popkova, E., Bogoviz, A. V., & Sergi, B. S. (2021a). Towards digital society management and 'capitalism 4.0' in contemporary Russia. *Humanities and Social Sciences Communications, 8*(1), 77. doi:10.105741599-021-00743-8

Popkova, E., DeLo, P., & Sergi, B. S. (2021b). Corporate Social Responsibility Amid Social Distancing During the COVID-19 Crisis: BRICS vs. OECD Countries. *Research in International Business and Finance, 55*, 101315. doi:10.1016/j.ribaf.2020.101315 PMID:34173410

Poultry World. (2022). *Russia again hit by hatching eggs shortage.* Retrieved December 27, 2021, from https://www.poultryworld.net/poultry/russia-again-hit-by-hatching-eggs-shortage/

Presidential Executive Office. (2019). *Decree "On the development of artificial intelligence in the Russian Federation" (together with the "National strategy for the development of artificial intelligence for the period up to 2030")* (October 10, 2019 No. 490). Retrieved March 27, 2022, from http://www.consultant.ru/document/cons_doc_LAW_335184/1f32224a00901db9cf4479 3e9a5e35567a4212c7/

Presidential Executive Office. (2021, November 30). *Russia calling! Investment forum.* Retrieved February 12, 2021, from http://kremlin.ru/events/president/news/67241

Pyzhikova, N. I., & Ozerova, M. G. (2018). Digitization of agriculture: Advantages and problems. In N. V. Gavrilets (Ed.), *The role of agricultural science in the sustainable development of rural areas* (pp. 1138–1140). Novosibirsk State Agricultural University.

Ratten, V., & Welpe, I. M. (2011). Special issue: Community-based, social and societal entrepreneurship. *Entrepreneurship and Regional Development, 23*(5–6), 283–286. https://doi.org/10.1080/08985626.2011.580159

Rêgo, B. S., Jayantila, S., Ferreira, J. J., & Carayannis, E. G. (2021). Digital transformation and strategic management: A systematic review of the literature. *Journal of the Knowledge Economy.* Advance online publication. doi:10.100713132-021-00853-3

Research Informatic. (2021). *Global agtech market – growth, share, opportunities and competitive analysis, 2021–2027.* Retrieved December 27, 2021, from https://www.researchinformatic.com/reports/agtech-market-32

RFI. (2021, November 21). *Sri Lanka backtracks on chemical ban in agriculture.* Retrieved December 27, 2021, from https://www.rfi.fr/fr/asie-pacifique/20211121-le-sri-lanka-revient-sur-l-interdiction-des-produits-chimiques-dans-son-agriculture

Rippa, P., & Secundo, G. (2019). Digital academic entrepreneurship: The potential of digital technologies on academic entrepreneurship. *Technological Forecasting and Social Change, 146,* 900–911. https://doi.org/10.1016/J.TECHFORE.2018.07.013

Ritchie, J., Lewis, J., & McNaughton Nicholls, C. (2013). *Qualitative Research Practice*. SAGE Publications.

Romanova, I. V., & Lavrik, T. M. (2021). Application of digital technologies in the sphere of corporate relations. *Law: History and Modernity, 2*(15), 137-142. doi:10.17277/pravo.2021.02

ROSINFRA. (2019, June 7). *The first PPP agreement in the field of IT has been signed in Russia.* Retrieved February 12, 2021, from https://rosinfra-awards.ru/press/2019-06-07-3.html

Russian Federation. (2021). Federal Law "On amendments to the Federal law 'On international companies and international funds' and on the suspension of certain provisions of the Federal law 'On joint-stock companies" and the Federal law 'On limited liability companies'" (February 24, 2021 No. 17-FZ). Author.

Rybin, M. V., & Voinov, A. I. (2020). Theoretical aspects and development of innovation management methods. *Economic Sciences, 185*, 37–43. doi:10.14451/1.185.37

Sahut, J. M., Iandoli, L., & Teulon, F. (2021). The age of digital entrepreneurship. *Small Business Economics, 56*(3), 1159–1169. https://doi.org/10.1007/S11187-019-00260-8

Sanders, T. (2021). Testing the Black Box: Institutional investors, risk disclosure, and ethical AI. *Philosophy & Technology, 34*(S1), 105–109. doi:10.100713347-020-00409-4

Schilirò, D. (2020). Towards digital globalization and the COVID-19 challenge. *International Journal of Business Management and Economic Research, 11*(2), 1710–1716.

Schilirò, D. (2021). Digital transformation, COVID-19, and the future of work. *International Journal of Business Management and Economic Research, 12*(3), 1945–1952.

Senyard, J., Baker, T., Steffens, P., & Davidsson, P. (2014). Bricolage as a path to innovativeness for resource-constrained new firms. *Journal of Product Innovation Management, 31*(2), 211–230. https://doi.org/10.1111/JPIM.12091

Serebryakova, T. Yu. (2016). Integrated accounting and reporting: Institutional approach. *Accounting. Analysis. Auditing, 2*, 24–33.

Sergi, B. S., & Popkova, E. G. (2022). Towards a 'wide' role for venture capital in OECD countries' industry 4.0. *Heliyon, 8*(1), e08700. doi:10.1016/j.heliyon.2021.e08700 PMID:35028473

Service New Brunswick. (n.d.). *Official website.* Retrieved February 12, 2021, from https://www2.snb.ca/content/snb/en.html

Shaba, E., Guerci, M., Gilardi, S., & Bartezzaghi, E. (2019). *Industry 4.0 technologies and organizational design - Evidence from 15 Italian cases*. Studi Organizzativi. doi:10.3280/SO2019-001001

Shelkovnikov, S. A., Kuznetsova, I. G., Petukhova, M. S., & Alekseev, A. A. (2019). Digitalization as a trend in the development of agriculture in the context of a new technological order. *Bulletin of the Transbaikal State University, 25*(8), 119–126. doi:10.21209/2227-9245-2019-25-8-119-126

Sheng, J., Amankwah-Amoah, J., Khan, Z., & Wang, X. (2021). COVID-19 Pandemic in the New Era of Big Data Analytics: Methodological Innovations and Future Research Directions. *British Journal of Management, 32*(4), 1164–1183. doi:10.1111/1467-8551.12441

Shruti, I. (2022). *Harnessing digital financial inclusion under the G20 Digital Economy Agenda 2023.* Retrieved February 19, 2022, from https://www.orfonline.org/expert-speak/g20-digital-economy-agenda-2023/

Shuisky, V. P. (2020). Digitalization of the Russian economy: Achievements and prospects. *Bulletin of the Institute of Economics of the Russian Academy of Sciences, 6*, 158–169. doi:10.24411/2073-6487-2020-10076

Siby, A., & George, J. P. (2022). Influence of customer relationship management for the success of E-business. In A. Joshi, M. Mahmud, R. G. Ragel, & N. V. Thakur (Eds.), *Information and communication technology for competitive strategies* (pp. 473–481). Springer., doi:10.1007/978-981-16-0739-4_45

Siggelkow, N., & Terwiesch, C. (2019, May-June). The age of continuous connection. *Harvard Business Review*. Retrieved January 19, 2020, from https://hbr.org/2019/05/the-age-of-continuous-connection

Silva, A. J., Cortez, P., Pereira, C., & Pilastri, A. (2021). Business analytics in Industry 4.0: A systematic review. *Expert Systems: International Journal of Knowledge Engineering and Neural Networks*, *38*(7), e12741. doi:10.1111/exsy.12741

Silvestri, L., Forcina, A., Introna, V., Santolamazza, A., & Cesarotti, V. (2020). Maintenance transformation through Industry 4.0 technologies: A systematic literature review. *Computers in Industry*, *123*, 103335. doi:10.1016/j.compind.2020.103335

Singapore Customs. (n.d.). *TradeXchange*. Retrieved February 12, 2021, from https://unece.org/fileadmin/DAM/cefact/single_window/sw_cases/Download/Singapore.pdf

Smales, L. A. (2021). Investor attention and global market returns during the COVID-19 crisis. *International Review of Financial Analysis*, *73*, 101616. doi:10.1016/j.irfa.2020.101616

South China Morning Post. (2022). *Mainland China was top importer of Japanese food in 2021, surpassing Hong Kong and the US, with sake, scallops and whiskey in demand*. Retrieved December 27, 2021, from https://www.scmp.com/week-asia/article/3166259/mainland-china-was-top-importer-japanese-food-2021-surpassing-hong-kong.

Spohrer, J. (2002). NBICs (nano-bio-info-cogno-socio) convergence to improve human performance: Opportunities and challenges. In M. C. Roco & W. S. Bainbridge (Eds.), *Converging technologies for improving human performance* (pp. 101–116). Edvard Press.

Statista. (2021). *Average company lifespan on Standard and Poor's 500 Index from 1965 to 2030, in years*. Retrieved February 18, 2022, from https://tinyurl.com/mw24zkw2

Statista. (2021). *The amount of venture capital investments in the US by branches for the 4th quarter of 2020*. Retrieved March 18, 2021, from https://www.statista.com/statistics/277506/venture-caputal-investment-in-the-united-states-by-sector/

Statista. (2022a). *Digital payments*. Retrieved February 08, 2022, from https://www.statista.com/outlook/dmo/fintech/digital-payments/worldwide#transaction-value

Statista. (2022b). *Overall cryptocurrency market capitalization per week from July 2010 to February 2022 (in billion US dollars)*. Retrieved February 08, 2022, from https://www.statista.com/statistics/730876/cryptocurrency-maket-value/

Statista. (n.d.). *Agricultural technology (Agtech) market value worldwide from 2020 to 2025*. Retrieved December 28, 2021, from https://www.statista.com/statistics/1222528/worldwide-agricultural-technology-market-value/#statisticContainer

Steininger, D. M., Kathryn Brohman, M., & Block, J. H. (2022). Digital Entrepreneurship: What is New if Anything? *Business & Information Systems Engineering*. doi:10.1007/s12599-021-00741-9

Suits, V. P., Horin, A. N., & Sheremet, A. D. (2020). *Comprehensive analysis and audit of integrated reporting on sustainable development companies*. INFRA-M. doi:10.12737/1072676

Sustainable Infrastructure Foundation (SIF). (n.d.). *Multilateral platform for sustainable infrastructure*. Retrieved February 12, 2021, from https://public.sif-source.org/

Tadviser. (2021a). *Artificial intelligence (Russian market)*. Retrieved March 27, 2022, from https://www.tadviser.ru/index.php/

Tadviser. (2021b). *Artificial intelligence (World market)*. Retrieved March 27, 2022, from https://www.tadviser.ru/index.php/Статья:Искусственный_интеллект_(мировой_рынок)

Tao, H., Sun, X., Liu, X., Tian, J., & Zhang, D. (2022). The impact of consumer purchase behavior changes on the business model design of consumer services companies over the course of COVID-19. *Frontiers in Psychology*, *13*, 818845. doi:10.3389/fpsyg.2022.818845 PMID:35310236

Tarasov, A. N., Kavardakov, V. Ya., Semenenko, I. A., & Maksutova, L. G. (2018). *Innovative and technological development of animal husbandry in the Russian Federation in the context of the industry's transition to a bioinformatic technological structure: Theory, methodology, practice*. AzovPrint.

Tasavori, M., Kwong, C., & Pruthi, S. (2018). Resource bricolage and growth of product and market scope in social enterprises. *Entrepreneurship and Regional Development*, *30*(3–4), 336–361. https://doi.org/10.1080/08985626.2017.1413775

Tavera Romero, C. A., Ortiz, J. H., Khalaf, O. I., & Prado, A. R. (2021). Business intelligence: Business evolution after Industry 4.0. *Sustainability*, *13*(18), 10026. doi:10.3390u131810026

Teece, D. (2010). Business models, business strategy and innovation. *Long Range Planning*, *43*(2-3), 172–194. doi:10.1016/j.lrp.2009.07.003

The Japan Agricultural News. (2022). *How will digital introduction agriculture change?* Retrieved February 08, 2021, from https://www.scmp.com/week-asia/article/3166259/mainland-china-was-top-importer-japanese-food-2021-surpassing-hong-kong

Tikhomirova, V. A. (2019). *Ensuring food security: International and Russian experience* (Dissertation of Candidate of Economic Sciences). Moscow, Russia: RUDN University.

Tikhomirova, V. A. (2021). Innovations in agro-industrial production as a driver for increasing the sustainability of national food systems. *RUDN Journal of Economics*, *29*(4), 773–784. doi:10.22363/2313-2329-2021-29-4-773-784

Tjahjadi, B., Harymawan, I., & Warsidi, N. S. (2020). Implementation of integrated reporting: A cross-countries' study. *Entrepreneurship and Sustainability Issues*, *7*(4), 2832–2850. doi:10.9770/jesi.2020.7.4(17)

TomTom. (2021). *Traffic index ranking, 2021*. Retrieved February 12, 2021, from https://www.tomtom.com/en_gb/traffic-index/ranking/

Torkanovskiy, E. (2021). National competitiveness in the era of industry 4.0 and new individual freedoms. *World Futures*, *77*(2), 137–153. doi:10.1080/02604027.2020.1755213

Trade Map, I. T. C. (n.d.). *Trade statistic for international business development.* Retrieved January 08, 2022, from https://www.trademap.org/Index.aspx

Trongtorsak, S., Saraubon, K., & Nilsook, P. (2021). Collaborative Experiential Learning Process for Enhancing Digital Entrepreneurship. *Higher Education Studies, 11*(1), 137. doi:10.5539/hes.v11n1p137

Tsenzharik, M. K., Arenkov, I. A., Steshenko, V. I., & Ivanova, D. V. (Eds.). (2021). *Business Management in the Digital Economy: Collection of abstracts of speeches Fourth International Conference.* St. Petersburg, Russia: St. Petersburg State University of Industrial Technologies and Design.

UNCTAD. (2021). *Digital Economy Report 2021. Cross-border data flows and development: For whom the data flow*. United Nations.

UNEP. (2021, February 24). *Integrated approaches in Action: A Companion to the International Good Practice Principles for Sustainable Infrastructure.* Retrieved February 12, 2021, from https://www.unep.org/resources/publication/integrated-approaches-action-companion-international-good-practice-principles

United Nation. (2017, June 21). *World population projected to reach 9.8 billion in 2050, and 11.2 billion in 2100.* Retrieved December 04, 2021, from https://www.un.org/development/desa/en/news/population/world-population-prospects-2017.html

United States Environmental Protection Agency. (n.d.a). *ECHO Data Services.* Retrieved December 28, 2021, from https://echo.epa.gov/

United States Environmental Protection Agency. (n.d.b). *EnviroAtlas.* Retrieved December 28, 2021, from https://www.epa.gov/enviroatlas

Valdez-Juárez, L. E., Castillo-Vergara, M., & Ramos-Escobar, E. A. (2022). Innovative business strategies in the face of COVID-19: An approach to open innovation of SMEs in the Sonora Region of Mexico. *Journal of Open Innovation*, *8*(1), 47. doi:10.3390/joitmc8010047

Vardari, L., Bytyqi, Q., & Lumi, A. (2022). The impact of information technologies on business during the COVID-19 pandemic outbreak. *Contemporary Studies in Economic and Financial Analysis*, *108B*, 143–158. doi:10.1108/S1569-37592022000108B038

Vazirani, A., & Bhattacharjee, T. (2022). Necessity or opportunity: A case of business venturing decision during COVID-19 pandemic. *Managerial and Decision Economics*, *43*(3), 768–778. doi:10.1002/mde.3417

VEB.RF. (2021a). *Urban economy.* Retrieved February 12, 2021, from https://вэб.рф/biznesu/finansirovaniye-proyektov/gorodskaja-ekonomika/

VEB.RF. (2021b). *City life index*. Retrieved February 12, 2021, from https://www.pwc.ru/ru/publications/assets/indeks-kachestva-zhizni/indeks-kachestva-zhizni.pdf

Venier, F. (2017). *Digital transformation and organizational capacity. Italian companies and the challenge of change* [Trasformazione digitale e capacità organizzativa. Le aziende italiane e la sfida del cambiamento]. EUT Edizioni Università di Trieste. https://www.openstarts.units.it/handle/10077/19885

Verdoliva, V., & Schiavone, F. (2021). Technologies 4.0 and business development. *European Management Journal*, *39*(3), 315–316. doi:10.1016/j.emj.2021.05.001

Verhoef, P. C., Broekhuizen, T., Bart, Y., Bhattacharya, A., Qi Dong, J., Fabian, N., & Haenlein, M. (2019). Digital transformation: A multidisciplinary reflection and research agenda. *Journal of Business Research*, *122*, 889–901. doi:10.1016/j.jbusres.2019.09.022

Vial, G. (2019). Understanding digital transformation: A review and a research agenda. *The Journal of Strategic Information Systems*, *28*(2), 118–144. doi:10.1016/j.jsis.2019.01.003

Voinov, A. I. (2015). China's national science and technology policy. *Birzha intellektual'noj sobstvennosti, 3*, 38-41.

Voinov, A. I. (2014). Evolution of the concept of "nanotechnology.". *Izobretatelstvo*, *14*(11), 35–39.

Voinov, A. I., & Lomakina, O. B. (2022). Nanotechnologization – the determining factor of the VI technostructure of the world economy. In T. M. Isachenko & L. S. Revenko (Eds.), *A new paradigm for the development of international economic relations: Challenges and prospects for Russia* (pp. 129–137). MGIMO University.

von Briel, F., Recker, J., Selander, L., Jarvenpaa, S. L., Hukal, P., Yoo, Y., Lehmann, J., Chan, Y., Rothe, H., Alpar, P., Fürstenau, D., & Wurm, B. (2021). Researching digital entrepreneurship: Current issues and suggestions for future directions. *Communications of the Association for Information Systems*, *48*, 284–304. https://doi.org/10.17705/1CAIS.04833

Vuppuluri, P. (2020, December 3). Investing in innovation: The rise of the smart city. *Forbes*. Retrieved February 12, 2021, from https://www.forbes.com/sites/forbesfinancecouncil/2020/12/03/investing-in-innovation-the-rise-of-the-smart-city/?sh=40a03ce75ba6

Wang, S. S., Goh, J. R., Sornette, D., Wang, H., & Yang, E. Y. (2021). Government support for SMEs in response to COVID-19: Theoretical model using Wang transform. *China Finance Review International*, *11*(3), 406–433. doi:10.1108/CFRI-05-2021-0088

Warner, K. S., & Wäger, M. (2019). Building dynamic capabilities for digital transformation: An ongoing process of strategic renewal. *Long Range Planning*, *52*(3), 326–349. doi:10.1016/j.lrp.2018.12.001

Welter, F., Baker, T., & Wirsching, K. (2019). Three waves and counting: The rising tide of contextualization in entrepreneurship research. *Small Business Economics*, *52*(2), 319–330. https://doi.org/10.1007/S11187-018-0094-5

Wierenga, M. (2020). Uncovering the scaling of innovations developed by grassroots entrepreneurs in low-income settings. *Entrepreneurship and Regional Development, 32*(1–2), 63–90. https://doi.org/10.1080/08985626.2019.1640478

Woetzel, J., Garemo, N., Mischke, J., Hjerpe, M., & Palter, R. (2016, June 14). *Bridging global infrastructure gaps: Report.* McKinsey Global Institute. Retrieved February 12, 2021, from https://www.mckinsey.com/business-functions/operations/our-insights/bridging-global-infrastructure-gaps

World Bank & GFDRR. (2015). *Investing in urban resilience: Protecting and promoting development in a changing world.* Retrieved February 12, 2021, from https://www.gfdrr.org/sites/default/files/publication/Investing%20in%20Urban%20Resilience%20Final.pdf

World Bank. (1990-2021). *Private participation in infrastructure: ICT.* Retrieved February 12, 2021, from https://ppi.worldbank.org/en/snapshots/sector/ict

World Bank. (2017, April). *Why We Need to Close the Infrastructure Gap in Sub-Saharan Africa.* Retrieved February 12, 2021, from https://www.worldbank.org/en/region/afr/publication/why-we-need-to-close-the-infrastructure-gap-in-sub-saharan-africa

World Bank. (2020, April 20). *Urban development overview.* Retrieved February 12, 2021, from https://www.worldbank.org/en/topic/urbandevelopment/overview#1

World Bank. (2022a). *Global economic prospect.* The World Bank.

World Bank. (2022b, January 11). *Global Growth to Slow through 2023, Adding to Risk of 'Hard Landing' in Developing Economies.* Retrieved January 18, 2022, from https://www.worldbank.org/en/news/press-release/2022/01/11/global-recovery-economics-debt-commodity-inequality

World Bank. (n.d.). *Private participation in infrastructure.* Retrieved February 12, 2021, from https://ppi.worldbank.org/en/ppi

World Economic Forum. (2019). *Fourth Industrial Revolution: Beacons of Technology and Innovation in Manufacturing.* World Economic Forum. https://www.weforum.org/whitepapers/fourth-industrial-revolution-beacons-of-technology-and-innovation-in-manufacturing/

World Economic Forum. (2022). *Global Cybersecurity Outlook 2022.* World Economic Forum. https://www3.weforum.org/docs/WEF_Global_Cybersecurity_Outlook_2022.pdf

World Health Organization (WHO). (2022). *WHO Coronavirus (COVID-19) dashboard: Globally, as of 8:36 pm CEST, 14 April 2022.* Retrieved April 18, 2022, from https://covid19.who.int/?gclid=Cj0KCQjwrIf3BRD1ARIsAMuugNsIqvkZ smIoto8RJ964Wv1YdYlla CbKloYu2Z9HLeUkZuatNROZyzgaAvEiEALw_wcB

World Organisation for Animal Health (OIE). (2021). *Global control of African swine fever: A GF-TADs initiative (2020–2025).* Retrieved May 19, 2021, from https://www.oie.int/fileadmin/Home/eng/Animal_Health_in_the_World/docs/pdf/ASF/ASF_GlobalInitiative_Web.pdf

World Organisation for Animal Health (OIE). (2021). *Situation reports for avian influenza.* Retrieved May 19, 2021, from https://www.oie.int/en/disease/avian-influenza/

Xie, X., Wu, Y., Palacios-Marqués, D., & Ribeiro-Navarrete, S. (2022). Business networks and organizational resilience capacity in the digital age during COVID-19: A perspective utilizing organizational information processing theory. *Technological Forecasting and Social Change, 177*, 121548. doi:10.1016/j.techfore.2022.121548

Yankovskaya, V. V., Kelina, K. G., Chutcheva, Y. V., & Alekseev, A. N. (2021). The consumer economy and the pleasure economy: Similarities and differences in developing countries in industry 4.0. *International Journal of Trade and Global Markets, 14*(4-5), 507–515. doi:10.1504/IJTGM.2021.116737

Ye, B. H., Barreda, A. A., Okumus, F., & Nusair, K. (2019). Website interactivity and brand development of online travel agencies in China: The moderating role of age. *Journal of Business Research, 99*, 382–389. https://doi.org/10.1016/J.JBUSRES.2017.09.046

Yi, J., Lee, Y., & Kim, S. H. (2019). Determinants of growth and decline in mobile game diffusion. *Journal of Business Research, 99*, 363–372. https://doi.org/10.1016/J.JBUSRES.2017.09.045

Zahra, S. A. (2021). International entrepreneurship in the post Covid world. *Journal of World Business, 56*(1). https://doi.org/10.1016/j.jwb.2020.101143

Zhai, W., & Yue, H. (2022). Economic resilience during COVID-19: An insight from permanent business closures. *Environment and Planning A. Economy and Space, 54*(2), 219–221. doi:10.1177/0308518X211055181

Zhang, C., & Kovacs, J. M. (2012). The application of small unmanned aerial systems for precision agriculture: A review. *Precision Agriculture, 13*(6), 693–712. doi:10.100711119-012-9274-5

Zharikova, E. P., Grigoriev, Y. Y., & Grigorieva, A. L. (2021). Applications of computer vision in cross-sectoral tasks. In O. G. Shakirova, O. V. Bashkov, & A. A. Khusainov (Eds.), *Current problems and ways of industry development: Equipment and technologies* (pp. 415–426). Springer., doi:10.1007/978-3-030-69421-0_45

Zhou, L., Li, S., Li, C., Shen, G., Yang, H., Zhu, P., Han, H., & Li, B. (2022). Spatial congruency or mismatch? Analyzing the COVID-19 potential infection risk and urban density as businesses reopen. *Cities (London, England), 123*, 103615. doi:10.1016/j.cities.2022.103615 PMID:35095162

Zolotová, I., Papcun, P., Kajáti, E., Miškuf, M., & Mocnej, J. (2020). Smart and cognitive solutions for Operator 4.0: Laboratory H-CPPS case studies. *Computers & Industrial Engineering, 139*, 105471. doi:10.1016/j.cie.2018.10.032

Zysman, J., & Kenney, M. (2018). The next phase in the digital revolution: Intelligent tools, platforms, growth, employment. *Communications of the ACM, 61*(2), 54–63. doi:10.1145/3173550

About the Contributors

Elena G. Popkova is a Doctor of Science (Economics), the founder and president of the Institute of Scientific Communications (Russia) and Leading researcher of the Center for applied research of the chair "Economic policy and public-private partnership" of Moscow State Institute of International Relations (MGIMO) (Moscow, Russia). Her scientific interests include the theory of economic growth, sustainable development, globalization, humanization of economic growth, emerging markets, social entrepreneurship, and the digital economy and Industry 4.0. Elena G. Popkova organizes Russian and international scientific and practical conferences and is the editor and author of collective monographs, and serves as a guest editor of international scientific journals. She has published more than 300 works in Russian and foreign peer-reviewed scientific journals and books.

* * *

Irene Borreca grew up in the province and graduated with distinction from the classical high school in Benevento. She continued her studies at the University of Sannio where she took a degree in Business Economics with a thesis in Business Organization. As her peers, she has witnessed several changes in the Internet and technologies in general as a phenomenon that evolves so quickly to give the impression of not being able to keep up. Therefore, in line with her choice of studies, she focused on the digital transformation at company level, but above all on future prospects.

Stefano Di Lauro is Postdoctoral Researcher at the University of Sannio (Italy). He teaches Organization studies related topics at the University of Sannio and University of Molise. He recently completed his PhD in Management (focused on organizational identity, corporate identity and social media) at the University of Naples Federico II. During his PhD, he was a visiting researcher at the Business School of the University of Edinburgh. Prior to PhD he accumulated an extensive international work experience in digital communication and marketing. His current areas of research include people analytics, organizational values, and competencies.

Irina O. Ignatova was born on May 19, 1998 in Moscow. In 2016 she graduated with honors from the State Budgetary General Education Institution of Moscow "School № 17". In 2022 Irina O. Ignatova graduated with honors from Moscow State Institute of International Relations (the School of International Economic Relations, specialty "International Accounting, Analysis and Audit"). Since 2020 she has been working in the Limited Liability Company "SVAROG": first as a financial analyst, then as a head of the Financial Department. Since 2021 Irina O. Ignatova has been working in Moscow State Institute of International Relations as a lecture of the Department of Accounting, Statistics and Audit. In 2020 she received the grant of the President of the Russian Federation for outstanding abilities and high achievements in science. Irina O. Ignatova is double Primakov scholarship winner. She has over 20 scientific publications.

Oleg V. Ivanov, Department of Economic policy and Public-private partnership, MGIMO, Professor, Doctor of Science (Econ.). He is the author of 15 monographs, books and textbooks, including "Theory and world practices of Public-Private Partnership", "Mechanisms of Public-Private Partnership in the economic policy of Russia", "Public-Private Partnership in Russia. Institutional Frameworks and Best Practices" (in Eng.), "Public-Private Partnership in the countries of the Asia-Pacific region", "Public-Private Partnership as a tool for infrastructure development and economic modernization", "State regulation of foreign economic activities in Russia: organization, functions, legal forms", "The fight against the dragon "kogai" (experience of ecological management in Japan)", etc.

Suha Jalloul completed her primary, secondary, and high school education at Amjad High School in Lebanon and ranked 10th in the baccalaureate official exams. Her undergraduate education was at Beirut Arab University in Lebanon, BA of Accounting, with a CGPA of 3.93, and her master's degree at Lebanese American University with CGPA of 3.97 Department of Business Administration. She works as a Graduate Assistant at Lebanese American University of Beirut and she had been awarded the CPA after passing the 4 exams.

Elvira A. Khalikova is a Ph.D. in Economics, Associate Professor of the Department of Corporate Finance and Accounting Technologies in Ufa State Petroleum Technological University, Head of the School of Scientific Development of the Institute of Oil and Gas Business of Ufa State Petroleum Technological University. Elvira A. Khalikova organizes Russian and International Scientific and Practical Conferences; she is the author and editor of collective monographs. Her research interests include economics and management in the oil and gas industry, business planning and budgeting, controlling, cost management, corporate finance, and management accounting. Elvira A. Khalikova is the author of over 169 works published in Russian and foreign publications. In particular, 10 of her works were published in journals included in the Scopus, and 8 in the Web of Science.

Olga V. Khmyz, PhD (Economics), is a docent, an associate professor in the International Finance Department, MGIMO University (Moscow State Institute of International Relations, Moscow, Russian Federation). She specializes in international finance, international capital markets, institutional investors. She holds a PhD in international economy and global finance from the Moscow State Institute of International Relations. She has led numerous workshops and courses with particular reference to mutual funds, hedge funds, pension funds, foundations, endowments, exchange-traded funds and, more generally, to institutional investors, investment strategies, foreign direct and portfolio investments, international capital flows, international monetary relation, finance. Her research interests focus on international capital markets dynamics and various aspects of institutional investors' activity. Author and co-author of more than 25 monographs and over 300 research articles, 20 textbooks. She has practical experience in the field of international finance.

Yulia A. Lukina graduated with honors from MGIMO University: Bachelor of Arts in Commerce (2020), Master of Arts in Economics, International accounting, analysis and audit (2022). She completed advanced training programs, including professional development program «Information analytical systems in work, study and business» (MGIMO, 2021), professional development program «Digital International Relations 2022» (MGIMO, 2022) etc. She has been working at the PhD and post graduate studies department of MGIMO-University since 2018. She has been giving lectures on accounting and taxation since 2021. Yulia Lukina has more than 20 scientific and academic publications. Her research interests lie in the area of investment valuation, investment attractiveness, financial and economic analysis, international taxation.

Mikhail V. Rybin In 1992, M.V. Rybin was awarded a scientific degree of Doctor of Technical Sciences, and in 1993 he was awarded the scientific degree of Senior Scientific Associate. From 1995 to 2020, M.V. Rybin worked at Gazprombank, heading its Board of Administration for 16 years. He was actively involved in development of innovation and transformation processes and implementation of the latest banking and managerial technologies. Since 2018, he has been Head of Innovation Management Department of Moscow State Institute of International Relations (MGIMO). He has 22 years of teaching experience. He has taught at MGRI-RGGRU, MGI-NITU MISIS, N.E. Bauman Moscow State Technical University, and MGIMO. Has received awards and commendations: Commendation from Ministry of Energy of the Russian Federation, Certificate of Merit from PJSC Gazprom, Honorary Employee of Gazprombank. He is the winner of the Top 1000 Russian Managers Rating three years in a row from 2010 to 2012. M.V. Rybin is the author of 78 scientific papers. He specialises in theoretical and practical aspects of management in large organisations, effective innovation management and corporate governance.

Daniele Schiliro is associate professor of Economics at University of Messina, Department of Economics B.A. (Laurea) in Economics, Catholic University of Milan. Researcher and Member of the Scientific Committee of the Centre of Research in Economic Analysis (CRANEC) Università Cattolica di Milano. Scholarship "Bonaldo Stringher", Bank of Italy, Rome. M-Phil program in Political Economy at the University of Cambridge (U.K.) Special Graduate Student at the University of Yale (U.S.A.) Research scholar in macroeconomics and history of economic analysis at the Universities of Cambridge (Selwyn College and Sidney Sussex College), Oxford (Bresenose College) (U.K.) , and Twente (NL).Visiting Professor, University of Dubai (UAE), University of Valencia (ES). Research Fields in International Economics, European Economy, Economics of Structural Change, Microeconomics and Industrial Organization, Coopetion Strategies, Behavioral Economics, Knowledge Economy, History of Economc Analysis.

Khodor Shatila is a Master in Business Administration, Sagesse University, Furn El Chebbak Baabda, Lebanon. Researcher in iProcares international research center, Beirut, Lebanon. Research interests: international logistic, transnational supply chains, human resources management, multinational management. Published more than 5 papers in internationally indexed journals, participated in 4 international conferences.

Larisa V. Shmarova was born on March 22, 1964 in Monino, the Moscow Region. In 1981 she graduated from comprehensive school № 313 in Moscow. In 1986 Larisa V. Shmarova graduated with honors from Moscow Institute of Civil Aviation Engineers with "Economics and Air Service Provider". Since 1998 she has been working at Moscow State Institute of International Relations: first as an assistant professor of the Department of International Tourism, then as an associate professor of the Department of Accounting, Statistics and Audit. In 2003 Larisa V. Shmarova defended her thesis on the specialty "Accounting, Statistics" on "The statistical Survey of International Tourism Service Market" in the specialized Board of Plekhanov Russian Academy of Economics. In 2010 she got a certificate of an associate professor in the Department of Accounting, Statistics and Audit. Larisa V. Shmarova has scientific publications of over 200 printer's sheets.

Vera A. Tikhomirova, from 2007 to 2012, studied at the Moscow City University of Management. Yu.M.Luzhkova - qualified Manager in the field of "State and municipal management", specialization "State regulation of the economy". From 2013 to 2016, she completed postgraduate studies at the Diplomatic Academy of the Russian Foreign Ministry. From 2017 to 2019 - an intern at the Department of International Economic Relations of the Faculty of Economics of the Peoples' Friendship University of Russia. In 2019 she defended her dissertation for the degree of candidate of economic sciences in the specialty 08.00.14 on the topic "Ensuring food security: international and Russian experience".

Evgeny P. Torkanovskiy's is currently a research fellow in the Russian Academy of Sciences Institute of Economics. He obtained Ph.D. in Economics from the Russian Academy of Sciences Institute of Economics and graduate degree from the French Sciences-Po Paris. His research program examines innovation in finance (collective investment vehicles, crowdfunding) and business (management of innovations, sustainability, international trade). He is particularly driven by research of economic autonomy/autarky and its implications for individual, corporation and nation. Dr. Torkanovskiy's project of sustainable climate fund developed in collaboration with Ukrainian and Belarus colleagues won Award of Climate Innovation Summit in Dublin in 2018. Besides academic career, Dr. Torkanovskiy has gained rich business and professional experience working for major Russian and international business groups in executive and board positions as well as for the Russian government. He headed Russian State Fund for Industry Development and served as Deputy Chairman of Russian State Investment Corporation.

Alexander I. Voinov worked as a project manager in the companies "Mosprodimpex," "Art-Happening Center Ltd.," "PANSAT Enterprises Inc." until the mide-2000s. After receiving academic degree, he held the position of head of the scientific development group at "Armoproekt Company LLC." He has a Ph.D. in Economics, Docent of Innovation Management Department of MGIMO University, Docent of the Department of Innovation Management and Commercialization of Intellectual Property at RGAIS. He has published over 30 articles in professional journals and 8 books as author, and co-author. Primary research expertise embraces breakthrough technologies, national innovation systems, and venturing.

Ekaterina Yu. Voronova is a head of the Department of Accounting, Statistics and Audit, School of International Economic Relations of MGIMO-University, Doctor of Economic Sciences, Associate Professor. She graduated from MGIMO-University in 1985 (Diploma in International economic relations). She has been working at MGIMO-University since 1991 giving lectures on Theory and fundamentals of accounting, Accounting, Accounting of foreign economic activity and reporting, Fundamentals of management accounting, Management accounting (Russian and international theory and practice). Prof. Voronova has more than 170 scientific and academic publications. She completed advanced training programs, including professional development program «Development and implementation of the main educational program in accordance with the requirements of the Federal state educational standard» (National Accreditation Agency, 2020) professional development program «Practical aspects of the development of accounting, statistics, audit and finance in the digital economy» (MGIMO, 2020), professional development program «Digital international relations 2022» (MGIMO, 2022) etc.

Olga A. Zainullina senior lecturer of the Department of Visual Communications, Synergy University. Head of Marketing Department Advertising agency "Optima", Research interests - strategic marketing. Publications: 3 monographs, co-author of the monographs "Standards of corporate culture in the 21st century", "Corporate Social Responsibility", Digitalization of corporate culture as a factor influencing ESG investment in the energy sector// January 2021 International Review","Current Problems of the World Economy and International Trade", 20 scientific articles, including the article "Modification of the marketing strategy in the conditions of the" Great Depression "as a factor of economic security". Place of employment: Head of Marketing Department Advertising agency "Optima", Head of the Marketing Department of JSC "USZ" under the Ministry of Industry and Trade of Russia.

Sergei B. Zainullin, Professor of Department of Visual Communications, Synergy University, Associate Professor of Department of National Economy of the RUDN University. Also taught at Samara State University and, as a visiting professor, taught at Middle East Technical University (Ankara, Turkey) and the University of the Basque Country (Spain).Research Interests- Corporate governance, Corporate security, Assets protection, Mergers&Acqusitions . Publications: 11 monographs and manuals, including the textbook "National Economy", 40 scientific articles (Higher education commission, SCOPUS ,WoS, AGRIS). CEO of consulting company "Astakhov, Khoroshev, Zainullin and Partners". Member of the Board of Directors of companies as JSC "Kryazh Breeding Plant", JSC "Central Research Institute of Leather and Footwear Industry", JSC "Central scientific research institute of film materials and artificial skin", JSC "Institute of Applied Biochemistry and Mechanical Engineering". Social activity: Member of the Association of Professional Directors, Member of the Board of the Moscow of the Russian Red Cross.

Index

A

B

C

D

E

T

www.ingramcontent.com/pod-product-compliance
Lightning Source LLC
LaVergne TN
LVHW061538290926
849162LV00004B/840